Terry has written a much neede
serious about planting the gospel i.. _ .
context. Rightfully so we must begin by exploring or even
rediscovering a healthy Christology if we dare to advance
the gospel. Terry helps us do just that.

—David Putman, co-author of *Breaking the Missional
Code* and *Breaking the Discipleship Code*, author of
Detox...for the Overly Religious, and founder of Planting
the Gospel (www.plantingthegospel.com).

This book is a pertinent word from a front-line leader
trying to start new churches and catalyze kingdom advance.
Terry writes authoritatively and passionately as a biblical
missiologist who has lived a missional life for decades.
More than point out problems, he proposes solutions that
will revive the American church as well as launch vital new
churches. Read it and be prepared for action!

—Dr. Jeff Iorg, President, Golden Gate Seminary,
author of *The Painful Side of Leadership*, *The
Case for Antioch*, and *Live like a Missionary*.

I'm excited about this book. Terry is the combination of an
academic, practitioner, and social observer which allows him
to bring a very unique perspective to this conversation. We
have to get "Jesus" right–if we don't our mission is over. Jesus
really is the answer...even for the church.

—Bob Roberts, Jr
Senior Pastor Northwood Church, Keller, TX
Blogger–www.glocal.net
Author of *Transformation* and *Bold as Love*.

In *Facing the Change: Challenges and Opportunities for an American Missiology*, Terry Coy provides thoughtful answers out of his lifelong experience in missiology and church planting to the key three questions confronting the church today: What are the non-negotiables of our belief?, What does it mean to be the church of Jesus Christ in contemporary American culture?, and What must we do to reach our nation and world for Christ? This is a must-read book for all church planters and mission-focused pastors.

—Dr. Steve Lemke, Provost, Professor of Philosophy and Ethics, Director of the Baptist Center for Theology and Ministry, and Editor of the *Journal for Baptist Theology and Ministry* at New Orleans Baptist Theological Seminary

If *Facing the Change* were a publicly traded company, I would be a major shareholder. Terry Coy has a sort of missiological swagger in this text that makes you thirsty to keep turning the pages. His handling of contextualization singlehandedly makes you need to read this robust and refreshing book.

—Dr. Jeremy Roberts, Lead Pastor, Church of the Highlands, Chattanooga, TN, Radio Host, "Gospel Dynamite" 94.9FM WDYN

Dr. Coy brings a theologian's perspective and missiologist's application of the ancient command of Christ in the Great Commission to go, make disciples of all nations. As a theologian and practitioner, he demonstrates the timeless relevance of the gospel, and the church it creates, for the current North American context-one that is ever changing in demographics and worldview. His work brings to light our current setting in North America with its increasing multi-cultural diversity and challenges to a proper understanding of Jesus Christ, while issuing a clarion call for the church to awaken to current demographic realities and proclaim the timeless message of Jesus Christ to our changing world. *Facing the Change* is a must read for pastors, laity, missionaries, theologians, and missiologists who want to understand what is means to be faithful to the Great Commission in our generation. In an unprecedented age of the mass migration of peoples and discernible shift in evangelical strength from the West to the Global South, Dr. Coy clearly explains the challenges and opportunities that both present to the church.

—John Massey, Ph.D.
Associate Professor of Missions
Southwestern Baptist Theological Seminary

This Missiology is up to date, insightful, and comprehensive. Terry Coy has provided us with a clear path to fulfill our mission in America. This work begins where we should begin, a thoroughgoing biblical presentation of Christ that speaks to the context of religious pluralism in America. Coy asks the hard questions and responds to the issues and realities in our culture and daily life that simply must be addressed. There is an honest and helpful assessment of the American church written with a love for the church and church planting. He will motivate you to do what is necessary and provide you with concrete steps to implement an effective missiology. This book will help you understand the most salient American realities the church faces. If you are looking for the place to begin understanding American missiology today, *Facing the Challenge* is the place to begin. If you are a seasoned and studied practitioner, you will learn a great deal from this work. I plan to return to it repeatedly.

—Mark McClellan, J.D.; Ph.D., Dean of the Herschel Hobbs College of Theology and Ministry, Professor of Theology and Missions, Oklahoma Baptist University; Former International and North American Missionary Church Planter; Co-Author, Introducción a la Misiología

Terry Coy's ability to provide insight into the challenges and opportunities we face in the American mission field is impressive and helpful. The chapters are crystal clear, very well-organized and engaging. It is a must-read for those who are serious about getting "out of the box" and not only facing but reaching the world here at home. This is an outstanding book!

—Tony Mathews
Pastor, North Garland Baptist Fellowship
Vice President, SBTC African American Fellowship

Terry Coy in *Facing the Change* moves between the past in terms of the Biblical record in relationship to our understanding of Christ and the early church and to the future in terms of the trends and challenges facing the church in America and stops in the present in terms of bringing our attention of the missionary opportunity within our borders. He looks through global eyes to see the diversity in America not only in ethnicity but also in the post-modern culture and speaks about by changing the methods used in evangelism/ church planting with the centrality of the unchanging message through the appropriate contextualization principles. Now to move ahead and embrace the opportunity in America!

Joe Hernandez, Ph.D.
Church Planting Equipper and Strategist
Retired, North American Mission Board

I met Terry Coy decades ago and was captivated immediately by the combination of his impressive intellect and clear commitment to the gospel. No person working to build or revive a church, to win or restore disciples, or simply to grasp how to serve the gospel in today's world should overlook this work.

Barry K. Creamer, Ph.D.
Vice President of Academic Affairs
Professor of Humanities
Criswell College, Dallas, TX

In *Facing the Change*, Terry Coy sets out to provide a text that will realistically address the issues of the Christian church and spur the reader to think biblically about the challenge of missions and to act boldly for Christ amid a changing culture. *Facing the Change* does both, and would be a welcome addition to any pastor's or missionary's library.

Ed Stetzer, Ph.D.
President, Lifeway Research

As the American church has sought to live out its mission, it has come to a crossroads in how to define and live that mission out. Will the church continue to try to make God in its image or be made into His? Will the church continue to allow popular culture to define its mission or will we look to Christ? In *Facing the Change*, my friend Terry Coy addresses these issues head-on and challenges us to seize the opportunity to live out a Christ-centered missiology. If you are a Pastor, Church Planter, or leader in the church, I encourage you to read this book and let its words challenge and encourage you!

Loui Canchola
Pastor & Church Planter
Cornerstone Church
McAllen, Texas

In *Facing the Change*, Dr. Terry Coy addresses many of the key issues facing the modern context for doing missions that genuinely impacts culture, and more importantly, the souls of men! From the point of being a field practitioner and a scholar for many years, this book took a lifetime of mission's service and passion to write . . . and it shows on every page!

David A. Wheeler, Ph.D.
Professor of Evangelism,
NAMB Field Missionary, &
Director of CMT
Center For Ministry Training
Liberty University, Lynchburg, VA

I wish I had had the vision, experience, and skills to write this book. In *Facing the Change* Terry Coy puts his finger on a number of issues that too frequently are treated separately. In particular, too often Missions and Culture are discussed apart from serious academic Theology (Christology in particular), or academic Theology is done with no concern for Missions. Coy has done the American church a great service by bringing these important subjects together in one book. One may quibble with his positions at points but one must take seriously what he has to say on all points. I, for one, appreciate this book very much. I highly recommend it!

Robert B. Stewart, Ph.D.
Professor of Philosophy and Theology
Greer-Heard Professor of Faith and Culture
New Orleans Baptist Theological Seminary

As someone who grew up immersed in missions from his childhood, Terry Coy knows his stuff. A lifelong missionary (his parents served in Chile), Terry has written a book for pastors who feel more like a guest residing in the visitor's clubhouse rather than having home field advantage that many American evangelical Christians used to enjoy. Many pastors have a passion for leading a Great Commission church but are not sure how to proceed forward on American soil. They have desire to see their churches flourish but lack the knowledge necessary to get their hands around the problem. *Facing the Change* addresses this problem as it offers a detailed explanation of the contours of biblical theology alongside a description of the tsunami wave of changes facing church leaders in the twenty-first century.

This book by my friend, Terry Coy, will assist pastors just like me. I pastor a church situated in the middle of the

Dallas/Fort Worth metro area and need to know how to think like a missionary. Terry brings his experience in planting and guiding churches along with his formal training in theology to converge on behalf of church leaders. Whether read straight through and referenced again and again, *Facing the Change* will assist you in positioning your church for the Great Commission.

Scott Maze, PhD.
Senior Pastor, North Richland Hills Baptist Church
North Richland Hills, Texas

Facing

— the —

Change

Terry Coy

Facing

 *the*

Change

Challenges and Opportunities
for an American Missiology

TATE PUBLISHING
AND ENTERPRISES, LLC

Published by Tate Publishing & Enterprises, LLC
127 E. Trade Center Terrace | Mustang, Oklahoma 73064 USA
1.888.361.9473 | www.tatepublishing.com

Tate Publishing is committed to excellence in the publishing industry. The company reflects the philosophy established by the founders, based on Psalm 68:11,
"The Lord gave the word and great was the company of those who published it."

Book design copyright © 2013 by Tate Publishing, LLC. All rights reserved.
Cover design by Junriel Boquecosa
Interior design by Honeylette Pino

Published in the United States of America

ISBN: 978-1-62902-077-8
1. Religion / General
2. Religion / Christian Life / General
13.10.30

To my daughters and their husbands:
Lindsey and Charlie Durham and
Meagan and Patrick Wells
To my grandchildren: Kennedy, Landrie, Gentry, and Gibson.
May they and their generation be gospel salt and
light in an ever darkening world.

Acknowledgments

My thanks must be expressed to numerous people. First, I thank Dr. Jim Richards, Executive Director of the Southern Baptists of Texas Convention for taking a chance in hiring me as a church planting strategist in 2001. The opportunity to serve on the missions team at SBTC has been the most challenging and fulfilling ministry opportunity of my life. The opportunity I now have to be part of the most talented missions team in the country is an enormous blessing. I thank them for their hard work, loyalty, and constant support and encouragement of me. Most of this book is the result of my ministry at SBTC – reading, conversations, theological reflections, and interactions with pastors, planters, and other missionaries. I am ever grateful to the SBTC for providing an environment for the book to be conceived and come to fruition.

I am also thankful to those who read part or all of the manuscript as I was writing. I received encouragement along the way from mission team members Barry Calhoun, David Alexander, Chad Vandiver, and Tiffany Smith. Dr. Sam Douglass of Just Coach Me regularly offered enthusiastic encouragement. Most importantly, my good friend and predecessor, Dr. Robby Partain, now Director of Missions of the Bluebonnet Baptist Association in New Braunfels, Texas, read every single word with a critical eye. He offered invaluable critique, encouragement, suggestions, and ideas. I credited him once for an idea in an endnote, but soon realized I would greatly increase the number of endnotes if I gave him credit for every one of his helpful suggestions. Thanks, Robby!

Immeasurable thanks go to my parents, Frank and Betty Coy. They have been my missionary heroes for as long as I can remember. Their commitment, perseverance, hard work, and practical daily faith continue to be a standard by which I measure myself. Dad also read every word of the manuscript as I completed each chapter. He was full of fatherly encouragement, as every chapter was simply the greatest thing he had ever read. That's a Dad for you!

Finally and most joyfully, to Sandy, my wonderful wife of almost forty years – thank you for loving me, encouraging me, and faithfully supporting me through every crazy twist and turn in our lives together. Thank you, especially, for your encouragement and understanding as I headed many an evening and Saturday to my "man cave" to write. Your patience, grace, kindness, and Christ-like love toward all people are an inspiration to me.

Terry Coy
1 Cor. 2:2

Table of Contents

Introduction

I have spent much of my life around missionaries and in missions. I grew up in Chile, where my parents served thirty-five years as Southern Baptist missionaries. I traveled some with my father as he visited churches, preached, and encouraged pastors. I listened to missionary conversations about establishing new works, training leaders, teaching seminary students, and working closely with national leadership. Missionaries were my "aunts" and "uncles," and biannual mission meetings were the highlights of the year as we got to see and play with our missionary "cousins." Even today, I have an immediate connection with missionaries and missionary kids (now called third culture kids) I meet. My connection with Chile continues as my brother and sister-in-law currently serve there as Southern Baptist missionaries. Several return visits to Chile to preach and teach have strengthened my love for that country and its people.

I was a thirty year old businessman when I responded to God's call to ministry. My first vocational ministry experience was with a Biblical counseling ministry in Oklahoma City. It was only after I moved my family to Fort Worth to complete my studies at Southwestern Baptist Theological Seminary that I found myself involved in missions again and, for the first time, as an adult. A connection through a retired missionary at the

Tarrant Baptist Association (Fort Worth) led to a part-time job as an associational Hispanic Consultant. I had the privilege of working with both established Hispanic churches and new church plants (or missions, as they were usually called). That experience opened my eyes to the changing demographics in Texas and the U.S., and to the concept of my own country as a mission field. Eventually, I was able to serve as the Director of Church Planting for the association, where my horizons were expanded to include a variety of church planting models and relationships with various ethnic groups living in the Dallas-Fort Worth metroplex.

In 2001 I went to work for the new Southern Baptists of Texas Convention as the Ethnic Church Planting Strategist. After ten years, several title changes, and many experiences later, I am more convinced than ever that the United States is a diverse and complex mission field. Changing demographics, a diversity of cultures and worldviews, growing socio-economic disparity, the effects of globalization, and a growing postmodernity, have all resulted in the marginalization of the gospel and perceived irrelevance of the church.

The gospel has been marginalized more and more on several fronts – the academy, the public square, pop culture, and in the daily life of the average American. I would argue, however, that some of this marginalization is more our (the evangelical church) perception than reality, and that it is in all cases a great opportunity. Note, however, that I do not say irrelevance of the gospel. The gospel is never irrelevant. Actually, the church is never irrelevant either; but sometimes the expressions, ministries, and life of the church and the average churchgoer are or are seen as irrelevant. If the mission of the church – of every church – is the Great Commission (to make disciples of all nations, teaching them to obey all that Jesus commanded), then where is the mission field? Around the world and among all peoples, yes. And that includes the United States of America.[1]

Purpose of the book

My purpose, therefore, is to define, explore, and discuss the implications of what I see as three overarching issues or realities the American church[2] must be aware of and address in order to faithfully and effectively communicate the gospel and make disciples of Jesus Christ. These three issues are:

One, contemporary challenges to a Biblical Christology. The gospel is all about Jesus, who he is, what he did, and what he commanded. Biblical and orthodox Christology, as understood and taught by the American church (again, read evangelical), has certainly been challenged throughout all of history from numerous perspectives. It could be argued, however, that the contemporary challenges are more numerous and more pervasive than ever. The first part of this book will examine fourteen challenges to a Biblical Christology, some of them imported from world religions, some of them homegrown, and some even coming out of both historical and contemporary expressions of Christianity. In these challenges Jesus Christ is radically redefined, or minimized and marginalized, or manipulated (consciously or unconsciously) to fit a contemporary and all too human centered need.

These challenges will then be answered by examining and exploring what the Bible says about Jesus – what he said about himself and what other Biblical writers said about him. This first section will end with some missiological conclusions, applications, and implications leading to the bottom line question: "What are we going to do about Jesus?"

Two, contemporary challenges to the mission of the church. The mission of the church is the Great Commission, but that mission does not take place in a vacuum. Opposition, overt or covert, has always been part and parcel of the mission. In America, the contemporary challenges (which may be positive, negative, or, more likely, a mix of the two) include cultural changes, "ownership" and definition of the culture, immigration and demographic issues, urbanization, rapid and discontinuous change, technological advances, and the growing diversity of lifestyles and lifestyle choices. These define to some degree who we have been and who we are as a country. They also shape and challenge the church in its mission to make disciples. The second part of the book will examine the context, nature, and characteristics of the American mission field, making missiological applications along the way as they relate to the mission of the church.

Three, contemporary responses of the church. The challenges to our Biblical understanding of Jesus are many. The context in which we live and minister is ever changing and diverse. So how does the American church respond to and in the American mission field? The third part of the book will address several responses the church can take to faithfully and effectively carry out its mission. These are not all of the possible responses, and the applications of those presented are often controversial. Yet they are, I will argue, our priorities as Great Commission believers. The hotly debated issue of contextualization will be addressed and defended. Contextualized evangelism, church planting, and preaching are critical responses. A few aspects of both individual and corporate Christian life will be examined as our responses to contemporary challenges must not be solely theoretical, but applicable to daily life.

Working assumptions

I write with some basic presuppositions, which, to some degree betray a few of my conclusions. These are:

1. The Bible is God's true, inerrant, and authoritative word, and is the standard by which all ideologies, philosophies, methodologies, and cultures should be judged. This is not always easy and we do not always agree on interpretations

or the particular judgment conclusion; however, this must and should be our starting point.

2. Change is inevitable and always a mixed bag of good and bad. In some ways things are better than they used to be and in some ways they are worse. However, change is happening faster and is more discontinuous than ever. This type of change intensifies both the anxiety of the church and the desire for understanding and for answers.

3. We can't go back to the way things were, and pining for the good old days is futile. Christianity is eschatological; that is, it looks forward with hope to the return of Christ, the consummation of the Kingdom, the fulfillment of all his promises, the resurrection of the body, and the new heaven and new earth. Our faith, although it appreciates, remembers, honors, and is solidly grounded in history, should always look and move forward. Here, too, we may not agree on all the eschatological details, but we should agree to look forward with anticipation and excitement.

4. Christians always struggle with being in but not of the world. Once again, we will not always agree on how that looks in daily life and church practice. The call and challenge is for humility and charity. Let's talk and debate, but let's be slow to attribute motives and to judge intentions.

5. The United States is a mission field. This presupposition, therefore, includes the idea that missions can (and should) be done in America. Now, there are numerous definitions of "missions," some of which are quite narrow. Others are too broad (for example, to say that "everything the church does is missions" simply means that nothing is really missions). Moreover, the relationship and

difference between evangelism and missions has also been widely discussed and debated. I am defining missions as "carrying out the Great Commission beyond one's cultural, socioeconomic, ethnic, or language groupings; through a variety of strategies and ministries; for the purpose of planting New Testament churches."[3] If this is the case, and because America is more than one tightly knit homogeneous group, then it is a mission field, and becoming one more and more every day.

Who this book is for

I am writing with the thoughtful pastor, minister, student, and lay person in mind. That is, this is not a book with the academician in mind, although some of the topics can be rather academic. It is not a book, necessarily, for the comfortable lay person either. It is for the evangelical Christian leader, vocational or lay, who is aware of, bothered by, and concerned about changes in the United States. It is for that leader who senses and has experienced the struggle of the American church – their own church, perhaps – in addressing its context and culture. It is for that leader who is trying to get a handle on the meaning of these changes and how the church should respond.[4]

My assumptions about the reader, therefore, are: An acceptance of the Bible as God's true and authoritative word, a desire to take the gospel to all peoples in America, and openness to wrestle with difficult issues and be comfortable with humble, and sometimes tentative, answers. Without a doubt, there will be a certain amount of dogmatism that may come through in my writing, particularly as we examine Biblical Christology. I believe God has revealed himself in his written word and most fully in his incarnate Word, about whom we learn in his inerrant written word! That said, however, as a fallen and limited human being,

I seek to be humble, although strong, in my interpretations of culture and the world and in the applications of God's truth in the world. I assume my readers will be and do the same.

PART 1

Introduction
Who Do People Say That I Am? The Christological Foundations

Why Begin With Christology?

Why begin developing an American missiology with Christology? Because America is plagued with inadequate and deficient Christologies. The average American disciple of Jesus who holds to an orthodox Christology encounters daily challenges to a biblical understanding of Jesus. In the academy, in popular culture, in community and political life, and in much of cultural and historical American Christianity Jesus is seen as an ethical teacher, as a special human being, as prophetic, and even sometimes as supernatural. These common perspectives are correct and are all based on a partial reading of the Bible, yet they are also all incomplete, inadequate, and deficient. Regardless of the religion, philosophy, worldview, or cult, challenges to an orthodox Christology spring from basic disagreements over the person and work of Jesus Christ and culminate at his exclusive claims.

Certainly, a fully developed missiology would deal with theology proper: the nature and character of a missionary God.

It would also have to address the inspiration, authority, and veracity of Scripture, the role of the Holy Spirit, and other critical Christian doctrines. It would address epistemological, philosophical, cultural, and sociological issues. At some point, however, a Biblical missiology will have to deal with the question, "Who is Jesus and what did he do?" That question has never been more relevant than in today's diverse American context. The answer to that question, which should be given confidently and respectfully, will drive evangelism, missiology, ecclesiology, and all of Christian life.

The Inadequate Jesus of World Religions and American Spirituality

> Jesus went out with His disciples to the villages of Caesarea
> Philippi. And on the road He asked His disciples, "Who
> do people say that I am?" They answered Him, "John the
> Baptist; others, Elijah; still others, one of the prophets."
>
> Mark 8:27-28

In this passage, Jesus has just fed the four thousand and healed
the blind man in Bethsaida. As he and his disciples walk together
among rural villages, he asks them a question that sets up the
question he really wants to get to in verse 29 (see next chapter).
"Who do people say that I am?" he asks. As they have travelled
with Jesus, mingled with the multitudes, and attempted to answer
people's questions, surely the disciples have picked up on the buzz
in the crowd. Surely they have heard discussions about Jesus, not
only among the vocal Pharisees and Sadducees, but also among
the multitudes that constantly followed Jesus. "Fellows," Jesus is
asking, "what's the consensus about me? What do you hear is the
conventional wisdom about me?"

There is not, however, a consensus among the people. The disciples answer that some think Jesus is John the Baptist resuscitated. Some people think he may be Elijah come back. Still others think he may be one of the other prophets come back to life. Each answer reveals that the people did, in fact, think highly of Jesus. That is, they knew he was extraordinary, different from them, perhaps even supernatural. He was a messenger from God, he had something to say, he performed miracles, he was…well, special.

The problem is that no matter how special Jesus was according to the people, their appraisal of him was inadequate and incomplete. Their view of Jesus was deficient. Specifically, they were blinded to the fact that he was Messiah, the anointed One of God. Their presuppositions, misunderstandings, personal agendas, low and misplaced expectations blinded them to all that Jesus was and came to do. Granted, Jesus had not yet chosen at this particular time to reveal himself completely to the people – even his disciples did not yet understand the full implications of his messianic nature and mission. The point still stands, however, and is confirmed time and again by reading the rest of the New Testament: we humans can hardly resist the temptation to mold Jesus into our image, to shape him according to our expectations, our presuppositions, our culture and worldview, and to our agendas. And, as with the people then, that manipulation inevitably leads to an inadequate and deficient Christology. What are some of the inadequate Christologies on the American landscape?

Jesus Redefined:
World Religions in America

Whether or not America truly is or has been a Christian nation will be explored in Part 2. Regardless of one's conclusion in that debate, it is undeniable that Christianity, in all its variegated forms, both influenced the founding of the country and the development of what is popularly conceived as the American Way of Life. For good or for bad, Christianity is part of the American historical and cultural fabric.

Historically, for many Americans, and particularly for those in the Bible Belt, the American culture was, if not shaped and dominated by evangelical Christianity, at least a reflection of a Christian outlook and ethic. This did not mean that every American was "born again." It did mean, however, that the prevailing cultural outlook was supposedly that of biblical Christianity. How much of a reality that was is debatable. What is not debatable is that it is less and less so. One of the reasons it has changed is the influence of world religions in America. This is not a recent development. The great immigrations from countries like Ireland and Italy in the late nineteenth century changed the American Christian complexion from predominantly Protestant to include significant Catholic features. The influx of Eastern European immigrants in the first half of the twentieth century strengthened that Catholic influence and increased the already existing Jewish presence. Hinduism, Buddhism, and Islam have been present on the American landscape for two hundred years, but these, too, have escalated in visibility and to an arguably disproportionate influence during the last thirty years as new waves of immigrants have arrived from Asia and the Middle East. In each case, religion was an important part of immigrants' lives, so much so that their beliefs and practices have and continue to increase our cultural diversification, "making the American religious landscape more complex."[5]

Judaism: The messianic pretender

Although there has been a Jewish presence in America since colonial days, the first "large groups of Jews arrived in the United

States in the early nineteenth century from German-speaking areas of central Europe." Between 1881 and 1900 hundreds of thousands of eastern European Jews arrived through Ellis Island, greatly transforming both the American culture and their own culture in the process. In fact, the Jewish contribution and influence on American culture and lifestyle is astounding. From education, science and medicine, economics and banking, to the arts and popular culture, Jewish influence has permeated the American way of life.[6]

Theologically, however, Judaism is far from a monolithic religion. In fact, being Jewish is as much an ethnic identification as it is a religious belief or practice, a reality grounded in a history of persecution, especially the holocaust.

There are three main branches of Judaism: Orthodox, Conservative, and Reformed. Their core belief is that Yahweh is the one and only true God. His promised Messiah has not yet come. The Orthodox branch holds that the Messiah is a human being who is not divine. When he comes, he will restore the Jewish kingdom and rule over the earth, serving as the judge who will make right all the wrongs in the world. The Conservative and Reformed positions take a more secularized position and do not see the Messiah as a person and much less as a divine being. Rather, they favor the concept of a utopian age toward which humanity is progressing, which is sometimes called the "Messianic Age." Prophecies such as the "suffering servant" passages in Isaiah refer to the "individual Jew's experience of the Jewish people, of its corporate life, way and history which mediates for him between the individual and God."[7]

For most modern Jewish thinkers, the doctrine of the Messiah is a fluid one open to a "bewildering diversity." Most interpretations are naturalistic, ranging from the idea of the emergence of a better human being to the political Zionist movement, which rejects a personal Messiah but embraces the restoration of Israel.[8]

34

Therefore, whatever the branch of Judaism, Jesus is most certainly rejected as the Messiah. This rejection is not necessarily because Jesus was the "wrong" man as much as it is a rejection of the entire Christian understanding of the Messiah. That is, because Jesus did not fulfill the messianic mission as understood by the Jews, than he cannot be the Messiah. That does not mean, however, that Jesus' historicity is denied. To the contrary, his historical existence is usually acknowledged; Jewish thinkers often speak of him with great respect and admiration, for "he was a man whose personality discloses the Jewish character." He was "a complete, believing Jew" who wanted nothing more than to be a "devout son of Israel."[9]

Obviously, any hint of trinitarianism is rejected as incompatible with Jewish monotheism. As one Jewish writer puts it,

> We have not believed that Jesus was the Messiah; we have not been willing to call him Lord; we have not believed that the Logos became incarnate as Jesus; we have not believed that Jesus was, or is, the very Godness of God....To us Jesus is never more than a man, and deeply as some of us Jews are to sympathize with the tragedy of his life and death, we do not see in it any special working of the divine....for we never go beyond regarding him as one more good man in the long history of good men, and in that line we do not place him as pre-eminent.[10]

So, Jesus was a messianic pretender. He was rejected as such at his trial (Matt. 26:62-67). He is rejected as such by the modern day Jew, who sees the affirmation of Jesus as Messiah as "Christian romanticism," because we have been too blind to see the evil and wrongness in the world that the true Messiah was to set straight. Whether or not Jesus was Messiah is where, as Jewish thinker Jacob Neusner said it well, ". . . Judaism and Christianity, in all their dazzling varieties, must part company, and without regret on either side."[11]

Islam: a prophet of Allah

Islam first came unwillingly to America with captured African slaves, but did not thrive because it was suppressed by slave owners. Although some Muslim immigrants arrived in the nineteenth century, the greatest growth of Islam has come in the last few decades of the twentieth century, both through immigration and by conversion. This latest growth has been such that Muslims may soon outnumber Jewish believers in the United States.[12]

Islam's core belief is an absolute and radical monotheism. There is only one absolute, unified, and transcendent God who cannot relate with anything or anyone outside of himself. Only his will can be known. It is this specific "view of the divine that places Islam most sharply at odds with Christianity." The Quran states numerous times that God has no son, for one because it would imply that God had physical relations with a woman. Thus, Islam totally rejects any idea of the Trinity (equated with worshipping three Gods) and of the deity of Jesus Christ. In reality, Jesus was one of the major prophets – a most honored prophet, certainly – but not to be associated with God (which is blasphemy), and ultimately superseded by the prophet Muhammad. Muslims do affirm the virgin birth of Jesus and acknowledge that he was sinless and performed miracles, but he did not die on the cross, much less atone for sins. Rather, he ascended into heaven while Judas died in his place, for God would not have allowed one of his prophets to be crucified. [13]

Because Jesus was no more than a prophet, salvation is obtained by following the five pillars of Islam: recitation of the Shahad ("There is no God but Allah, and Muhammad is the prophet of Allah"), five daily prayers, almsgiving, fasting, and a pilgrimage to Mecca. Salvation is clearly by works, having "one's good deeds outweigh one's bad deeds."[14]

According to the Quran, Jesus himself knew he was only a human being. When God challenged Jesus after his ascension, Jesus denied that he told people to take him (and his mother) as two additional deities. Historically, says Islam, the problem is that the Apostle Paul obscured the humanity of Jesus and elevated him to godhead, creating the myth that Christians now believe. It is the Quran, Muslims claim, which restores Jesus' humanity and his historical prophetic mission. It is the Quran that encourages Christians not to raise Jesus to godhead and not to ascribe to him beliefs that were never his. Christians have "deliberately falsified the scripture he brought" and thus worship the "Messiah blasphemously." Finally, Jesus taught the kingdom of God, which is "the practical kingdom of Islam for all people, irrespective of race or ethnic origin, who believe in one God."[15]

The historical and prophetic Jesus is acknowledged by Islam. However, he has no divine connection with God – that is both impossible and blasphemous to even consider. A special human being, yes. One who displayed supernatural characteristics and acts such as the virgin birth and miracles, yes. But also one misinterpreted by Paul and the early church, superseded in importance by Muhammad, restored to his proper place by the Quran, and most certainly not one who can act as mediator and savior for human beings. Jesus is, therefore, redefined to fit a supposed newer revelation involving a superior prophet of God.

*

Hinduism: an incarnation of God

Hinduism has been historically centered in India. It is made up of many branches and many forms, to the extent that "it has developed the most complex and extensive philosophy ever known."[16] It came to the U.S. at different times and took different forms, especially as it was popularized and Americanized. One of its earliest introductions into America was through the Vedanta Society in the late nineteenth century. In the 1960s the Hare Krishna Movement greatly influenced the American hippie countercultural movement. Hinduism is still growing in both presence and influence as more refugees, immigrants, and students arrive from India, Nepal, Bhutan, and other south Asian countries.

The core belief of Hinduism has been described as a "polytheistic view, with a unified monotheistic concept." That is, there is one true God, who can take on many different forms. These forms or manifestations (avatars) are "representatives of the endless natures and layers that make up" God. Human beings are subject to Karma, or the law of judgment, and are trapped in the wheel of reincarnation and rebirth. The goal in life is to eventually transcend or escape Karma and achieve Moksha, or liberation.[17]

Our problem as humans is that we are ignorant of our divine nature, that we are essentially one with Brahman, the ultimate Reality, or the impersonal oneness that is all in all. Consequently, we are attached to desires and our own individual existence. Through the process of Karma, reincarnation and rebirth, we can eventually be liberated from the illusion that the self, or Atman, is reality. Enlightenment, therefore, leads to oneness with Brahman; it leads to understanding that Atman *is* Brahman.[18]

How does Jesus fit into this scheme? One way is to see him as one among many. That is, he is one of those avatars, one of the many manifestations of the impersonal Brahman. He is one of the special creations of God along with other special incarnations throughout history. He is one of the manifestations of the Word, but certainly not the only one. The incarnation of Jesus, therefore, is not rejected. Hindus, however, believe that his was not the only incarnation because incarnation is not just a one-time historical event. It is an eternal truth in that the Word incarnates itself many times over the course of human existence, according to the needs of humankind. Thus, Sri Krishna, Buddha, Jesus Christ, others from the past and others yet to come are incarnations of the Word or Brahman. His incarnation is real, but redefined and certainly not unique.[19]

Another way for Hindus to interpret Jesus is to see him as the fulfillment or the perfect manifestation of all that Hinduism stands for. He was one of the incarnations of God, but he was the best. He is venerated as a great teacher of righteousness, a selfless and sacrificial saint serving as a model for all people, the best example of God-in-man rather than God-as-man. The cross is the symbol of all this; that is, it is the ideal of self-denial in the interests of humanity. The cross was a redemptive act because it serves as an example to the rest of us. Therefore, Jesus Christ is the "quintessential Hindu, the one who lived Hindu ideals as they ought to be lived and teaches the essence of Hindu truth as it ought to be taught."[20]

It is not difficult for Hindus to believe in Jesus, either as one of or the best of the incarnations of God, or as one who lived out the best of Hindu ideals. What is difficult for a Hindu is to acknowledge the uniqueness of the incarnation of Jesus Christ and that the importance of the incarnation and the passion of Jesus as far more than an example of selfless sacrifice. As an Indian pastor in America put it to me after he led a Hindu to Christ, "I know he confessed Jesus Christ as the Son of God. Now I need to make sure he acknowledges and confesses him as the unique Son of God." That is, he wanted to make sure that this individual did not just "accept Jesus Christ," but that he "accepted Jesus Christ *alone*."

Buddhism: an enlightened one

As one of the most universal of the world's religions, Buddhism dominates much of East and Southeast Asia, although most every country in the world has some Buddhist representation.

Like Hinduism, it has spread to and been popularly received in the West, including the United States (it is the dominant religion in Hawaii). It was introduced in the U.S. in 1844 at the convening of the American Oriental Society, but arrived *en masse* through immigration, particularly by Chinese workers in California during the 1849 gold rush. It influenced Transcendentalists such as Thoreau and Emerson, was popularized in 1893 at the World's Parliament of Religions in Chicago, and continued to grow through immigration and popular cultural acceptance, especially in the 1950s and 60s.[21] In the last few decades, its influence has accelerated through the influx of immigrants and through popular culture.

Although there are at least five major divisions or groups in Buddhism some common core beliefs can be identified. The most basic Buddhist belief deals with suffering or pain in human existence. For the Buddhist everything is in reality impermanent and ever-changing. Humans suffer because we do not recognize this and because we desire impermanent things. The goal of life is to stop desire and seek the permanent – Nirvana. In Buddhism there is no personal God; ultimate reality is Nirvana, which is an abstract void. By overcoming desire, by overcoming emotions, and realizing the non-existence of the self, a person enters into oneness with Nirvana where the ego is extinguished. Thus, although there is no personal God, there are "many paths to God" if "God" is understood as Nirvana.[22]

The founder of the religion, Siddhartha Gautama, was the first to understand these truths, achieve enlightenment, and be called the Buddha. After Enlightenment his mission was to teach others how they, too, could find deliverance from human suffering and enter Nirvana. Most Buddhists are willing to accept "clear parallels" between Buddha and Jesus. They can appreciate him because his miracles show that he was "an extraordinary individual," although they "do not prove that such a person is God or that he or she is enlightened or worthy of worship." Miracles are basically acts of magic and thus theologically neutral for Buddhists. Jesus' teachings in the Beatitudes on loving one's enemy, repaying evil with kindness, and giving alms all resonate with Buddhist teachings.[23]

The biggest problem Buddhists have with Jesus is that Christians portray him as God. They do not object to the claim that Jesus is an incarnation or a manifestation of a deity, but they do deny both the uniqueness of the incarnation and the characterization of the deity whose manifestation Jesus is said to be. They deny the uniqueness of Jesus' incarnation because, depending on the branch of Buddhism, there could be a "wide range of deities" and of "selective incarnations that are embodiments of selective aspects of the enlightened state." That is, Jesus could certainly be a manifestation of a deity, of Wisdom, or of the Word, but that is just "as good explanation as any." Furthermore, the universe is filled with beings that have a real relationship with a variety of deities. They object to the kind of God that Christians say Jesus manifested because there is no god who is originally pure, who is the creator of the universe, who is perfect. All the evil and suffering in the world give evidence to the contrary. Thus, Jesus cannot be the incarnation of such a God.[24]

Buddhists, like Hindus, have no problem accepting Jesus as one of many incarnations of some form of deity, but never of *the* one, true, personal God, for such a personal God is rejected. He is at best one who, like the Buddha, understands the nature of suffering and the need to escape this impermanent world and become one with the abstract void, Nirvana. He was, thus, an enlightened one who gave up all desire and all selfhood at the cross in an act of sacrifice and was finally one with Nirvana.

Mormonism: growing into godhood

Of the five world religions examined, Mormonism is the one that is all-American homegrown. Founded by Joseph Smith, led westward from Illinois after Smith's murder and geographically established by Brigham Young in Salt Lake City, the Church of Jesus Christ of Latter Day Saints (LDS) is now a worldwide phenomenon. By 2000, its membership passed 11 million and is now one of the largest denominations in the U.S. It is experiencing phenomenal growth in Latin America and is rapidly growing in Asia and Africa.[25]

An ongoing debate is whether Mormonism is a branch of Christianity or a cult; whether or not Mormons can legitimately call themselves Christians. Mormons certainly argue that they are Christians. In fact, according to Stephen Prothero, Mormons have been working on reinventing themselves since the 1890s, as they "Americanized and Protestantized their tradition."[26] This effort has intensified in the last few decades, and is especially important to them as their numbers and influence continue to grow outside their Utah base and into business, education, and even presidential politics.[27] Besides the fact that no one would really want to be considered a cult, Mormons have argued they have a Biblical and restored (through Joseph Smith and the Book of Mormon) view of Jesus Christ. I would argue, however, that, although so much of their terminology sounds orthodox, when those terms are defined and explained, they have redefined Jesus to fit an extra- and non-biblical theology.

For Mormons, Jesus Christ pre-existed, as did all men and women, in the premortal realm. He was the firstborn spirit child of God the father and thus the literal elder brother of all the spirit sons and daughters of the Father. In this premortal realm, Jesus Christ grew in light and truth, knowledge and power until he became like God the Father. He was above his spirit siblings because he did the best in faith and good works. God the Father had a plan of redemption and salvation for his children, which would allow them to become gods. The plan, however, involved the sons and daughters of God becoming mortal and walking "by faith in this second estate without full knowledge of what they did and who they were in the life before." God the Father called together the Grand Council of heaven, laid forth his plan, and asked for volunteers to implement his plan on earth. Lucifer, Jesus' brother, volunteered first. He was, however, full of pride and ambition, believing that he could save all human souls, so that none would be lost. His will and plan was contrary to the Father's. Jesus, on the other hand, was more humble in his offer. He admitted that he would not be able to save all and submitted fully to the Father's plan. Jesus, the Firstborn, therefore, was chosen by God the Father to be the Mediator for man and the Way to the Father. It was at this point that Lucifer and a third of the spirit children rebelled and were cast down to earth.[28]

Following his selection as Mediator and under the direction of the Father, Christ created this world and "worlds without number." He was known by the ancients as the "Lord Omnipotent," as the "Father of heaven and earth, the Creator of all things from the beginning." He was the one called Jehovah by the ancient Hebrews. In due time, this "almighty Jehovah, the premortal God of the ancients," was born as the man Jesus, conceived through sexual relations between a flesh and bones Father and Mary. This Jesus was perfectly obedient and was thus entitled to a fullness of the Spirit. Being that Jesus was the son of God, he was a glorified immortal being with the capacity to rise up from the dead. He kept the law of God and was thus in the Father and the Father in him, and "though they were two separate and distinct beings, they were one." Our duty is to be like Jesus and strive to be one with the gods.[29]

Mormons reject the doctrine of human depravity and "do not subscribe to a belief in an 'original sin'." That is, we are neither condemned nor accountable for the fall of Adam. The consequences of the fall, rather, are limited to a "propensity for and susceptibility to sin." The atonement of Jesus, which is the gift of God, therefore covers only the sin of Adam and sets up the availability of forgiveness of all other sins. It is the beginning of the process of salvation, which includes baptism and the necessity of good works. Jesus, therefore, initiates salvation, but every individual must complete the process through good works and faithfulness to the church. Brigham Young summed it up by saying,

> It requires all the atonement of Christ, the mercy of the Father, the pity of angels and the grace of the Lord Jesus Christ to be with us always, and then to do the very best we possibly can, to get rid of this sin within us, so that we may escape from this world into the celestial kingdom.[30]

The Jesus of the Latter Day Saints is, therefore: the literal spirit son of the Father, begotten at some point in premortal time, and the spirit brother of Lucifer/Satan and the rest of the spirits in heaven who became mortal. This means that Jesus is different only in *degree* and not in *kind* from his brother the devil and all other premortal offspring. In this premortal existence he grew to become like God. His incarnation and atonement provides the first step in the forgiveness of sins, the process of salvation, and the journey towards becoming like the gods, a process that is never certain until the end.[31]

Based on this brief overview of Mormon Christology it can be seen that Jesus Christ is radically redefined. Yes, he is pre-existent, the Son of God, able to act supernaturally and able to "save." But his fundamental nature, relationship to the Father and to the Holy Spirit,[32] his identification with Jehovah, his manner of incarnation, and the nature of his atonement are all so radically redefined that Mormons surrender any legitimate claim to being Christian or Biblical. It is only by using extra biblical sources and ongoing "revelation" that such a redefinition is possible. The Christology of this world religion sounds the most biblical and orthodox, but it is arguably the most dangerous and deceptive. Mormon Christology is simply the old Arian heresy revisited; that is, claiming that there was a time, however long ago, when the Son did not exist. He may be divine, but in Mormonism his is a deity far less than the Father's.

Conclusion:
Just one among many others

The five world religions examined define Jesus along a spectrum from the most naturalistic to supernatural. In every case examined, Jesus has been redefined and made inadequate in his deity, in his humanity, or in his work of atonement. The reality for twenty-first century America is that we are no longer a three religion nation (Protestant, Catholic, Judaism). Immigration, and especially the post-1965 "new immigration," means that religious diversity is now our norm.[33] As we evangelicals define our most basic belief – Jesus Christ as the Son of God, the second person of the Trinity, fully and truly God and man, unique in his incarnation and atonement – where does that put us in relation to our neighbors from other religions? Where does "tolerance" fit in, and what does it really mean? What about our missionary duty? Perhaps even more subtly, how is our understanding and practice of Christianity changing as more and more American Christians are no longer from a western background? These are issues that will be addressed later. But, there are still challenges to a biblical Christology from other sources.

Jesus in Our Own Image:
Anthropocentric American
spirituality and "religions"

The United States of America is a religious country. True convictional atheists are few and far between. Certainly there those materialists who believe that the natural world is ultimate reality and all there is. Most Americans, however, are at worst agnostic about spiritual matters, with most open to and interested in religion and spirituality, however those may be defined – usually defined through personal opinion and experience.

In the midst of a religious America dominated by Christian denominations, non-Christian spirituality in America has also thrived from colonial days. Whether through the influence of Enlightenment Deism, spiritualism, rationalism, empiricism and evolution, scientific or economic materialism, and numerous other sects and cults, the American religious and spiritual landscape is broad and diverse. In many ways this is simply an outcome of the American experiment. We are all about the new and the creative, the practical and the achievable, and about making things personal and relevant. In itself, this tendency is not altogether a bad thing. When it comes to religion, however, and specifically to Christianity, we too often push aside history and traditions (after all, as a nation we are fairly anti-tradition and even anti-history), and this makes us vulnerable to the latest cultural pressures and influences. Evangelicals, especially, tend to reject or marginalize creeds and traditions. This can result in anthropocentric spirituality and religion – shaping the religion, in practice if not in belief, to our own image. As far as Jesus is concerned, we interpret, shape, manipulate, and force him into our cultural experience, our ideological stands, our material and psychological needs, and our latest scientific discoveries. We all do it. Atheists and agnostics do it, secularized intellectuals do it, religious compromisers do it, and well-intentioned evangelicals do it.[34]

The Modern Jesus: Tested and found wanting

America has always been about progress. We love scientific knowledge and technological advances to the point that faith in science and technology has arguably been one of our biggest national idols. Although postmodern Americans in the twenty-first century are far less confident in science and technology (we still love technology, we are just not as confident in its ability to solve our problems), our forefathers embraced new knowledge and inevitable progress. The three Christologies examined below grew out of the attempt to adapt the Biblical account to new scientific discoveries and new philosophies. If these happened to contradict or correct Scripture, so be it.

Moralism: a good and moral teacher

The understanding of Jesus as simply a good and moral teacher grew out of prevalent Deism on the early American intellectual scene. The deistic view of God – that he created the universe, set up natural laws to govern its functioning, and then let it run without interference – was fashionable in upper class circles in Colonial days. Earlier in England the deist sentiment had been "to overcome the divisions among Christians by suggesting that only those affirmations on which all Christians agree are essential articles of faith." In other words, what are the irreducible minimums all can agree on? Unfortunately, the starting point was not Biblical revelation, which was rejected, but new understanding from science and from unaided reason. The essentials would be "those truths which can be known by human reason alone without the aid of special revelation." This independent use of reason was free from church authorities, divine revelation, or any other person. As the philosopher John Locke would argue, "If something is contrary to reason, we must reject it no matter what religious authority it claims." Using the new methods of historical-critical research, the search was on for the "true" historical Jesus. Doctrinal developments such as the Trinity were pushed aside, for they were too abstract and too unreasonable. Instead, Christianity ought to be based on "morality and commonsense." Yes, there is a God, the deist would say; yes, he is to be worshipped, but true worship is simply the practice of virtue. What we can know of him, however, is only what our reason can tell us.[35]

Some of the most notable deists in early American history were George Washington, Thomas Jefferson, Benjamin Franklin, and Thomas Paine. They rejected orthodox Christology. For them, the essence of religion was virtue, which was certainly best learned from Jesus. According to Franklin, Jesus left us the best system of morals, but he was not divine. These founding fathers were, without a doubt, religious and steeped in the Judeo-Christian tradition. They were not atheists. They believed in Jesus as a moral teacher, but, rejecting the revelation of Scripture, they denied the deity of Jesus. They were essentially pragmatic moralists, "Christian" in the sense that they followed Jesus' moral and ethical teachings (or so they claimed). Despite that claim to be Christian, they time and time again rejected the orthodox beliefs about Jesus' person and work. Original sin was rejected so atonement is not needed. Jesus was reduced to a good man, a good teacher, and one who leads the way in virtue, ethics, and morals. Salvation, if it can be called that, comes by following him in his teachings.[36]

This moralist view of Jesus, or "the first of human Sages," as Jefferson called him, spread as America grew, most notably among Unitarians, Reformed Jews, and liberal Protestants. The result is that many Americans, especially in our contemporary setting, have sought to remove and "disentangle" Jesus from creeds, statements of faith, and doctrinal declarations. To them his exemplary life is what matters and is far more important than his atoning death – because we don't need it. As Prothero puts it, we are a nation of "Golden Rule Christians," where true religion is about doing the right things rather than believing the right things, where good deeds means more than right doctrine or right worship.[37]

Liberalism: he's almost but not quite enough

The term liberal, like many other terms, is frequently misused and abused. Too often, we evangelicals use it to describe anyone with whom we have a slight disagreement, and often, at that, over a second or third tier doctrine. In this particular case, my interest is an overview of the classical liberal view of Jesus.

As mentioned above, during the Enlightenment religion (and particularly the Bible) was subjected to criticism from new ideas and philosophies. Classical liberalism is that movement following the Enlightenment "that sought to reconstruct Christian belief in light of modern knowledge" by adapting it to these new scientific and philosophical mindsets. The Bible was to be studied scientifically, with more trust placed in that particular analysis and in human reason and human experience than in revelation. Liberalism, however, is not a monolithic belief system, but rather a set of presuppositions, approaches to the Bible, and theological methodologies.[38]

In reaction to earlier rationalists and Deists who had reduced Jesus to an ethical teacher, Friedrich Schleiermacher, the father of liberal theology, put the locus of religion not in morality or even knowledge, but in feeling. This religious feeling is the "consciousness of being absolutely dependent" on God. Therefore, he argued, doctrines are based in religious consciousness rather than in external reality. Jesus Christ is both divine and human, and is redeemer. He is redeemer, however, in that his life demonstrated his perfect God-consciousness. His death was not in our place but rather the result of the world's hostility toward that God-consciousness. Being a Christian means to become conscious of Jesus' life and move in our God-consciousness from sin to perfection. That is, Jesus' God-consciousness is different from other human beings only in degree and not in kind. His God-consciousness developed and is thus the "archetype" and example of what all of us should be in our consciousness of God. This father of liberal theology, therefore, put the emphasis on feeling, "discovery," and religious consciousness rather than on revelation.[39]

Other liberal theologians, like the Deists before them, focused on the ethical dimensions of Christianity and avoided the abstract metaphysical doctrines of Christology. For them, religious truths were not fixed doctrines to be believed, but were rather "developmental and evolutionary in nature." The Bible, therefore, is simply the interpretation of the specific "religious experiences of the authors. In a nutshell, classical liberal Christology: 1) opposed the Christ of the early church creeds, 2) were suspicious of Paul and John, claiming they over-interpreted Jesus, 3) focused, therefore, on the Synoptic Gospels (especially Mark) and sought to reconstruct the "real" Jesus from these based on a psychological description of Jesus' inner life and development, and, 4) consequently downplayed the classical view of his divinity and emphasized his humanity.[40]

A Christology built on these assumptions led to various unorthodox conclusions by liberal theologians, including the belief that it was the piety of the early church that "turned the historical Jesus into a divine figure," that Jesus' teaching about the Kingdom of God was purely "ethical in nature," which was interpreted to mean "humanity organized according to love," and that Jesus's "consciousness of himself as the Son of God was nothing but the practical consequence of knowing God as the divine Father." The Gospel, therefore, was not about Jesus but about the Father only, although Jesus showed how one could come to the full realization of God consciousness.[41]

Liberal Christologies are found today in various shapes and forms and in many denominations. Perhaps the two most common versions are the ones that focus on personal devotion and personal religious experience. Similar to the moralistic view, Jesus Christ is reduced to a moral example and Christianity is reduced to "a set of moral platitudes." This view goes hand in hand with minimizing or redefining Biblical revelation, which then leads to a diminished view of sin and an elevated view of humanity. There is certainly an affirmation of faith in Christ in this kind of liberalism, but neither faith nor Christ is defined in the same terms as orthodox Christians would understand them. Jesus is simply the model character for us all. He is a "superhero of human goodness," but his divinity is understood only as an inner quality of life. Furthermore, all humanity possesses this inner quality; it is not unique in Jesus, he is just more spiritually attuned than the rest of us.[42]

The other common liberal version of Christ is exemplified by the famous, or infamous, Jesus Seminar of the 1980s and 90s. In line with previous "quests for the historical Jesus, the goal of this group of scholars was to free Jesus from his supposed bondage to traditional Christian creeds." What actually happened each time is that the newly discovered Jesus somehow wound up looking like those doing the quest. Liberal Protestants in the first quest of the nineteenth century, it has been said, managed to "dig down the well of Catholic history" only to find "their own reflections." The second quest of the mid-twentieth century reflected the neo-orthodox and existentialist trends of the age and petered out when these "went out of fashion." The third quest – the Jesus Seminar – was mostly an American one. According to Prothero, it was "designed to provoke" and presented Jesus as a "subversive sage," an iconoclast, a rebel, a hippie. The Seminar group studied and discussed Jesus' sayings and then voted (after all, they were democratic Americans) on the probability of the authenticity of those sayings. They essentially repeated what Jefferson did with his Bible, and, like all quests, cast Jesus in their own image. Most of the Seminar participants had grown up in the beatnik 50s or hippie 60s, so their real Jesus was somehow an "enlightened sage, but a groovy one." He was like Jack Kerouac and Timothy Leary – "subversive," "irreligious, irreverent, and impious."[43] Lest we jump to joyful criticism, however, as we shall see later, the temptation to mold Jesus in our own image is one we all face to one degree or another.

Scientism: a quaint, mythological figure

The western world's infatuation with science and technology has inevitably led to what is called scientism, which is "the view that all real knowledge is scientific knowledge – that there is no rational objective form of inquiry that is not a branch of science." This view is grounded in naturalism and materialism, the belief that the natural and material world is ultimate reality. Scientism consequently denies the supernatural, including miracles and any concept of God, personal or otherwise. What is real is what can be observed and measured. Religion has "no scientific foundation," and therefore, "has no rational foundation." Faith is pitted against science and science is made synonymous with reason. It appears that, as Daniel Dennett observed, "[W]hen it comes to facts, and the explanation of facts, science is the only game in town."[44]

It should be noted that scientism is not simply a rejection of religion and the supernatural. It is its own worldview, a comprehensive way of understanding, interpreting, and explaining the universe. As the home page for the Center of Naturalism states it, their purpose is to promote "science-based naturalism as a comprehensive worldview," which would serve as "a rational and fulfilling alternative to faith-based religions and other varieties of supernaturalism." As a worldview it is supposed to give purposeful and fulfilling answers to life's questions and problems.[45]

Perhaps no one more famously embodies the worldview of naturalism than the scientist Stephen Hawking. For him scientism is the worldview that explains all natural phenomena, that rejects supernatural speculations, and which embraces the "twin pillars" of reason and empiricism as a philosophy of life.

The hope is that scientism will "courageously" give naturalistic answers "that supplant supernaturalistic ones and in the process" provide "spiritual sustenance for those whose needs are not being met by…ancient cultural traditions."[46]

Note that last sentence about "spiritual sustenance." Scientism is more than just a worldview. If not a religion in the traditional sense, it is certainly a religious worldview, for it claims to answer ultimate questions about existence. It is a worldview driven by ideological presuppositions, presenting itself as the ultimate authority on life and meaning.[47]

This is not to say that all scientists hold to scientism. Some are believing Christians, some practice other religious traditions, and many are simply agnostic. Moreover, I am not saying that evangelicals ought to fear science or be anti-science. If God is the Creator and Sustainer of the universe and if he has revealed himself in his creation, then we should lead the way in studying and investigating his magnificent creation. What we do need to be concerned about is the growing popularity of scientism and the often unquestioning acceptance by the media and the public of its adherents' statements about life and ultimate reality. This is when scientists meddle in theology and at that with scores of unrecognized assumptions and presuppositions. They speak, the media reports their conclusions as absolute truth, and the public often receives them as such.

So what would a naturalist or scientific materialist or one who holds to scientism say about Jesus? What would his Christology entail? Not much. By rejecting the supernatural, by denying God, or at minimum any kind of personal God, and by rejecting the Bible as nothing more than a book of stories, Jesus is relegated to a simple man who taught and did good things. He is at best a good teacher, but is more apt to be seen as a quaint mythological figure, for there is little about him that can be verified through the scientific method. To believe in him, or anything the Bible says, is to admit to being superstitious, non-scientific, and maybe even delusional.

Conclusion:
Just a Step Ahead of the Rest of Us

The Jesus in these influential American Christologies has been knocked down to size through rationalism, an excessive dependency on science, an unwillingness to accept the supernatural, or simply to fit him into an ethical box, a personal experience, or an intuitive feeling. This reduction of the Biblical understanding of Jesus as the Christ, the unique Son of God, results in a deficient and marginalized Jesus. He is at best a human being or special individual who has received more light and more understanding than the rest of us. He is a step or two more advanced, making him different from us in degree, but certainly not in kind. Even in scientism, where Jesus is considered as nothing more than a human being, he is still considered somewhat special, because he is remembered and thought of fondly by most.

In every case discussed, Jesus is inadequate from the evangelical point of view to be or to do anything more than teach, guide, or be an example. For many people in America this is enough. They follow his teachings (or at least some of them) and his example and even call themselves Christian. To declare any uniqueness or exclusivity about Jesus, however, is to fall into intolerance and superstition.

The Cafeteria Jesus: Pick and choose

American Sects and Cults:
Keeping him manageable

Entire books have been written about the many American sects and cults. Only a few will be briefly examined here. There are also different definitions of the terms "sect" and "cult." Sometimes they are used interchangeably, but they do mean different things. As I use them, a sect is a Christian schismatic group that is generally orthodox in its beliefs, especially in its Christology. They hold, therefore, to orthodox understandings of the person and work of Jesus Christ. They do have, however, some different or heterodox doctrines and/or some debatable out of balance emphases. A cult has unorthodox or heretical beliefs, especially about the person and work of Jesus. This does not mean every cult is extreme or violent as was, for example, the Jonestown cult or the Branch Davidians.

The largest and most influential American cult, the Church of Jesus Christ of Latter Day Saints, has already been considered separately. Other groups, however, not nearly as large or as influential, arose on the American religious landscape in the last two centuries, an illustration of both the inherent religiosity of Americans and of our emphasis on individualism. In a society where tradition and traditional authority are regularly questioned and where individual freedom is celebrated, all it takes is for one creative and influential person to have a new and different idea. Whether it is a new way of reading and interpreting the Bible or whether it is a desire to harmonize the Bible with other religious beliefs, reinterpreting Jesus to fit or harmonize new ideas were common.

The Transcendentalists, whose most famous figures are Ralph Waldo Emerson, Henry Thoreau, and Walt Whitman, were an eclectic movement that is hard to characterize specifically. The movement is the result of the Rationalist tradition, which rejected orthodox doctrines such as the Trinity and the two natures of Christ, colliding with the age of Romanticism. This led to a mysticism that insisted on God's immanence in creation, a dependence on an individual's intuition as able to grasp the truth, and "a rejection of all external authority." This being the case, the individual soul, which is linked to God, has no need for a redeemer. Jesus is not conceived as the rationalist's moral teacher, but is the romantic's supreme Beauty and Goodness, the "Poet of the Spirit."[48]

Some cultic groups actually rose out of evangelical revivalist movements. These revivals often emphasized an "immediate confrontation with God," the possibility of perfect sanctification in this life, and the "millennial expectation of a golden age to come." Whereas many evangelical groups today would argue that any or all of those emphases are Biblical, many groups grabbed hold of one or another emphasis and took it to extremes. Utopian groups such as the Shakers argued that original sin and the foundation of human depravity was the actual sex act. The communities they established were therefore celibate and could grow by conversion only. The founder of the Shakers, "Mother Ann," taught that she was Christ in his second coming and had inaugurated the millennium. Another utopian group, the Oneida Community, went to the other extreme, was antinomian and lived in "complex marriage" arrangements.[49]

Millenerian groups focused on, and often tried to predict, the second coming of Jesus. The Millerites or Seventh Day Adventists sect, for example, set 1844 as the date for Jesus' coming. When he did not return, many were disappointed and the movement almost fell apart. It was only after one leader explained that Jesus had in fact come in secret for his "investigative judgment" that the group recovered and grew to the international denomination it is today.[50]

The Jehovah's Witnesses also tried to set the second coming of Jesus in 1914. When he failed to return, they explained that he had come in spirit. As a cult, the Jehovah's Witnesses are growing in number and influence around the world, and are especially making inroads among American Hispanics. Their Christology is the old Arian heresy revisited, which stated that there was a time when the Son was created. They interpret, and re-translate, the "Word" or *Logos* in John 1 as "a god," making the Son less than God himself. He was God's first creation, was with the Father in heaven from the beginning of creation, and was used by God in the creation of all things. This god was made human as Jesus and did suffer death to produce the ransom for obedient man – a salvation by works. He was not, however, the immortal God, otherwise, "he could not have died." The atonement removed the "effects of Adam's sin" from humans and "laid the foundation of the New World of righteousness including the Millennium of Christ's reign." Jesus was raised from the grave, but as a spirit only and not bodily. The Trinity, therefore, is rejected. There is the Father, the created Son, and the force of the Holy Spirit of God.[51]

There are also numerous spiritualist cults. One of the earliest groups was the Theosophical Society, founded by Madame Blavatsky in the nineteenth century. Hers was a combination of Spiritualism and Buddhism, and she claimed to be in the line of other gifted seers, such as Moses, Krishna, Confucius, Buddha, Christ, and others. Perhaps among the most well-known of the "mind" or "spiritual" groups are the Christian Scientists, founded by Mary Baker Eddy. For these the Eternal Mind is the source of all being and matter is non-existent. Because all is actually an illusion, disease is caused by erroneous thinking and death is simply passing on to reality. Similar is the Unity School of Practical Christianity which believes in reincarnation, spirit-communication, positive thinking, and which taught an early version of prosperity theology.[52] In every case, Jesus is simply one who is further along than the rest of us. He understood the illusion, was enlightened by that knowledge, and is the example and guide for the rest of us. The influence from both Hinduism and Buddhism is obvious, and it could be argued that the spiritualist-types of cults are the American version of eastern religions.

Finally, and most dangerous, are the numerous cults that arose in the late twentieth century that fit the common perception of a cult. These are usually characterized by a dictator type leader, by secret rites, by demands for absolute devotion that may include turning over possessions to the leader, by closed and secretive communities, and in the most extreme cases, mass suicide or violent acts. If Jesus enters into the picture at all, he is radically reduced to a manageable level for the leader's agenda. The leader himself is often a self-proclaimed Messiah or even claims to be the reincarnation of Jesus. Disastrously, the name of Jesus is used to manipulate people to give up their possessions, their will, their bodies, and even their lives.

The Post-modern Jesus: Have it your way

We are, it is often argued, in a time of philosophical and cultural transition. We are transitioning from modernity to that reaction against modernity, most commonly referred to as post-modernity. Both, it should be noted, are a mixed bag. There is good and bad in modernity, and there is good and bad in post-modernity. The jury is still out as to how comprehensive the transition will be and what will come out on the other side, but trends and emphases are recognizable. At the risk of oversimplification, modernity can be understood as the worldview that grew out of the Enlightenment. The rational autonomous human self was elevated to the center of the world and knowledge about the world. Faith rested in science and technology, with the expectation of continuous if not inevitable progress in which all of our human problems could be solved. We have seen how this view inevitably rejects the revelation of Scripture, denies the miraculous and the supernatural, is at best agnostic about an impersonal God and at worst atheistic. In Modernity, human knowledge is certain and objective, inherently good, and even absolute.[53] Jesus, as we have seen, is at best a good man who taught moral and ethical lessons we all can choose to follow.

In reaction to that human centric optimism and absolutism, and growing out of the twentieth century's plethora of wars, threat of nuclear holocaust, and technological failures, the postmodernist denies absolutes and tends toward pessimism. Science and technology are used as never before, but they are no longer trusted as the solution for human problems. In fact, it is dependency on technology that has led to our current ecological disasters. Truth is a construct of the community; that is, there is no one absolute narrative or truth. It all depends, rather, on the context, the people, and the situation. Truth is what one determines is truth. Any attempt to impose a metanarrative or overarching truth is viewed as an act of oppression and violence. This relativism both rises out of and leads to a fractured, tribalistic, and non-linear view of the world. Diversity is celebrated. Niche marketing rules – there is no one style or fashion of clothing or music or art that is "in style." Whatever you choose at the moment is right. Past and future merge into a perpetual present (T.V. shows with multiple plots that continue week to week); near and far are always here (instant communication means global events are experienced immediately); truth and fiction are often indistinguishable (note the popularity of so-called "reality" shows). In the end, relativism and pluralism rule. The postmodernist argues that because there is a multiplicity of human communities, then there is a multiplicity of truths. No one is supreme over the other.[54]

The good news for evangelicals is that post-moderns are open to spirituality and the supernatural. They are willing to accept that there is more to the universe than what the eye can see and what the rational mind can conceive. Unfortunately, they also see spirituality as relative. It is both the construct of a particular community and ultimately whatever a person decides it to be – you simply choose, and if the situation merits, lose your religion. The postmodern Jesus, then, is truth…if that is your truth. He is the true manifestation of God, even God incarnate, if that is what you choose to believe. As was stated in a sermon I once heard, "If you are Christologically oriented, then these verses mean . . ." leaving it wide open for those who were not Christologically oriented to apply the words of Scripture to another manifestation of God, if they were so inclined. Have it your way. Feel free to believe in the Jesus of the Bible if that is your preference. Just don't impose that narrative, story, or truth on anyone else, because there are no absolutes.

Of course, saying that there are no absolutes is itself an absolute statement and thus self-refuting. But never mind that breakdown in logic, and never mind all the absolute statements Jesus himself made. In reality and in practice the post-modern individual pieces together various spiritual beliefs, including some taken from the Bible and about Jesus. Even in pop culture, "God is in; spirituality is hip." It all sounds encouraging until further examination reveals that the "prophets of our day" are not teaching a Biblical message.[55] Jesus is cool, he is hip. Spirituality is every one's quest. But for the most part it is a cafeteria religion with a bit of this and a bit of that, all meshed together to create "truth for me."

New Age: An enlightened manifestation of God

The New Age movement is really not new, but is rather a conglomeration of schools of thought, organizations, movements, teachings, and spiritual practices influenced by eastern religions, the ancient mystery schools, parapsychology, astrology, and the occult. It is an "umbrella term," because there is no specific founder or central headquarters or hierarchy. This multiplicity of beliefs and streams of influence means that only generalizations and sweeping statements can be made. Still, as John Newport points out, there is an "amazing unity" of ideas, which include:

- All is One (Monism). Everything that is, is connected. There is no clear line of difference between the creation and the force or energy that creates it. Separation in the creation, and separation between humans, is an illusion. Humans "are expressions of one another and of the universe."

- Everything is God (Pantheism). This One is what holds all things together and is beyond personality.

- God is within you. Each one of us has the divine spark within us, so "we are God in disguise."

- Reincarnation and Karma. Every person must go through a series of lifetimes to reach oneness with God or the One.

- Changing your consciousness. We need to get over and past the illusion that is the world and be enlightened by true spiritual reality and karma.[56]

The Jesus of the New Age is all over the map; however, he is essentially a special man who was endowed with the spirit of the Christ, something that many others have experienced and many of us could grow into. He was, therefore, an enlightened manifestation of God. In any case, New Age believers have to reinterpret the teachings, actions, and events of Jesus's life. For example, reading through the index of Manly P. Hall's massive book *The Secret Teachings of All Ages*, he explains how Jesus was confused with "*Christos*," which he blames on later Christian writers. Jesus' crucifixion and death was "a recital of the myth of the dying god." He was "identified with Bacchus" and "identified with personal consciousness." There were records found about him in Tibet, he "revealed [the] purpose and nature of Christos," he was the "personification of the Divine Mind," and his "true story [has] never [been] unfolded to the world."[57]

This untold or "true" story of Jesus is one of the common Christological themes in New Age thought. His secret life was not recorded in the Bible, and it was during these so-called "lost years" that he travelled to India, Persia, Tibet, Assyria, and Greece, reading and studying the scriptures of the religions in those lands. He read the Hindu scriptures, he was initiated in Egypt into the mystery religions, and he eventually became an enlightened one whose great commission was that his followers should also teach others about their own inherent and ultimate divinity. This Jesus, however, was not unique. The "Christ" has also been incarnated in many other men, including Adam, Joshua, Melchizedek, Enoch, and may other "World-Teachers." [58]

Another common Christological theme in New Age is the Gnostic Christ, commonly seen in the popular book *A Course in Miracles*. Influenced by eastern religions, this view claims that historic Christianity has misunderstood both the world and Jesus' mission in the world. The physical world is an illusion that only appears real because of our unenlightened perception. The only reality is eternal. Jesus' incarnation, crucifixion, and resurrection were to give us an opportunity to discover that both individual existence and death are illusions. Through Jesus' experience we can discover that we are all Christs and can come to the same state that he achieved, a "God-realization." That is, he became what we all must become; he is an older brother and a guide and can show us who we are and what we are to become. His mission is to show us our oneness with God. Furthermore, since the physical world is an illusion, there is no need for miracles or healings. There is no real sickness or death, and there is no need to worry about poverty or social justice. All is an illusion. [59]

The bottom line for most New Age Christologies is that Jesus was a mere human vessel inhabited by the Christ. This Christ may be defined in different ways by different groups, but he is always divine, cosmic, impersonal, or the personification of God. Jesus is, therefore, a "way-shower." His life and death was to show that we, too, are divine, how we can become divine, how we can achieve enlightenment about reality, and how we can unite – achieve *"at-one-ment"* – with the ultimate reality or the divine Self. He discovered the truth; he was the embodiment of higher wisdom and truth, he was perfect, and he shows us how to be perfect, also.[60]

Conclusion: Just Pick and Choose

Our individualistic American culture, our emphasis on personal freedom, and our cherished freedoms of thought and speech led the modern world to seek for the one objective, absolute truth. When there was not agreement on truth, there was freedom to do whatever was needed to disavow one philosophy, religion, or church and look for or start up another. No matter how unorthodox or unusual the belief or practice may have been, it was the right of every American to seek and practice truth, however it may be defined.

Not much has changed in the postmodern world when it comes to the search. The difference is that the modernist was looking for *the* truth. The postmodernist is free to *discover* and even *make* her truth. There are no absolutes, so there is no final *Truth* to find. There are truths that are constructs of one's context, community, and experience, and that should be discovered, embraced, and never imposed on anyone else. In either case, modern individualism or postmodern community, the result is a pick and choose cafeteria Christology – design your own "personal Jesus" based on your personal experience.[61]

Jesus Manipulated for Me and Mine

The Great American Experiment is founded on many ideas, beliefs, and truths. Perhaps no ideas from our founding are more ingrained in our American psyche than these: that God has given us the right to our own lives, the freedom to do as we choose, and the right to pursue happiness. This is the American dream. This is why millions of immigrants have come to our shores. Without a doubt, books have been written, sermons have been preached, and arguments have taken place from the dinner table all the way to the Supreme Court over the interpretation, priority, and practice of these.

My concern in this section is the intersection of those ideas with the previous phrase "endowed by their Creator." These are God-given rights we believe. No argument there. But what happens when Jesus is attached to the American Dream? Even more critically, what happens when Jesus is yanked out of his Biblical context and manipulated to justify a particular interpretation and application of that Dream?

The Consumer Jesus: He is there to give me what I want

Part of the American dream involves home ownership, good personal transportation, owning nice things, and taking nice vacations. With rare exception, no American wants to be poor. Most Americans do want to improve their economic lot, and most want their children to be better off than they were. Problems arise, however, on two fronts. One, when the individual "right" to have possessions and own things is driven more by materialism and greed rather than real need, and, two, when the structures and systems of society are shaped and driven more by consumerism than by actual demand and supply. Consumerism is the American dream – the pursuit of happiness – out of control. Consumerism begins to inform us as to our identity and our status in the world. It pulls and pushes at us from all directions and at all times. In its extreme, it leads to the "empty interior," to "broken relationships," to "the craving for more," and a hardening or callousness toward injustice and the wounded in the world. The American Dream becomes the "American Fairy Tale," which leads us to believe that "more possession mean more happiness" and that a "person who does or produces more is more important" to society.[62] On the one hand, the bumper sticker promotes consumerism: "He who dies with the most toys wins." On the other hand, financial counselors warn of "buying things we can't afford with money we don't have to impress people we don't like." Thus, the double edged sword of the Dream and of economic blessings.

Unfortunately, Christians and the church have not been exempt from the temptations of materialism and consumerism. We have co-opted Jesus and faith in him to build empires – communications industries that include television, radio, publishing, radio, and recording labels. Christian success is identified not with an ethic of self-denial, but with Christian networks, corporations, and megachurches.[63] Perhaps all these have good intentions, and perhaps all do in some form spread the gospel message. The problem is when the economic health and survival of the organization becomes as important, or even more important, than the gospel of Jesus. More money has to be raised, more products have to be sold, more commitment is needed from more people or the "ministry" can't continue. Too often, the message of the gospel is marginalized at the expense of the organization. Jesus is manipulated, and faith in him becomes simply an economic buzzword.

Churches themselves have often been criticized for being too consumer oriented and materialistically driven. In too many churches, every ministry and program is geared toward the perceived need, want, and desire of the person in the pew. Offending that person is avoided at all costs. The question driving the church is: "What do you want us to be?" The demands of Jesus – repentance, taking up one's cross, following him – are rarely spoken of. Instead, sermons deliver either an outright prosperity gospel where Jesus is obligated to bless financially, or a prosperity-lite message where Jesus is all about "meeting your needs." That is, the invitation is not to repent and come to Jesus for forgiveness of sin, the hope of eternal life, and a continued life of service. It is to come to Jesus to have all your needs met as you continue in the pursuit of happiness.

There are at least three outcomes to the consumer Jesus:

One, Jesus' person and work are reduced to the absolute minimum for consumption. He is tamed. His demands are toned down or ignored. His life, message, death, and resurrection become all about values and principles for living. He is the wise sage, the good teacher, the nice guy. No repentance is needed. Our sinful condition is ignored. There was no real sacrifice on his part, and certainly none needed on ours. Jesus is merely everyone's best friend. After all, you can buy Jesus action figures, Jesus bracelets, bumper stickers, pencil toppers, backpacks – you name it – Jesus is on it. No one hates this Jesus, everyone believes in him, but no one is really his disciple.

Two, Jesus is commodified in and for the Christian subculture. We think we are honoring him by using him to promote sales; however, instead of Savior and Lord he is a product. We think we are offering "safe" alternatives to a dangerous secular world, thus we have Christian self-help books, Christian financial planning, Christian cruises, Christian sex manuals, Christian TV and celebrities, Christian athletes and rock stars, Christian T-shirts, and even Christian karate and yoga. One problem is that we are not offering "safe" alternatives, but are creating a fortress – a ghetto – mentality and reality, where we can avoid all contact with a world that desperately needs us to be salt and light. We may think it is a good idea to look in the Christian yellow pages for a Christian plumber, but wouldn't it be a better idea to call a qualified plumber, regardless of his faith, and take the opportunity to share Christ with him?[64] Another problem is calling all these products and services "Christian" to begin with. What makes them Christian? Is it because they are made by, sold by, or delivered by a Christian? And yet we worry about the commercialization of Christmas! Commodifying Jesus simply trivializes him.

Three, contrary to common belief, it probably doesn't really help our witness that much. The non-believing world sees this materialistic-consumerist Christianity and is either turned off by it or simply laughs. On the one hand, some argue, putting Jesus on everything we make, wear, buy, and do is an evangelistic strategy. Surely there is the possibility that someone might come to Christ because of that bold witness. Yes, that is true. But, as Nichols warns, commodifying Christ becomes too easy. It only trivializes him and "becomes all too problematic, if not lethal, for the church and the gospel." The truth is, he argues, that for the watching world this consumer Christianity is "sacriligeous, not to mention that it just plain looks silly."[65]

Noticing how silly it can be and laughing (and being angry) at it is just what the journalist Robert McElvanie does in his book *Grand Theft Jesus,* a cringe inducing criticism of conservative evangelicals, whom he refers to as evangelical-lites. He notes that he sees "'Christian' profitcy in practice all around me. You name it, and somebody in our area is doing it for Jesus – at a profit. There are Christian house painters, Christian coffee shops; there's a place where you can do 'karate for Christ' – there are even Christian pest-control companies." He goes on to complain about some of the apparent hypocrisy when he says there used to be "a gas station with a sign saying, GOD IS THE OWNER OF THIS BUSINESS; I JUST RUN IT FOR HIM. It had the highest prices in town, and was open on Sundays. Apparently God is a Sabbath-breaker, if there's a profit to be made."[66]

I have numerous disagreements with McElvanie's opinions, assumptions, and certainly with his method of Biblical interpretation. He does make, however, some valid and painful points. Jesus is appropriated by too many for all sorts of reasons, many of which have little or nothing to do with the gospel. Too often we have bought into the consumerist worldview of the American Dream gone out of control. Too many Christians buy and buy, go into exorbitant debt, worship at the all you can eat buffet until morbidly obese, and yet claim to be meticulously following Jesus. The consumer Jesus, it appears, has "blessed" us to the point of obsession and addiction to sports, entertainment, possessions, and food. And when pastors are as guilty as the rest, there won't be many sermons preached on gluttony, materialism, and sports obsession.

Certainly, not all are guilty and there are many exceptions. This consumer Jesus, however, is one evangelicals are faced with every day. Whether explicitly through the Prosperity Gospel (often masquerading as "victorious Christian living") or implicitly through the cultural status quo, Jesus is trivialized in the name of materialism and consumption. We make him into a "nice, middle-class, American Jesus" who doesn't really "mind materialism and who would never call us to give away everything we have." The church too often, points out Michael Horton, no longer preaches a "religion for the poor, the meek, the downcast and downtrodden, the oppressed and broken." Instead, he laments, "Christianity today is for the rich, the proud, the achievers, the powerful, and the successful...or for people who want to be." Jesus becomes simply the genie in Aladdin's lamp, obligated to give us what we want when we want it. Horton praises the zeal of American Christianity, but bemoans its shallowness and lack of doctrine, for he says, "we *are* living out our creed, but that creed is closer to the American Dream than it is to the Christian faith."[67]

The Therapist Jesus:
He is there to make me feel better

Not too different from the Consumer Jesus is the Therapist Jesus, whose main job is to help me feel better about myself and my circumstances. The growth and popularity of psychotherapy in the twentieth century led evangelicals to surrender too much authority to therapists for interpreting and giving meaning to our lives. Therapists, and even pop psychology, have been given an authority and respect that even preachers or the Bible don't get. We see therapy as "science and as good medicine" and give up opportunities to enhance and guide spiritual growth during critical and formative times in life. Instead, because of the ever-present pressure, temptation, and expectation to feel good, love yourself, have your needs met, and self-actualize, we bow to the answers of secular therapy.[68]

One of the earliest proponents of a therapeutic Christianity was Norman Vincent Peale. Much of what he said was Biblical and true, especially in his earlier writings. He emphasized repentance and faith in Christ alone for salvation and eternal life. His intention and desire was to help people live out daily Christian life in an encouraging and positive way. He correctly believed and taught that the power to face daily struggles and difficulties comes only by a commitment to Jesus Christ, whose Spirit empowers each and every believer. The challenge is for each person to believe and appropriate that truth. This was possible through "positive thinking," which he equated to "faith in God, faith in Jesus Christ, faith in life, and faith in yourself." It appears, however, that Peale's emphasis turned more and more human centered, in which Jesus' role was to help the individual accomplish what he wants in life. He quoted the "truth" that all need to believe and follow, "I can do all things through Christ," for "Christianity is also a technique for personal life change." As his writing progressed, and as he famously told stories about people whose lives were changed through positive thinking, what seems to stand out is an individualistic emphasis. The point of the Christian life, what Jesus is supposed to be about, it could even be said, is to give *me* the strength to stand up to problems, to give *me* "a realistic faith" in myself, help *me* in my business, in my health, in all my circumstances, and to give *me* the "power to attain what I really want."[69]

Again, there is certainly some truth to what Peale taught. Jesus Christ is our power for living. There is a noticeable absence, however, of any talk about taking up one's cross, about self-denial, about sacrifice, about suffering, even about service to Christ or to others on behalf of Christ. Commitment to Christ is so that *I* will have the power to live life, rather than admitting my dependency on Jesus and letting him live through me. Peale does quote Philippians 4:13 ("I can do all things through Christ . . .") but does so without context, and with an apparent emphasis on the *I can* rather than the *through Christ*. Peale's Christology is not necessarily incorrect, it is just woefully incomplete and inadequate.

An even more glaring example is Robert Schuller's "new reformation" and "new theology" of self-esteem. Schuller redefines sin as "any act or thought that robs myself or another human being of his or her self-esteem," and hell as the place where a person is "when he has lost his self-esteem." This is, he says, the most basic and important of human needs – to have one's self esteem restored. It is our "emotional birthright as children [of God] created in his image." In this world, when we speak of sin, evil, demonic influence, or systemic evil, what we are really talking about "at core" is our "lack of self-dignity." When we speak of a lack of faith, what we are really talking about is our "profoundly deep sense of unworthiness." Therefore, self-esteem, or "pride in being a human being," is our greatest need.[70]

This calls for a "theology of salvation" that begins with the human "hunger for glory." Jesus Christ, therefore, is the "Ideal One, the Ultimate Person, the Universal Standard" for self-esteem. In fact, the Lord's Prayer, which has as its central theme the "priceless value of every person, points us to him, who is "the Person, the power, and the pathway to real self-dignity." This person, Jesus, "honored the human race" in his incarnation. He "placed unlimited value on the human race" in his crucifixion. In his resurrection, he passed on to us the ministry of "sharing self-esteem love with every person we meet." That is, we "must tell people everywhere that God wants us to feel good about ourselves." Thus, one can be born again, which is that change from "a negative to a positive self-image" or from "shame to self-esteem."[71] In Schuller's Christology, everything about Jesus is to help me feel better about myself.

Once again, Jesus is trivialized.[72] Whereas the good news of the gospel is that sinners can be saved from sin and that born again saints can be continually transformed by the Holy Spirit into the image of Jesus, today too many messages are more about how basically good people can accept themselves for what they are – no repentance, change, or sacrifice required. The gospel is less and less about God's glory, less and less about our purpose being his pleasure and honor, but more and more about our self-esteem. It is not Jesus worship, but me worship. He is there to help me feel better about myself rather than to be my Lord, demanding that I take up my cross and follow him.[73]

Certainly, part of the message of the gospel is that the person who places in faith in Jesus Christ is saved not only eternally but also has abundant life now. As believers, we are new creations in Christ with a new identity as sinners saved by grace, now saints imputed with the righteousness of Jesus. That means that there is a place for proper self-esteem, which is really Christ esteem. It is not feeling badly about myself or feeling good about myself. It is, rather, understanding who Christ is, what he has done for me and in me, and living life in the power of his Holy Spirit. It is, as Paul says in Gal. 2:20, "no longer I who live, but Christ lives in me." This is sanctification – more of Christ and less of me. The more that happens, the "better" I feel about myself. . . if that concept even has to be used.

This view of sanctification (and it is incomplete and oversimplified), is founded on the sacrifice of Jesus Christ on the cross to pay for my sins. It is founded on the reality that he calls me to be more like him, to sacrifice for his glory and for the sake of others. Amazing grace, therefore, is not some vague and trivial goodness God feels toward anyone and everyone. It is the fact that he gave his only Son to suffer on my behalf on the cross. If my understanding of myself, of the gospel, and of the process of sanctification is only about my self-esteem, my happiness, and making "good decisions" in this life, then non-Christians can wonder what the big deal is. As Horton points out, they could legitimately ask, "What right do you have to say that yours is the only source of happiness, meaning, exciting experiences, and moral betterment? Jesus is clearly not the only effective way to a better life or a better me. One can lose weight, stop smoking, improve one's marriage, and become a nicer person without Jesus."[74] Horton is right. If being all you can be, having your best life now, and feeling good about yourself is all Jesus is about, then he is not indispensable, he is not the only true Savior, and he is not Lord. The world will gladly take all the practical advice we can offer as long as we stay away from the offensive truth of original sin, the scandal of the cross, and the call for death to self and to sacrificial discipleship.

The Ideological Jesus:
He's there to fight my cause

Throughout history Jesus has been taken captive by political ideologies of every kind. Whether it was Constantinian Christianity, feudal Lords of the middle ages, both sides in any number of civil wars, the brutal conquest of Latin America by the sword and the cross, slavery in America, genocide of Native Americans, God and King of the British Empire, Prussian imperialism, and even Nazi-supporting Germans, there are few political points of view that are innocent of co-opting Jesus and abusing his name for the sake of ideology. In America, both the Right and the Left are guilty.

Some time back, I was at a national meeting of Christian leaders. One of the plenary speakers was a former Army officer, who is a true patriot and hero. Without a doubt he loves his country and has served her selflessly most of his adult life. Unfortunately, he is also quite an amateur theologian. At the end of his one hour speech, I was both confused and disturbed, for he had conflated patriotism, nationalism, the Kingdom of God, right wing politics, and his own vision of what America should be. My issue was not necessarily with any one of those viewpoints, but the ease with which he appropriated Jesus for his particular causes, whether right or wrong. Besides that, he was almost dismissive of the church. Because he was trying so hard to emphasize his vision and interpretation of the Kingdom of God and appeal across denominations, he seemed to confuse the Bride of Christ with the negatives of denominationalism. The end result was a highly political, nationalistic, militarized, and almost churchless view of the Kingdom of God in America.

In *Grand Theft Jesus*, McElvanie is quick to criticize, from the left wing's point of view, what he calls "literalist evangelicals" for using the name of Jesus, and the Bible in general, to promote the right wing agenda. He points out, for example, how often conservative evangelicals condemn homosexuality and abortion, but somehow are trending more and more towards overlooking divorce. Jesus, he points out, said nothing about the first two but was quite clear about divorce. He also notes that Jesus spoke over three hundred times about helping the poor, yet poverty does not seem to dominate anyone's right wing agenda. Does he have legitimate points to make? He certainly does about many evangelicals' failure to speak prophetically and consistently to all social and political issues regardless of where these may fall on the right-left political spectrum.

But as it turns out, McElvanie is just as guilty of a kind of reverse literalism. That is, his "argument from silence" is essentially the same thing. If Jesus did *not* say anything about a particular issue, the assumption is that we do not have any guidance in dealing with that issue and certainly should not oppose it, regardless of what the Old Testament or the rest of the New Testament may say. If Jesus did not mention it, it must not be important. This is so for McElvanie because he pits Paul, as liberals are wont to do, in opposition to Jesus. He assumes that Paul misunderstood Jesus, that he interpreted Jesus incorrectly, and, he argues, since evangelicals tend to follow Paul instead of Jesus we are truly more "Paulinists" than Christian. This approach obviously rejects the unity and authority of the entire Bible and is grounded in a non-historical and non-theological hermeneutic. Yes, the right wing does overlook too much of what Jesus said, too often appropriating only that which fits an ideology. But McElvanie's solution is woefully inadequate.[75]

The left wing is just as guilty. To ask "What would Jesus drive?" in order to promote an ecological agenda trivializes Jesus as much as any consumerist approach. Others on the left argue that "Jesus taught a liberal creed, while Paul preached a right-wing screed" that twisted the social values of Jesus. It seems that in most cases the only way for the left to "Biblically" uphold the practices of abortion or homosexuality is to argue from Jesus' silence, the Old Testament's supposed irrelevance, and Paul's confusion and misunderstanding of Jesus. The (selected) sayings of Jesus are all that matter, not his work on the cross, not his fulfillment of the Law and the Prophets, not his place in the history of Israel or in God's redemptive purpose.[76]

Both the right and the left at times demonstrate a "confusion of the gospel with a partisan agenda." This is particularly the case for the right now that the evangelical vote is so critical for a politician's election. And lest we forget, that politician's ultimate goal is to get elected. He will say what he needs to say to get the votes. He will worry later, if he really worries at all, about disappointing those who supported him. In the end, does it really matter what the issue is, left or right, if the gospel agenda is eventually supplanted by human ones? As Horton pleads, can we "stop using 'gospel" and 'evangelical' for anything and everything we think is best in achieving the common good?" because the gospel "is an announcement that we have to deliver, not an agenda that we have to negotiate with our fellow citizens."[77]

This does not mean that individual Christians or the church needs to be passive and uninvolved politically. We must be good citizens and conscious of our civic duty. Even more than that, the Kingdom of God as inaugurated by Jesus Christ includes redemption of the entire creation and demands both social ministry and social action. It does mean that if we identify ourselves – or worse yet, identify Jesus and his words – with either the right or the left, with Democrat or Republican, with any political ideology, we lose our prophetic voice. When we reduce the gospel message or the Kingdom of God to a select few of Jesus' sayings, with no consideration for the full counsel of Scripture or a comprehensive theology, we are abusing Jesus. The unfortunate reality is that not one of us can be totally free from an ideology – we have values and opinions and hold beliefs that are grounded in our background, culture, and worldviews. We all have a hermeneutic, a way of approaching Scripture, that can sometimes skew our understanding of Scripture. Consequently, we must admit that we see through a glass darkly, have cultural lenses and biases, be aware of these as much as possible, and work hard at not manipulating the gospel of Jesus to fit our view. It cheapens and minimizes him and the gospel. My task is to align myself with him, not the other way around. My task is to let Scripture – the whole of Scripture – judge every culture and every political view. I may take a particular position, belong to a particular party, and vote for particular candidates, but I must be very careful about fully identifying any of those with Jesus. Historically, as stated in the first paragraph of this section, any time the church, a denomination, or any religious worldview gets too close to the state, a party, or a political ideology, they both end up corrupted.[78]

Americans need to remember this. We should love our country and appreciate both her achievements and promise; however, we cannot forget that America, too, is "Babylon." As a country, the "American Proposition is provisional, not eschatological." In the end, it is not about any one country, race, people, or ideology, whether left or right. It is about the Kingdom of God, which is anticipated and demonstrated now in the church, the Body of Christ, not by any particular country, race, party, or political ideology.[79]

Conclusion:
Just keep expectations low and comfort high

The Consumer Jesus and the Therapist Jesus are products of a comfortable and affluent society in which the values that drive much of our worldview are our own comfort, physical and mental well-being, and success in all we do. We prefer not to talk much about sacrifice, service, and self-denial. Ayn Rand's Objectivism is arguable as ingrained in our American psyche as Jesus' Sermon on the Mount, for, after all, "God helps those who help themselves."

The Ideological Jesus is centuries old, and he won't go away anytime soon. This is because we struggle with the Biblical call to apply the whole gospel message to and in the world. It is an unavoidable, difficult, and legitimate struggle. We can, however, learn to be aware of our ideological presuppositions and the temptation to pin Jesus' name to them.

All three Christologies reduce the demands of Jesus. Rather than read his words and view his person and work in a theological context, they manipulate what he said and did to fit a predetermined political philosophy or philosophy of life. Again, it is not that Jesus does not provide, bless, or heal our emotional hurts. It is not that Jesus cares nothing for social issues, justice, and how people are governed. It is that if Jesus is only "life coach, therapist, buddy, significant other, founder of Western civilization, political messiah, example of radical living, and countless other images" then we are distracted from "the stumbling block and foolishness of 'Christ and him crucified'." Are we telling His story, or our own story?[80]

Jesus, Weak and Wimpy: The Easy Way Out

There are many other deficient attempts, both in America and around the world, to understand and explain Jesus and I have admittedly not addressed the majority of them. Some are related to specific religious groups and belief systems, some spring from attempts to highlight Jesus' relevance to a particular culture or race and some are specific emphases attempting to relate Jesus to a particular experience or need. Usually, they are the result of overlooking the full Biblical record or allowing culture and experience to shape far too much of one's Christology. This is not an exclusive American phenomenon, but has been a temptation and struggle throughout church history.[81]

I have addressed the fourteen Christologies above because I believe they are both the most dangerous and influential in America, and the ones that have the greatest impact on an American missiology. These all tell *some* truth about Jesus (in some cases very little truth). The Biblical record affirms that Jesus was fully human, that he was a good teacher and a prophet, that he did teach an ethical system, and was misunderstood. He does provide for us, he does bestow blessings, he does give wisdom and guidance and direction, he does heal, he does want the best for us, his teachings do have relevance to politics, and so on.[82] One failure of all these Christologies, however, is that they do not tell the full truth and, in most cases, don't even attempt to do so.

Another failure is that they often use orthodox terminology but inject new and different meaning. The result is a weak and wimpy Jesus. He is redefined, recast in our image, and manipulated. In some cases he is barely recognizable to an evangelical; in other cases, he is almost there, but deficient enough or manipulated just enough to raise concerns. In a sense, this is the easy way out. For some, the best way to deal with difficult Biblical texts, the best way to deal with Jesus' hard sayings, and the best way to deal with what does not line up with our presuppositions, our experience, and our culture is to simply cut it out, ignore it, redefine it, and manipulate it. It is hard work to take the entire Bible, all that Jesus said and did, and even all of what Paul, John, and Peter said about him, wrestle with it, let it challenge our assumptions, and put it into imperfect practice in our lives.

Not to struggle with the full Biblical record results in either Pluralism or a designer spirituality, and these are rapidly becoming the religious dogmas of America. Believe whatever you want to, because all roads lead to God, however you may define him. If that is the case, then propositional statements and dogma about Jesus are unnecessary or at best, a guide. Take what you like from here and there and design your own niche spirituality. Whatever you do, just don't offend anyone else with your beliefs! That is precisely one of the characteristics of so many contemporary Christologies – they have emerged in a non-offending culture. The uniqueness, exclusivity, and demands of Jesus Christ are redefined, reduced, or marginalized because someone may be offended by that narrow perspective

What is needed for an American missiology is a bold, balanced, and holistic Christology. The full Biblical record must be taken into account, Jesus must not be ripped out of his historical context, and his life, teachings, deeds, death, and resurrection must be placed at the center of a full Biblical theology. This will be my attempt in the next few chapters: a Christology that drives an American missiology, firmly grounded in the Bible, taking into account all that Jesus said and did, understood in his historical context, and cautiously applied to the present day setting. That is, the following is my cautious attempt at developing an offensive Christology, offensive because its purpose is missiological. My assumption is that America is a predominantly lost mission field and the answer is in the exclusive, unique, and offensive person and work of Jesus Christ.

The Jesus of the Bible

"But you," He asked them again, "who do you say that I am?" Peter answered Him, "You are the Messiah." And he strictly warned them to tell no one about Him.

Mark 8:29-30

Jesus has listened to the responses the disciples have given to his earlier question, "Who do people say that I am?" There appears to be little consensus among the people. Some think he is John the Baptist or Elijah come back to life. Others think he may be one of any number of prophets. Jesus hears these responses and then asks the question he is really interested in: Who do the disciples themselves say that he is?

Impulsive, bold Peter answers: "You are the Christ, the Messiah, the Anointed One." You are, Peter implies, the one the nation of Israel has been waiting for, the one the prophets have told us about, the one who is to redeem us and establish the Kingdom of God. Peter had the answer right. He had the terminology down – Jesus is the Christ. What he had yet to fully understand was the meaning of Messiah. He had yet to fully understand what the prophets had meant, what redemption meant, what the Kingdom of God meant, what kind of suffering the Messiah was preparing for. At this point his understanding of Messiah was not completely what Jesus himself meant by the term Christ or Messiah.

Jesus, however, does an interesting thing. He does not immediately elaborate on messianic definitions. He simply asks that the disciples not tell anyone the truth as stated by Peter. The clear indication is that Peter had spoken correctly;[83] in other words, Jesus is saying, "Hold that information close to the chest for now." Jesus knew that the majority of people would misunderstand the true nature of his messianic mission and could possibly interfere with his goals and purposes. He knew that Peter and the others still had a lot more to understand. The time would soon come when both the disciples and the multitudes would hear and see from Jesus what his mission as Messiah really was. Here's my point: There is a correct answer to the question "Who do you say that I am?" The answer is definitely "Christ" or the "Messiah." But simply saying that is not enough, as Peter and the disciples would discover. Jesus himself gets to define what Christ/Messiah means. Moreover, the entire inspired Bible has to be taken into account to develop a Christology. But having already discussed defective Christologies, admitting to the reality of presuppositions, cultural influences, and personal biases, is a true Biblical Christology even possible?

I believe the short answer is yes. It is also, however, a challenge that should not to be taken lightly or flippantly. Because the Bible *is* God's inspired revelation to us and because we *do* live in a culture, have personal experiences, and even different personalities and needs, we must be careful as we put forth our answer to "who do you say that I am?" The task of answering requires two attitudes: confidence and humility. How so?

First, we can have *confidence* that the inspired, authoritative, and inerrant Bible is a unity. It is God's revelation to us, telling us from Genesis to Revelation about Jesus Christ, who is the fullness of God's revelation to us. It is not a random collection of histories, wisdom, prophecies, and letters. Not only did the Holy Spirit inspire the individual writers, he led and directed the process of collecting, preserving, and canonizing the Scriptures. The entire Bible points to Jesus and, as important as his actual words are, the rest is also inspired and contributes to the development of a Christology.[84] We should express *humility* because although the Bible is God's true, authoritative, and absolute word, we are not. Our translations, interpretations, and applications are fallible. We may even get it ninety-nine percent correct, but that one percent is enough to require humility.

Second, we can have *confidence* in our knowledge and tools to study Scripture. For two millennia Godly men and women have read, studied, and defended Scripture. They have studied the Hebrew, Greek, and Aramaic. They have dug up a good portion of Israel studying archeology. They have studied extra-biblical sources. They have pored over and debated so-called "gospels" and other books rightly left out of the canon. They have written commentaries, theologies, preached, taught, and prayed. They have taught us how to study the Bible. They have explained Jesus to us. They have used philosophy, history, technology, sociology, anthropology and other disciplines to study and explain the Bible. Are they infallible? Of course not! More often than not they have numerous disagreements among themselves. But on the whole, their desire has been to better understand God's word and the person and work of Jesus. God has supplied his children with the intelligence and the curiosity to pursue knowledge of him. We should not be afraid to use these gifts.

At the same time, we should express *humility* for the obvious reason that we are fallen human beings. Our knowledge is imperfect. Our intelligence is lacking. Our motives are often selfish and impure. Not all who have searched the Scriptures, used historical methods, or spoken in philosophical categories have done so as disciples. Sometimes their desire is to destroy confidence in the word of God. Sometimes the tools, resources, and knowledge we have at our disposal are abused and misused to support a misguided presupposition. The tools, our intelligence, and even *my* motives are tainted by sin. We need to be careful and humble.

Third, we can have *confidence* in our Christian experience. Jesus often spoke in parables "Because the secrets of the kingdom of heaven have been given for you to know, but it has not been given to them." (Matt. 13:11). That is, simply, not everyone is going to get it. There are many who will read Scripture, who will study what Jesus said, and at best conclude, as we have seen, that he was a nice man who taught a good ethic. Others may even be able to verbalize a more comprehensive and academic Christology, but only as "one" of the ways to understand Jesus. Why? Because it takes a Spirit-renewed heart and mind to understand and to apply the word. It takes a real personal encounter with Jesus Christ as Savior and Lord to open one's eyes to the truth of Jesus. It is only after that experience of personal salvation that a person begins to read and correctly understand who Jesus is and what he has done. We can have confidence in that experience and in our ongoing experience with him, which opens the door for our understanding, shapes our understanding, and is confirmed and enhanced by new understanding.

We should express *humility*, however, because our experiences can fool us. They need to be interpreted and evaluated according to Scripture. We must realize that, because we are fallen, our experiences and emotions are fickle, unpredictable, and are in large part shaped and interpreted in light of our personalities and background. Therefore, as we read Scripture and develop a Christology, our personal experience with Jesus informs that Christology but does not determine it. It helps us understand Jesus, but must be submitted to Jesus and corrected, redirected, or even ignored if it contradicts his word. We must also be careful not to let our personal experience overshadow the need for community correction and accountability. One of the great evangelical distinctives is that every person can read and interpret the Bible for himself. That truth, however, must not deteriorate into hyper-individualism. It must be held in tension with the need for theology to be done in community. The believing individual is the temple of the Holy Spirit (1 Cor. 6:19), but so is the body of believers (1 Cor. 3:16-17). There is value in historical creeds and confessions. There is value in what we have struggled with and learned throughout history. Certainly, there are times for a Wycliff or a Luther to stand up to the majority; however, if I am the only one around with a particular understanding of Jesus, I may be wrong. Accountability to and correction by the body of Christ is essential.

Is a Biblical Christology possible? Yes, and it will be characterized by four qualifiers:

1. It will be true but not perfect. Jesus is perfect. His words are perfect. His work is perfect. My understanding, statements, and explanations are not. They will be true – that is, they can state the truth about Jesus – but they are not perfect. This is not a contradiction and it does not have to lead to relativism. I truly love my wife, but I don't love her perfectly. I am a true disciple of Jesus, but I don't follow him perfectly. What I believe and say about him may be true to him and to the word, but it is not perfect.

2. Similarly, a Biblical Christology will be faithful but still correctable. It will seek to confidently, accurately and correctly interpret the full counsel of Scripture regarding Jesus (including the Old Testament and even Paul). At the same time, it will acknowledge that the community of believers is needed for evaluation, accountability, and even correction of what is stated.

3. It will be propositional but also experiential. Doctrinal
    statements about Jesus have to be made. Some of these
    will even be theologically abstract and in philosophical
    terms. A Biblical Christology may begin "from below"
    and look first at Jesus the man, his earthly ministry, and
    what he said and did. It may begin "from above" and
    look first at the cosmic Christ, the pre-existing Son of
    God, the Second Person of the Trinity come in the flesh.
    Either way, the result must be a balanced Christology.[85]
    Either way, at some point explanatory and doctrinal
    statements are needed. A Biblical Christology, however,
    could deteriorate into a cold, academic exercise if it does
    not both reflect and result in individual and corporate
    transformation. Knowing about and explaining Jesus
    goes hand in hand with knowing and experiencing him
    and his sin-forgiving, life-giving, and life-changing
    power. Thus, an experience with Jesus requires coherent
    explanation, and propositional explanations call for a
    personal response.

4. Finally, a Biblical Christology will be comprehensive but
    not exhaustive. Thanks to God's revelation in the Bible
    and in the person of Jesus, we can have comprehensive
    knowledge of him and his ways. We can know as much as
    we need to know. Yet we don't and can't know everything.
    A Biblical Christology will be comprehensive in the sense
    that it will take into account the Old Testament prophecies
    and how Jesus fulfilled the law and the prophets. It will
    consider his sayings, commands, parables, miracles, and
    his actions during his three year ministry, while on the
    cross, and as resurrected Lord. It will also take into account
    what he further revealed through his Spirit to the inspired
    writers in the rest of the New Testament. It will also be
    comprehensive in the sense that it will consider what Jesus

did and said about personal ethics, justice, treatment of the poor, the worship of God, the church, relations to the government, peace, war, violence, and a multitude of other issues. Finally, it will be comprehensive in that it will judge, evaluate, and apply to every aspect of human life. Yet, a Biblical Christology will not be – cannot be – exhaustive. As fallen human beings we simply do not have that ability. When we see him in heaven, however, we will have an eternity to learn so much more about him.

For the purposes of this book, developing a Christologically driven American missiology means that what he said, what he did, and the explanation the Biblical writers give us about him must be the starting and ending points. These can and should be affirmed and explained through philosophical categories, church history, and personal experience; however, all of these are always judged by and never take the place of the Biblical witness. I will attempt to develop a truthful albeit imperfect, faithful but certainly correctable, and propositional yet personally applicable Christology (I will not attempt to be comprehensive due to the missiological focus of this book). I expect that, within the evangelical family, there will be differences of opinion, differences in emphases, and differences in application of what Jesus said and did. But these are "family fights," and my hope is that these would not overshadow our agreement that Jesus himself sets the agenda for understanding his nature and mission. In the end we need to remember that the "living Jesus Christ is greater than all of our confessions and creeds and surpasses all of our theological reflection on him." We can state the truth about him, but he is greater that all our statements, and often "upsets our neat categories and classifications of him."[86]

So, back to Jesus' question to the disciples: "Who do you say that I am?" Here is my answer.

Jesus of Nazareth: Fully and truly human

> He went away from there and came to His hometown, and His disciples followed Him. When the Sabbath came, He began to teach in the synagogue, and many who heard Him were astonished. "Where did this man get these things?" they said. "What is this wisdom given to Him, and how are these miracles performed by His hands? Isn't this the carpenter, the son of Mary, and the brother of James, Joses, Judas, and Simon? And aren't His sisters here with us?" So they were offended by Him.
>
> Mark 6:1-3

The humanity of Jesus is not frequently challenged in contemporary academic theology or world religions. To the contrary, as we saw in chapter one, more often than not he is relegated to being only human.[87] Although not generally an issue, establishing that Jesus was fully and truly human is important for several reasons:

Historical misconceptions

There have been occasions when the true and full humanity of Jesus has been outright denied, questioned, or imperiled out of fear of making him too human. The first Christological heresy was Docetism, which flourished during the late first and into the second century. It incorporated the Gnostic idea that matter, and therefore the body, is evil. Consequently, it would be impossible for the Son to have an actual physical body. Jesus only appeared to have a body; he only seemed to be a man. The first Epistle of John was probably, in part, a response to an early form of this heresy. John emphasized that Jesus was "seen," "observed," "touched" with hands, and "has come in the flesh" (3:1-4; 4:1-3). Later heresies included Modalistic Monarchianism, which "obscured the full humanity of Jesus" by claiming that he was only a "mode" of God, and views that argued Jesus did not have a "human rational soul," or a "human spirit," or that his two natures were so radically separated that he was basically two persons, or even that his humanity was "swallowed up by his deity." In every case, these early heresies arose as the church grappled with how to understand the Jesus described in Scripture – as apparently fully human and fully God.[88]

Historically, the struggle has been not only among theologians and church leaders. It is perhaps most noticeable by the average church member as she views religious art in a museum, looks at the illustrations in children's Bible story books, or even looks at the illustrations in her adult Bible for that matter. Whether it has been popular piety influencing art or the other way around, throughout history Jesus has been usually portrayed with a halo, flawless in appearance, clean and neatly groomed, and usually as the only one in a spotless white robe. His skin appears smooth, his gaze trancelike or like that of a mystic, and his hair recently coiffed. Worse, he is often feminized and appears more like a good looking bearded lady than a manly carpenter. Even as a baby in the manger, we sing "no crying he makes." His humanity is not denied, but it is suppressed so as not to be an embarrassment. We like him human, just not fully down and dirty with the rest of us.[89]

More recently there have been views that do not deny the humanity of Jesus, but greatly de-emphasize its importance. In theological circles this is most notable in Rudolf Bultmanns' existential Christology. He did not deny the reality of Jesus' humanity and the facts of his life, but he de-emphasized their importance. What matters, said Bultmann, is not the Jesus of history (actual facts), but the Christ of faith.[90] Whether the Biblical accounts about Jesus and his life can be proven to be factually true does not matter as much as the existential content of the story about him does and how that leads to life transformation. Some of the defective Christologies examined in chapter one, particularly those in Buddhism, Hinduism, and the New Age, have similar results. Jesus was certainly human and what he did as a human was important; however, once enlightenment is achieved or once the "Christ" spirit comes upon him, his humanity no longer matters. It is pushed aside and even denigrated.

Evangelical overreaction

Evangelicals sometimes unintentionally diminish the importance – and even at times the reality – of Jesus' humanity in three ways:

One, too often we are guilty of an overreaction to liberal denial of his deity. Because Jesus' deity is so often downplayed or outright denied, evangelicals have to defend that Christological doctrine more than any other. Unfortunately, what comes across too often in preaching and teaching is an unintentional diminishing of his humanity out of fear of appearing to diminish his deity. We say he was fully human, but are afraid of talking too much about it or even of his life lest we be accused of somehow downplaying the cross or the resurrection. We seem afraid at times to emphasize too much his life and teachings or we might be charged with preaching the social gospel. In our contemporary American setting we have to explain and defend the true nature of Jesus' deity more than ever, for it is so often denied, redefined, or misinterpreted. That should not keep us, however, from fully expositing the true nature of his humanity.

Two, it appears that the average Christian a little embarrassed to attribute too much humanity to Jesus. Some still hold to a material dualism, unwilling to attribute goodness to

God's creation, especially the human body. Consequently, we agree that Jesus had a body, that he got hungry, tired, and that he slept. But, we don't want to think about him having body odor or bad breath, and he certainly was not susceptible to gross bodily functions. He was human, so he laughed, wept, experienced sorrow, and even got angry a time or two. But, he is portrayed as mostly somber (at least according to most art and most movies), mostly emotionless, and we like to think he only had to stand up to temptation that one time. We seem to have a hard time attributing too many emotions to Jesus, and it never occurs to us that he regularly faced temptation to a degree that we cannot fathom because we give in while he always rejected it.

Three, sometimes we suffer from a variation of Bultmann's existential Christology. Whereas a personal relationship with Jesus is absolutely necessary and at the core of what evangelicals stand for, we cannot disengage that personal experience from history. This is the danger of preaching solely topical sermons (no context for the sermon), and focusing primarily on Jesus "meeting all your needs." When disengaged from his historical context, including his full humanity, his three year ministry, and what he meant as fulfillment of Israel's hope, Jesus becomes a deity-on-demand and a magical "needs-meeter." Whatever happened way back then is not that important. What matters, to borrow from Bultmann, is what my personal Jesus can do for me now. Do not misunderstand me. Jesus does meet all my needs; however, I must let the historical, fully human and fully divine resurrected Jesus define my needs, and they are usually not what I thought they were.

Our need for a fully human savior

And here is our greatest need: a savior. That savior, however, must be fully human. The gospel is that God himself graciously provided the means for us to be reconciled through him. He did that by sending his Son, the Second Person of the Trinity and thus fully God (see below), to become fully human, mysteriously yet truly two natures in one person. That person, Jesus Christ, knew no sin, but became sin – took on all our sin – on the cross to pay the penalty we deserved. The benefit of that sacrifice is forgiveness of sin and new life in Christ, both eternally and in this world. But why was it important for Jesus to be fully human? What does his humanity imply for us?

One, a human sacrifice had to be offered by a human priest, both of which needed to be perfect. Hebrews 10 speaks of the deficiency of the Old Testament sacrifices, for they "can never perfect the worshipers by the same sacrifices they continually offer year after year," and serve as a "reminder of sins every year" (vv.1-3). The reality is that "it is impossible for the blood of bulls and goats to take away sins" (v.4). What was needed was a perfect sacrifice offered by a perfect priest, and that sacrifice had to be perfectly effective and permanent. Jesus was that perfect human sacrifice and the perfect human priest, and was able to do what the animal sacrifices could never do – "make propitiation for the sins of the people" (Heb. 2:17), the result of which, according to 10:10, is that "we have been sanctified through the offering of the body of Jesus Christ once for all."[91]

Two, a fully human savior is needed for our full redemption. As fallen human beings, every aspect of our humanity has been infected by sin. Our physical, intellectual, emotional, volitional, and spiritual faculties have been affected. We are, in fact, spiritually dead according to Scripture. That does not mean these faculties are ineffective or that every human being is as bad as he could possibly be. It means that every faculty is not truly human as God intended it to be and in need of redemption. If Jesus is our Redeemer and he redeems every aspect of our humanity, he himself had to be fully and truly human, yet without sin. The great church father Gregory of Nazianzus stated this truth in the fourth century as he countered views that limited the humanity of Jesus: "For that which He has not assumed He has not healed; but that which is united to His God-head is also saved."[92]

Three, Jesus' full humanity means that he fully identified with us. He experienced what we experience; he knows what we feel, and what we struggle with. He understood, more than we can imagine, pain, sorrow, joy, love, disappointment, anger, and the fullness of all emotions, yet without responding to any of those emotions in sin. Perhaps more importantly, as Hebrews 4:15 says, "For we do not have a high priest who is unable to sympathize with our weaknesses, but One who has been tested in every way as we are, yet without sin." Some translations say that he has been "tempted in all things" (NASB). The point is, Jesus experienced *every kind* of testing and temptation (not just in the wilderness) that we could possibly experience, yet, instead of giving in as we so often do, he resisted to the point of sinlessness. When we are tempted and when we are tested, we can be comforted in knowing that our Savior really knows what it is like.

Finally, Jesus' full humanity lets us see our humanity as it was intended to be and as it will be in the resurrection. This should alleviate some of our evangelical over reaction mentioned above; i.e. our fear of attributing too much humanity to Jesus. The problem is that we attribute to him our fallen humanity. We define humanity as we know and experience it. We need to understand that his humanity is true humanity, ours is not. His emotions are selfless and never sinful, ours rarely are. His human needs and desires are fulfilled within God's will, ours sometimes are not. His humanity is the model and the example of what we are to be when we strive to be "more like Jesus." This means that the human body and human nature are originally and inherently good. Thus, the incarnation is eternal; that is, Jesus Christ sits at the right hand of the Father now in his resurrected body. We will see the scars on his hands and feet. It means that we should not really excuse our failings and our sins by saying "I am only human;" in reality, we should say "I am less than truly human." It means that when we are resurrected and see him as he is, we will begin to experience our humanity as God originally intended.

The Biblical Record

A summary of the Biblical evidence for Jesus' full humanity should include:

Old Testament Prophecy

One of the most significant Messianic passages in the Old Testament, Isaiah 52:13-53:12, describes in detail the human characteristics of the Suffering Servant. It predicts his growth ("He grew up before Him like a young plant"), speaks of his not too attractive physical appearance, contrary to most art ("He had no form or splendor that we should look at Him, no appearance that we should desire Him"), and describes him as one who "knew what sickness was," understood suffering, and was one well acquainted with the human experience of rejection and hatred ("He was despised and rejected by men . . . He was like one people turned away from"). Physically, he was tortured ("His appearance was so disfigured that He did not look like a man"), "was pierced because of our transgressions," and killed ("They made His grave with the wicked").

His birth and childhood

The gospels of Matthew and Luke give us two perspectives on the birth of Jesus, who, although conceived by the Holy

Spirit, was born to Mary. His conception was miraculous, but Mary's pregnancy and his actual birth were apparently as normal as any one's. At eight days Jesus was circumcised just like all Hebrew males (Luke 2:21), giving evidence that his was a flesh and bone body and not just having the appearance of humanity. Of his childhood we have only the account of him staying behind in the temple at age twelve. Luke's account (2:41-50) suggests a precocious boy growing into an awareness of his unique nature and relationship with the Father. Immediately, in the next two verses, Luke notes Jesus' physical, intellectual, emotional, and relational growth. He was obedient to his parents; he grew in wisdom (which includes intellectual, spiritual, and emotional aspects), stature (physical maturity), and "in favor with God and with people" (increase in spiritual and relational maturity). [93]

His physical limitations

Jesus experienced the physical limitations and needs that are common to human physiology. He got tired, he needed rest (Matt. 14:13; John 4:6) and sleep (Luke 8:23). He was hungry (Matt. 4:2; 21:18) and thirsty (John 4: 7; 19:28). Thus, he had to eat (Matt. 9:10; 11:19) and care for his physical needs like the rest of us. There is no indication anywhere in the gospels that anyone thought of him as less than a physical human being. They touched him and felt him, and he touched others (Matt. 20:34; Mark 10:13; Luke 8: 45; John 20:27), more often than not for healing purposes.[94] Jesus also felt pain and suffered. At his arrest, he was manhandled, slapped, flogged, and tortured. He finally died an actual physical death on the cross. His body was taken down, prepared for burial, wrapped in burial cloths, and put in the tomb. This was no spirit or appearance only. He still has the scars to prove it.

His human personality

Jesus experienced human emotions, including those we often think of as "negative." They were not in his case, however, because the emotion is perfectly normal, natural, and neutral. It is how the emotion is used or reacted to that determines whether it is sinful. After all, the Bible attributes emotions to God. Although not every emotion is called by name in the following passages, the emotion is implied or demonstrated by Jesus' words and actions. He experienced love toward Mary, Martha, and Lazarus, and toward the rich young ruler (John 11:5: Mark 10:21). He speaks of his joy (John 15:11; 17:13). He feels sorrow and distress ("troubled") in the Garden of Gethsemane and when he predicts his crucifixion (Matt. 26:36; John 12:27). He knows grief over Lazarus's death and the grief of his loved ones (John 11:35); anger over desecration of the Temple and over the power of death and the hardness of hearts (John 2:13-17; 11: 33, 38; Matt. 12:34). He could feel disappointment in his disciples and in Peter specifically (Matt. 26:45; Luke 22:61), amazement at an expression of faith (Matt. 8:10), and compassion over the hurts and needs of others (Matt.14: 14; Luke 7:13). It even seems he could be irritated by the lack of faith and comprehension in his disciples (Matt. 15: 16; 16: 8, 23) and indignant over their attitude and actions (Mark 10:14). Moreover, it is difficult to read about the wedding at Cana, Jesus' encounter with children, and the multiple times when he reclined to eat at someone's table and not believe that he experienced joy, laughter, and happiness in the presence of people.

The scope of Jesus' intellectual qualities is a little harder for us to fully grasp. There were times when he displayed knowledge far beyond normal human ability. At other times he asked questions and confessed to ignorance (not error) about a matter. He could discern the thoughts of his disciples (Luke 9:47). He could discern both the thoughts and intentions of his enemies (Luke 6:8; Matt. 22:18; Mark 12:15). He knew all about Nathanael's character and the Samaritan woman's past (John 1:47, 4:18). He correctly anticipated that he would be betrayed by Judas and denied by Peter (Matt. 26:25, 34). He had "a remarkable knowledge of the past, the present, the future, human nature and behavior."[95] At the same time, however, Jesus asked questions that were not to make a teaching point but to gain information, as he did with the father of the paralytic boy in Mark 9:21. He also clearly told his disciples that no one but the Father knew the day or the hour when he would return (Matt. 24:36).

Conclusion

Without a doubt Jesus was fully and truly human. Although his humanity may not seem to be a critical issue for American missiology, in order to present and proclaim him as Savior and Lord, the fullness of his person must be acknowledged. Consequently, his humanity must not be minimized on the one hand, nor be made the totality of his person on the other. Moreover, we must communicate the proper version of his humanity: like ours in kind, but different than ours in degree in that it was a sinless humanity and therefore what God originally intended humanity to be. We must not, therefore, evaluate his humanity based on ours, but ours based on his. We must neither minimize his humanity out of fear of making him too human nor make his humanity so much like ours that we make him sinful. The fullness of his person, however, *is* unique and quite different than ours, because his true human nature was united with his true divine nature.

The Eternal Word:
Fully and Truly God

In the beginning was the Word, and the Word was with
God, and the Word was God. He was with God in the
beginning. All things were created through Him, and
apart from Him not one thing was created that has been
created.

John 1:1-3

Although it is still important to understand and affirm the true
humanity of Jesus in contemporary theology and missiology, it is
even more important to clearly and confidently affirm and explain
his deity. Of the fourteen Christologies examined in chapter
one, ten affirm Jesus' deity to some degree, with only three in
any orthodox sense.[96] The others limit his deity, redefine it, or
remove its unique reality in the person of Jesus. The challenge
in developing a Biblical Christology, therefore, is not simply
establishing Jesus' deity, but establishing the uniqueness of his
divine nature.

Historical misconceptions

In the early church the greater concern was proving the full
humanity of Jesus rather than his full deity. This was due to
the prevalence of supernatural world views that emphasized
metaphysical dualism. Contrary to most modern viewpoints, the
worldviews surrounding early Christianity struggled to accept
that God could or would interact with his physical creation.
Consequently, Jesus's humanity was deemed apparent only or
modified to a large degree.

There were still, however, those who denied the divinity of Jesus. The earliest were the Ebionites. Although we don't know much about them, these were generally either strong Jewish monotheists who could not fathom the divinity of anyone other than the one Jehovah God, or later adoptionists who claimed that the exceptionally good man Jesus was adopted by God at his baptism and given the Spirit of the Christ, who then left him before the crucifixion. A more developed, influential, and eventually explosive view in church history was Arianism, which claimed that Jesus' was a limited deity. The claim was that Jesus was created at some point in the pre-temporal past by an absolute transcendent Father, served as the agent of creation, and was incarnated to be redeemer and savior. Jesus Christ, the Son of God, was therefore divine, but less so than the Father (and thus a demigod). He was a perfect creature, but a creature nonetheless. He was certainly a greater being than the rest of us humans, but definitely less than fully God, for "there was a time when he was not."[97]

In chapter one, we addressed several Christologies that redefine, limit, or deny the deity of Jesus Christ. Historically, and oversimplifying, views that deny the full deity of Jesus are based on rationalist, empiricist, or religious objections.

The rationalist objections point to the supposed illogicality of the incarnation and the unity of two natures, divine and human, in one person. The deists and the moralists examined in chapter one belong here. For them God is certainly real, but what they read in Scripture and what orthodox dogma claims about the incarnation and the deity of Christ is unreasonable and illogical. Appealing to mystery is not accepted; only what can be understood and explained by human reason is. The result is a rejection of the Bible as final authoritative revelation, and the denial of God become flesh in the person of Jesus Christ. At best, Jesus was a special person inspired by God, who became a good teacher and showed us God's way.

The empiricist objections are more naturalistic and deny the supernatural. There may be a God, but we can only know him by what we observe, measure, and describe, which is not much. Jesus may have been a historical person, but he was no more than a special teacher, prophet, and ethical teacher. The miracles he performed prove nothing, for they are regarded as church myths.

Both of these views regard the incarnation, and most of the supernatural events recorded in Scripture, as faith expressions of the disciples and the later church. As the church grew and aged, it began to reflect on and theologize about the impact the man Jesus had. They made use of current philosophical categories and concepts which only muddled the simplicity of Jesus and his teachings. Consequently, what orthodoxy says are the teachings of Jesus are really the musings of a growing church far too influenced by philosophy.[98]

The religious objections were noted in the examinations of Judaism, Hinduism, Buddhism, and Islam. For these, Jesus is merely a man, one incarnation of God or gods, an enlightened human being, or a mere prophet.

Contemporary objections

The objections to the deity of Christ – that God would become man and be both fully man and fully God – have not changed that much. The rationalist still claims that it is illogical, the empiricist still says there is no way to scientifically prove it, and the naturalist simply denies God and the supernatural. From a missiological perspective, however, the greatest contemporary objection in our postmodern but yet highly spiritual world is not so much to the deity of Jesus Christ as it is to the uniqueness of this God-man. Again, we saw this objection in our earlier review of world religions: Hinduism, Buddhism, New Age religions, and others are willing to admit to Jesus being one of many incarnations or having the Spirit of Christ or having some kind of special presence and relationship with God; however, they deny either the uniqueness of the deity that is Jesus Christ, however that deity may be understood, or the uniqueness and once-for-all nature of his incarnation.[99]

Two prominent and influential voices who have objected to the orthodox understanding of the incarnation and the subsequent deity of Jesus Christ are John Hick and Paul Knitter. Hick has objected to the orthodox claim of the deity of Christ because "almost certainly Jesus himself did not teach that he was God incarnate." This doctrine actually "emerged" in the early church at a time when "it was not uncommon to speak of a great human figure as a son of God." The bottom line for Hick is that the "Christian image of the divine incarnation" is "but a religious myth," whose function is to evoke a desire to follow Jesus as the way to salvation, but not because Jesus saves in the sense that evangelicals understand salvation. To the contrary, it is the heavenly Father who saves. Jesus' role was as "God's agent, so completely conscious of living in God's presence and serving God's love, that the divine reality was mediated through him to others." That is, salvation is found in Jesus only in the sense that, as a very special human being, he mediates God's love to us. The clear implication for Hick is that Jesus is just one of many ways to salvation. Jesus is the Christian concrete image of God; however, the salvific image of God can also be found in other key individuals in other world religions.[100]

Paul Knitter agrees with Hick in that Jesus "gave us no Christology" for he did not claim to be the Son of God or have "any kind of awareness of divine sonship." Jesus saw his role and mission as the final or eschatological prophet "announcing and enacting the good news of God's final rule." Jesus was deeply aware of God as his Father, which, according to Knitter "indicates specialness, uniqueness," but does not "automatically imply exclusivity." The key to Jesus is to understand that he was "theocentric" and pointed to God and his kingdom, not to himself. Jesus was a "particular" revealer and savior, but other religions and cultures need their own particular revealers and saviors. Consequently, Christians cannot lay any claim to the exclusivity of Jesus. Knitter is clear in this when he says that the "experience of faith necessarily includes the conviction that Jesus is God's revelation and grace. It does not necessarily include the conviction that he *alone* is this revelation and grace."[101]

Per our missiological interests, Hick and Knitter are simply giving an academic exposition of the pluralism that many Americans believe, practice, and verbalize more and more. The academy, popular culture, much of the media, and more and more civic leaders – even those who may claim to be Christian – are expressing doubts about or disbelief in either the deity or the uniqueness of Jesus Christ. The influence of academic postmodernism's denial of a metanarrative, the reality of globalism's shrinking world, and the influx of world religions demand, most Americans now say, a tolerance of all worldviews and religions (unfortunately, tolerance is redefined as acceptance and equality). Jesus may be *your* God and Savior, they say, but he is not the only one. The challenge for the church is the same as during the first century: proclaiming and demonstrating through word and deed that Jesus Christ our Lord is fully human and fully divine and unique in his person and work. Some ways to fulfill that challenge will be addressed in Part III.

The Biblical Record

The Biblical evidence for the deity of Jesus Christ can be broken down into four general categories:

Statements about his pre-existence

Any talk about the deity of Jesus Christ must begin with his pre-existence. Without the existence of the Word (*Logos*) before the incarnation, then no claim can be made that the Savior is God.[102] The most famous and most often quoted passage related to the pre-existence of Christ is probably John 1:1-3. The Word, clearly identifiable later in vv. 10-18 as Jesus Christ, was "in the beginning" and "was with God," and "was God." He had an immediate and direct hand in creation, for all things were "created through Him." The passage parallels Genesis 1:1 in some of its wording, which "is not a mere coincidence." John's point is to identify the Word as existing before and involved in creating all that is, which reveals Christ to be "eternal and uncreated – two attributes of God."[103] Furthermore, to say that the Son was God and with God implies "both *unity* and *distinguishability* within the Godhead – elementary features of triune teaching."[104]

Jesus himself referred to his pre-existence when he told the Jewish leaders that "Before Abraham was, I am," (John 8:58) a statement that implies "eternality as a distinctive attribute of the speaker." In John 17, as Jesus prays to his Father, he speaks of the "glory I had with You before the world existed" (verse 5) and of the love the Father had for him "before the world's foundation" (verse 24).[105]

The great "kenotic" (emptying) passage of Philippians 2:5-11 clearly indicates that Jesus "existed in the form of God" prior to the incarnation and then "emptied Himself by assuming the form of a slave, taking on the likeness of men." Similarly, Colossians 1:15-20 refers to Christ as the "firstborn over all creation," indicating his priority over all creation rather than being *of* the creation. This is confirmed in the same passage, where it says that "all things have been created through Him and for Him. He is before all things, and by Him all things hold together." The same creator emphasis is found in Hebrews 2:10, where the Son is the one "for whom and through whom all things exist."

What Jesus claimed

A common apologetic approach to the deity of Jesus Christ is what Josh McDowell calls the "Trilemma." If Jesus claimed to be God, either he was telling the truth and is our God and Lord, or he was not God and was either a liar or a deluded lunatic.[106] McDowell's point is well taken, for it forces us to seriously consider what Jesus said about himself. Thomas Oden calls this the "Scandal of Self-reference;" that is, unlike other great religious teachers who are usually self-effacing, Jesus "was constantly saying outrageous things about himself." There must be, Oden insists, a "plausible premise behind" these sayings in order to make any kind of sense. Without that plausible premise – that Jesus was in fact God – what he said about himself would certainly have to be classified as absurd, delusional, or outright manipulative lies.[107] Furthermore, claims by Jesus to be deity, if true, obviously only add to the arguments for his pre-existence. If he was God, then he is eternal pre- and post-temporally.

Jesus claimed *titles*, an *identity, prerogatives*, and a *position or a relationship* that either should only belong to God or which clearly indicate that Jesus understood that he was one with God.[108] First, he claimed the *title* "Son of Man" for himself over fifty times in the Gospels (excluding parallel passages).[109] The full meaning of this favorite title of his is hotly debated in academic circles. It appears Jesus used it to speak of and affirm his humanity, to refer to his work on earth, to allude to the suffering of the Son of Man, and to point to his future glorification. It is generally agreed upon, however, that this was a Messianic title taken from the books of Daniel and Ezekiel. The title defined his mission as "a heavenly Messiah fulfilling on earth a ministry on men's behalf which would culminate in scenes of final glory."[110] It must be emphasized, however, that the title also implies deity. The scenes described in Daniel 7:13-14 portray a figure coming in the clouds, with an everlasting dominion, with glory, and with a kingdom over all peoples, nations, and languages. Surely this is a divine figure, and Jesus is claiming that he is this Son of Man. It is no wonder that the High Priest Caiaphas screamed "blasphemy" when Jesus answered his question (Matt. 26:63-65; Mark 14:61-64; Luke 22:67-71). In his response Jesus was "claiming to be a heavenly, divine figure who would be seated at God's right hand, exercising rule forever over all people everywhere."[111]

Jesus also claimed or accepted the *title* "Son of God" either explicitly or implicitly. In the wilderness temptation account, the Devil twice begins his challenge with "If you are the Son of God." The Greek "makes it clear that there is no casting of doubt on the sonship of Jesus," and Jesus certainly does not reject the title. In Matt. 11:25-27 Jesus speaks of the revelation that "My Father" has entrusted to the Son. Calling himself "Son" in this passage is not a reference to a generic son of God, but is an "absolute form" of the "'the Son' as a self-description." It is clear that Jesus is conscious of his "unique filial relation" with God ("No one knows the Son except the Father, and no one knows the Father except the Son") and that he understood himself as "the sole agent" for revealing to others "all things" the Father has entrusted to him. When speaking of his own second coming, Jesus says in Mark 13:32 that "concerning that day or hour no one knows – neither the angels in heaven nor the Son – except the Father." Again, a close filial relationship is described, although in this particular case, the incarnate Son is ignorant of a particular future time. This does not imply inferiority of the Son, but is a manifestation of his self-limitation while in the flesh (see next chapter).[112]

Finally, there is the overwhelming evidence of the Gospel of John. John states that his purpose is so his readers might believe that Jesus is the Son of God. To that end, he records the actual title "Son of God" several times, but also records over "a hundred occasions" where "Jesus speaks of God as Father." This is a dominant theme for John and leaves no doubt that he was interested in giving the reader a "glimpse at what it means to be in a unique sense the Son of God."[113] The most famous example that expresses that unique relationship is Jesus' encounter with Nicodemus (John 3:1-21). Here Jesus states that God "gave His One and Only Son," and "did not send His Son into the world that He might condemn the world," but to save whoever might believe "in the name of the One and Only Son of God." Another example is found in 5:22-23, where Jesus says that the "Father, in fact, judges no one but has given all judgment to the Son, so that all people will honor the Son just as they honor the Father. Anyone who does not honor the son does not honor the Father who sent Him."

Second, Jesus claimed an *identity* that put him on par with God. The most striking of these identity claims are the "I Am" sayings in John's Gospel. They not only identify Jesus with an Old Testament description of God, they also identify him, through the use of metaphors, as the one who embodies and reveals God and God's gifts. Several times the saying is used in the absolute sense. In 8:58 Jesus states says that "Before Abraham was, I am," clearly intending "to convey in an extraordinary way such exclusively divine qualities as changelessness and pre-existence." The uses of "I am" in 8:24 and 13:19 similarly imply deity and indicate a unique relationship with Yahweh God. The "expression is in the style of deity."[114] The other "I Am" sayings are connected with metaphors indicating that Jesus is revealing God in a unique way: bread (6:35), light (8:12), door (10:7), shepherd (10:11), resurrection and life (11:25), way, truth, and life (14:6), and vine (15:1). These sayings identify who he was and what he did: divine and *uniquely* sent to be the revealer of God the Father.

Third, Jesus claimed *prerogatives* that should belong only to one who is deity. He forgave sins: In Matt. 9:2 he publicly forgave the paralytic's sins, and then in verse 6 claimed the authority as the Son of Man for doing so. He gave to the disciples the keys of the kingdom of heaven (Matt. 16:19) and claimed that he will rule the kingdom (Matt. 19:28), which is his kingdom (John 18:36). He claimed ownership as the builder of his church (Matt. 16:18). He claimed Lordship over the Sabbath (Matt. 12:8). He claimed that belief in him was the basis for eternal life (John 6:40; 8:24), and claimed the right to judge and separate the sheep from the goats at the end time (Matt. 25: 31-33). He claimed authority to ask the Father to send the Holy Spirit to the disciples (John 14:16, 26), which is the same as the Son sending the Spirit (John 16:7), and later claimed that "all authority" had been given to him, both "in heaven and on earth" (Matt. 28:17). He claimed (in the sense that he accepted as one deserving) worship from the disciples after he walked on water (Matt. 14:33), from the man born blind who was then healed (John 9:38), from the children who were shouting in the temple (Matt. 21:15-16), specifically from Thomas after the resurrection ("My Lord and my God," John 20:28), and then again from the eleven before his ascension (Matt. 28:17). Over and over again, Jesus either directly claimed or accepted as deserving prerogatives that could and should only be those of deity. Either he was God or he was deeply disturbed, or he was a gross manipulator of people.

Finally, Jesus claimed a unique *position* in his relationship to God the Father, for his Sonship and his relationship to the Father was one unparalleled and unmatched in history. As fully divine, he was one with the Father in essence, in mind, and in will. He claimed oneness with the Father (John 10:30, 38) to the point that to see and know Jesus is to see and know the Father (John 12:45; 14:8-11), and to receive Jesus is to receive the Father (Luke 9:48; John 13:20). Conversely, to reject Jesus is to reject the Father (Matt. 10:32-33; Luke 10:16). How one feels toward the Son is intimately tied with how one feels toward the Father; that is, to love the Son is rewarded by the Father's love (John

16:27), but to hate the Son is to hate the Father (John 15:23-24). This unique relationship is also seen in the fact that the Father has sent the Son (Luke 4:43; John 4:34; 5:37-43; 17:18, 23), the Son reveals the Father (Matt. 11:27; John 6:46), speaks for the Father (John 12:49-50), and they glorify each other (John 13:31-32). Finally, to believe in Jesus is to believe in God (John 14:1), meaning that their relationship is such that no one can come to the Father except through Jesus (John 14:6). No person in history could ever claim this kind of positional relationship with God unless he were divinely related to God.

The titles, the identity, the prerogatives, and the position Jesus claimed all point to his self-consciousness as the divine Son of God. The only plausible conclusion echoes the trilemma presented above. He must have been a lying manipulator, a deluded mad man, or the unique divine Son of God come in the flesh. Further evidence for the latter option is found in what he did.

What Jesus did

Jesus not only claimed titles, an identity, prerogatives, and a position that verified his divine nature, but he also acted upon these in his interactions with people. His desire was not simply to state who he was, but to act in accordance to who he was – God's perfect, unique, and divine Son come in the flesh. Consequently, he demonstrated power and authority over sin, sickness, nature, the demonic, and over death.

Jesus demonstrated power and authority *over sin* by not only claiming the prerogative to forgive sin, but by actually doing so. He forgave the paralytic (Matt. 9:2; Luke 5:17-20), he declared that the woman who anointed his feet as an act of faith had been forgiven of her sins (Luke 7:47-48), and most famously forgave the woman caught in adultery (John 8: 1-11). Although he did not say the actual words "You are forgiven," he did refuse to condemn her and sent her on her way clearly implying forgiveness.

Jesus demonstrated power and authority *over sickness* numerous times as he healed disease, sickness, and restored broken down bodies. He healed Peter's mother-in-law (8:14-16), a woman who had suffered bleeding for twelve years (Matt. 9:20-22), and two blind men (Matt. 9:27-31). He healed a man with a paralyzed hand (Matt. 12:9-13), ten lepers (Luke 17:12-19), an invalid man at the pool of Bethesda (John 5:1-9), and people with all kinds of infirmities (Matt. 15:29-31). His power and authority over sickness was such that it was publicly recognized by a Roman Centurion, with the result that Jesus healed the man's servant long distance (Matt. 8:5-13; Luke 7:1-1), a divine feat repeated for a royal official (John 4:46-54).

Jesus demonstrated power and authority *over the creation* in several ways. He turned water into wine (John 2:1-11). He walked on water (John 5:16-21) and calmed the wind and the waves (Luke 8:22-25). Twice he took a small amount of bread and fish, blessed them, and created more than enough to feed thousands, with plenty left over (Mark 6:30-44 and 8:1-10). He even cursed a fig tree, causing it to wilt, as an object lesson to his disciples about the spiritual deadness of Israel (Matt. 21:18-22).

Jesus demonstrated power and authority *over the demonic* when he confronted and cast demons from the possessed. In Matt. 8:16, after he healed Peter's mother-in-law, the people "brought to Him many who were demon-possessed." Jesus had such power and authority over these that he drove them out "with a word." Again, in Mark 5:1-17, he confronted a "Legion" of demons in the region of the Gerasenes, driving them out into a herd of pigs. He cast out a demon from a mute man (Matt. 9:32-34), an action which caused the Pharisees to accuse Jesus of being in cahoots with the ruler of the demons.

Finally, Jesus demonstrated power and authority *over death*. A synagogue leader named Jairus asked him to heal his critically ill daughter. By the time Jesus made it to the little girl, she was dead. Although he was laughed at by the mourners, he resuscitated the little girl and brought her back to life (Mark 5:21-43). On another occasion (Luke 7:11-17) he encountered a man already dead. His compassion for the grieving mother led him to raise the young man to life, resulting in both great fear and praise among the onlookers. In the most dramatic occasion of raising a dead person to life, Jesus waited for three days after his friend Lazarus was dead before he acted. This three day wait prevented anyone present from denying that Lazarus was actually dead. After declaring that he was "the resurrection and the life," Jesus called Lazarus from the tomb (John 11:1-44).[115]

All these actions performed by Jesus point to and give evidence of his divine nature. Perhaps one could argue that any one of these miracles could have been done by a non-divine person who was simply submitting himself to a supernatural power. The Pharisees made this accusation, in fact, when they accused Jesus of casting demons out by the power of the devil. Without a doubt, there have been many in history who have performed miracles similar to the ones Jesus performed, perhaps even raising someone from the dead. Reports of such supernatural activity are not uncommon in missionary and ministry reports – just because something is supernatural does not mean it is of God! Taken all these accounts together, however, and putting them with all that Jesus claimed for and about himself, the only reasonable conclusion is that this person, Jesus Christ, was God. Furthermore, the reasonableness of the evidence is compounded once the statements of others are taken into account.

What others said: The Synoptic Gospels

The birth narratives found in both Matthew and Luke give ample indication of the deity of Jesus. Mary discovered that she "was pregnant by the Holy Spirit" (Matt. 1:18), a fact communicated to Joseph by an angel ("what has been conceived in her is by the Holy Spirit," 1:20). Luke 1:26-38 details Mary's own encounter with the angel Gabriel, who told her she to be overshadowed by "the power of the Most High."

When Jesus began his public ministry, God spoke from heaven affirming him as His beloved Son (Mark 1:11; Matt. 3:17; Luke 3:22). During his temptation in the wilderness, Jesus was even acknowledged twice as the Son of God by the devil (Matt. 4:2,6; Luke 4:3,9). Although the Devil says "If you are the Son of God," he is not questioning Jesus' divine sonship, but rather acknowledging it.[116] Not only did Satan acknowledge his divine sonship, so did the demons Jesus confronted and cast out. When a man with an unclean spirit met Jesus in the synagogue, he shouted out: "What do You have to do with us, Jesus – Nazarene? Have you come to destroy us? I know who You are – the Holy One of God!" (Mark 1:24; Luke 4:34). After Jesus walked on the water and got into the boat with his disciples, they declared "Truly You are the Son of God" (Matt. 14:33). When Jesus later asked his disciples who they said that he was, Peter proclaimed "You are the Messiah, the Son of the living God" (Matt. 16:16). At the transfiguration, once again God spoke from heaven affirming Jesus as his "beloved Son," in whom he takes delight and who should be listened to (Matt 17:5). At the crucifixion the Roman Centurion could only come to the conclusion that "This man really was God's Son (Matt. 27:54).

What others said: The Gospel of John

The Gospel of John is so different from the Synoptics that some critics believe it to be less factual and somewhat untrustworthy. They claim that John's obvious theological interest means he had little historical interest and did more theological interpreting than he did reporting. Theological interpretation, however, "does not necessarily mean distortion of the facts. Indeed the absence of interpretation may sometimes mean distortion." Thus, if God the Son did indeed become flesh, "then this interpretive document is of the utmost importance for those who want the fullest light on the facts."[117] I bring this up because the Gospel of John is chock full of statements, arguments, and interpretations that are intended to prove that Jesus Christ was the divine Son of God.[118] This is John's express purpose as stated in 20:31, when he says he wrote about only a few of the signs Jesus performed "so that you may believe Jesus is the Messiah, the Son of God, and by believing you may have life in His name." These seven signs or miracles that for John prove Jesus was the Messiah, the Son of God, (some already mentioned above), are: turning the water into wine (2:1-11), healing the royal official's son (4:46-54), healing the paralyzed man at the pool of Bethesda (5:1-15), feeding the five thousand (6:1-15), walking on water (6:16-21), healing a man born blind (9:1-41), and raising Lazarus from the dead (11:1-44).

John says and records so much more, however, about the deity of Jesus. As already discussed, in 1:1-18 he eloquently argues for the pre-existence, and thus deity, of the Word, the One and Only Son, who became flesh and lived among human beings. In 3:31-36 he says that this One "comes from heaven" and "is above all." God "sent Him, and He speaks God's word." He is the Son who is loved by the Father, who "has given all things into His hands." After his encounter with the Samaritan woman at the well, the villagers told the woman that they believed Jesus for themselves because they knew "that this really is the Savior of the world" (4:42). In 5:18 John reports what Jesus said that got him into so much trouble with the Jewish leaders, something that John obviously believed: "He was even calling God His own Father, making Himself equal with God." John reports statements of Peter ("You are the Holy One of God," 6:69), the disciples as a group ("By this we believe that You came from God," 16:30), and Thomas ("My Lord and my God," 20:28).

Granted, it could be argued that any one of the incidents or statements recorded by John is inadequate in and of itself as absolute proof of the deity of Jesus. Certainly, in many cases the person making the statement did not have a fully developed theology of the human and divine nature of the person of Jesus Christ. But the abundance of statements and miraculous signs, taken together with John's interpretive statements, makes John's Gospel a treasure trove of evidence that Jesus Christ is the "very incarnation of God," fully man and fully God.[119]

What others said:
The rest of the New Testament

Liberal scholars will often pit the Gospels (in particular the Synoptics) against the rest of the New Testament (in particular the writings of Paul). Their argument is that the first century church (read Paul, in most cases) distorted the simple ethical message of the historical Jesus into one that was over spiritualized, exclusivist, and triumphalist. In particular, they do not appreciate Paul's focus on the atonement and the resurrected Lord. Those who question or deny the full deity of Jesus often point to Paul (and John) as the one who deified Jesus after the fact. To say this, however, is to obviously deny the inspiration and authority of the entire New Testament. It is also requires one to either ignore or minimize all that we have already seen recorded in the gospels. If we approach the Bible as a unity, and if we can allow that the Holy Spirit continued to explain and interpret all the Jesus events and teachings to "you" (John 16:12-13), then interpretation and explanation by Paul and other writers is exactly what was needed and intended to fully understand the person and work of Jesus.[120]

In summary, the rest of the New Testament affirms and explains the divine nature of Jesus Christ:

In Acts, his ascension and the promise of his return is recorded (1:9-11); Peter refers to Jesus as the resurrected Messiah and as Lord during his Pentecost sermon (2:14-36). Later Peter is speaking to a crowd and refers to Jesus as the "Holy and Righteous One" and "the source (or author) of life" (3:14-15), terms rooted in Old Testament terminology and indicative of a divinely appointed King and Savior.[121] At the end of his testimony, Stephen "gazed into heaven" and "saw God's glory, with Jesus standing at the right hand of God." Telling the Sanhedrin that he saw "the Son of Man standing at the right of God" enraged them so much that he was martyred (7:54-60). After Saul met the Lord on the road to Damascus, he "began proclaiming Jesus in the synagogues: 'He is the Son of God'" (9:20). In his testimony to Cornelius, Peter referred to Jesus as "Lord of all" and as the "One appointed by God to be the Judge of the living and the dead" (10:34-43).

In his writings, Paul leaves no doubt that he considered Jesus Christ to be God. Rarely did he begin a letter without including in his salutation the fact that Jesus was God's Son and the "Lord" (Rom. 1:3; 1 Cor. 1:2; 2 Cor. 1:2; Eph. 1:2; 1 Tim. 1:2,12). Other uses of "Lord" by Paul (Rom. 10:9; 13:14; 1 Cor. 1:7-10 [four times]; 6:11; Eph. 1:17; 1 Thess. 2:15, 19;1 Tim. 1:6:14) indicate that he saw Jesus Christ as "risen and exalted," the Son of God "in power."[122] Lest one object that Paul's use of "Lord" is one of high honor and respect, but not necessarily one that acknowledges deity, how Paul describes this "Lord Jesus Christ" clarifies that he meant Jesus was deity.[123] The Lord Jesus is the Son of God (1 Cor. 1:9; Eph. 1:3; 4:13), the power and the wisdom of God (1 Cor. 1:24), the ultimate judge of all (2 Cor. 5:10), the One through whom God worked to reconcile the world, and to offer forgiveness and salvation (2 Cor. 5:19; 32; 1Thess. 5:9; 1 Tim. 1:15). Jesus is the "promise of life" and the "Savior" (2 Tim. 1:1,10). In Titus

1:3-4, Paul refers to both God and Christ Jesus as "our Savior," speaking of one just as he could the other. No Pauline passages speak to the deity of Jesus Christ, and put all other statements in context, better than Phil. 2:5-11 and Col. 1:15-20 (and 2:9-10), where Jesus is said to have "existed in the form of God," to have had "equality with God," to be "the image of the invisible God," the One who created and holds all things together, "before all things," and the one in whom the "fullness" of God dwells. Finally, Paul had no problem referring to the Father, the Son, and the Holy Spirit in multiple orders "so as to imply a relationship among the three," highlighting the "Three-in-Oneness" found in the New Testament and which obviously assumes the deity of the Son (see 1 Cor. 12:4-6; 2 Cor. 13:14; Eph. 1:1, 5, 6, 13; 2:18; 4:4-6).[124]

Hebrews says God spoke "to us by His Son" and speaks of the Son as the one "through whom He made the universe" (1:2). This Son is also mentioned in 1:8 and 5:8, and is clearly presented as one who is much higher than the angels and whom the angels worship (1:4-6). He is also the perfect high priest, "holy, innocent, undefiled, separated from sinners, and exalted above the heavens" (7:26), now at the "right hand of the throne of the Majesty in the heavens" (8:1; 12:2), and the one who is changeless, the "same yesterday, today, and forever" (13:8).

Peter blesses God, the "Father of our Lord Jesus Christ" (1 Peter 1:3), who was "destined before the foundation of the world" (2:20) to be our "Savior" and "Lord" (2 Peter 1:1,8,11,14,16; 2:20; 3:18). In his epistles, John repeats much of what he stated in his Gospel: Jesus is the "Son" in 1:3, 7; 3:23; 4:10, 15; and seven times in 5:5-13. In 2:22-23, John ties acknowledgment or denial of the Son with the Father. John does the same in 2 John 9. In Revelation, John emphasizes the eternality and the glory of Jesus Christ the Son: He is the "First and the Last, and the Living One" (1:18) and the "King of Kings and Lord of Lords" (17:14; 19:16). This King and Lord is also the "Lamb who was slaughtered" and the one who is "worthy to receive power and riches and wisdom and strength and honor and glory and blessing…forever and ever!" (5:12-13), praise and worship that should be only offered to one who is God.

Implications:
Our need for a fully divine savior

Why is it important to establish that Jesus was fully divine? That he was in fact the Son of God, the second Person of the Trinity, come in the flesh? Why is it not good enough to accept him as an exceptional man who was adopted by God, who was inhabited by the Christ Spirit, or a good man who became fully God-conscious? What are the implications of this full deity?

Just as Jesus had to assume full and true humanity in order that we would be fully redeemed, so he must have been fully and truly God in order that our redemption would have been possible. A perfect human being who was only human would not have been enough. A human being who was only partially divine would not have been enough. If Jesus Christ were not fully and truly God, co-equal and co-eternal with the Father, then our redemption would have been the work of a creature, and that would have been in itself impossible. This was recognized in the fourth century AD during the Arian controversy when Arius stated that the Son, although divine, was less than fully God. If there was a time when the Son came into being, then he was a creature, and creatures, even one of a higher degree, cannot redeem other creatures. To the contrary, an infinite God, "who did not have to die, died."[125]

Similarly, any reduction, minimizing, or denial of the deity of Christ means that sin has not been fully dealt with. A good human being or even a demi-god could have taught a good ethic and even been a good example for us. He could not have, however, efficaciously and permanently dealt with either our inherited sinful human nature or our chosen sinful acts. If Christ is not fully God, then he is a creature, and if that is the case then "there is no way to speak of the liberation of humanity from sin."[126]

If Christ is fully God, then we "can have real knowledge of God." Jesus told his disciples that they needed only to see him in order to see the Father. The same holds true today. If we want to know God, we simply need to know Jesus. If we want to understand God's nature, character, and will, we can look at Jesus. If we want to understand how we should respond to God, we should look to Jesus. To know Jesus is to know the Father.

The deity of Jesus also implies that worship of Jesus Christ is fully appropriate. His disciples were justified in worshiping him, and so are we. He is fully God, and is "as deserving of our praise, adoration, and obedience as is the Father."[127] Moreover, the full deity of the incarnate Son of God implies that only he, of all supposed saviors, is worthy of that worship. Again, he is not one among many to be worshiped. He alone is worthy to be considered Savior and Lord, and is above all names on heaven and earth.

Finally, the deity of Jesus Christ means that he is also our resurrected Lord and lives today, seated at the right hand of the Father, ever making intercession for those who are his. Unlike all other founders of philosophical movements, religions and religious orders, he is alive today. Our faith is not merely in a historical figure. Our faith is not merely in God incarnate who was crucified. Our faith is in the *living* historical Jesus Christ, Son of God, incarnate, crucified, and resurrected.

Conclusion

Jesus Christ was certainly fully and truly God. He was not given divinity, he did not achieve divinity, and he was not a created demi-god. The deity he possessed was not simply the image of

God in all human beings and was not a "spark" of deity that grew and developed. He was, rather, fully and truly God, as divine as the Father and the Holy Spirit. Whereas his humanity is the point of identification for human beings (he was like us, yet without sin), his deity is a point of utter difference. The only way to deny this reality is to discount the vast record of his sayings, his actions, and the testimonies of those who lived with him. Taking all this evidence into account, the only valid conclusion is that Jesus was God or he and those around him were deceived or acting with malevolent intent. Accepting his full humanity and full deity still leaves the question, how could he be both at the same time?

Jesus Christ, the Son of God: Fully and truly Savior

The mystery of the incarnation and the subsequent two natures of Jesus Christ, human and divine, is one that has perplexed humans for two thousand years. It has driven some to skepticism and outright denial of one or the other nature (usually the divine). It has led others to confusion and even heresy as they have tried hard to fully and clearly explain how one person could exist with two natures. An explanation is certainly possible; however, it is possible only as long as one is willing to hold to mystery, paradox, and faith.

The Biblical Record

The passages already examined under the sections on the humanity and deity of Jesus Christ are sufficient to conclude that the Biblical writers "represent Jesus Christ as having a divine nature and a human nature in a single undivided personality" (John 1:1-18; 9:48-59). This conclusion is not, therefore, an addition that arose in church history that was added to Scripture but is a "premise required by Scripture" understood and verbalized by the church.[128] Over and over again the Scriptures "allude to both the deity and the humanity of Jesus, yet clearly refer to a single subject." We are told that "God sent forth his Son, born of woman, born under the law" (Gal. 4:4) and that "He was manifested in the flesh, vindicated in the Sprit, seen by angels, preached among the nations, believed on in the world, taken up in glory" (1Tim. 3:16).[129] In Rom. 1:1-4 Paul speaks of "His Son, Jesus Christ our Lord," who was both "a descendant of David according to the flesh" and "established as the powerful Son of God by the resurrection of the dead." The Philippians 2 passage examined above clearly speaks of the union of both natures in one person.

Thomas Oden points out that this "theandric premise" (God-man union) is actually necessary in order for a reading of the New Testament to even make sense. The names and titles given him – Jesus Christ, Son of God, Son of Man, Word become flesh – all speak of one person. When Jesus refers to himself, there is no "we," just an "I." This Jesus is "paradoxically 'before Abraham' yet 'born in a manger,' 'suffered under Pontius Pilate' yet the same yesterday, today, and forever." The one through whom all things were created and hold together is the same child Mary carried and the same boy left behind at the temple. The one who was before the foundation of the world does not know the day or the hour of his second coming. The one who is eternal and all-knowing is the same one who was crucified and died – the same one who now sits at the right hand of the Father. Only one person with two natures can fit these descriptions.[130]

Embracing both History and Mystery

Throughout history people have tried to intellectually grasp and faithfully explain the "Christian paradox" of the incarnation and the unity of God and man in Jesus Christ. The difficulty is that we are using "the historical to talk about what is historical and more."[131] In other words, our intellectual categories and our words may come close, but ultimately fail us. Furthermore, we have absolutely no experience to which we can appeal.

Some historical attempts to explain this unity that have fallen short include: Nestorianism, which so separated the human and divine natures of Jesus Christ that the result was virtually two persons in one fleshly body. At the other extreme, Eutychianism taught that the humanity of Jesus was so absorbed by his divinity that it was like a drop of water cast into the sea. A similar heretical teaching is that at the incarnation, the divine and human natures were fused into a *tertium quid*; that is, a third thing or one nature that was neither truly human nor truly divine.[132] Adoptionism simple states that the man Jesus came to a point (most likely at his baptism) when God adopted him as his Son. The descent of the Spirit upon Jesus was the point that he became "divine." Similarly, Dynamic Incarnation states that the active power of God inhabited Jesus in a special way. All of these attempts to "solve the problem" have required diminishing one or the other nature.[133]

The most intriguing attempt at explaining the paradox of the human and the divine in one person was *kenotic* Christology, which was popular in the nineteenth century. Coming from the Greek word for "emptying," the explanation keys in on Phil. 2:7 (". . . He emptied Himself by assuming the form of a slave"). Assuming the veracity of the Biblical materials that describe Jesus as both human and divine, the question is "what does this emptying say about God's nature?" That is, what did he do and what happened when God the Son emptied himself? Some proponents of this view went so far as to say that the eternal Son of God laid aside – even abandoned – some of his divine attributes when he became human. Others argued that he kept the divine attributes, but abstained or ceased from using them temporarily. A more moderated view denied that Christ laid aside or actually emptied himself of any divine attributes. Instead, he "deliberately limited his divine consciousness" through a "self-reduction" or "self-retraction." That is, in the incarnation Christ continued to have the divine attributes, which occasionally were displayed; however, they were, generally speaking, in "a new mode of being in which they were concentrated and came to expression in different form."[134]

Although there are several variations and nuances of kenotic Christology, the general criticisms are that they seem to treat the person of Jesus as oscillating between God and Man, never fully both at the same time, or imply some sort of "temporary theophany," or limit the divine nature far too much by defining some of the divine attributes as "potential" only. The reality is that the Son *did* empty himself according to Phil. 2:7. Verse six, however, says that he "did not consider equality with God as something to be used for His own advantage." That phrase is the antecedent of "He emptied Himself" – he gave up equality with God to become a "slave." Consequently, emptying does not mean that he became *less* divine in his nature, but that in taking on humanity, "he became functionally subordinated to the Father for the period of the incarnation." That is, he voluntarily became man and willingly limited the functioning of his divine attributes (not lost, not abandoned), because he took on human nature *in addition to* his divine nature. Christ chose to give up "the independent exercise" and functioning of his divine attributes for a particular time and a particular mission.[135]

That Jesus Christ could be fully divine and fully human and that those two natures could perfectly exist in one person in unity just seems too illogical and too irrational for human minds to accept. Perhaps so, but as already argued, although we can truly know God, we cannot know him perfectly and exhaustively. Thus, what it means for Deity to condescend to become human really does not fit our fallen mental categories. We object to it because we limit God, but if God is omnipotent, why should the incarnation be impossible for him? Furthermore, as fallen human beings we are really less than what humanity was meant to be. Jesus' was a perfect humanity. Who's to say what God can and cannot do with such sinless humanity?

The challenges of this doctrine are three:

1. There is a unique historical incarnation to believe. Unlike so many of the "incarnations" found in other religions, the Biblical account of God in Jesus Christ is unique. It was the *one* God taking on flesh *one* time for a specific and *once-for-all* purpose. No other religion claims this uniqueness. No other religious leader claimed what Jesus claimed for himself.

2. There is a paradox, viewed from our fallen human perspective, to accept. In spite of all the explanations about the union of the divine and the human in Jesus, the rest of us humans have no experiential categories and few mental categories in which to fit them. At some point, we have to be comfortable with a divine paradox.

3. There is a divine mystery to embrace by faith. That the union of the divine and the human seems paradoxical means that we have to embrace it by faith. We do not embrace this mystery by ignorance or blind faith. We study, we explain, we ponder, we do all we can do grasp the incarnation; however, at some point faith must lead.

Conclusion: The simplicity of the gospel

What we should not lose sight of in the discussion of Christ's divine and human natures, and how these co-existed and functioned in one person, is the basic simplicity of the gospel.

Certainly, these theological discussions and debates are extremely important. To misunderstand or to misstate the true nature of Jesus Christ is to run at least two serious risks: One is an evangelistic risk, of preaching about and testifying to a non-salvific and false Jesus. I am not saying that one's theology saves a person from sin. It does not. Jesus saves, not one's theological understanding. What I am saying is that Jesus stated that *he* was to be believed in (John 3:16; 6:29,35; 7:38; 14:1), and belief in him must be accurate. Jesus saves, but the sinner must understand in the simplest way possible that he is lost and that Jesus, the Son of God, died on the cross to save him. Theological understanding will certainly (hopefully) grow and become clearer after one has received Christ and is indwelt by the Holy Spirit, but the gospel of Jesus Christ must be presented clearly from the beginning for through its presentation the Holy Spirit brings conviction "about sin, righteousness, and judgment" (John 16:8).

The second risk is a discipleship risk. If a person hears the basic gospel of Jesus Christ, repents, believes, and receives the forgiveness of sin, and then is later led astray by incorrect teaching about Jesus the consequences are serious. The believer could be rendered ineffective and fruitless, may be subject to the Lord's discipline, and in turn may lead others astray. The church suffers division, disunity, disruption, and the existence of the local church may even be threatened. The Apostle Paul dealt with these issues regularly in the churches of Corinth, Galatia, and elsewhere. Continued incorrect teaching on the person and the work of Jesus will not only kill the growth of believers, but will stifle evangelism, and open the door for God's discipline and correction.

Understanding Jesus and building a Christology is critically important for missions in North America. There are simply too many inadequate Christologies creating confusion and gaining ground in the culture to minimize the importance of this doctrine. The implication of such a Christology upholds the simplicity of the gospel. If Jesus was truly and fully the God-man, what does that say about the rest of humanity? Simply that we are much less than that. We are not God and we are far less than the humans we were originally intended to be. We are fallen, sinners and sinful, and in need of a savior. And, that Savior is not a set of ideas, a belief system, or behavioral ideals, as important as these may be. That Savior is a person, and a person to be individually and personally encountered.[136] The next chapter looks further into one of the greatest challenges facing evangelicals today: the claim for the exclusivity of Jesus as *the* way.

Jesus, the Way: His Exclusivity and His Worth

> Then He began to teach them that the Son of Man must
> suffer many things, and be rejected by the elders, the chief
> priests, and the scribes, be killed, and rise after three days.

> Mark 8:31

Jesus has asked the disciples who they would say that he is, and
Peter has correctly answered that Jesus is the Messiah (the Christ).
Jesus tells the disciples to keep that information to themselves for
the time being. There were too many popular expectations and
conceptions of the prophesied Messiah that did not line up with
the reality of Jesus' mission.[137] It was too early to publicly proclaim
that Jesus was the Messiah. Jesus still had much to teach his
disciples about his true Messianic mission. Contrary to popular
militaristic and triumphalist expectations, his Messianic mission
was to include suffering, rejection by the religious leaders, and
death. His person and his mission, however, would be vindicated
three days after his death by his glorious resurrection. Therefore,
he is the Messiah, but just as he gets to define the nature of the
person who is the Messiah, so he gets to define the nature of the
mission of the Messiah.

Missiologically, there is a critical need to be clear about the full humanity and full deity of Jesus Christ. It is also critical, and arguably even more important in our pluralistic society, to be clear about what he came to do. Historically, as has been seen, Jesus' person has been redefined, reduced, or manipulated. Even when his deity is acknowledged, it too often is diminished or not accepted as unique. The inevitable consequence is that his mission is also redefined or reduced to that of teacher of an ethical system, example of a good life, inspiration for sacrifice, model of enlightenment, practitioner of God's love, or achiever of God-consciousness. Certainly, he is and did many of these, but his mission cannot be reduced to any one of them. His mission certainly cannot be explained without full consideration of his suffering on the cross, his death, and his resurrection. His mission cannot be considered without finally concluding that, like his person, that mission was unique – it was radically different than that of any other religious leader or philosopher, and is thus the overarching or meta-narrative that answers the religious pluralism of American society.

Jesus the Messiah

Although the actual title "Messiah" is "nowhere used of the coming deliverer" in the Old Testament, much is said about the coming Messianic age (Is. 26-29; 40ff; Ezek. 40-48; Dan. 12; Joel 2:28-3:21). In fact, Messiah (meaning "anointed one") is often used of patriarchs, kings, priests, and prophets. It was used initially to refer to a special office, but later of the one who would be "God's chosen instrument in the deliverance of his people." Therefore, the Old Testament prepared the way for the coming Messiah, with many of its passages used by the New Testament writers (and Jesus himself) as evidence of his Messianic person and mission.[138]

Similarly, Jesus did not claim or acknowledge the title of Messiah or Christ for himself that often. As noted, part of his concern was confusion among the Jewish people about the nature and mission of the Messiah. The three main passages where the title is used are Peter's confession that he was the Christ, which we have examined at the beginning of each chapter, Jesus' interaction with the Samaritan woman, and Caiaphas's question of Jesus at his trial before the Sanhedrin. When the Samaritan woman at the well states she knows that Messiah is coming, Jesus explains that "I am He" (John 4:25-26). Because he is in despised Samaria, isolated from the religious leaders and demanding multitudes, Jesus can publicly assert who he is without fear of premature arrest or inappropriate attempts at coronation.

At his trial, Caiaphas asks Jesus, "Are you the Messiah?" (Mark 14:61; "Tell us if You are the Messiah" in Matt. 26:63). "I am" or "You have said it," Jesus answers (Mark 14:62; Matt. 26:64). Why would Jesus now openly accept such a title when he avoided it, at least publicly, for three years? Because the imminent crucifixion and resurrection – the suffering many things, being killed, and being raised that he earlier taught his disciples – now "rendered impossible a purely political interpretation of the messianic mission."[139] The passion and resurrection fully defined and explained who the Messiah was and what he came to do.

Inauguration of the Kingdom

"Jesus was going all over Galilee, teaching in their synagogues, preaching the good news of the kingdom, and healing every disease and sickness among the people" (Matt. 4:23). Without a doubt, a great part of Jesus' teaching was on the Kingdom of God. Moreover, it is clear that he viewed "his work to involve in some way the inauguration of the kingdom of God." ("The time is fulfilled, and the kingdom of God has come near. Repent and believe in the good news!" Mark 1:15). The idea of Kingdom is present in the Old Testament in several senses. God is the king of both Israel and of all men. This reign of God is both present and future. It is present in the experience of Israel; however, it is future in that they looked forward to both the earthly restoration of the Davidic line and to "the apocalyptic idea of some kind of heavenly kingdom."[140]

By the time of Jesus the prevailing understanding of the coming Kingdom was apocalyptic – the kingdom would "break into the present" only "to bring the present to the end." Thus, when Jesus came preaching that the "kingdom of God is among you" (Luke 17:20-21), he was drawing a sharp distinction between his teaching and that of Judaism.[141] That is, the Kingdom of God was present, but the present continued. The Kingdom in the present was real, but its consummated reality would be in the future. According to Jesus, what are some characteristics of this Kingdom?

The Kingdom is so valuable that it is to be sought above all other things (Matt. 13:44-46); in fact, it is to be sought first and then all else will be provided (Matt. 6:33). The coming of the Kingdom should also be prayed for (Matt. 6:10), for the Father wants to give us the Kingdom (Luke 12:32). The Kingdom grows slowly but surely, and its true membership will not be known until the end of time (Matt. 13:24-50). The Kingdom is one in which forgiveness prevails and un-forgiveness is judged (Matt. 18:21-35). Entrance into the Kingdom is by the narrow gate and is difficult (Matt. 7:13-14), especially for the rich (Matt. 19:23-24; Luke 18:24-30). Entrance requires that one's righteousness exceed that of the scribes and Pharisees (Matt. 5:20), which only happens to those who recognize their spiritual poverty and dependence on God (Matt. 5:3), and who rely solely on his grace (Matt. 20:1-16; 22:1-14) rather than on position, performance, place in society, or ethnic heritage. This means that only those who are born again can see the Kingdom (John 3:3,5).

The consummation of the Kingdom will be unexpected and everyone must be ready (Matt. 25:1-30). There will be many signs announcing the "days" that are coming, yet no one knows exactly when the Kingdom will come (Matt. 17:20-37). The Kingdom is also a mystery which only the few can really understand (Luke 8:9-10). Proclamation of the Kingdom included healing the sick and casting out demons (Luke 9:1-6). Finally, life in the Kingdom demands perfection as the heavenly Father is perfect (Matt.5:48) and the practice of an ethic with both personal and corporate applications (Matt. 5-7), demands that would be impossible if not for the work of Jesus the Messiah on the cross. The Kingdom, therefore, is first and foremost a "soteriological concept," beginning with the regeneration of the individual, but also replete with social, structural, and political implications for the here and now, some of which will be addressed in later chapters.[142]

The Cross of Christ

Jesus radically redefined the prevailing understanding of Messiah and of the Kingdom of God. Many were expecting a triumphant national kingdom headed by a military-political leader, who would free the nation of Israel from their Roman oppressors just as God had once delivered his people from Egypt. That is not what Jesus brought. Yes, it was God's Kingdom and it was one of power and salvation. The deliverance, however, was from "an oppressive power greater than Pharaoh." It was a "redemption from far more powerful foes than Rome, including the evil of the human heart," which is why Jesus called for repentance and a "corresponding transformation of being."[143] Yes, this ruling and kingly Messiah inaugurated the Kingdom, for it was manifested and revealed in his person and work. It was not, however, a kingdom "of this world" (John 18:36) as he had stated over and over again through his teachings and his parables. It includes this world and the present life, but it will be perfectly and fully consummated when the Son of Man comes with "power and great glory" (Matt. 24:30). Yes, this ruling and kingly Messiah calls for the kind of acceptance, commitment, and obedience that a king deserves. Unlike all other kings, however, this King suffers judgment on behalf of the world. Unlike all other kings, Jesus did not come to be served, but to serve (Matt. 20:28). He came not to Lord it over mankind, but to seek and to save the lost (Matt. 18:10-14), to call sinners to repentance (Luke 5:32), and to give rest to the weary (Matt. 11:28-29).

Thus, Jesus' mission was to go to the cross. Three times he predicted his suffering, death, and resurrection (Matt. 16:21; 17:22-23; 20:18-19). He spoke of giving his life as a "ransom for many" (Matt.20:28), and the night of his arrest he explained how the Lord's Supper portrayed his "body, which is given for you," and his blood, which "is shed for you" (Luke 22:19-20). What does it mean that this God-man Jesus Christ, the unique incarnation of the Second Person of the Trinity, the only Son of God, suffered, died on the cross, and then rose again? The best way to understand such a sacrifice is to let those speak who knew him, witnessed the passion event, or encountered him as risen Lord.

Peter

As much as anyone, Peter was an eye witness to all that Jesus said and did and to all that happened during his passion. The Day of Pentecost arrives, the disciples are filled with the Holy Spirit, and Peter gets the opportunity of a lifetime to publicly proclaim what he has seen, heard, and come to understand about Jesus. He opens his sermon in Acts 2:14-40 by explaining that the phenomenon being witnessed is simply the fulfillment of prophecy found in Joel. He then calls on the crowd to listen to what he has to say about "this Jesus the Nazarene": Jesus was "pointed out to you by God with miracles, wonders, and signs," which were themselves God's work. Jesus was delivered up "according to God's determined plan and foreknowledge," nailed to the cross, and killed. God then "resurrected this Jesus" and exalted him "to the right hand of God," while Jesus has both received and poured out the promised Holy Spirit. Finally, this crucified Jesus has been declared and announced by God to be "both Lord and Messiah." The crowd heard these clear words explaining Jesus and immediately came under conviction. "What must we do?" they asked Peter. He responds: "Repent, and be baptized, each of you, in the name of Jesus the Messiah for the forgiveness of your sins, and you will receive the gift of the Holy Spirit." Thousands did exactly that and were "saved from this corrupt generation."

Sometime later Peter addressed another crowd of people at Solomon's Colonnade. He repeats his appeal that the people "repent and turn back, that your sins may be wiped out," an appeal based on the fact that "His Servant Jesus" was the Messiah who suffered, was killed, and raised from the dead (Acts 3:11-26).

Time and again, in sermons, speeches, or letters, Peter explained the meaning and benefits of Jesus' crucifixion and resurrection: There "is salvation in no one else, for there is no other name under heaven given to people by which we must be saved" (Acts 4:12); there is "forgiveness of sins" in this "ruler and Savior" who was murdered (Acts 5:30-32); the Gentiles and the Jews are both "saved through the grace of the Lord Jesus" (Acts 15:11). The resurrection of Jesus Christ means that God has given "us a new birth into a living hope" and "into an inheritance that is imperishable, uncorrupted, and unfading." This has happened through "the genuineness" of faith expressed by believing in Him, resulting in the "salvation of your souls" (1 Pet. 1:3-9). Moreover, nothing could be more clear about Jesus' mission and the purpose of the cross than when Peter writes that Christ, who "did not commit sin" also "suffered for you," was reviled, and "He Himself bore our sins in His body on the tree, so that, having died to sins, we might live for righteousness" (1 Pet. 2:21-24). Again, "Christ also suffered for sins once for all, the righteous for the unrighteous, that He might bring you to God" (1 Pet. 3:18). The result of such a sacrifice is that we have "everything required for life and godliness" (2 Pet. 1:3).

John

Like Peter, John saw, heard, and witnessed all that Jesus said and did, and was present at the crucifixion. He was the one to whom Jesus entrusted the care of his mother (John 19:26-27). Certainly, there are few eye witnesses to the ministry and passion of Jesus more capable of interpreting the cross of Christ. In his Gospel, John regularly adds commentary to what Jesus said and did. Those who "receive Him" and "believe in His name" are given "the right to be children of God," for it is through him that "grace and truth came" (1:12,17). In 2:21 he explains that Jesus was talking about his own bodily resurrection and not about the actual temple. Again, in 3:36 John comments that believing in the Son means eternal life, but "the one who refuses to believe in the Son will not see life; instead, the wrath of God remains on him." This wrath of God against sin, John writes, was turned away at the cross through the death of Jesus (1 John 2:2), which was, without a doubt, fulfillment of Old Testament prophecy (John 19:35-37). John himself saw the empty tomb (20:3-10) and the resurrected Lord (20:19ff). All the signs – and we must certainly include teachings, miracles, suffering, death, and resurrection – were recorded, he says, so that the reader may believe in Jesus and have "life in His name" (20:31).

In his first epistle, John states that "the blood of Jesus His Son cleanses us from all sin" (1:7), and twice declares that because

God loved us he "sent His Son to be the propitiation for our sins" (2:2; 4:10), turning away the wrath of God that we deserved. The Father, therefore, sent "the Son as Savior of the world," and "whoever confesses that Jesus is the Son of God – God remains in him and he in God" (4:14-15). Eternal life – being "born of God" – is in the confessing, believing in, and having the Son (5:1,11-12). Finally, believing in Jesus as the Son of God not only guarantees eternal life, but gives one victory over the world (5:5).

In Revelation, John includes in his salutation to the seven churches praise to "Him who loves us and has set us free from our sins by His blood" (1:5b). During the amazing vision of the throne room of heaven, John sees the "slaughtered lamb" (5:6), who "redeemed [people] for God by Your blood" (5:9c) from all nations and peoples, making them a "kingdom and priests to our God, and they will reign on the earth" (5:10). Over and over again, John describes this crucified, slaughtered Lamb as the victor, as King of kings, as Lord of lords, as the one who holds the past, the present, and the future in his hands, and as the one who will return "quickly" (22:20).

Paul

Apparently, Paul's first encounter with Jesus was on the road to Damascus as resurrected Lord, an event that radically changed his life. Fourteen years in Arabia, Syria, and Cilicia gave Paul the time to pray, reflect, and listen to God. He had the opportunity to meet Peter, James the brother of Jesus, and other Christians (Gal. 1:17-2:1). Although he was not dependent on these for his understanding of the gospel (Gal. 1:12, 16), surely he both learned something from them and was endorsed by them. Although liberal theologians may claim that the gospel according to Paul is not that of Jesus, i.e. that Paul misinterpreted and misapplied Jesus' teachings, the claim does not hold up.

Paul notes in Gal. 2:7 that these early pillars of the church "acknowledged the grace that had been given to me" and agreed "that we should go to the Gentiles and they to the circumcised" (Gal. 2:9). Surely these leaders would not have sent Paul off with an incorrect version of the Gospel. Even when Paul later confronted Peter over a doctrinal issue (Gal. 2:11-21), it was Peter who was wrong! After his missionary journeys, Paul would report to his home church in Antioch (Acts 14:27), was affirmed by them, and later was affirmed in his teaching by the Jerusalem Council (Acts 15:1-35). Luke never questions Paul in his recording of the Acts. Peter calls attention to Paul's writings, placing them on the same level as "the rest of the Scriptures" (2 Pet. 3:16). At a time before the canon of the New Testament had been established, the oral teachings of the Apostles were predominant. In fact, letters that circulated were judged according to authoritative oral tradition; i.e. what the Apostles taught.[144] There is no Biblical instance of any of the original Apostles or early Christian leaders opposing or questioning Paul's preaching, teaching, writing, or methodology. When he was opposed, it was from Judaizers, false teachers, or those who sought personal gain from the gospel.

Furthermore, to denigrate Paul's theology, as some do, because he does not speak of the virgin birth, discuss much about Jesus' earthly ministry, or say as much as Jesus did about the kingdom is to miss the point. Paul wrote all he did *assuming* the reality of these; he did not believe he needed to add to what the apostolic teaching already stated. From his perspective – of the reality of the crucified and risen Messiah, of being "in Christ," of the presence and power of the Holy Spirit – his task was to preach Christ Jesus and the glory and the benefits of the cross. That this risen Christ was the same as the historical Jesus was not in debate; the perspective had simply changed.[145]

Because Paul's great passion in preaching was "Jesus Christ and Him crucified" (1 Cor. 2:2), the vast Christological content of his sermons in Acts and his thirteen letters can only be summarized. In Antioch of Pisidia Paul preached that Jesus has been raised from the dead that "through this man forgiveness of sins is being proclaimed" and that those who believe in Him are "justified from everything" (Acts 13:37-39). He later told the Philippian jailer that all he had to do to be saved was to "believe on the Lord Jesus" (Acts 16:31). While under house arrest he taught the visiting Jews about the kingdom of God, attempting to persuade them that Jesus was the fulfillment of "both the Law of Moses and the Prophets" (Acts 28:23).

In his epistles, Paul first sets out the human condition, which is that "all have sinned" (Rom. 3:23), are "enemies" of God (Rom. 5:10), condemned (Rom. 5:18), and, therefore, "slaves to sin" (Rom. 6:20), and "dead" in "trespasses and sins" (Eph. 2:1; Col. 2:13). God, however, "predestined us to be adopted through Jesus Christ" (Eph. 1:5) and sent His own Son to die on the cross as a "sin offering" (Rom. 8:3; 1 Tim. 1:15). Jesus Christ, who "did not know sin" was made "to be sin for us" (2 Cor. 5:21), thus "died for the ungodly" (Rom. 5:6-8; 15:3), became "a curse for us" (Gal. 3:13), reconciled us to God (Rom. 5:10-11; 2 Cor. 5:18-19; Col. 1:22), made us righteous (Rom. 5:1,9,19; Phil. 3:9), justified us (Rom. 4:25; 5:16,18), and redeemed us "through His blood" providing "forgiveness for our trespasses" (Eph. 1:7; Col. 2:13). The cross means that we have new life in Christ (Rom. 6:4-11; 2 Cor. 4:11), that we are new creations (2 Cor. 5:17), that we have the presence and power of the Holy Spirit (Rom. 8:9; 1 Cor. 12:11-13; 2 Tim. 1:14), and that we have been sealed for the day of redemption, having been promised eternal life (Rom. 6:23; 2 Cor. 5:1-4; Eph. 1:14). This salvation is through God's grace, mercy, and love alone, is appropriated by faith alone, and is in Christ alone (1 Cor. 1:4; Eph. 2:4-9).

Paul's is, without a doubt, a cruciform or a cross-formed theology. Whereas the purpose of the Gospel writers was to tell the story of Jesus in the flesh up to his sacrifice and resurrection, Paul's purpose is to tell the story of Christ Jesus from the resurrection. Whereas the Gospel writers recorded Jesus' hints and veiled explanations about his death and resurrection, Paul fully explains what that sacrifice and resurrection means for those who are in Christ Jesus, have the Spirit of Christ, and look forward to the promise of eternal life. Paul thus assumes and builds on the teachings of Jesus. His Christology assumes the historical Jesus and all of his sayings and actions. Paul's ethic for the individual and for the church living in a world between Jesus' advents, assumes and builds on Jesus' Kingdom ethic. Paul has come to identify "the Messiah with Jesus, crucified and risen," and thus his previous "understanding of the Messiah has been revolutionized."[146] He is able to consider the person of the historical Jesus and draw a straight line to the resurrected and exalted Christ, whom he has personally encountered and whom he now preaches.

Hebrews

According to the author of Hebrews, the Son made "purification for sins" (1:3) and turned aside God's wrath as a "propitiation for sins of the people" (2:17) when he suffered and became the "source of eternal salvation" (5:8). The primary image Hebrews uses for Christ is that of perfect high priest (4:14-15) and perfect sacrifice for sins. The Messiah did not take on this honor himself, but was given this role of high priest by God (5:5,10). As an intercessor, this high priest, "is always able to save," for he was "holy, undefiled, separated from sinners, and exalted above the heavens." Unlike other priests, however, he does not have to continue to offer sacrifices, for "He did this once for all when He offered Himself" (7:25-27) as "one sacrifice for sins forever" (10:12). He now is exalted and sits "at the right of the throne of the Majesty in the heavens," waiting for the "until His enemies are made His footstool" (8:1; 10:12-13).

This mission of suffering and dying and taking on the sins of the world is unique in world religions and of religious figures. In fact, it is the cross of Christ that informs us best about the character, nature, and will of God. According to Alister McGrath, the "basis of responsible Christian discussion of God is given to us – not chosen by us! – in the crucified Christ." Moreover, he says, we are actually "*authorised* to base our discussion of God upon the crucified Christ." To discuss God based on anything other than the cross is "idolatry."[147] The cross appears to our human minds as irrational, foolish, and absolutely the wrong way for God to achieve his purposes and declare his glory (I Cor. 1:18-25), but it was exactly what God intended in order to fully display his love and his wrath, his glory and his servant heart, and his victory through apparent defeat.

His Exclusivity and His Worth

This brief overview of the mission of Christ has focused on three key aspects. First, we have seen that Jesus was the promised Jewish Messiah, come to free Israel from her sins. Those he came to first, however, "did not receive him" (John 1:11; Luke 17:25), because he radically redefined the popular understanding of Messiah. Although his own people rejected him, he was also the Messiah for the entire world, so that "many will come from the east and west, and recline at the table with Abraham, Isaac, and Jacob in the kingdom of heaven" (Matt. 8:11), for "to all who did receive Him, He gave the them the right to be children of God, to those who believe in His name" (John 1:12). He is, therefore, not only the Messianic Redeemer of Israel, but of the whole world.

Second, this Messiah – Jesus Christ – also came to inaugurate the Kingdom of God in his person and ministry. All aspects of the Kingdom, both the present "already" realities and the future "not yet" realities, "find their content in the identity and mission of Jesus as Messiah." He is the "Kingdom of God in person."[148] Without a doubt, he also redefined the common expectations of Kingdom. Rather than one of worldly power and ambitions, his Kingdom is one of cross bearing, service, and being last according to the world's standards (Luke 9:23; John 13:14-15; Mark 9:35). The Kingdom, however, is not just "otherwordly," but is now, too, with an ethic not just for the individual but also with social implications for the life of the church.

A fully developed Kingdom theology is beyond the scope of this work; however, two important missiological points need to be made: One, the Kingdom of Christ is at its core soteriological, and thus has as its "priority of the redemption of sinners." The Messiah came as a suffering servant, the Lamb who was slain for the sins of the world. This is the beginning point – the entry point – to the Kingdom. Two, the Kingdom cannot and should not be limited to the salvation of individual souls. The implication and result of the "salvation of the whole person" is "that it achieves social reconciliation, justice and community in the 'already' aspect of the Kingdom" as the first-fruits in God's movement toward the reconciliation of the entire creation in Jesus Christ. Thus, the Kingdom is evangelism, disciple-making, social ministry (meeting human needs), and social action (having a prophetic voice and actively challenging unjust social, economic, and political structures). The challenge for the church, of course, is how this is understood and practiced while allowing the Scriptures to judge even our own cultures and ideologies.[149]

Third, this Jesus Messiah went to the cross. In doing so, he took upon himself the sins of the world, paid the debt and suffered the punishment for these, and thus providing the gracious means of entrance into the Kingdom for all who look to him, repent, believe, and receive him by faith (John 3:14-16). These actions defined who the Messiah was and for what purpose he was sent by God. Furthermore, his suffering, death, burial, resurrection, and ascension began the "last days," which we are in until he returns again. In fact, the entire creation "eagerly waits" and "has been groaning" (Rom. 8:19-22) for full redemption. While we wait, living in the already inaugurated but not yet consummated kingdom, the missiological question is whether this Biblical Jesus is the true Jesus Christ. More relevant for our missiological purpose, is this fully human, fully divine, incarnate Son of God, who went to the cross for the forgiveness of sins the story that answers all stories? Is he the exclusive and only worthy meta-narrative that corrects all other Christologies? That answers all worldviews? That answers all other religions? That answers individual sin and corporate sin? Is his mission, his Kingdom, and his work on the cross the answer for America?

Once again going on the assumption that the Bible is our only source of authority, the answer has to be "yes." As was pointed out above in the section on Jesus' deity, over and over he claimed a unique relationship with the Father. More pointedly, he states that his is a unique mission. He claimed that he is "the way, the truth, and the life," and that no person "comes to the Father except through Me" (John 14:6). He is not one of the ways, a portion of the truth, or one who shows how to have life, he is *in his person and his work* the way, the truth, and the life. To see him, Jesus claims, is to see the Father. To believe in Him is to believe the One who sent him. If others claim that Jesus was one of the incarnations of God, or one of many good men who was adopted by God or who achieved enlightenment or God-consciousness, Jesus certainly does not speak of himself in that manner. The entire corpus of his sayings indicates that *he* believed he was in a unique relationship with the Father, that he had a unique mission, and that he was the only one who could do what was needed for the salvation of all people. Once again, we are faced with the choice of a Jesus Christ either speaking the truth, lying and manipulating, or being totally self-deceived.

Consequently, Jesus is far more than a good example, an ethical teacher, one source of enlightenment, and a special prophet. He is unique and exclusive, meaning that no other religious teacher or spiritual savant can claim the same relationship with God, can claim to be fully God and fully human, nor claim to be the payment for sin and the means of salvation. In fact, no other religion comes close to making such bold claims.

What of other religions and other spiritual "truths"? Are they to be rejected as worthless? Two answers: One, any person who believes and practices another religion, however that may defined, should be taken seriously, treated with respect, and listened to. There is no reason to offend him before he has heard the gospel of Jesus Christ. If he is offended and refuses to listen, may it be the message of the cross that offends him and turns him away. Two, there may indeed be "truths" in other religions, but these are simply broken responses from fallen humanity to God's general revelation in the world (Acts 17:16-33; Rom. 1:18-23). These religions may have pieces of truth and teach and practice truths; however, they are inadequate and ultimately "worthless," because they lack the Truth of Jesus Christ. He is the only one who is able to bring fallen humans, fallen humanity, and a fallen creation back into relationship with the Father.

Jesus, therefore, is the only one who is clearly and finally worthy. He was the only one worthy to be slaughtered as the lamb for our salvation (Rev. 5:9). He is the only one worthy of setting the agenda for life (*contra* the consumer, the ideological, and other "manipulative" Christologies). He is the only one worthy of worship, adoration, obedience, and Lordship. He is the one who stands over and above all other distorted Christologies and all other religions and spiritual systems. As dogmatic and intolerant to contemporary ears as this may sound, the Biblical evidence demands that the exclusivity and worth of Jesus alone be the driver, the content, and the goal of an American missiology.

Avoiding Rebuke: Missiological Implications, Opportunities, and Challenges

> He was openly talking about this. So Peter took Him aside and began to rebuke Him. But turning around and looking at His disciples, He rebuked Peter and said, "Get behind Me, Satan, because you're not thinking about God's concerns, but man's!"
>
> Mark 8:32-33

After Peter made his confession that Jesus is the Messiah, Jesus began explaining to his disciples what that meant. Contrary to the prevailing expectations, he had not come as a political and military conqueror. He was, rather, going to suffer and be killed. This radical redefinition of Messiah was something he was "openly talking about." Apparently, it was more than Peter could take. Yes, he was willing to confess that Jesus was the Messiah, but this was not what he expected! Surely, Jesus must be confused about his role, his purpose, or at least his timing. Whatever the case, Jesus does not need to be talking like this.

Bold, impulsive Peter takes it upon himself to privately rebuke the One he has just admitted to being the Messiah. Scripture does not tell us exactly what Peter said, but it was enough for Jesus to jump right back at Peter and rebuke him in front of the disciples. More than likely, although Peter was speaking to Jesus "aside," he was speaking on behalf of the others, and Jesus knew it. The rebuke is so strong that Jesus calls Peter "Satan" and accuses him of putting a human agenda before God's.

As we consider the missiological implications, opportunities, and challenges of a Biblical Christology, there are three things to avoid: One, we never want to put ourselves in the position of rebuking Jesus. We may not understand what he said and we may not even like what he said, but if he said it, we should not argue about it. Two, we should seek to listen, believe, and obey so that he would not have to rebuke us. This is perhaps a far more likely scenario than the first, for we fail regularly at fully believing and obeying. Still, Jesus gets to define what he said and set the agenda for both his purpose and for our lives. Three, when he does have to rebuke us, it is because we are usually setting a human agenda ahead of his. It may be our agenda or someone else's, but we are either trying to define him or his mission according to our fallen understanding and our sinful intentions. We are thinking of human concerns and not God's.

How then to draw some missiological implications and make applications of a Biblical Christology to the American mission field? The list can certainly be quite long, but let me suggest the following:

1. It is the first century all over again. Many cultural observers have noted that the twenty-first century is more like the first century than any other in terms of spiritual interest, spiritual pluralism, and cultural change. The first century was one of great advances. The *Pax Romana*, as odious as it may appear to our modern democratic minds, had forced an

end to tribal and territorial wars, had established a relative peace and prosperity throughout the known world, and had put into place a common administrative system. This "peace," along with the building of a road system, allowed for greater commerce, travel, and exchange between nations and peoples. Great cosmopolitan cities grew, ideas flourished and exchanged, and religions of all kinds moved beyond their territories of origin. The end result was a world in transition, of people movements, and of spiritual interest and awakening. Pagan religions, mystery religions, syncretistic practices, and a pluralism not seen in previous days prevailed. Perhaps the most distinguishing characteristic of the first century world, which was both its greatest challenge and greatest opportunity, was that the majority of the world was lost. The harvest was "abundant," as Jesus said in Luke 10:2; the fields were "ready for harvest" (John 4:35).

This was the world in which the first Christians found themselves. They were alternately persecuted, received, scattered, listened to, praised, and ridiculed. Whatever the case, people came to faith in Christ, churches were planted, and the church as a whole grew. In a predominantly pagan and hostile society, with intermittent (and later consistent) persecution, this small minority "turned the world upside down" (Acts 17:6).

The twenty-first century is similar in many ways, one being that the "harvest is great once again," especially in America. The growing secularization of society,[150] disappointment in modernity and the move to post-modernity (however that may be defined), the great movements of people, the new "road system" called the internet, growing acceptance of world religions, new syncretisms, and the almost assumed values of tolerance and pluralism make twenty-first America much like the first century world. True philosophical atheists are relatively few, even considering the rise of the "new atheism."[151] Practical atheists, however, are growing. They certainly have an underlying philosophy to their actions and lifestyle, but they are driven more by apathy and human selfishness rather than serious philosophical reflection. They simply don't care.[152]

Some argue that spiritual hunger, searching, and experimentation are more prevalent than ever. This provides both a great opportunity and a great challenge for the evangelical church: On the one hand, many people may be spiritually interested and hungry; on the other hand, they too easily follow the latest amateur celebrity guru, or simply practice cafeteria religion, picking and choosing what they want to create their "religion for one." On the one hand more people may want to know about Jesus and what the Bible says; on the other hand, they do not automatically accept the authority of the Bible (much less that of the church), and add Jesus to other well-known gurus. On the one hand, the church has the answer: Jesus Christ, the only, eternal, crucified, and living Son of God; on the other hand, we are not always very good at communicated that reality in the American culture. We bemoan the changes and the deterioration of the culture at large, but are too blind to our own cultural captivity. The only conclusion is the argument made in the Introduction: America is a mission field. Further discussion of these cultural conditions and some suggested solutions will be offered in subsequent chapters.

2. Our message must be about Jesus Christ. The great temptation of the last two thousand years is to make Jesus into our image by fitting him, his teachings, and his work

into cultural, ideological, personal, or religious categories that do not fully reflect Scripture. This is a temptation for *all* of us, which we sometimes succumb to intentionally in order to support a presupposition, but which more often we are unaware of as we assume Jesus fits into a personal or cultural mold or pattern. The missiological challenge for the evangelical church in America is to strive to faithfully present the Jesus of the Bible. This is not always an easy task, but it is a necessary endeavor. One flip of the television channel or one visit to the popular Christian book store reveals that careless Christology creates confusion within the church and scorn in the world. With the multiplicity of deficient Christologies clamoring for attention, we must continually return to the Scriptures for the historical facts, for explanation, for correction, and for instruction. We must regularly appeal to and learn from orthodox Christological statements for affirmation and clarification. Finally, we must intentionally converse within the evangelical community for greater contemporary understanding, correction, and application.

3. Our message must be about the totality of Jesus Christ. Avoiding the temptation of presenting our own personal Jesus also means we must strive to present all of Jesus Christ. A holistic, balanced Christology requires presenting him as the incarnate and only begotten Son of God, fully divine and fully human, and yet sinless. It also means we must present all of what he said and did, *and* what the inspired writers of the New Testament confirmed and explained about him and his work. Certainly, there are hard sayings of Jesus; yes, there are challenging passages by Paul. We can and should move forward confidently with a missiology driven by a Christology based on the entire New Testament and not on some personal "canon

within the canon," whether liberal or conservative. Either way, we are shortchanging Jesus.

4. Our message must begin and end with Jesus Christ. By that I mean two things: One, Jesus Christ is the overarching, all-encompassing metanarrative. His "story" answers and covers all other stories. Therefore, our message cannot be compartmentalized to say that Jesus answers only spiritual needs, or only the needs of the individual, or only the Western person's quest, and that there are other answers for other peoples or other aspects of life. Rather, all people and all of life are addressed by all of Jesus. Two, although there are specific personal, family, and social issues the church must address and respond to, these cannot be dealt with apart from the person and work of Jesus. Yes, poverty must be addressed, but the ultimate answer is Jesus Christ. Yes, the breakdown of the family must be addressed, but the ultimate answer is Jesus Christ. And so on. This is not to denigrate or minimize any particular passion, issue, or ministry, but to say that any passion, issue, or ministry devoid of a balanced and holistic Christology may be a good work, but ultimately spiritually unsatisfactory and eternally lacking.

5. Our message must be all about Jesus Christ, and him crucified. Taking point number four even further, the scandal of the cross cannot be avoided. In fact, not only should we not avoid the scandal of the cross, we should rejoice in it. It was a stumbling block to the Jews and foolishness to the Greeks (1 Cor. 1:23), and it still is so for many today. To some world religions the cross still is foolishness. To others the cross is merely the unfortunate death of a good man. To us who believe, however, it is wisdom, power, salvation, love, and joy. Therefore,

whatever our particular message may be to individuals and to American society, whatever particular aspect of life and culture we are addressing, whatever portion of Scripture we may be preaching and teaching, our message must at some point lead to the cross of Christ. Whether the cross is explicit or implicit in our message, whether it is our beginning point or our conclusion, or even when it may not be specifically mentioned, it must be the foundation, the core, and the driver of our message.

6. Our message must be about Jesus Christ and his Kingdom inaugurated. The crucified and resurrected Messiah is central to God's Kingdom purposes. The work of Christ on the cross means that forgiven and justified sinners have been united to Christ, are members of the Kingdom, and are now, as saints, participating in God's redemption and restoration of the creation. Because salvation and membership in the Kingdom includes all aspects of redemption – "spiritual, physical, bodily, social, relational, and political" – the church acts as the present, universal, and most importantly and effectively (albeit imperfectly) localized sign and agent of the Kingdom.[153] As a community of the Spirit (and as local communities), the church lives, loves, and acts differently than the world, confronting not only personal sin, but also entrenched corporate and structural sin. This is because the loving and just God who dealt with the individual's sin on the cross is the same loving and just God who deals with all sin in the fallen creation. He is the same God who is restoring the entire creation, partially now in the "already," but ultimately, completely, and finally with the new heaven and the new earth. Missiologically, this means that, once again, the story of the resurrected and living Lord Jesus Christ is *the* story, the overarching story,

the metanarrative, that addresses personal sin, individual destiny, *and* the fallen-ness of the world. Whether poverty, war, economics, environmental stewardship, or any other societal ill, it matters in the Kingdom of Christ.

7. Our message must be about Jesus Christ and his attitude. Having the right theology, the correct Christology, the conviction and passion about America as a mission field, an understanding of missiological methodologies, and an unswerving confidence in the Bible and the message of the gospel of Jesus Christ is absolutely fundamental to the task. Yet, without the attitude of Jesus Christ, as expressed most profoundly in Phil. 2, we will have only sporadic and short-termed fruitfulness. Besides having a missiological theology and missiological methodologies, let me suggest that we ought also to practice certain missiological attitudes:

One, boldness tempered by humility. The American mission field needs to hear a consistent and constant word about the uniqueness of Jesus Christ and his saving work on the cross. We must be confident and bold in that assertion. At the same time, the message must be communicated with an attitude of humility. That is, we must have the attitude of Paul, who was "not ashamed" (2 Tim. 1:12) of the gospel of salvation for sinners, but who was also well aware that he was the "worst of them" (1 Tim. 1:15-16). Although the gospel of Jesus Christ is absolute and true regardless of our behavior and attitudes as believers, sinful behaviors and wrong attitudes are unnecessary obstacles to preaching, hearing, and responding to the message. Consider that Jesus saved his harshest words for the religious establishment and not for the lost. His rebukes were strongest toward his disciples, who should have known better. Yes, he confronted the world, but when people rejected him it was because of the truth and not because of an attitude.

Two, truth telling tempered by love. Similarly, the message must always be the truth about *the* Truth – Jesus Christ. Yet we should not use expressing the truth as an excuse to lambast someone we don't like, agree with, or approve of. There are times to confront, to speak boldly, to not back down. Is our driving motivation, however, to win an argument or to show the love of God for the sinner?

Three, passion tempered by acceptance. Our passion for the gospel, to see individual lives change, and to see the transformation of communities and society should not blind us to several realities we must accept: lost people are usually going to act like lost people, and Jesus promised the world will hate us. Why, then, are we surprised in America when that is the case? Not everyone will believe. Results will be mixed. There will be both wheat and tares. And, even when we agree as evangelicals on the central premises of the gospel and are unified on the primary purpose of the church, we will still not agree on the details and the applications. We will continue to have "family fights" until Jesus returns. Therefore, we need passion, but we must also accept that we are still imperfect people who belong to an imperfect church ministering in a fallen world.

For an American evangelical missiology to be effective, the first question to be answered is: "What are we going to do about Jesus?" That is, who do we say that He is? What are we saying about Him in our preaching, our teaching, our lifestyles, our churches, and our attitudes? On the one hand we must confront the false and deficient Christologies found in world religions. On the other hand, there are times when the evangelical world has to examine the Jesus it proclaims. Have we misrepresented Him?

Manipulated Him? Preached a deficient, incomplete, and wimpy Jesus? Have we allowed Him to be captive to our ideology, our culture, and our personal experiences? Who do we say that He is and what are we going to do about it?

PART 2

Introduction
Who Do We Think We Are?
Culture and Change

Once a Biblical Christology has been formulated, the task has just begun. If "Christ Jesus came into the world to save sinners" (1 Tim. 1:15), then the world needs to hear the message. Part 3 will deal in more detail with how the message can and should be communicated. This section is concerned with the world that needs to hear it. Three premises concerning culture in general and American culture in particular will be explored and their implications unpacked in the following chapters:

One, Christ came as a *real* person in a *real* culture. That is, the incarnation of the Son of God – the fully human and fully divine Jesus Christ – took place at a real time in history and among real people. He was not an ethereal alien barely connected to the world or to his culture. He was an authentic first century Jew who had genuine relationships with people and a genuine interaction with his culture. This is part of the "scandal of particularity," that God became flesh as *one* man, at *one* time, and in *one* place. Part of this particularity means that Jesus Christ was born, lived, walked, taught, and performed his miracles in real time and in a real place: first century Palestine. He came into a particular culture with a particular language and a particular religion. It was a world of real conflict and troubling transition in politics, commerce, and economics, all of which Jesus was keenly aware of. Certainly, he was more than merely human and was at the center of a divine plan, but his life and his plan took place within a particular culture.

Two, *all cultures change.* The culture in which Jesus came was undergoing change, and all cultures change, for change is inevitable. Sometimes it is good and sometimes it is bad, but it is certain. Whether God in his sovereignty directly causes or simply allows every particular change is not to be settled here. It can be confidently asserted, however, that God is never surprised by change, can use it all for his purposes and his glory, and that his plan for the world involves change. Our new birth in Christ changes us individually. Our witness and ministry in the world should change others, communities, and the world. The world, and all of history, is moving forward – changing – to the second coming of Christ and the end of history as we know it.

Three, communicating and living out the message of Christ requires a *theology of culture.* How we witness, what we say, how we minister in the world will be driven by our understanding, appreciation of, or rejection of culture. This implies that we all have a theology of culture, whether we know it or not – whether we have articulated it or not. For an American missiology, the Christological foundations are essential. They must be articulated and understood. Who Jesus is and what he has done must be clear, for that understanding – that Christology – will drive missiology. The target or recipient of that missiology, in this case the American culture, must also be understood as much as possible in order for Christology not to remain a purely academic endeavor. We know Jesus is the answer. We even know, from the Bible, what the questions are. Do we know, however, what those questions sound like, how they are phrased, and who is asking them in our particular context, the American culture?

The House We Live In:[154] Developing a Theology of Culture

In the beginning God created the heavens and the earth.... Then God said, "Let Us make man in Our image, according to Our likeness. They will rule the fish of the sea, the birds of the sky, the livestock, all the earth, and the creatures that crawl on the earth." So God created man in His own image; He created him in the image of God; He created them male and female. God blessed them, and God said to them, "Be fruitful, multiply, fill the earth, and subdue it. Rule the fish of the sea, the birds of the sky, and every creature that crawls on the earth."... God saw all that He had made, and it was very good.

Gen. 1: 1, 26-28, 31a

When the creation story is discussed, the emphases are usually the physical creation of the universe and the creation of Adam and Eve. Certainly the tasks given to the newly created humans are acknowledged, i.e. fruitfulness and multiplication, stewardship of the creation, and dominion over all living things. The creation is not discussed often enough, however, as the beginning of physical and human *culture*, albeit in its most basic forms and principles. Genesis shows us that God is the creator of the physical universe and the "originator of social culture." The first few chapters of the book show how God instituted marriage, gave mankind work, and instructed him to organize and govern, thus establishing cultural relationships among humans and with the creation. Granted, these relationships had not yet developed into a human culture with all its intricacies and complexities, yet what God had created "was very good."[155]

Then came sin and the fall. Just as the fall marred the image of God in mankind and condemned Adam and Eve and every one of their descendants, so culture was affected in both its physical and social aspects. The marriage relationship would be marked by conflict, as would all human relationships. Work would become difficult and tedious. Human stewardship of the physical creation would too often deteriorate into abuse. Human government would be marked by greed and conflict. Human culture was a victim of the sin of Adam and Eve.

We are, therefore, fallen human beings living in a fallen creation partaking in a fallen culture, all groaning for redemption. What God had created and declared "very good" – human beings *and* human culture – was now infected by sin and unable to redeem itself. This does not mean that God abandoned culture. He created it and still sustains it through his gracious providence, and although culture is marred by sin, with a mixture of good and evil elements, God desires that human culture should, the same as individual humans, reflect his image and nature. Of course, this is possible only through the transforming grace of Jesus Christ.

One of the problems in talking about culture is our various definitions and understandings of the term. Too often, without any prior definition, arguments are started over the goodness or evil of culture resulting in pronouncements that this one or that other is for, against, anti-, counter-, or sold out to culture. With tempers flaring and accusations flying, no one realizes that the discussion has been about different issues.

To begin with, most common understandings of culture are too narrow and limiting. Some people think of culture only as "pop" culture. Such is often rightly criticized because so much of it is vulgar, shallow, and un-, if not outright anti-Christian. However, all of pop culture in and of itself is not necessarily objectionable. It depends on the content and the purpose of that content. Although some content may not necessarily be Christian, it still may not be objectionable and have redeeming value. Even pop culture can be a vehicle of beauty, joy, and thought provoking themes. Therefore, pop culture can give us movies such as *Life is Beautiful*, *Bella*, *Seabiscuit*, *The Help* and even *Schindler's List*, *Saving Private Ryan*, and *The Matrix*, each with more redeeming value than any number of slasher movies full of gore. The content of U-2's rock music is vastly different than that of Marilyn Manson's. Country music may tell us about traditional values of home, family, and work, or glorify cheating, lying, and killing. There are numerous reasons *To Kill a Mockingbird* is read in high schools but *Tropic of Cancer* is usually banned. Besides, most people like their pop culture (usually what they grew up with) but cringe at another's (usually the "younger" generation's). Furthermore, popular culture is often understood to be only whatever is trendy, in style or fashionable at the moment.

Others go to the opposite extreme and think of culture as only "high-brow" art, literature, and classical music. The knee-jerk reaction is to think of this type of culture as inherently more acceptable and desirable; however, elitism is a danger and there is plenty in high-brow culture that is vulgar, shallow, and anti-Christian. In and of itself, this type of "culture" is neither acceptable nor objectionable. Again, it depends on the content and its purpose.[156]

A difficulty in many Christian circles is confusing culture with the Biblical concept of the "world." If they are to be equated, then culture must be rejected, because Christians are told to "not love the world or the things that belong to the world" (1 John 2:15). However, the term "world" in this particular context (and elsewhere, e.g. John 15:18; 16:11; 17:25) refers to an "evil system totally under the grip of the devil." It does not here refer to the physical world we live in, or the world that God loves and for which he sent his Son to die (John 3:16). It is rather the world of mankind – individuals, structures, systems, worldviews – "hostile to Christ and all that He stands for," ruled by "world powers" of darkness (Eph. 6:12).[157] The distinction between the "world" that is hostile to Christ and culture, however, is certainly not always clear and distinct, for much of culture is also hostile to Christ. Perhaps the simplest way to express it would be:

1. God created all that is. His human creation included spiritual, emotional, and intellectual aspects, all of which were "very good." This implies that human beings had the ability to worship and interact with God, interact with fellow human beings on many levels, and interact with the physical world. Furthermore, humankind could be creative, could learn, could organize, could govern, could build, and could develop institutions to carry out these tasks. In essence, humankind could develop culture and cultures. Therefore, God was the initiator or creator of human culture in its most basic form, endowing humans with the abilities to further create and develop their respective cultures.[158]

2. The fall "created" the "world." That is, humankind's fall into sin resulted in the marring of the image of God in humans, the scarring of the entire creation, including cultures, and opened the door for Satan's ongoing activities in the world. The result of Adam and Eve's choice to sin was not only death for human beings but

also the fracturing "of the harmony of the universe," an "allegiance alien to God's design," and a break between God and His creation.[159] The result was "total depravity" in human beings and, by implication, "total depravity" in creation. The "world" as a force of opposition to God was formed. Although no human being is as bad as he could possibly be and there are elements (thoughts, attitudes, and actions) that are good in every person, every aspect of the person is tainted by sin. Every human is by nature and choice a sinner and is thus in need of redemption, something he cannot do in and for himself. Similarly, the creation is fallen, but not as bad as it could possibly be. There are good elements (sunsets, flora and fauna) and bad elements (drought, disease, natural disasters), and the entire creation is in need of, and groans for, redemption.

3. The "world" vies with God for our allegiance in creation and culture. The entire creation – physical, animal, human – is fallen and in need or redemption. Yet, because God sustains his creation through his gracious and merciful providence, there are still elements of beauty and goodness midst elements of violence and destruction. Because the creation is fallen, human culture and all human cultures, are fallen. In them are elements both good and bad because the "influences of God, Satan, Christ, and humanity are intertwined in the same culture and even within the same heart." Again, it is what and who humans are – the house we live in. It is how we think, speak, communicate, govern, work, and play, and although culture as a whole is tainted by sin, not all elements of culture are in and of themselves evil. Our challenge is the "world," that mindset, worldview, Satan-infested belief system that permeates all of creation vying for our attention and our allegiance. Yes, Satan is the ruler of this age and his influence penetrates all aspects of

the creation; however, God is sovereign over all, his Holy Spirit is at work in the world, and disciples of Jesus are salt and light. Thus, like the wheat and tares, the good and bad fish, the creation, culture, and our lives in general are a mixed bag until the end comes.[160]

Most people realize, however, that culture involves much more than just pop culture or "cultured" activities. It is language, customs, attitudes, values and expectations, and a way of life. Their definition may not be sociologically or anthropologically sophisticated, but it does include elements of a world-view, of belief systems, and behavior. The challenge for us culture bound beings, however, is threefold:

The first is being able to evaluate one's own culture. Because we are born in and of a culture, because it is "the house we live in," we are blind to many aspects of our own culture, how it affects us, and especially to many of the negative elements in our culture. Therefore, total objectivity towards our own culture is impossible. Even if we agree that all cultures are to be judged by the Scriptures, we are reading, interpreting, and applying the Scripture from within our own culture. The practical result is that I am able to see the deficiencies in another culture better than those in my own culture. For example, as one who has worked and worshipped in both the Anglo and the Hispanic cultures, I am frequently part of the conversation related to timeliness and order. The Anglo culture often points out the lackadaisical attitude towards time in the Hispanic culture. The impression is that Hispanics are disorganized and disrespectful of order, previously set agendas, and the schedules of others. Perhaps there is something to those observations. Hispanics, however, note that the Anglo obsession with time, keeping to the schedule, and going by the book implies that the clock and the schedule are more important than people and relationships. And there is something to learn in that observation.

The second challenge is cultural comparison. Because I am a product of my culture, I will generally tend to see mine as better than any other. I am comfortable with it. Because I am blind to the failings of my own culture, I will tend to see it as the norm, the standard, or the benchmark by which all other cultures are to be judged. This can lead to an unwillingness to listen to, learn from, and appreciate other cultures. The end result could be arrogance, prejudice, paternalism, and eventually, conflict. This does not mean that all cultures are morally and ethically equivalent. Biblically and historically, such cultural relativism is unsustainable. Some cultures do approximate a Biblically based morality and ethic more than others. For example, few would argue that the Taliban culture is on the same moral ground as, say, the Swiss. Or that the Nazi worldview was relatively equal to the Samoan. There are absolute Biblical grounds on which to judge the failings of cultures, including my own. The point still stands, however, that although the American culture may not treat women as the Taliban does, we have plenty to repent of when held up to the standard of Scripture. The solution is not moral and cultural relativism, nor the complete rejection of another culture, nor the complete rejection of one's own culture. It is to look to the Bible and be willing to judge all cultures, starting with one's own, according to a Kingdom culture,[161] acknowledging the limits of one's own perspective.[162] According to Leslie Newbigin, the "only way in which the gospel can challenge our culturally conditioned interpretations of it" is by listening to those from other cultures who have other perspectives and are also reading the Bible. They too, of course, are shaped by their cultures, in which there is both good and bad. But when the global Body of Christ talks and listens and learns from each other, assumptions are challenged, biases are discovered, and "mutual correction" takes place, which is "sometimes unwelcome, but...necessary and...fruitful."[163]

A third challenge is one that is becoming more and more prevalent in a globalized world, and that is the mixing, melding, and transposing of cultures. On the one hand, some aspects of the American culture (primarily consumerism and popular entertainment) are sweeping the globe. On the other hand, it appears that the rising cultures of China and India may globally dominate the twenty-first century in many ways. At the same time, almost all developed and developing countries are experiencing migrations and immigrations of peoples, resulting in the rise of multiculturalism. This means that fewer and fewer cultures are as "pure" and distinct as they were even a quarter of a century ago. Some celebrate this multiculturalism, while others respond with growing prejudice, tribalism, and nationalism. The missiological challenge in America is that many of our strategies are culturally specific. In church planting, for instance, the general starting point in planning (and I am generalizing) is an eleven a.m. worship service, an attractional model of church, a time driven order of service, and expectations still driven by the church experience of the twentieth century southern white church – usually bigger is ultimately better. Only recently have cultural issues such as our 24/7 work culture, cultural differences in time and order, overlooked sub-cultural niches, and relational models of church come into play. Whereas many of our traditional culturally driven strategies may still be effective, they are less and less so as younger generations become more "third culture" than anything else (these issues will be dealt with in more detail in a later chapter).

So, how can culture be defined? In its broadest sense, "culture embraces all of life." It is a "design for living" by which a society adapts itself to its "social and ideational environment." More specifically, it involves worldview, ways of thinking, language and linguistic patterns, behavioral patterns, ways of communicating, social structures and institutions, and motivational/deciding sources.[164] Essentially, it is the social environments in which we are born, reared, and live. It is who we are as a people, as a nation, as a group, as a community. Obviously, a culture can be as broad as "Western civilization," the "American culture," or the "Judeo-Christian" culture, or as narrow as the "second generation Mexican-American" culture or the "south Louisiana Cajun" culture. Taking it even further, communities, regions, families, churches, and multiple affinity groups have their own cultures. The American missiological challenge is to avoid the extremes of defining culture so broadly that significant sub-cultural differences are overlooked, or to be so narrow and reductionist that culture is no more than individual differences and preferences.

If culture is what and who we are, both good and bad, what should be our attitude toward culture? More importantly, how to we begin to formulate and attitude and a way of evaluating culture? As usual, the best place to begin is the Bible. Although Scripture "offers no definition or even discussion of culture in the abstract,"[165] it provides numerous glimpses into God's hand in initiating culture, mankind's hand in developing culture, and sin's destructive influences on culture.

The Old Testament and Culture

The beginnings of human culture – the first relationships, works endeavors, and life tasks – are laid out in Genesis 1 and 2. Adam was placed in the Garden "to work it and watch over it" (2:15). God called upon Adam to see and name the animals (2:19). God created the institution of marriage when he made Eve and "brought her to the man" (2:21-24). Obviously, we can only speculate what human culture might have looked like had sin not intervened. When it did, all of human culture, including the marriage relationship and work was affected.

God did not, however, abandon mankind after the fall. Children were born to Adam and Eve; Abel became a shepherd and Cain became a farmer. Later descendants introduced or developed other human skills and abilities, such as city building, animal husbandry, music, and metallurgy (4:17-22), abilities that only continued to grow and expand through the generations.

Some basic aspects of human culture described throughout the Old Testament include:

Building and construction

The ark Noah was commanded to build was a masterpiece of both nautical engineering and zoological organization. The instructions God gave Moses for the construction of the Tabernacle and its accouterments involved master workmanship and artistic skills, including wood carving, metal work, sewing, jewelry, tapestry, and tailoring. Likewise, the construction of the temple by Solomon involved trade with foreign countries, massive organization of human labor, and the height of craftmanship in Israel. The rebuilding of the walls by Nehemiah and of the temple by Haggai and Zerubbabel required organization and delegation. In every case, the talents and the abilities required for the task are grounded in what God created and endowed in the first human beings, i.e. the ability to think, create, and work with purpose.

Art and Music

Without a doubt, much of the tabernacle and temple furnishings were works of art, whether in wood, metal, precious jewels, tapestry, or priestly clothing. Much of what modern archeologists have learned about Biblical cultures has been precisely through artistic remnants: architecture, pottery, carvings, murals, and such. In the case of the tabernacle, the men who did the work were "skilled" persons "in whose heart the LORD had placed wisdom" (Ex. 36:2), led by one who was "filled with God's Spirit, with wisdom, understanding, and ability in every kind of craft" (Ex. 35:31) They were men both endowed with natural God-given abilities and filled with the Spirit of God for this special task.

We know David was a musician, that he was called upon to play for Saul (1 Sam. 16:23) and later wrote many of the Psalms. More than that, he appointed men to be in "charge of the music in the Lord's temple" (1 Chron. 6:31). Throughout the Old Testament there are accounts of music, at "times of farewell (Gen. 31:27), at times of rejoicing and feasting (Ex. 32:17-18; Is. 5:12; 24:8-9), at military victories (2 Chron. 20:27-28), and for work (Num. 21:17)."[166]

Commerce and Economics

From the most basic nomadic commercial exchanges during the age of the patriarchs (Gen. 37:25) to the complexities of running Solomon's vast kingdom, commerce and economic systems have been a part of human culture. Jacob sent his sons to Egypt to purchase grain in order to simply survive. Solomon had multiple and complex exchanges with Hiram, king of Tyre, instituted a system of taxation and forced labor, and became world renown for his wealth and power. Although Solomon's macroeconomics were impressive, none of it would have been possible without the common trades, occupations, and government positions that were part and parcel of Biblical life. The Bible speaks of ambassadors (Is. 30:4), bakers (Jer. 37:21), carpenters (2 Kings 12:11), cupbearers (1 Kings 10:5), farmers (Is. 28:24-27), fishermen (Is. 19:8), gatekeepers (2 Kings 12:9), merchants (1 Kings 20:34), potters, (Is. 29:16), recorders (2 Sam. 8:16), silversmiths (Ex. 26:19-25), soldiers (Ex. 14:9), and many others.[167]

Government and Organization

From the basic family unit to the kingdom, human culture requires organization and governing, whether from a parent, a clan leader, a prophet, a judge, or a king. In the Old Testament we encounter nuclear families like Isaac and Rebekah's, extended families like Jacob and his sons and their families, and tribal organizations such as the twelve tribes of Israel. Governing also took place through the Judges (although not technically organized government; Gideon even refused to "rule over you" [Judges 8:23]), through prophets such as Samuel (1 Sam. 3:20-21), and eventually through the kings, beginning with Saul and ending with the last kings of a divided kingdom.

Lifestyle and Cultural Traditions

The Old Testament is replete with examples of lifestyle and cultural traditions that may seem quite different and even odd to a Western worldview and modern sensibilities. They are usually recorded in Scripture non-judgmentally; that is, they are described simply as the way people were, whether for good or for bad. Some of these cultural traditions include: placing one's hand on another's "thigh" while making an oath (Gen. 24:2-3), sending someone as proxy to find a wife for a family member (Gen. 24: 3-4), giving the first born a binding blessing that cannot be revoked (Gen. 27), working to earn the right to marry a daughter (Gen. 29:13-30), and pride in one's beard (2 Sam. 10:4-5). The book of Ruth describes the tradition of the family redeemer and the method (exchange of sandals) by which the redemption was made legally binding (4:7-7). Esther describes multiple cultural and royal traditions, including the manner in which a new queen was selected. Arranged marriages, betrothal, the payment of a bride price, burial practices, mourning, festivals and entertainment, clothing and adornments, the practice of hospitality, and many other cultural identifiers are described in the Biblical text and have been better understood through archeological exploration. All these were part and parcel of who the ancients were. They are what distinguished nations, peoples, and tribes from each other.[168]

The reality is that many of the customs and traditions practiced in the Old Testament were theologically driven. That is, they were God given laws and commandments for the purpose of identifying the Israelites as his people, separate from the other nations, and as ways to show their commitment to him in daily life. They were meant to visibly express God's will in daily life; they were practical ways to express holiness in dealings with the family, with neighbors, and even with one's enemies. These God given instructions, however, were themselves not given in a cultural vacuum. For example, two of the most significant practices of the Israelites were circumcision and sacrifice. In both cases, God took an already common cultural practice and infused them with new meaning. Other nations may have also practiced circumcision and sacrifice, but they were empty and non-covenantal practices with non-existing gods.[169] In other cases, even quotidian dress, cooking, and eating practices were designed to distinguish Israel's culture from that of her neighbors' (Lev. 13:47-59; 19:27; Ex. 34:26; Deut. 14:3-21).

In times of individual or national exile, there could be a radical culture clash. If the host culture did not violate Israel's religion, then the people could adapt themselves to the culture of their captors. Joseph did this when he found himself in Egypt. He shaved (Gen. 41:14), put on Egyptian dress, took an Egyptian wife (Gen. 41:45), and identified himself with the Egyptian way of life to such a degree that rising through the ranks of government was not surprising to the Egyptians. If the host culture demanded a violation of God's law, then it was rejected, often at the risk of death (Dan. 3:1-30; 6:1-24). Daniel and his friends refused to partake in eating what they believed would defile them (Dan. 1:8) and certainly refused to engage in idolatry. Yet, they were able to live and serve in a culture that was quite alien from their own. Most notable, perhaps, are the instructions the exiles received from God through Jeremiah. They were instructed to settle down in Babylon and build their lives within the host culture (Jer. 29:4-7). Without a doubt, these "cultural concessions" were the exception and not the rule, but they demonstrate that culture, in and of itself, is not evil. Elements of every culture, however, certainly can be.[170]

Conclusion

Cultural elements and practices in the Old Testament, whether those of Israel or of her neighbors, are often simply described without judgment. There were two significant exceptions: One, when cultural practices were used or misused by God's people themselves for sinful purposes. Examples of culture gone wrong, so to speak, include the building of the tower of Babel (Gen. 11:1-9), deceptive use of circumcision (Gen. 34), the making and worship of the Golden Calf (Ex. 32), and the making of rash unbreakable oaths (Judg. 11:29-40; 1 Sam. 14:24-46). Two, when those cultural practices were derived from or corrupted by foreign pagan religious practices. When that was the case, cultural practices – marriage, worship, sacrifice, whatever – were roundly criticized by God and his prophets. In Israel, the reality is that many cultural practices were theologically driven. They were implemented, appropriated, or corrected by God to demonstrate his holiness and what holiness should look like in his people. Foreign practices, even ones similar in appearance or practice, were to be avoided because they were associated with idolatry and false gods.

The New Testament and Culture

Jesus came into the Jewish culture of first century Palestine a "full-blooded" Jew. Mary and Joseph had gone through the traditional practice of betrothal, and Joseph, upon discovering that Mary was pregnant, had intended to "divorce" her according to common practice (Matt. 1:19). Jesus participated in the religious and cultural traditions of the day: he was presented in the temple on the eighth day; he traveled with family and friends to Jerusalem at age twelve for the Passover Festival, even getting "lost" because his parents assumed he was traveling with the extended group. As an adult, he attended a wedding in Cana, he attended festivals, fellowshipped over meals, and encountered funeral processions. He incorporated everyday life into his teachings and parables, drawing on familiar images and experiences from fishing, farming, viniculture, commerce, and simple household chores. He knew his context, he knew his people, and he knew what to say to help them grasp the truths he was teaching.

When cultural and religious traditions contradicted his teaching, however, he did not hesitate to confront these. He confronted the traditions of the Pharisees and Sadducees (Matt. 12:3-5; 15:1-9). He told the people that they had often "heard it that it was said" but "I tell you" right before he laid out a new and radical counter-cultural teaching (Matt. 5:21, 27, 31, 33, 38, 43; Mark 10:1-12). He violated ungodly cultural mores when he spoke to the Samaritan woman at the well (John 4:1-42). Jesus was also careful to distinguish people and culture from "the world," which hated him, rejected him, and hated the disciples (John 15:18-20). The "world," that Satan-led system of falsehood, violence, and evil, hated Jesus and his disciples. That "world" infected and influenced people and the culture. Jesus, however, does not tell his disciples to reject people and their culture per se, but to stay among people and the culture as salt and light in order to defeat the "world." This is the tension he experienced: in the world, but not of the world. It is the tension all his disciples must live with. Jesus was therefore not rejecting the Jewish culture or human culture in general. He was, rather, calling the people to return to culture – beliefs, attitudes, and practices – as God had originally intended it to be.

The rest of the New Testament takes a similar attitude to culture. There were times when cultural differences caused conflict. This was acknowledged and dealt with (Acts 6:1-6). There were times when cultural traditions had to be rejected, such as Peter's attitudes towards the Gentiles (Acts 10:1-48). There was a key time in church history – the Jerusalem Council (Acts 15:1-35) – when cultural differences were acknowledged, when it was also acknowledged that neither "Jews nor Gentiles were compelled to forsake their cultures to become Christians," but that they should still "make concessions to the cultural sensitivities of the other." This decision meant that "the gospel was primary, and culture was secondary."[171] Thus, Paul could become to the Jews "like a Jew" and to "those outside the law, like one outside the law" and be "all things to all people" for the sake of the gospel (1Cor. 9:20-23). At the same time, however, if a particular cultural practice offended or misrepresented Christians to the world, he would forbid or discourage it; e.g. eating meat that had been sacrificed to idols, the length of hair for both men and women, and head coverings for women (1 Cor. 10: 25-33; 11: 4-16).

Conclusion

The tension we encounter in the New Testament is that of being "in the world" but not being "of the world." This concept is expressed by Jesus particularly in his prayer for the disciples in John 17, by Paul in verses like Rom. 12:1-2, and by Peter when he calls believers "aliens and temporary residents" who are still to "submit to every human institution" (1 Pet. 2:11-14). I have already argued that the "world" should not be strictly identified with culture, and that contributes to the tension. There are times and circumstances in the New Testament when cultural elements, mores, customs, and traditions are participated in, assumed, or mentioned with no particular evaluation or judgment. There are plenty of times, however, when other elements, mores, customs, and traditions are questioned, challenged, condemned, and corrected. Culture may be "simply the word we use for the way in which a whole community of men and women behaves,"[172] but the "world" that is hostile and opposed to Christ has also infiltrated and infected culture – all cultures – with sin. Therein is the tension: the Bible does not reject culture wholesale, but it does not fail to pass judgment either when necessary. It does not simply affirm or totally reject culture, and neither should we. We cherish culture as God's gift to us, but remember that it also falls under his judgment. Our task, and our challenge, is to live in that tension ever thankful yet always watchful.[173]

The Church and Culture

The Bible is clear that our ultimate allegiance as individual Christians and as the Body of Christ – the Church – belongs to Christ. The Bible is also quite clear that Christians are not to be of the "world" and not to love the things of the "world," as long as the "world" is understood as explained above. The Bible is not quite as dogmatic, however, when addressing our relationship – as individuals or as a church – with the culture at large. Consequently, theologians and churchmen have struggled with and debated over this issue for the last two millennia. How are we to understand and hold to the tension we see in Scripture, where some passages seem to condemn culture both generally and in specifics while others take a neutral or positive stance toward human culture?

Christ and Culture

In the academic world that tension has often been referred to as the issue of "Christ and Culture." In particular, that was the title of an influential book by H. Richard Niebuhr, written in 1951, in which he examines five different historical approaches, positions, or options to the question of how Christ (that is, Christianity, Christians, or the Christian community or church) and culture have related throughout history. His five options were:

1. Christ against Culture, which is the answer "that uncompromisingly affirms the sole authority of Christ over the Christian and resolutely rejects culture's claims to loyalty." This simply means that culture is generally considered evil and is to be rejected by the church. There is no real distinction made between the "world" and culture.

2. The Christ of Culture, which occurs when Christians "seem equally at home in the community of culture" as they do in the community of believers. They "interpret culture through Christ," picking and choosing from his teachings, his actions, and from Christian doctrine "such points as seem to agree with what is best in civilization." This occurs when there is not enough distinction made between the "world" and culture. That is, the sinfulness of the "world" is downplayed so that culture, church, and world are blended into a "Christian" society or a civil religion. Sin is only an individual issue, not a corporate or societal ill. The attempt, therefore, to "harmonize Christ and culture," which inevitably results in a tamed Christ and a watered down gospel.

3. Christ above Culture, which Niebuhr actually subdivides into the *synthesists*, the *dualists* (#4 below), and the

conversionists (#5 below). In this approach the duality of Christ and culture is acknowledged; however, that duality is not dealt with by separation as in the first option or accommodation as in the second. In the most common of all historical approaches, the synthesists do not say "Either Christ or culture," because God is in both. They do not say "Both Christ and culture" as if there were no great difference between them. Synthesists do say "Both Christ and culture' in full awareness of the dual nature of our law, our end, and our situation." That is, Christ is certainly above and sovereign over culture, but an attempt must be made to unite the demands of Christ and the demands of culture, to ". . . give back to Caesar the things that are Caesar's, and to God the things that are God's" and to be subject to the governing authorities who have been instituted by God. Christ and culture, therefore, are united in one great system.

4. Christ and Culture in Paradox, which is also a dualist (Christ above Culture) position, but which differs "considerably from the synthesist in its understanding of both the extent and the thoroughness of human depravity" and in its "conception of the nature of corruption in culture." A tendency, therefore, is to let "state and economic life…continue relatively unchanged," because the primary issue is the relationship between "God and us." That is, the spiritual conflict is not primarily between God and culture, but between God and sinful human beings. Christ has come to redeem and save sinners, who now live in the tension "between time and eternity, between wrath and mercy, between culture and Christ." Like the Christ against Culture position, the dualist sees culture as primarily evil and sinful; yet, there is no other option but to be in the world while not being of the world.

The dualist's speech and conduct, therefore, are full of paradoxes: "He is under law, and yet not under law but grace; he is a sinner, and yet righteous; he believes, as a doubter; he has assurance of salvation, yet walks along the knife-edge of insecurity. In Christ all things have become new, and yet everything remains [the same]." God has revealed himself, yet remains hidden, and the believer believes, yet walks by faith. There is no synthesis between Christ and culture, there is a life of tension and paradox.

5. Christ the Transformer of Culture, is the answer given by "conversionists," who have a "more positive and hopeful attitude toward culture." These, too, believe that Christ is above Culture; however, because culture is "under God's sovereign rule, ... the Christian must carry on culture work in obedience to the Lord," thus transforming the culture. The conversionist (cultural conversion, not individual) is more positive and affirming of God's creation, emphasizes the role of Christ in the creation, distinguishes the effects of the fall from the original and ultimate goodness of creation and the material body, and emphasizes more of a realized eschatology – that is, what God can and is doing in the world today. Although he doesn't explicitly say so, this is apparently Niebuhr's preferred position. [174]

As influential as Niebuhr's book has been, his assumptions and his typology have regularly been critiqued and revisited. Craig Carter has appropriately noted that Niebuhr's typology is grounded in the "unarticulated presupposition" of Christendom, which is a "passé era,"[175] and was formulated when public life in America was dominated by "liberal Protestantism." [176] Carter's "revisiting" of Niebuhr is thought provoking and even convicting at times, but it is rather reductionist. D.A. Carson rightly notes that Carter does not do justice to the full gospel, the complexities of all the Christ and culture issues ("Carter paints only in black and white"), and the realities of history.[177] Carson himself critiques Niebuhr's typology along three main lines:

One, Niebuhr's definition of "culture" is lacking. Carson notes that Niebuhr restricts "culture to the domain of the 'temporal and material realization of values,'" more in line with what the "New Testament means by 'world'." Thus, when he says "culture," Niebuhr "means something like 'culture-devoid-of-Christ'." This "slipperiness of the 'culture' terminology is palpable." Carson correctly argues instead that "the categories 'Christ' and 'culture' are not mutually opposed in every respect."[178]

Two, Carson runs Niebuhr's typology through the grid of Biblical theology and arrives at two conclusions: First, the "Christ of Culture" position is so devoid of the "non-negotiables" of Biblical theology that is cannot even be considered a Christian option. Second, Niebuhr approaches Scripture as a set of "discrete paradigms" rather than a unitary canon that should be approached as a whole. The result is that he can assign Paul to several of the options, quote John as support for two different views, and at times set the New Testament authors against each other.[179]

Three, and as a result of these two criticisms, Carson again correctly argues that the options in "Niebuhr's fivefold scheme" should not be thought of as all equally "warranted by individual documents of the New Testament" and thus available to pick and choose as we prefer. To the contrary, the appropriate canonical approach is to take in the whole counsel of Scripture "attempting a holistic grasp of the relations between Christ and culture," knowing that the situation of Christians in today's world varies dramatically. In some countries Christians are the majority and dominate the culture. In others, Christians are under severe persecution. Consequently, in some circumstances we may have to "emphasize some elements" of the answer and "other elements in another situation." Therefore, Carson does not offer a typology or list of options. There is no "ideal stable paradigm" that will fit every situation and every time. Cultures are constantly changing, political situations are constantly changing, and there is thus no "political structure" that offers a "permanent 'solution' to the tension."[180]

Carson is certainly correct that the historical, political, and cultural context, and the attitude in any specific culture toward Christianity, will largely determine the response of both the individual Christian and the church. How Christians understand and define culture and the world, whether equating them or not, will also influence their response. If equated, the tendency will be withdrawal. If separated completely, accommodation may occur. Leaving aside some of the more technical and academic language, but like Niebuhr, I suggest there are five primary approaches to culture among American evangelicals:

1. Withdrawal or Separation. Historically, when culture and the "world" have been closely identified, the tendency of Christians is to withdraw as much as possible. The most extreme form of withdrawal is intentional martyrdom, actually sought after by some persecuted Christians in the centuries before Constantine. Another form of withdrawal is monasticism, from contemplative meditation to hermit monasticism.[181] Other forms of withdrawal include groups like the Amish, who only partially withdraw and selectively reject culture and the world. Among contemporary evangelicals, the most common form of withdrawal or separation is intentionally building a Christian ghetto. That is, churches build and provide all the social and entertainment needs for the Christian family, the Christian yellow pages provides opportunities to do business with only believers (regardless of competence), all forms of "worldly" entertainment are rejected so that only Christian music is listened to and Christian novels are read, and children are homeschooled or sent only to Christian schools.

Now, I am not criticizing any one of these practices in and of themselves. I would love to send my own grandchildren to a Christian school! My concern is whether there is any missiological thinking behind these practices, especially when all of them are preached and practiced. Certainly, the biblical tension between holiness (being set apart) and being salt and light in the world is real. The example of both Jesus and Paul, however, compels us to go into the world, as nasty and ugly as it may be. That should be done, certainly, with accountability, with partners, and with caution. At the same time, the church, the local body of believers, is separate and withdrawn from the world to some degree. But to withdraw too far means a loss of influence and the danger of becoming ingrown, irrelevant (that is, not salt and light), and maybe even cultic. In the end, the church may have a prophetic voice, but it is not heard.

2. Accommodation. When Christians (and the church) accommodate to the culture, they do so based on one of two presuppositions: One, that culture is inherently good or neutral at best, or, two, that the culture is, in fact, "Christian" and representative of the best of Christian life. Historically, the most egregious examples include Constantininism, which was the forced unity of state and the church, "more of a political than a religious decision,"[182] and later the state churches of European nations. In these cases there was rarely a distinction between what was supposedly Biblical and God's will, and the practices and the will of the Emperor, the King, or the ruling government. The prevailing culture was the best expression of Christianity, and the church rarely objected. The church, therefore, too often accommodated, accepted, endorsed, and even encouraged whatever the

state was involved in, with historical examples ranging from colonialism, slavery, invasions and wars, genocide, and even the rise of Hitler.

Even in countries where there is no state religion and an official or practical separation of church and state, the church, or at least individual Christians and different representatives of Christianity, can sometimes confuse patriotism with nationalism and both with Biblical Christianity. In America, we have historically experienced confusion with slavery, the genocide of Native American nations, and several wars. Even in our own Civil War each side was convinced that its cause was holy and righteous. Perhaps less extreme, but still Biblically questionable and missiologically challenging, are efforts to identify the nation, the culture, or the history with Christianity. This will be examined more closely in the next chapter, but to call America a Christian nation requires a significant redefinition of Biblical Christianity.

However much accommodation takes place, the strategy is to take the "path of least resistance," or perhaps more accurately, the "path of least offense." Whenever Christ – the church, the gospel, Christianity – is accommodated to the prevailing culture, the church loses its prophetic voice. Whereas in the withdrawal option a prophetic voice is heard, in the accommodation option, the church loses its right to have a prophetic voice.

3. Two-Tiered or Dual Reality. This option most simply considers that Christ and culture – the church and the world – are two separate and different realities, both of which must be lived in. On the one hand are the "synthesists" who seek a "both-and solution". They reject both the withdrawal from and the accommodation to

culture. Christ is sovereign over culture, they insist, so it is not either one or the other, but both. Trying to have a both-and approach, all tied up in a neat unified system, however, inevitably leads to a culturally conditioned and error-filled system. What synthesists too often fail to realize is that they themselves are culturally conditioned and are building a unified system on a culturally bound mindset. Thus, Thomas Aquinas's system was medieval and hierarchical. Similar attempts in synthesis may involve unifying capitalism, socialism, middle-class values, nationalism, the empire, or the Father land with Christiainity, none of which are inherently or ultimately Christian.[183]

On the other hand, are the dualists. This position acknowledges the realities of Christ and culture and certainly understands the reality of sin and evil in human culture. The dualist comes to the conclusion that life is paradoxical (thus Niebuhr's category) in which one must live torn, pulled, and struggling between two realities. This pull, however, often leads to either "antinomianism" – basically giving up and living without concern for God's law – and "cultural conservatism;" that is, focusing on religion to the exclusion of social and political justice.[184]

Practically speaking, this two-tiered or dualistic approach is seen far too often in the average American Christian's life. That is, the Christian treats reality as dual – there is the everyday life of business, work, play, and community, and then there is church life, which may or may not include family. The practical consequence of such dualism is piety in church on Sunday or in the company of other believers, but cut-throat and unethical practices at work. There is love for God and neighbor at church, but greed, envy, and injustice during the week. The result is a privatized religion that is no one's business, and a little, personal Jesus stored away for use in personal moments of crisis.[185]

Although this dualism is commonly preached against in evangelical churches, the application usually goes only far enough to cover the obvious sins of the flesh. Although that application is correct, it is incomplete. Christ-like behavior also addresses pride, gossip, ethics, justice, and peace. The difficulty is addressing these (particularly the latter three) in our culture without encroaching on assumed and emotional political positions.

4. Counter-Cultural. This position is similar to the withdrawal position in that it recognizes the sin and evil in the world and in human culture. The rhetoric and the attempted practice, therefore, are to live counter to what is seen and experienced in culture. Christians are encouraged to demonstrate a different worldview, live a different way of life, and demonstrate a different way of doing community. The intent is to demonstrate that the Christian culture is above – superior – to the prevailing culture. This approach is most commendable and one that can and should be practiced. Several warnings should be heeded: One, there is a danger of considering all of culture as the enemy, when, as demonstrated above, much of culture is good. Two, the elements of culture that are to be "countered" are often arbitrarily picked from an already culturally conditioned perspective. The result is that we counter what is not our culture or what we are uncomfortable with rather than what is unbiblical. Three, as with dualism, the easy tendency is to focus on the obvious sins of the flesh and overlook corporate sin and the sinful structures of society.

5. Transformation. The presupposition in this position is that culture is fallen and primarily sinful, but can be redeemed. There have been four basic approaches to this transformation:

One, as with Constantine, there has been the coercive approach. The nation, the culture, or the people are declared to be Christian and then obligated by law or force to live as such. The most notorious example of this coercion was the conquest of Latin America by the "Cross and the Sword." Entire peoples were forced at the point of the sword by the Spanish and the Portuguese to "convert" or die. The end result was both the eradication of native peoples and a Christo-pagan syncretism that exists to this day in parts of Latin America.[186] Other examples include the Crusades, the Spanish Inquisition, and numerous European wars, most of which were "Christian against Christian," but all with the intent of transforming what was wrong in culture.

Two, there have been attempts to transform culture through structural and corporate change. The Social Gospel proponents tried to unite "sociology, new economic theories, and contemporary socialists and reformers" in an effort to promote enough social services, education, social solidarity, and legal reforms that God's kingdom would be manifest as "a social reality that involves the entire life of humanity."[187] This approach collapsed under the reality of cultural evil during World War I and the Great Depression. More common today is the approach by evangelicals to elect Christian officials, lobby for laws, and protest unjust laws. Although this approach is commendable and absolutely necessary at times, the danger is becoming too identified with a particular politician, political party or system, and believing that just "one more law" will get things where they need to be. Laws will certainly hold back the unrighteous (to a point), but they will not create righteousness. Having said that, however, the challenge for Christians is to address not only the sinful acts of society such as abortion, but to address the sinful structures of society that permit or encourage racism, poverty, and other injustices. Again, identifying and dealing with these takes us into the difficult and controversial realms of economic and political theory.[188]

Three, the standard conservative evangelical approach has been to transform society and culture one person at a time. Acknowledging the biblical truth that any transformation of culture must begin with the conversion and transformation of the individual, this position opts for the "grassroots" approach. Lead enough people to Christ and culture will be transformed. Although this is certainly true, there are two problems: One, how long will it take? Two, what do we do in the meantime? If this had been William Wilberforce's strategy to bring down slavery, or that of the reformers attacking child labor in the nineteenth century, how long would change have taken? It is not an either-or proposition.

Four, and related to number three, is the popular American evangelical rhetoric of "returning our country" to God or to what it once was. I will address this in more detail in the next chapter, so suffice it to say that a "return as transformation" or "transforming so as to return" approach is futile and unbiblical. The issue is "what" we may want to return to. That is not always clearly stated, and, there are plenty of Christians who do not want to return to the old days. Besides, Biblical history moves forward, so we ought to seek transformation in anticipation of the coming of Christ. More on that in the next chapter.

Culture is simply who we as a race, a people, a nation, an ethnicity, a tribe, and a population segment. But simple it is not. It is not always simple to identify a culture. Many people are products of multiple cultures (although usually a dominant one), especially if they are urban, have lived in several geographic locations, are the products of a mixed marriage, have grown up in different cultures, or have migrated. Our flattened and globalized world means that more and more of us are multi-cultural or at least influenced by various cultures. It is not always simply to speak theologically of culture. There are various conceptions of the fallenness of the world and of creation. There are various shades of meaning of the "world." How we interact with and live in culture has been an ongoing debate throughout church history. Do we adapt, reject, ignore, or transform? Let me offer some missiological thoughts on American culture.

A Missiological View of Culture

1. Culture is God's gift to us. However, just as humans are fallen, so is culture, for it is made up of, by, and for humans. There is both good and bad in culture. The challenge is to biblically identify which is which.

2. We are all culturally bound. In other commonly used words, we are all "sold out to culture." Some of being "sold out" is simply who we are and how we do things. They are what make us different from and hopefully interesting to each other. Some of being "sold out" is unbiblical, and we are often blind to those aspects of our culture. We like them, we are comfortable with them, we have never even thought about them. The challenge is to allow Scripture to challenge our own cultural presuppositions before we challenge those of others.

3. All culture and all cultures are subject, therefore, to the evaluation and judgment of Scripture. The challenge is to do that in partnership with other cultures, all being open to reproof and correction.

4. Biblical Christian culture is above all other cultures. Being a disciple of Christ and living in Christian community rises above and transcends all culture and cultures. The challenge for us is that it is impossible to live the Christian life in a cultural vacuum. Consequently, even as the Christian life and the Christian community is experienced within culture, it must never be identified fully with any culture.

5. The missiological challenge, therefore, is to present that Christian lifestyle, community, and culture – to present the gospel of Christ, which is timeless and culturally transcending – packaged culturally when appropriate, counter cultural when necessary, accommodating (contextualizing) to the culture at times, always in culture, but never fully identified with culture. Our challenge and the ongoing debate is how to do these faithfully without giving up the truth of the gospel message. The options offered above, therefore, as Carson says, are not necessarily mutually exclusive. In particular, depending on the situation, there are times when we must withdraw and be against culture, but there is always a time to transform culture. Our perpetual challenge is how to do so. Some ministry options and suggestions will be offered in Part 3.

Buckle Up Your Seat Belt: Change in the 21ˢᵗ Century

There is an appointed time for everything. And there is a time for every event under heaven –

A time to give birth and a time to die;
A time to plant and a time to uproot what is planted.
A time to kill and a time to heal;
A time to tear down and a time to build up.
A time to weep and a time to laugh;
A time to mourn and a time to dance.
A time to throw stones and a time to gather stones;
A time to embrace and a time to shun embracing.
A time to search and a time to give up as lost;
A time to keep and a time to throw away.
A time to tear apart and a time to sew together;
A time to be silent and a time to speak.
A time to love and a time to hate;
A time for war and time for peace.

What profit is there to the worker from that in which he toils? I have seen the task which God has given the sons of men with which to occupy themselves. He has made everything appropriate in its time. He has also set eternity

in their heart, yet so that man will not find out the work
which God has done from the beginning even to the end.

Eccl. 3:1-11 (NASB)

In this passage of Wisdom literature the preacher reflects on life,
time, constancy, and change. At first glance the poem states the
obvious: from birth through death various events fill the lives of
human beings. Some of these are significant and even traumatic;
others are part and parcel of daily existence. The poem initially
seduces the reader into identifying and agreeing with what is
being stated, leading him to conclude that most of these events
are typically under human control. The reality, however, is that
these times are determined by God. The belief that changing
times and events are "manageable and under human control"[189]
is a delusion shattered by the preacher's subsequent strong
statements of "divine determinism." These are God's times.
He sets them up, he controls them, he decides what and when
everything is "appropriate" according to his plan. Human beings
may think they have the times figured out, but we cannot know
the full significance of them.

Perhaps the reader is tempted to fall into hopeless fatalism,
to push God's sovereignty well past an appropriate Biblical
determinism. To do so, however, would virtually eliminate the
need for any kind of a meaningful missiology. All the intricacies
related to the tension between the twin Biblical realities of God's
sovereignty and human free cannot be resolved here. Suffice it
to say that from this passage five truths about change can be
gleaned: One, human life is filled with changing events and
events that change. Although there is constancy in some – birth,
toil, war, death – there is also uncertainty in how these events
unfold and affect human existence. Two, change is inevitable.
Life goes on, events come and go. The types of events may be
predictable, but their content and impact are not. Consequently,

three, there is both constancy and change in human life. That is why the old cliché that says "the more things change, the more they stay the same" is both true and false. Four, humans can effect and affect change to some degree and in some cases. The farmer may decide when and where and what to plant, but he does not control the seasons. But, five, in the end, as the preacher notes, God is in control of all events and all change. Acknowledging his sovereignty over such can either frustrate or comfort, depending on one's view of God and faith in him.

Whether one ends up theologically and philosophically a determinist or a free will advocate, the realities from a cultural, experiential, and missiological point of view are that change happens and that it is happening faster and faster. Perhaps one may agree reluctantly or grudgingly, but most people see change as inevitable. Whether intentional radical change, intentional incremental change, or unintentional evolutionary change, it happens. Change may be resisted or celebrated. It may be anticipated and planned, unexpected and dreaded, orderly or chaotic. One may argue whether change is good or bad, whether a particular change was necessary, or even argue over the ultimate meaning of change. The fact is change happens, and people, organizations, and missiologists must learn to deal with, respond to, and often create change. What are some characteristics of change in the 21st century?

It is Discontinuous and Chaotic in Nature

History is all about change: wars, kingdoms and governments rising and falling, people migrations, inventions, explorations, expanding knowledge, famines and calamities. If anything, history teaches that nothing on this earth is permanent. Although historical change is often radical in its worldview and its eventual application, it has usually been fairly linear (you can trace its line of development), continuous (you can point to *cause and effect*, such that change was even predictably), evolutionary rather than revolutionary, and sporadic in its spread beyond its point of origin (it just took longer for things to be known). Consider, for example, the medieval centuries of feudalism, where change simply meant more of the same throughout generations. Economic, political, and technological changes took place but were linear, slow, and evolutionary. On the other hand, think of the American and the French Revolutions as idea-driven change, for example, which, although they relied on centuries of philosophical insights and decades of persuasion, radically changed the world, often in unpredictable fashion.

The difference between continuous and discontinuous change is significant, in particular for developing a missiology. Continuous change follows from that "which has gone before," and is thus "expected, anticipated, and managed." The development of children is a natural example. The traditional growth of a business, especially a Mom and Pop operation is another. On the other hand, "discontinuous change is disruptive and unanticipated" and challenges our assumptions. What we already know and can do is not very helpful in this scenario. Working harder with existing skills won't cut it; new skills are needed for such an unpredictable environment, and "there is no getting back to normal." That is, the change is such that the culture is transformed forever, "tipping it over into something new."[190]

The end of the Cold War and 9/11 are certainly the most recent and painful examples of discontinuous change for Americans and even much of the world. It has often been observed that during the Cold War the enemy was clearly (if not always accurately) identified. The rules of the game were known and generally followed by all sides (MAD – mutually assured destruction doctrine – being the most infamous). Global strategies followed known and accepted alliances, global change happened along expected and anticipated ideologies and global themes, and political ideologies separated the good guys from the bad. Then came the fall of the Berlin Wall and the collapse of the Soviet Union, the rapidity of which was a surprise to many observers. The rules of the game changed as new alliances were formed, economies changed, and entire nations and cultures were in upheaval. Change was rapid, discontinuous, and disconcerting for many.

The decade of the 1990s was one of economic boom, relative peace, and the "end of history" as Francis Fukuyama famously put it. What he meant was that the world would no longer be divided by great ideologies and that liberal democracy would continually and eventually prevail in future conflicts. But on September 11, 2001 it all changed. For Americans, the inconceivable happened. We were attacked on our own soil and that by a nebulous and relatively unknown enemy who was not identified with any particular nation. Efforts to describe the enemy only created more confusion: it was not any particular nation, but we invaded two. It was not Islam but radical Islam and then an undefined entity called "terrorism." Military doctrine, global alliances, religious differences and understanding, ethnic tolerance, our own American language, travel habits, economics, and view of the world changed radically. In both instances, the fall of the Soviet Union and 9/11, change was predominantly unanticipated, unknown, and discontinuous with what was before. Certainly, in hindsight so much of it seems obvious. But that is just the point of radical discontinuous change: you can't see it coming.

Now, take that discontinuous change and speed it up. Anyone who has lived in or studied the 20th century knows that change has come more rapidly than ever before, whether political, economic, and certainly technological. Anyone who has lived during the last quarter of the 20th century – through the end of the Cold War and 9/11 – knows how accelerated and chaotic that change has become. Anyone paying attention in today's world knows that change is even more discontinuous, rapid and radical, non-linear and chaotic, and seemingly instant in its global impact,[191] especially in the amount of information available to us.[192] In reality, the changes don't have to be as dramatic as 9/11. This is especially true because of the migrations of people and the advances in information technology. Cities that just twenty years ago were fairly ethnically homogeneous or clearly divided along white-black lines are now rapidly becoming minority majority due to rapid immigration patterns. And think of this: when 9/11 happened Facebook, the iphone, ipads, the cloud, and Skype did not exist, and itunes was only nine months old. The increase in information, the speed of communication, and the rapid development of social networking is mind boggling.

A practical outcome of all this, as Alan Hirsch points out, is that the ability to forecast the "future with high levels of predictability" fifty years ago allowed us to develop strategic plans that would eventually lead to desired results. This was because the "future was just a projection of the past with some adjustments." However, today the rapid pace of technological innovation, the "redundancies of whole industries" (that means lots of competition – dog eat dog), "hypersensitive" and interdependent global markets, terrorism, and the constant shift of geopolitical forces, and the immediate impact of these worldwide means that "change for us is *discontinuous*, and it is increasingly rapid," and, it could be added, less and less predictable.[193] Bottom line, the world is becoming far more complex and chaotic every day.

It is Postmodern in Content

Plenty has been written about the shift from Modernity to Postmodernity; the good and bad of each continue to be debated.[194] There is probably a symbiotic relationship between postmodernism and rapid discontinuous change – one relies on the other, one could not have happened without the other, it is hard to know which caused the other, and where one begins and the other ends. It could be argued, however, that rapid technological change and a flattened, globalized world, do contribute to the ease by which postmodern thought develops, is communicated, and spreads virally around the world. A brief explanation of postmodernism was given the first chapter, so a list of some primary characteristics of postmodern thought and life will suffice here. These include:

1. A refusal to see change, and particularly technological change, as inherently good or as inevitable progress. In popular culture, the modern visions of the future were usually utopian and of a better standard of living. The postmodern vision of the future is usually that of *Terminator* and *The Matrix* – technology and science gone rogue.

2. A rejection of an overarching metanarrative or truth. Instead, truth is what you make it; it is a social and community construct. Rapid and discontinuous change only seems to confirm this as nothing appears to be lasting and absolute.

3. Consequently, there is no such thing as an "ethic." There are only personal values and a personal spirituality. Since there is no absolute truth, there is nothing upon which to build an absolute ethic. If reality and truth are constructs, then so are ethics and morality.

4. Consumerism, which is materialism out of control. Much of what we experience as change in daily life is consumer oriented. Supply and demand is no longer the economic principle, rather it is supply, create a perceived demand, and

sell as much and as quickly as possible. That is, products do not exist because they are needed; they are created simply to sell. The consumer is king. The game is to give him more and more options as quickly as possible. Thus, for many people, change is most evident in consumer goods.

5. Fragmentation in a digital area. There is fragmentation of style, of music, of art, of tastes, of people, of attention spans, and in storytelling. Note that television programs are no longer linear and of one story per episode. The most popular have a large cast ensemble and carry several concurrent and overlapping story lines at once, often including an overarching myth that mysteriously directs the characters' lives. Yet, at the same time, fragmentation does not necessarily mean cognitive dissonance or intrapersonal conflict in postmodern thought and lifestyle. Ambiguity, paradox, and even incongruity are part of the postmodern person's cafeteria lifestyle. Clothing styles may clash, tastes are eclectic and change quickly, and even contradictory beliefs are held in tension. All is acceptable and all is in style, so pick and choose what you want from the vast plurality of options.

Much more could be said about postmodern thought and lifestyle. The point is that the fast and discontinuous change of the 21st century is a close companion of postmodernism. In the end, the primary missiological concern is the resulting rejection of absolutes, metanarratives, and the assumption of pluralism and contextual relativism.

It is Global in Scope

Change in the 21st century is certainly global in scope, both causing and being facilitated by a flattened world. Distance is irrelevant, both in the physical reality of travel and in the virtual reality of events. What is taking place on the other side of the world right now is also happening everywhere right now. Digital accessibility and commentary make any event everyone's event. Certainly, there are gaps in countries and cultures, but rapid, discontinuous change is happening everywhere.

In fact, it could be argued that change is even more rapid and discontinuous in non-developed and under-developed countries. Whereas in the United States and other industrialized nations we have experienced incremental technological progress, in many majority world countries that progress has jumped several steps. For example, in America, telephone communications went from switchboard operated to party land lines to private land lines in the forties, fifties and sixties. The seventies and eighties saw the introduction of cordless and push button phones. In the nineties, cell phones, fiber optic cables, and the internet took off. By 2012 we can barely imagine a world without smart phones, Skype, and Bluetooth technology. In many African and Asian countries, however, the last twenty years saw a jump from relatively few and very expensive land lines straight to vast, effective, and relatively cheap cell phone networks. The incremental steps in between were simply skipped. Therefore, on a recent visit to a village in India I was in a home without electricity or running water, but with the ubiquitous and indispensable cell phone.[195]

It is Potentially Tribal in Outcome

Travel, the internet, multi-national corporations, and global markets mean that America is both changing the world and being changed by the world. That is, a flattened world, a globalized culture, and interdependent economies allow for, and in fact, encourage the postmodern paradox of homogenization (one culture and one economy) and tribalization (niche marketing, emphasis on ethnic identity and pride). Across the globe there is less and less distinction between what is national and what is foreign. Because of our multinational heritage, that has been a perpetual debate in America, an issue that will be addressed in the next chapter. Thus, there is on the one hand, a globalized homogeneity, or, as some have derisively called it, the "McDonaldization" of the world. Where can you go without seeing American influence, products, and culture? Our movies and TV shows are viewed worldwide. McDonalds, Starbucks, WalMart, and American styles, automobiles, and music sometimes appear to overwhelm other cultures. At the same time, America is vastly and deeply influenced by Hispanic and Asian culture. Everything we buy, it seems, is made in China. India is handling more and more of our information. Worldwide there is growing cultural uniformity and cultural confusion.

On the other hand, and as a result of global homogeneity, there is a growing cultural tribalization. In the face of overwhelming cultural homogeneity, many racial, ethnic, and cultural groups seek to protect and even re-establish their identity. Sometimes they are establishing their "lost" identity for the first time or for the first time in a long time. They are establishing and promoting their "tribe." In some cases this can lead to violent protests and even violent revolutions by groups that feel threatened. The paradox is that while globalization and global change is creating and promoting a "one-world" culture (unfortunately driven more by consumerism than anything else), ethnic, religious, and cultural conflict threatens to divide the world even more.

This is also true of the Unites States. As Americans we often find ourselves arguing for and defending both a broad "American" culture while at the same time exalting regional, state, ethnic, and sub-cultural differences. Historically, we have both celebrated and felt threatened by multiculturalism. We both celebrate and fear the American "mosaic" and "melting pot." The next chapter will address this more.

Taking the Good with the Bad

But is all this change good or bad, or a little of both? Too often, Americans, and especially American Christians, suffer from selective memory and historical myopia. We tend to remember the "good old days" of our youth and how things supposedly used to be better in America. Many argue that things are worse today than they ever were; that is, change is happening and it is mostly bad change. But is that so? It is a mixed bag, and it depends on how far back one is looking and what one is measuring. Does anyone really believe life was easier and better in centuries past anywhere in the world? Violence and wars have always been rampant. Disease, illiteracy, high childhood mortality, and childbirth deaths were all common occurrences.

How about the good ole U.S.A.? Well, does anyone really want to return to the days of tuberculosis, polio, small pox, measles, and the yearly ravages of influenza? Does anyone really think that African-Americans and Hispanics wish to return to the way things were in the fifties, much less earlier decades? What about literacy rates, pollution, and the much higher poverty index, not to mention medical care and education? Is crime worse than it used to be (not necessarily, according to FBI statistics) or is it just more reported – again and again?[196] Were the days of two World Wars and world depression better than today's world events and economic woes? But, the rebuttal goes, what about morality, common decency, manners, marriage and family, and a general Judeo-Christian ethic? What about rampant abortion and the ever radical gay agenda? Without a doubt, there has been a steady decline in morality and a steady attack on marriage and the family (some of these critical moral issues will be discussed in a later chapter).[197] The reality is that sin has always been rampant among human beings; it was just more private in the good old days.[198]

Are things worse now than they were fifty years ago? Were Ozzie and Harriet the reality of the fifties and is *Modern Family* reality today? The truth is that neither reflects the full reality of their times. We were probably not as Ozzie and Harriet as we thought we were, and we have probably slid further toward the *Modern Family* than we are willing to admit.[199] Change has always been and is a mixed bag. There is good change, there is bad change, and then there is just...change. It is inevitable, it is mostly out of our control, and it all creates a missiological challenge for the church in 21st century America, because there are more people undergoing more change who are less connected to each other and to any particular place. The missiological opportunity is to present an unchanging message that will anchor them to living truth now and forever.

Missiological Implications: A theology for evaluating, embracing, and resisting change

Missiologically, the temptation is twofold: to continue seeing and acting as if America is a homogeneous culture, and to confuse the acceptance of change with the endorsement of all its content. In the first case, even when we acknowledge that we are multicultural, we have too often dogmatized our missions methodology so that homogeneous methods are applied in heterogeneous contexts. In the second case, the church often fails to discern between what is uncomfortable but generally harmless with what is truly unbiblical and harmful. The first offends our sentimentality and preferences, the second offends God.[200]

America is changing daily – chaotically and discontinuously – and the postmodern, global, and potential tribal result of that change demands a Biblical missiology that acknowledges and embraces the following:

1. Change is inevitable. In fact, biblically and theologically, change is essential and part of God's creation. Creation involved change – from nothing, from the formless void, to a beautiful creation. Unlike many world views in which time is cyclical, inescapable, or meaningless, Biblical time is purposeful, forward moving, and climaxing in the fulfillment of God's promises and plan. Seasons change, living beings change, life is about change of all kinds, as the preacher so vividly points out in Ecclesiastes.

2. Not all things change. First, God does not change. That does not mean he is a static, inactive, and completely unknowable God. He is, rather, relationally dynamic; that is, he is personal and lovingly and graciously interacts with his creation. To be certain, being a personal God does not mean he is the malleable God of Process Theology or the uncertain God of Open Theism. He does not change in his nature, his character, or his attributes. Second, God's truth does not change. As the world around us changes we may state his truth in various manners, we may express his truth in different ways, and we may live out his truth in ever changing contexts. But his truth does not change, and that includes truth about himself and truth about ourselves.[201] Third, the human condition has not changed. From the fall of Adam and Eve, all humans who have every lived (save for Jesus) have been sinners by nature and by choice. No matter how good or how bad any individual person's actions may be, all have fallen short of what God expects and demands, and the only solution is the salvific work of Jesus Christ on the cross.

3. Change, even chaotic change, can be good. Studies in chaos and complexity have shown that any living system in a state of equilibrium it is at risk. Equilibrium leads to

stagnation which leads to death. Change, and even moving to the edge of chaos, is what causes living systems to adapt, find new solutions, and improve. The disturbances caused by change and chaos can be, in fact, life savers.[202] This is seen time and again in the life of Israel. When they forgot who they were, when they abandoned God's law and way, when they moved away from God's purposes, he introduced radical change – even chaos – to get their attention and lead them to repentance. Allowing the Assyrians and the Babylonians to invade, conquer, and exile the people radically upset the status quo! It was only through knocking the entire nation off balance that they would even consider returning to God.[203] Similarly, what could have been more of a radical change than Saul's Damascus Road experience? Experientially, contemporary Christians talk about the same principle regularly, when we speak of God "getting my attention," or "God using that bad experience to grow my faith." It is, I would argue, an indisputable Biblical principal that change, even "bad" change, is both determined and used by God to grow his people individually and corporately.

4. The missiological key, therefore, is how we evaluate change. Should we embrace it or resist it? We should ask the following questions:

   a. Can we control it? The answer is "probably not." I am not saying that God does not change people, systems, or structures. I am not saying the church should not stand up to injustice, poverty, and corruption or stand for pro-life, pro-marriage, peace, and other moral issues. Change in these and other issues can be brought about through persuasion, influence, and lives that reflect the salt and light of the gospel. What

I am saying is that we cannot totally nor ultimately control change, either by causing it or preventing it. The world moves on, time marches forward, and life happens. Missiologically, we should allow for God's control, his timing, and prayerfully act and respond according to the gospel, understanding that change happens only as the Holy Spirit moves in people's lives individually, corporately, and structurally. To put it in more business-like terms, it is the difference between attempts at strategic planning and strategic preparedness. There are similarities between the two, but also significant differences.[204]

b. What is actually changing? My main concern here, of course, is a missiological response. As America changes rapidly and discontinuously, the church must clearly identify the changes worth confronting. It seems that we spend an inordinate amount of time and energy addressing and focusing on changes that affect our sentimentality about life and culture and our preferences about the church. Or, we too often fall to the temptation of addressing symptoms rather than causes (and other than simply saying "sin," the causes are not always easy to discern and identify). Certainly, symptoms may need to be addressed, for they are, after all, what we see and immediately experience. Missiologically, however, until the root causes of these symptoms – greed, oppression, selfishness, hatred, and the love of money are addressed by the gospel of Jesus Christ, we will only move from feeble, politically driven efforts to correct one symptom to the next, at best a patchwork solution.

c. How can and will God use this change for His glory? As hard as it is, we need to work to see the biggest picture possible – God's. What is he doing through these changes? What does he want to do in my individual life, in my church, and through believers in America and around the world? How are these changes eschatological; that is, how are they moving toward the fulfillment of his promises? I am not suggesting that the answer lies in trying to interpret every current event according to some end time calendar. To the contrary, I believe we need to stop such futile end times interpretations. The Bible is clear that no one knows the day and hour of Jesus' return (Matt. 24:36, 42), and that it will be when we least expect it, not when we think we have it figured out (Matt. 24:44; 1 Thess. 5:2-3). The signs of the end times are "signs of the times for all times."[205] What I mean is that the Christian faith is an eschatological faith. It has a purpose and a hope and is moving toward completion and fulfillment. Whether that fulfillment is today or in another ten thousand years, how is God at work right now in the radical changes of the world to bring about his purposes: the fulfillment of the Great Commission and the growth of his kingdom? This is a question that can and should be asked for changes in one's individual life, in one's church, and definitely in our country.

d. Can I embrace, or at least accept, this change without compromising the gospel? If not, it needs to be resisted. Now, I am not asking whether change is compromising my style of doing church, my preference of music, my particular political party, my preferred economics, or my most comfortable cultural mores and habits. It may be painful when these are challenged by change, but they are not the gospel. I may legitimately choose to resist changes to these, but they are not the gospel. Missiologically, the church must learn to separate challenges to preferences, cultural styles, and traditions – as good as these may be – from the challenges to the gospel. If we don't, we are focusing on defending the cultural package rather than the unchanging and life-changing message. That is, for example, we may find ourselves arguing for a white, Republican, middle-class capitalist Jesus (or a hippie, liberal, pacifist, socialistic Jesus) in defense of our particular upbringing, culture, and ideology rather than the God-man who judges all persons and all cultures and calls all to repentance and faith in him.

Change is rarely comfortable. Our Sovereign God, however, rules over both the changeless and the changing. While we may need to confront and resist unbiblical change, I am convinced that more often than not God is waiting for us to seize the moment, "making the most of the time" (Col. 4:5b), to reach ever-changing America for Christ.

Looking for "America": Multicultural and Demographic Changes

Because He loved your fathers, He chose their descendants after them and brought you out of Egypt by His presence and great power, to drive out before you nations greater and stronger than you and to bring you in and give you their land as an inheritance, as is not taking place....The Lord has chosen you to be His special people out of all the peoples on the face of the earth.

Deut. 4:37-38; 14:2b

But you are a chosen race, a royal priesthood, a holy nation, a people for His possession, so that you may proclaim the praises of the One who called you out of darkness into His marvelous light. Once you were not a people, but now you are God's people.

1 Peter 2:9-10a

And they sang a new song: "You are worthy to take the scroll and to open its seals; because You were slaughtered,

and You redeemed people for God by Your blood from
every tribe and language and people and nation. You made
them a kingdom and priests to our God, and they will reign
on the earth."

Rev. 5:9-10

These passages trace the concept of God's "chosen" people
throughout Scripture. The Deuteronomy verses are clear
that Israel was God's elect nation. Because God loved "your
fathers," that is, Abraham, Isaac, and Jacob, he chose their many
descendants as his own, led them out of Egypt, and was in the
process of taking them to the land of promise that was to be
their inheritance. The Israelites were chosen out of all the peoples
of the world, not because of anything inherently special about
them, but because of God's own love, grace, and mercy. This was
both a privilege and a responsibility, and a never to be repeated
divine action. That is, no other single nation, whether defined as
an ethnic people, a particular geography, or a geo-political entity
could ever be God's elect.

Although no other nation will ever supplant Israel as God's
elect, Paul explains in Rom. 9-11 how Israel has rejected the
gospel of Jesus Christ. This did not mean, however, that God has
totally rejected Israel (Rom. 11:1-4). It means, rather, that election
now refers to and includes those who have believed in and have
experienced salvation in the Lord Jesus Christ. Those who are now
in and of Christ are the chosen ones, regardless of race, ethnicity,
origin, or residence. Therefore, Peter can call Christian believers
a "chosen race, a royal priesthood, a holy nation, a people for His
possession." The common ground of their election is acceptance of
God's grace by faith in the person and work of Jesus Christ.

Finally, the future reality described in Rev. 5 actually pictures
the ever growing present reality: Jesus Christ died for people of
"every tribe and language and people and nation." The chosen are

not only those believers in Jesus, but they represent *every* type of person. This is not simply a missiological theory or a multicultural ideal. It is, rather, a theological assertion and a Biblical promise. The gospel is for all peoples, people from all possible groups will respond, and *these* are God's chosen people.

What has this to do with an American missiology? For one, it means that the gospel has never been, can never be, and should never become ethno or culturally centric. It does not represent nor belong to any one people. It also means that no nation can ever claim favored status with God. Certainly, God can bless nations and use them in any number of ways for any period of time. But that same God can bring judgment, remove his hand of blessing, or even allow wickedness to prevail for a time for his ultimate purposes. He causes nations and empires to rise and fall; he can bless nations that honor him, but he can also use wicked nations to bring judgment. A careful examination of world history and all the economic, political, and military ups and downs ought to give us pause before we make declarations about God's intents and purposes with nations. Furthermore, it means that how we view America, both its origins and its current reality, must be driven by a multicultural and missiological worldview. We are one nation from many (*e pluribus unum*) and continue to draw the many to our shores. Finally, these passages help us see that our most important human relationship, after that with the Lord himself, is the eternal one to the family of God – his chosen people, royal priesthood, and holy nation.

The Meaning of Nation: America and Americans

This land is your land, this land is my land, from California to the New York island.

Woody Guthrie

Give me your tired, your poor, your huddled masses yearning to breathe free.

Emma Lazarus

We hold these truths to be self-evident, that all men are created equal, that they are endowed by their Creator with certain unalienable rights, that among these are life, liberty and the pursuit of happiness.

The Declaration of Independence

How should a "nation" be defined? The above three quotes, all familiar to most Americans, reflect three different understandings of what it means to be a nation. Although not mutually exclusive and with some overlap, they do reflect different emphases in describing a nation or a country, and to a certain degree reflect different understandings of patriotism. First, there is the understanding of nation as a place. This is perhaps the most common and foundational view among most peoples throughout history. The children of Israel left Egypt to go to the "promised land," an actual place that God had set aside for them. Explorers throughout history, especially in the New World of the Americas, immediately claimed the land where they landed for King or Queen. Innumerable wars have been fought to either defend or acquire land. Our own American history is one of land conquest. We bought Manhattan island from the Native Americans, we constantly conquered (or civilized, as was claimed) the western frontiers as we took land from the natives and pushed further west. We added land through the Louisiana Purchase, the Gadsden Purchase, and the Alaska purchase. We now are a nation of fifty states and several territories and the commonwealth of Puerto Rico. We have borders. We have entry points. We have a land that "belongs to you and me."

A second understanding of what it means to be a nation is to talk in terms of a people. The land may be important to a nation (or a tribe, clan, or family), but blood, ethnic, and racial ties run the deepest. For the people of Israel, the promise of a place went hand in hand with a covenant as God's people that transcended the land. Even in exile and when scattered, they were still God's chosen ones. Throughout history, being a Jew implied a connection with other Jews regardless of nationality and location. The "nation" was a people. Positively, throughout history the emphases on being a "people" has been what has drawn some nations together in crisis, as it did most famously with the British during World War II's air war known as the Battle of Britain. It has, unfortunately, also led to arrogance, hatred, and even ethnic cleansing as it did with the Turks against the Armenians, the Nazis against multiple groups, and the Serbs against the Croatians.[206] As Americans, we see ourselves as a people, too. Although we have struggled, and still do, in fully agreeing on what it means to be an American, we are a people. An interesting (perhaps unique) characteristic about being an American as compared to being from another nation is that anyone can become an American. That is, if someone becomes a citizen of Germany, Indonesia, or Kenya, he is called a "citizen" of that particular country. It is only after a few generations that his descendants are referred to as Germans, Indonesians, or Kenyans. When a person takes the oath to become an American citizen, he is immediately an "American."

A third understanding of nation is that it is held together by a set of ideas and ideals. The nation of Israel was a people, given a land, but also held together by their unique understanding of God and their relationship to that One God. Specifically, his law was their founding and guiding idea. Historically, as with the concept of a people, this has been both positive and negative. Some great ideas have led to freedom from tyranny, compassion for the needy, liberation for the enslaved. Think of the ideas that motivated William Wallace, the *Magna Carta*, Francis of Assisi, and William Wilberforce. Other ideas are chock full of evil and lead to violence, persecution, and suffering. Think of what drove Machiavelli, Hitler, Stalin, and Pol Pot. America's founding documents reflect the ideas that hold us together. Although we have imperfectly applied these, we are a nation of ideas and ideals. That is, regardless of the land, which has significantly increased since 1776, and regardless of the people, which in 1776 referred primarily to white, male landowners, we are a nation held together by ideals. We certainly argue, debate, disagree, vote, and go all the way to the Supreme Court in trying to interpret and apply those ideals, but we all point back to the same ideals expressed in those documents.

All three of these understandings of nation, and their resulting implications for defining patriotism, are intertwined in our American history and our American psyche. This is missiologically important. For one, if America is a mission field, the first task of a missionary is to understand his field. Assumptions, presuppositions, biases, and superficial understandings must all be challenged and replaced with a deep understanding of the world view of the people being reached. This also implies that the missionary must learn to love the culture and the people he is serving, while at the same time scripturally challenging the culture as needed. Secondly, the missionary must understand how a nation sees and understands itself, for there is a natural human tendency to think in terms of "us against them." Because all three understandings of nation are part of who we are as Americans, and because we are a nation of multiple peoples (see below), we live with an inclusive/exclusive tension. That is, how one defines "nation" and where one falls on the inclusive-exclusive spectrum (us vs. them; real Americans or not) will determine his missiological approach to our complex and diverse society.

What are, therefore, some of the issues that need to be considered in understanding America? What are a few of the missiologically important historical and current issues that shape who we are?

Who was First? Immigration and people movements

From time immemorial peoples have moved from place to place. At times they settled peacefully, at others they conquered militarily, either displacing or annihilating the existing inhabitants. Land was bought, traded for, or outright stolen. Sometimes the new group simply assimilated into the existing peoples, at others they remained separate. Usually, the vanquished and other minorities suffered persecution, lived in ghettoes, became servants or slaves, and rarely moved above second class citizenship. In one sense, this is what world history is all about: the movements of people through conquest, occupation, slavery, displacement by disaster and famine; that is, migration by choice or by force. And then, history is written by the victors,[207] or at least by the survivors.

This movement is evident throughout Scripture. Adam and Eve were banished from the Garden of Eden. Cain wandered, God scattered the people after the Tower of Babel, and Abraham migrated. Jacob and his sons moved to Egypt and four hundred years later Moses led the exodus to the Promised Land. By God's command the Canaanite nations were displaced. Both David and Solomon expanded the kingdom. Later on, God used the Assyrians and the Babylonians to disperse and exile his own people. The Persians, the Greeks, and the Romans all conquered, moved peoples, and changed the face of nations. One of the Apostle Paul's earliest missionary strategies was to first visit the synagogues of the Jews of the Diaspora. Whatever the world – nations, countries, empires, tribes, kingdoms, and peoples – may have looked like at any particular time in history, it has historically proven to be transitory and ever-changing.

The present global reality is no different. Although "only" 3% of the current "world's population has migrated across international borders," that still represents about 214 million people. If these "international migrants were counted as one nation," it would be the fifth largest. Moreover, about "one-in-five international migrants alive today" live in the United States.[208] Our American history is one of migration and immigration. Our "land" has seen the original inhabitants crossing over from what is present day Russia to Alaska and moving across the Americas. Our shores have seen the likes of Viking explorers, Spanish Conquistadors, French and British explorers and traders. The original thirteen colonies were settled by Puritans, merchants, wealth seekers, and those seeking freedom of religion or the freedom to pursue life and happiness (often just seeking a second chance). Those migration movements also involved the forced resettlement and even extermination of Native Americans, and the forced immigration of African slaves. As immigration exploded in the nineteenth and early twentieth centuries, hundreds of thousands of immigrants, mostly from Europe, arrived through Ellis Island and Galveston. Thousands more came from Asia, and particularly China, through San Francisco to work on the railroads. As mentioned earlier, the influx of thousands from Ireland, Italy, Poland, and other European countries in the nineteenth century changed the predominantly Protestant face of America. Some cities and states even became majority Roman Catholic. The great immigrations of the middle and late twentieth century continued to add that Roman Catholic influence from Mexico and other Latin American countries, and greatly increased the number and the influence of Islam, Hinduism, and Buddhism as more people arrived from Asia and Middle Eastern countries.[209]

So, who was first? Who does the country belong to? Who are the true Americans? Who are we, really? Consider that:

- We are a nation of immigrants. With the exception of Native Americans, who still "came here" millennia ago, we are all immigrants. Our fathers, grandfathers, and distant forefathers came to these shores for a variety of reasons, some noble and some more mundane. Our national soul is an immigrant one.

- We are an American culture consisting of multiple cultures. That is, we are a mosaic of cultures that are all part of the American culture. Can American culture even be specifically defined or described? Is there a typical American? Perhaps so; however, the reality is that American culture has regional flavors — New England Yankee, Midwestern farmer, Deep South, Texan, Pacific Northwest, Californian – and each region could be broken down even further. There are racial and ethnic elements in American culture, each with a multiplicity of sub-cultures: Native American, African-American, Asian-American, Irish, Italian, German, Scandinavian, Cajun, Hispanic, Lebanese, and Anglo-Saxon among others. There is the Cowboy/Western culture; there is Mormon culture; there is the maritime culture of various coasts, the rugged individualism of the Northwest, the urban culture of multiple cities, and more sub-cultures than can be listed here. Some argue that looking at America this way (to be hyphenated Americans) only serves to divide, segregate, and create resentment. This is a danger, but it is the reality of where we came from and who we are. People also want to remember their heritage and ensure they continue to have a voice in such a diverse culture. To a degree we have melted into the pot of a broad American culture, which makes us alike as Americans. The greater reality is that we have differences, some of which are significant, that identify us as part of the greater American Mosaic.

- Multicultural America can and should be celebrated. To be clear, a philosophical multiculturalism that claims no absolutes but rather moral and ethical equivalency for all cultures is not what I am proposing.[210] Scripture should judge all cultures and all elements of a culture. Cultural practices and beliefs such as polygamy, female circumcision, honor killings, racism, and wars of choice cannot stand the scrutiny of Scripture. What should be celebrated is that this nation was founded and settled by people from all over the world and all walks of life. In the present day God continues to bring the world to us. Of course, this is not without difficulties, controversies, and a multiplicity of problems. But the American mosaic is our history, our present reality, and undoubtedly, a future fact.

With our immigrant soul and our unique American multicultural reality, what does it mean missiologically? All the related political, civil rights, immigration, and social justice issues cannot be addressed or much less resolved here, as important as they may be. Suffice it to point out:

1. Missiologically, we must learn to "see" America as diverse. That means the missions task is more complicated and difficult than many assume. One missiological "size" and strategy does not fit all. A blanket geographic approach may miss a lot of people. This missiological challenge relates to the controversial homogeneous principle.[211] On the one hand, our multicultural and diverse society begs

for multicultural and diverse churches and ministries. We want to overcome the infamous "most segregated hour of the week," as Martin Luther King, Jr. called it. At the same time, to not see and directly address the multiplicity of groups – languages, colors, cultures, socioeconomic levels – inevitably means that someone will be overlooked and missed with the gospel. Churches and Christian institutions and organizations often say "all are welcome here," or "all have a seat at the table." What they don't realize is that the first statement implies "come and be a part of us as long as you are like us," and the second overlooks that a dominant culture still owns the table and sets the agenda. Certainly, we are doing better than we were even a few decades ago, but we still struggle with our diversity. Missiologically, the challenge is to hold the tension between the homogeneous principle as a beginning strategy and Biblical multiculturalism and equality as the intentional and desired result.

2. Missiologically, our diverse nation with its multiplicity of religions, cultures, and worldviews, means that we must be ready to explain why the Biblical narrative is the one and only meta-narrative. The great advantage of a free society where one can believe and practice whatever he chooses also means that he is free to reject whatever he chooses. We don't coerce, we don't deport for unbelief, and we don't gain converts simply through familial, racial, ethnic, or national ties. Neither coercion nor biology is an effective long term evangelistic strategy. In the current American pluralistic context we must be ready to persuade by telling the loving truth and by living the truth in love, fully expecting some to reject our message simply because they believe it is "one way out of many, and it is not my way."

3. Missiologically, the nations have come to us, so that should help us to fulfill the commandment to take the gospel to all the nations. That is, with thousands of international university students and millions of immigrants with connections back home, often in countries closed to the gospel, to reach them with the gospel of Jesus Christ only increases the chances of the gospel reaching around the world. This does not, of course, replace global missions, but can be a complement and asset to global missions. The first contact with the "ends of the earth" may be next door.

4. Missiologically, we need to rejoice at the Christian influence from many immigrants. The center of world Christianity has shifted to the Southern hemisphere; that is, the typical Christian today is probably Brazilian or African, Black and poor. The future of Christianity actually will be that brand rising out of Africa and Asia. Consequently, many immigrants coming to our shores are bringing with them different ways to read the Bible and do theology, new and different expressions of church, a deeper understanding of Christian community and community transformation, and often passionate commitments to Christ quite unlike the typical American Christian.[212]

So, what holds us together? To some degree it is the land we occupy. It is also our identity as an American people, nebulous, controversial, and confusing as it may sometimes be. More than anything, it is a set of ideals as expressed in our founding documents – life, liberty, freedom, the pursuit of the good life. Yes, we debate these, argue over these, and go to court over what they mean and how to apply them. Yes, they have been imperfectly and unevenly applied throughout history – we are still working on that. Yes, there are those who seek to upend and even destroy them. In the end, although few Americans and perhaps even fewer immigrants could accurately quote much of our founding documents, the American mythology (in the most positive sense) permeates the world to such a degree that millions have come here precisely because of those ideals, and millions more want to.

This is part of our American missiological challenge. We moved here, we are still moving here, and we continue to move even within our land. Transition, change, diversity, multicultural – that is who we are and that is who needs to be reached with the gospel of Jesus Christ.

What are we?
A nation of Christians or a
Christian nation?

In God We Trust

Motto of the United States

... one nation, under God ...

From the Pledge of Allegiance

An ongoing debate in American life, and one that has grown in intensity over the last forty years, is whether the United States was founded as, and continues to be, a Christian nation. At one end of the debate spectrum are those who argue that we were founded by mostly Christian men with the purpose of being a Christian nation. They place great emphasis on the statements of America's Founders and on the "traditional legal sanction granted Christianity in America." Their conclusion is, as Francis Schaeffer put it, that the United States was formed by a "Christian consensus" that gave us our "form and freedom in society and government." The problem, of course, is that the consensus has been lost and our "Christian-based system established by the Constitution" is being abused. The only solution is to return America to her traditional Christian foundation."[213]

One of the leading contemporary spokesmen for this view is David Barton of Wallbuilders. According to its website, Wallbuilders' goal is to "exert a direct and positive influence in government, education, and the family by (1) educating the nation concerning the Godly foundation of our country; (2) providing information to federal, state, and local officials as they develop public policies which reflect Biblical values; and (3) encouraging Christians to be involved in the civic arena." [214] By examining the writings of our founders and the documents of our founding, Barton and others argue that America was founded on Godly and Biblical principles, and more specifically, Christian principles.[215] Similarly, Pastor Robert Jeffress of the First Baptist Church of Dallas, argues that America's founders "did not hesitate to declare that America was a Christian nation," and that the "government can…show a preference for the Christian faith."[216]

At the other end of the spectrum are those who either deny or downplay the role Christianity played in America's founding and history. At best, some may acknowledge the religiosity (usually deism) of the founders, but insist that they "established a religiously neutral nation." These who deny the "Christian Nation Myth" also appeal to the Founders' writings and founding documents, particularly those of known deists and skeptics such as Thomas Paine and Thomas Jefferson.[217] Some argue that we were founded not as a Christian nation which was later corrupted by liberals and humanists. To the contrary, the founding Fathers, and specifically the writers of the Constitution, wanted a "godless document" and set up the United States as a "formally secular institution." It is fundamentalist Christians, they argue, who have latched on to a minority of quotes, a few writings from a few founders, and a vaguely defined Christianity to promote a doctrinal and political agenda.[218]

The truth is somewhere in the middle of the spectrum, although trying to hold a middle ground in no way lightens the debate. There are those Christian scholars who acknowledge the religiosity and even Christianity of many of the founding Fathers, but argue that these were not concerned with setting up a Christian nation but rather one built on clear separation of church and state. Coming from a background of oppressive European state churches, the Founders wanted a country not devoid of religion, but with clear religious freedom for all religions.[219] Historian John Fea notes that the religious references in the words of the Founders are misunderstood and misinterpreted by both evangelicals and the "secular left." The Christian Right runs "roughshod over the historical record" by "selectively choosing texts" from the Founders' writings without considering the historical context. At the same time, secularists "simply have no idea what to make of those same quotations," because they do not understand how faith can be important in any person's life.[220]

Other Christian scholars agree that America was founded by Christians … *and* also by "deists and others who embraced virtue and biblical morality." Ours is therefore "not originally a 'Christian' nation, but one in which the Founders certainly understood the importance of Christian morality and "the necessity of acknowledging God's supreme authority."[221] How that morality and humility before God played out, however, may be the real evidence of whether or not we are a Christian nation. Richard Hughes points out that the United States definitely "abounds in Christian trappings" but has historically and abundantly rejected "the values of Jesus" and thus loses all right to be called a Christian nation.[222] Richard Land agrees when he says that although "America was not founded as a Christian nation, it was certainly founded by people who were operating out of a Judeo-Christian worldview."[223]

Noted church historians Mark Noll, George Marsden, and Nathan Hatch offer perhaps the most non-political and balanced

TERRY COY

view. They argue that America has not been and is not presently a "uniquely, distinctly or even predominantly Christian" nation, *if* one means a "state of society reflecting the ideals presented in Scripture." This does not mean, however, that Christian values were absent from the founding of the country or from the nation's history. Christian principles, values, goals, and aspirations have been an integral part of the settling, founding, and growth of America. These positive Christian aspects must be recognized, for they make, these scholars argue, the United States "a singularly *religious* country." Thus, the two narrative extremes to be avoided are an idealized Christian past on the one hand and a tale of pure sinfulness, oppression, and exploitation on the other.[224] These extreme errors, according to Noll, are committed by both secularists and "Christian traditionalists" because neither makes a careful study of the past. The secularists pick out "bare phrases" from the founding documents, from the Constitution, and from later court decisions to make their case. The Christian traditionalists pick out "bold assertions" from the founders as proof of their Christianity and of God's providential action in the establishment of America. Both take quotations from earlier generations and use them to prove their respective points "without context, without evaluation, without understanding."[225] The historical truth, therefore, is little more complex than either side is willing to admit.

So, is America Christian or not? As Noll rightly puts it, the answer is both "yes and no." He rejects the "strong view" of Christian America which claims America as God's chosen nation, a "new Israel," and a nation specially ordained and thus "in some sense an extension of the history of salvation." Certainly, that may have been the view of some of the early settlers, especially the Puritans, but it was not necessarily the predominant view and much less is it a desirable view. Taken to its logical conclusion, this view leads to the establishment of a civil religion and conflates national patriotism with "American Christian patriotism." To the contrary, Noll argues, only Israel has even been and will ever be God's chosen nation, and, the dangers of conflating religion with patriotism have been evident throughout history. He notes that many other countries – South Africa, Russia, Poland, Germany – have claimed a special relationship with God; claims that now seem overreaching if not absurd. Furthermore, our own mixed American history of both good and evil should give us pause to claim too much in the name of God.[226]

Noll is far more comfortable with a "weak version" of Christian America, which he also believes best reflects the historical record. By "weak" he means that we cannot claim any "messianic" or special "salvation history" role. We can, however, argue that many of our political and social structures and institutions come closer to Biblical principles than those of other nations. On many occasions we have, as a nation, practiced well those principles, for we have pressed for (albeit imperfectly) the dignity and freedom of human beings. We have taken part in the liberation of many nations from the grips of tyranny. We have been a nation quick to respond compassionately to disaster, famine, and have certainly led the way in the global missionary movement. Overall, we are a generous and giving people. In this broad sense, we were founded and have been a Christian nation.[227]

As historically accurate and positive as this assessment is, Noll again rightly cautions against claiming too much. Although as a nation we have been responsible for much good, we cannot escape responsibility for much evil in our history: Native American genocide, slavery, out of control materialism and consumerism, wars of choice, political corruption, and more. If we do have a generally religious and a specifically Christian foundation, we certainly have not always lived up to it. Furthermore, divergent interpretations of our history will come out of different theologies, worldviews, and experiences. For example, some religious groups that believe and practice pacifism may not see our involvement in World War II as necessarily righteous. Similarly, minority groups who have experienced oppression and marginalization may be far less willing to see America as very Christian.[228]

What can we conclude, then about the religiosity of America? Were we and are we a Christian nation? We need to answer by considering context, definition, and behavior:

First, we must first remember the Christendom context in which the founding of America took place. For centuries the average Westerner saw no major distinction between Christianity, the state, and society in general. As to the first, state churches were the norm. These had varying degrees of influence over the government and vice versa – the tension was palpable and often violent. Kings and Queens were "defenders of the faith," and minority expressions of faith were usually persecuted in both Protestant and Roman Catholic lands. This was the precisely the church-state relationships our forefathers were trying to avoid. As to society in general, the average Westerner believed and accepted it was "Christian," whether that individual was any kind of practicing believer or not. Thus, the Bible was at the center of much of education (at least in Protestant lands), the cathedral or church was at the center of cultural life, and there was a "right" way and a "wrong" way to do things. In fact, for most "Christian" Westerners, the conquest of pagan lands entailed no real distinction between civilizing, Christianizing, and military, political, and economic conquest. The settling and founding of America, however, challenged some of these Christendom assumptions to a significant degree as the Enlightenment had as much influence on the Founders as the Bible did.

We see, therefore, that both sides in the Christian America debate are correct to a degree. Our founding was the confluence of Biblical Christianity with both "state church" and Free Church flavors *and* Enlightenment ideals which questioned the authority of Scripture, the nature of God, the Deity of Christ, and elevated the autonomy of man. Both of these worldviews are found in the writings of our forefathers and in the founding documents.

Having said that, the context was still Christendom. The beginning of the end for Christendom was certainly in sight, but the average person, and especially the educated moralist, had no problem in quoting Scripture, referring to Deity, and appealing to the ethics of Jesus. That was just the way people were then, whether truly born again believers or not.[229]

Second, taking it a step further, and something that is not done often enough in the ongoing debate, is defining what each side means by "Christian." If America was and is a Christian nation, what does that mean? Does it mean that the majority of the Founders or the majority of the population were believers? Most church historians note that the general population at the time of the Revolutionary War was only about 5% church attenders, a percentage that changed significantly only after the Second Great Awakening. The general population, however, still operated under a general Christendom worldview. They would probably have claimed belief in God and may even have had some Biblical knowledge. Does that qualify them as Christian? Are we a Christian nation because some of the principles upon which we were founded are Christian? Are we a Christian nation because the Founders were a majority Christian, or at least Deists? It appears to me that the meaning of "Christian" in the debate is either left undefined or is assumed to be so broad so as to mean nothing.[230] For example, if all it takes to be a Christian nation is a broad cultural Christianity, identified by some Biblical values and principles, or for certain founders and leaders to refer to Deity and the Bible, then every European nation with a state church is a "Christian" nation. They certainly believed they were (and still are in some cases) – remember Christendom. And what does that mean for predominately Roman Catholic countries, including Latin American countries? They are not Protestant or of the Free Church tradition, as the majority of our Founders were, but they claim to be Christian, claim the authority of the Bible, believe in the Deity of Christ, and are guided by some

Christian principles. In fact, it could be argued that some of the Roman Catholic countries were more Christian than many of our Deistic Founders who quoted an emasculated Bible and believed in a purely moralistic gospel.[231]

Third, taking the argument even a step further, what is the relationship between Christian claims and Christian behavior? As evangelicals we often argue that an individual's claim to be a Christian needs to eventually give evidence or show fruit. We know that sanctification is a life-long journey, but that there should be some evidence of growth and progress. Does that apply nationally? Does our national fruit give evidence that we are a Christian nation? Of course, as mentioned above, our history is a mixed bag. Furthermore, that is precisely the argument from the Christian Nation perspective: We don't give evidence anymore and we need to get back to what we were. Our growing crime rates, the disintegration of marriages and families, abortion, pornography, and so forth give evidence that we need to return to what we were. The mixed bag of history, however, reminds us of racism and slavery, genocide and wars of choice, abuse of children in the marketplace, and the absence of civil rights for numerous groups. It is true that many of the activists who attacked those social ills were Christian and were driven by Biblical truth – something the secularists conveniently overlook in their version of history. As discussed previously: Are we getting better or worse? Are we becoming less Christian, or in some senses, more Christian? Perhaps part of the answer lies in our definition of Christianity and Christian action, and that only increases the debate. In the end, Mark Noll is correct in his assessment – yes, we are a Christian nation is some respects; no, we are not in others. Without a doubt, we have been and continue to be a *religious* country.[232]

Given these observations about the religiosity of American, what are some missiological issues affected by our conclusions?

Does it matter missiologically whether or not one views America as a Christian nation? Five observations:

1. If America is a Christian nation, then it is not a mission field. Conversely, we will only see and treat America as a mission field if we don't see it as a Christian nation. Now, some would argue that is precisely the point: America is a mission field and we need to evangelize individuals and change structures through lobby and vote to return to what we once were. That is, being a Christian nation does not mean that every single person is a believer. Evangelism is still a high priority, but the results of conversion are not only eternal life but also another step in returning the country to its golden past. My counter argument is twofold: One, unless we see America as a mission field we will assume that our evangelism strategies and our "churchiness" of the last two hundred years will do the job of reaching our ever growing lost population. Two, regardless of one's conclusions about the Christian Nation debate and regardless of the civil and political implications of those conclusions, the gospel of Jesus Christ is *not* about returning any nation back to what it was or might have been. Making the gospel primarily about a national return to an idealized past is using the message of Christ for a temporal state of affairs, which is something other than evangelization. It reduces the gospel to politics and propaganda, and our role to simply that of polemicists instead of missionaries. It reduces our purpose from membership in the Kingdom of God and living as disciples of Jesus to membership in the city of man and being good moral citizens.[233] This may not be bad, but it is not enough.

2. That means if we focus too much on the "gospel" of a Christian Nation we are in danger of diluting the Biblical

gospel and what it means to live like Jesus. Unfortunately, the call for a "Christian Nation" has historically led to the establishment of a state church and/or civil religion.[234] A civil religion can do no other than create the appearance of a diluted Christianity. It may lead to and even enforce a superficial morality and ethic, but it is not the gospel. Civil religion may make life easier and more comfortable for those who agree with that version of religion (Protestant? Roman Catholic? Free Church tradition? Mormon?), but overtly or covertly coerces others to follow what they do not believe. This is not the gospel. This danger of favoritism, especially if initiated or upheld by the government, is the context of Jefferson's letter to the Danbury Baptists in which he famously argued for a "wall of separation" between church and state.[235] As a matter of fact, Baptists have long opposed any favoritism by government toward any religion, for whose version will be favored?[236] Again, to argue for a bland and generic version of "Christian principles," cultural Christianity at its lowest common denominator, is not ultimately helpful or healthy, and is not the gospel. [237] An example is the controversial topic of school prayer. Some argue that taking prayer out of schools is what led to the demise of our educational system, academically and morally. Whether the removal of prayer and the demise of our schools was a causal or correlational relationship is debatable. The greater question is what good would it do to have a generic prayer that many, if not most, in the classroom ignore or did not believe? What ultimate theological or missiological purpose would there be in coercing anyone to listen to a generic prayer? A generic gospel leads to cultural Christianity, and cultural Christianity leads to a bored, uncommitted, comfortable post-Christian society. See Western Europe.

3. If the content of the gospel is not recognizing that we are a Christian nation or that we should return to being a Christian nation, what is it then? Entire books have been written to define and explain the gospel. Suffice it to quote what the Apostle Paul says in 1 Cor. 15:3-8 about the gospel he proclaimed: "For I passed on to you as most important what I also received: that Christ died for our sins according to the Scriptures, that He was buried, that He was raised on the third day according to the Scriptures, and that He appeared to Cephas, then to the Twelve…to over 500 brothers…to James…to all the apostles…He also appeared to me." Briefly, and quite incompletely:

- "Christ died for sins." Jesus the Messiah went to the cross for the sins of mankind and for the sins of every person. Implied is that no one else did or could pay the price for sins. Implied also is that this Messiah was the one the Jewish people were looking for (Rom. 5:8; 1 John 1:7; 2:2).

- "According to the Scriptures." Christ's death for sins was the fulfillment of all the Scriptures, thus they all point to him and to his work on the cross. What happened was no accident, but the plan of God in and for history (Luke 24:27).

- "Buried…raised…according to the Scriptures." This Christ was a real man who could die, he was dead for three days, and then was raised on the third day. Thus, he conquered sin and death and lives today. Again, it was according to God's plan and purpose for Israel, the nations, and individuals (Acts 1:3).

- "He appeared...to me." The witnesses to this Christ who died and rose again are numerous and varied. The reality of his person and work led to the radical transformation of millions of lives, including that of the Apostle Paul, a former persecutor of Christ followers (Acts 9:1-25).

The gospel, therefore, is that Jesus Christ died for our sins. We may talk of our salvation, redemption, forgiveness, reconciliation, adoption, justification, eternal life, and new birth. We may speak of Christ as Savior, Lord, Mediator, Healer, Son of God, or Son of Man. Every one of these terms (and many others) is rich in meaning, but every one of them has at its core the idea that Jesus Christ did something for us that we could not do for ourselves: he died for our sins. All the Old Testament, and the entire life of Jesus, including his teaching, preaching, and healing, point to his sacrifice on the cross. All that was written in the New Testament after the cross and all that the church is and represents are because of the cross. That is, what we say and do as disciples of Christ is either the evidence or the fruit of that action on the cross. We have certainly been saved for good works; the fruit of the Spirit in our lives is love, joy, peace, and so on; we are being sanctified daily because we have already been sanctified by Christ. We love each other, treat each other well, pray for each other, live in peace with each other, care for widows and orphans, care for the poor, feed the hungry, stand up for justice and the disenfranchised *not* because these actions are the gospel, but because they are the *evidence and the fruit* of the gospel. A transformed life, family, community, society, or nation is not the gospel, but the fruit of the gospel. Transformation happens only because the gospel has been preached, believed, and then does its transforming work in both individuals and in society. Legislation, laws, and congressional bills, as good as important and they may be, are not the gospel and will not lead sinners to repentance. Laws can hold back the unrighteous...to a degree. Laws can guide us in good living...to a point. Laws, however, never preached the gospel or transformed a life.

I understand that some will accuse me of being reductionist by describing the gospel as such. I would rather say I am an essentialist. I, too, often speak of the "whole gospel" or of a "holistic gospel" that emphasizes social action and social justice (and the "Christian Nation gospel," by the way, is definitely one of social action). A clear distinction must be made, however, between the core or essence of the gospel – Christ dying for sins – and the results of believing in and being transformed by Christ; between the core of the gospel and the results of the gospel. Fighting against poverty is definitely the Christian thing to do. Fighting against injustice and oppression is definitely the Christian thing to do. Standing up for peace and against violence is definitely the Christian thing to do. They are not, however, the essence of the gospel; they are the fruit of lives transformed by the gospel. Yes, the gospel of forgiveness of sins without the evidence of good works is incomplete, ignores too much of Scripture, and has been the bane of too many evangelicals for too long. But social action and social justice without the gospel of the forgiveness of sins is simply temporal good works that lead to eternal perdition. Similarly, lobbying for and working to return America to a Christian nation may be comforting socially and culturally, but missiologically it is not the gospel and is not ultimately what will transform individuals and our nation.

4. Missiologically, to argue that America is or should be a Christian nation compounds the challenge of reaching immigrants with the gospel. First, for those coming as Christians already or from countries with a "Christian"

background, there is the possibility of being sorely disappointed in American Christianity or our claims to be Christian. At the same time we are arguing that we are a Christian nation, we give little evidence of it. Second, for those arriving from non- and even anti-Christian backgrounds and countries, our claim to be a Christian nation only confirms their misconceptions of Christianity. We claim we are Christian, but our lifestyle is full of divorce, drug abuse, violence, and immorality. As one converted Muslim immigrant tells it, her father feared for her life in America because he did not want her to become like those other Christian women, "like Madonna." Either way, to claim to be Christian in such a culturally generic way is missiologically unhelpful – it does not help our evangelistic task.[238]

5. Finally, to argue that America is or should be a Christian nation is unconvincing to a radically unchurched postmodern generation. Why would they want a gospel that simply gives them more of what we already are? If they are aware of our historical ambiguities – genocide, slavery, racism, injustices, wars of choice – why would they want to follow Jesus if that is the fruit? The gospel, of course, is not our history. The gospel is Christ dying for sins and transforming lives. The unchurched generation (and immigrants, for that matter) is not interested in going back to anything. That is not what will call them to repentance and belief. A crucified Messiah, fulfilling God's plan for the ages, dying for their sins – that is the message we must somehow communicate.

So, are we a Christian nation, a secular nation, or a pluralist nation? The answer is "yes," depending on what one means by the question and how one defines the answer. Our nation and our history is far too complex to give a simply yes or no answer. The present reality, however, is that we are becoming far more secular and far more pluralistic. The message of the gospel, of the one and only crucified Christ, is seen more and more as intolerant and narrow minded. Missiologically, what our country needs is a forward looking gospel. Looking back at what God has done in our past is a good thing. Israel was often called to remember what God had done, to reflect on and stand on his faithfulness. America needs to do the same. We can look back at his guiding hand, his blessings, and his protection and be thankful. The gospel, however, is about what God is going to do. Looking back is Biblically healthy, but looking forward is Biblically mandated. We look back at Eden with sorrow for what was lost. We look forward to New Jerusalem with anticipation for what we will gain. That is, our hope is in his promises for the future, individually and as a community of believers. Our hope is for better things to come, in this life and the next. Our hope is not in a return to what was, but in movement toward what God is going to do. Whether that means America will once again be what it was like or will grow into something completely new and different, God is faithful.

What is happening to us? This is not your father's America

Change is the only constant.

Heraclitus

The only constant is change, continuing change, inevitable change. That is the dominant factor in society today. No sensible decision can be made any longer without taking into account not only the world as it is, but the world as it will be.

Isaac Asimov

America is changing culturally and demographically. Of course, that has always been the case; however, as discussed earlier, changes are more and more numerous, discontinuous, rapid, and disconcerting. Some of our cultural changes regarding immigration have already been discussed. Other cultural changes will be addressed in the next two chapters. In this section I want to point out just three demographic changes (out of many) that impact the development of an American missiology.

Life in the Big City: Urbanization

As we consider the missiological challenges in America, one of the critical strategic issues is the rapid and continued urbanization of our nation.[239] We were once a rural and small town nation with rural and small town values. Neither rural and small town America nor those values have completely disappeared, but it is the city that leads the country. It is the city where most of the people live, where the centers of business and government reside, where the leading edge of art, music, entertainment, fashion, and sports is found. The reality is that the cities have the jobs, make the majority of the decisions, and strongly influence if not actually determine the direction of the country.

This urbanization trend is not something new (and is certainly not confined to the United States). In 1790, ninety-five percent of the American population was rural. The remaining five percent lived mostly in villages, with our largest cities having only fifteen thousand or more in population. A century later the industrial revolution contributed to the growth of American cities, and thirty-five percent of the population was urban, mostly in northern cities. It was in 1920 that the number of urban dwellers passed that of the rural population. In the last forty years, cities have continued to grow and now eighty-three percent of Americans live in metro areas – cities and suburbs. At the same time, the fastest growth has been in southern and western cities while many northern cities have actually declined.[240]

The dynamics of urbanization are far too numerous and complex to be fully discussed here. Suffice it to say that:

One, the American trend toward urbanization will continue (albeit it at a slower pace for now).[241] Family farms are no longer the norm as corporate farming grows. Jobs are scarce in rural areas and small towns, so these areas continue to experience a youth drain as kids go off to college and don't return, and a brain drain as those with competitive skills and education move to the cities for a better choice of jobs.

Two, urban areas will continue to grow particularly in the South and the West, and especially due to immigration and internal population shifts.[242] The 1990s saw the "largest numerical increase in immigrants this country has ever experienced." The first decade of the twenty-first century saw a slowdown in immigrant growth, but "the number of immigrants living in the 100 largest metropolitan areas increased 27 percent," with twenty-one of these gaining at least 100,000 new immigrants. Furthermore, contrary to nineteenth and early twentieth century immigration, immigrants are no longer settling in core or inner city neighborhoods. Instead, they are settling directly in the suburbs where there are usually better schools, affordable housing, and a lower crime rate. The result is that the suburbs are now as or more diverse than most central city areas.[243]

Three, an obvious effect of increased immigration and population shifts is a change in the racial and ethnic makeup of metro areas. Hispanics are now the largest minority group in major American cities. Furthermore, "over half of America's cities are now majority non-white," and even suburbs are at least thirty-five percent non-white. Some major metro areas like Houston, San Francisco, and Washington, D.C. are majority minority even in the suburbs. Is there still "white flight"? Yes, the fast growing "exurban areas" are still mostly white and depend on whites for growth. Interestingly, "black flight" has also accelerated as African-American move up the socio-economic ladder and move out of the cities to suburbs. Overall, cities and suburbs are more and more diverse and integrated.[244]

Finally, why should the urbanization of America be of missiological concern? Consider the following:

1. The majority of the population lives in the urban areas, and, consequently, the greatest percentage of lostness is in those cities. The influence of world religions, postmodern worldviews, and a growing secularism only add to the breadth and depth of that lostness. Additionally, in some cities up to fifty percent or more of the population lives in multihousing settings, the great majority of whom are unchurched. This fact is why some organizations, such as the North American Mission Board of the Southern Baptist Convention, are investing most of its personnel and resources in the large cities.[245] Missiologically, the priority should be where the people are.

2. The majority of immigrants arrive in and stay in the cities and suburbs. As stated above, the diversity in ethnicity, race, culture in the metro areas mean these are rich mission fields. At the same time, a missiological challenge is an increase in, and acceptance of, religious pluralism. Those who proclaim the exclusivity of Jesus Christ are seen as intolerant and hateful. This diversity and pluralism means that developing an American missiology for the cities entails multiple approaches and strategies for communicating the uniqueness of Christ. No assumptions can be made about worldview, Bible knowledge, or even a basic understanding of Christianity.

3. The centers of power of business, education, entertainment, and both high and popular culture are in the cities. From

these there is a "trickle down effect" to the exurbs, the small towns, and rural America. Missiologically, the challenge is to counteract the sometimes overwhelming influence of these with Biblical truth. In effect, to reach the city is to reach the country.[246]

4. The cores of the cities are being revitalized. This process, called gentrification, means that new people, new opportunities, new businesses, and new housing are springing up in areas that used to be run down, in disuse, and defined by poverty and crime. The downside is that real estate prices are being driven up and the poor have to move out.[247] Another downside is that the central city areas become less and less church friendly. In some cities churches, and especially new church plants, simply cannot afford property. Some American cities are passing zoning laws that discourage churches from future building or new churches from locating in the city.[248] Missiologically, this means that churches, and church plants especially, will have to think about *being* the church more than *having* a church building and facilities. They will have to be the scattered church in homes, in third places, and simply in everyday life. Even if millions of dollars could be spent on land and buildings, the question now is whether it is worth it.

5. Because of growing secularism and postmodernism, the cities are more "tolerant" to alternative lifestyles, in particular homosexuality and gay marriage. There is already a growing acceptance of homosexuality and gay marriage in all of America,[249] especially in metro areas. There will be a growing intolerance toward evangelical "intolerance" and "hate speech," which is simply our Biblical opposition to homosexuality and gay marriage. Missionaries, planters, and pastors in the cities must learn to expect rejection and

hostility. These must be encountered with the loving truth of the gospel, demonstrated through ministry actions. Furthermore, pastors have to face the reality that many of their congregants have already moved to acceptance of the gay lifestyle. Opposition will not only be from the outside, but also from within.

6. Suburbs, too, are more diversified than ever. There are significant pockets of poverty in American suburbs. The government is regularly building government assisted housing (section 8) in suburbs, which radically changes the ethnicities and socioeconomics of suburbs. The reality is that ethnically and racially there is less and less difference between the central city and the suburbs. It is only in the growing exurbs that one finds white homogeneity. Missiologically, in the cities and the suburbs, one size will not fit all. Both "homogeneous unit" and multi-cultural/racial/ethnic strategies must be employed.

7. A growing trend in urban life is what is called New Urbanism. In response to congested cities, urban sprawl, and suburban isolation, developers are building planned communities that reproduce town and village life. All that is needed for living is within walking distance – housing, shopping, medical care, entertainment, and even the workplace. To a large degree, these communities are in response to our American isolation and cry for community – the "old neighborhoods" with sidewalks and front porches.[250] The missiological opportunity is for the church to more aggressively be the example and the model of what true community is like.

Like it or not, for good of for bad, the city in America is "where it's at."[251] Complex, diverse, congested, pluralistic, and often hostile to the gospel and to churches, our American metro areas are ripe for missiological investment, creativity, and adventure.

The Rich get Richer: Economic Disparity

There are few issues in American life and politics as volatile and as personal as economics. Certainly, moral issues such as abortion, crime, drug abuse, and gay marriage are emotional and vital to our overall well-being, but the economy touches every single person. Whether rich, middle-class, or poor, improving one's economic lifestyle and ensuring that one's children are better off is a central theme of the American dream. Whether *laissez faire* capitalist, pro- or anti-government regulations, or even leaning toward socialism, every American politician has to address the economy and the financial well-being of every American. Furthermore, we are a rich nation and a nation of relatively rich Christians. Things, however, may be changing and this is missiologically important to know.

There appears to be a growing socioeconomic disparity in America. There is disagreement as to this reality and there are certainly a variety of opinions as to the causes and the solutions of the disparity if it is in fact true. On the one hand, some report with confidence that "income inequality in the United States in rising and is now greater" than in almost all developed countries. In particular, "the average income among the richest 10% is 14 times greater than the average income among the poorest 10%, up from a 10 to 1 ratio in the 1980s." In other words, the rich are getting richer than the rest of us faster and faster, with the richest of the rich and the poorest of the poor moving further and faster to their respective extremes.[252] One result is that the middle-class, the backbone of America, is declining.[253]

On the other hand, some argue that this income disparity is either a myth or statistically insignificant. A few of the rich are certainly getting super rich, but that simply skews the statistics and is not really at the "expense of other Americans." Yes, it is said, there is an income disparity at the very top, but the impact on most of us is "minimal" and inequality is simply the fruit of a system that rewards hard work and risk.[254] Others argue that there has been "absolutely no meaningful change" in income inequality since 1994,[255] and that most Americans are not that worried about it, calling the gap "an acceptable part of our economic system." That is, free markets work well and are efficient "partly *because* they distribute economic rewards unevenly."[256] If that were not the case, no one would invest, take risks, or work hard.

One of the most recent comprehensive studies of changes in American life is Charles Murray's *Coming Apart*. Murray's research on whites in America shows that a new elite or a new upper class has grown significantly in America since the 1960s. This group is, he says, enabled by wealth and characterized by high I.Q. and elite college educations. They are "cognitively talented people who live together" in "super zip codes" around the country, but primarily clustered in New York, Washington D. C., and San Francisco. They are our nation's policy influencers, but actually live in a "bubble" when it comes to their interaction and understanding of the majority of Americans.[257]

At the same time there is a growing "new lower class" in America which is characterized by a significant decline in traditional marriage, industriousness, honesty, and religiosity when compared to the lower or working class of 1963. The most counterintuitive discovery, Murray points out, is the lack of religiosity among the new lower class, while religiosity has remained fairly stable among the new elite. The conclusion, stated rather simply, is that there is definitely a growing economic disparity that is more than simply financial. It is also characterized by a growing disparity in traditional American values and attitudes. The rich are getting richer, but they are also getting smarter and holding on to traditional marriage and religion.[258]

So what is the economic reality? I am not an economist and have a minimal understanding of macro-economics. I also understand that political ideology often drives one's understanding, interpretation, and solutions to poverty and income inequality. Two things, however, must be considered: One, the raw census data does show an increase in poverty and a growing income gap. Some of this is due to immigration, some is due to the recent recession, and some may be simply due to an increase in our overall population. Perhaps part of the cause is due to a decline in our work ethic and "American values." The fact is, however, that the American poverty level "hit 15.3 percent, the highest level since 1993."[259] This increase affected almost all American metro areas and especially the suburbs, given that more and more poor immigrants are moving directly to these.[260] Two, because the economy affects every person, and because passionate politics surrounds so much of the understanding and the interpretation of economics, *perception* is as important as the reality. If most people believe they are losing ground, sense that their children will not be better off, and believe the government is not offering any real solutions then people will feel and express anger, despair, and hopelessness. Perhaps the economic downturn is only temporary, an historical blip. Still, a thirty or forty year blip is a lifetime for most Americans, affecting the outlook of entire generations.

Missiologically, there are several issues to consider:

1. Increasing poverty will mean churches will have both more social action and social justice opportunities. The first, social action, deals with ministry to and for the poor and needy. The second means addressing the structural and political issues that surround the causes and solutions to poverty. Although many evangelical churches often shrink from the politics of social justice, the Bible doesn't. Of course, the challenge is to let both social action and social

justice be driven by Biblical truth rather than ideological agendas, whether right or left.

2. If Murray is right about a growing lower class, it is a vast mission field in and of itself. Functional illiteracy rates, rampant divorce, cohabitation as the norm, single women with multiple children, deadbeat Dads, welfare dependency, hopelessness, lack of opportunity – all give the church ample reason to engage missionally. Too often, reaching the lower class is not on churches' missiological radar or considered an effective church growth strategy. We are to target, some would say, the influencers and movers and shakers of society. Yes, they need Jesus, too, and Jesus did not ignore the rich. But, in both the New Testament and throughout history, spiritual awakenings, revival, and church planting movements have usually started among those on the margins and the underbelly of society.

3. Whether the income gap is reality or perception, the opportunity is there to emphasize the temporality of material things, the ultimate emptiness of materialism, and the hope that is found in Christ rather than any economic system or investment scheme.

Don't Trust Anyone Over Thirty! Boomers finally get old.

The Boomer generation supposedly refers to those born between 1946 and 1964. The reality is that there are two Boomer generations, those who came of age in the turbulent sixties and those who came of age in the strange seventies. Perhaps it is an oversimplification, but they could be divided as those who turned eighteen sometime during the Viet Nam war and those who did after the war.[261] Whatever the case, that group of people (of which I am one) was the single largest generation block in American history – 76 million by 1964, or almost 40% of the population. All kinds of studies have been done and books written about the Boomers and their worldview, their rebellion, their selfishness, their contribution to declining morals, their positive contributions to civil rights, and their move from countercultural "hippies" to prosperous "yuppies" to seniors who refuse to age. The demographic point to be made here is that this group, many of whom stated in the sixties that you should never trust anyone over thirty, is now turning sixty-five, retiring, and changing the landscape of America. Boomers currently number about 72 million, although there are actually almost 77 million people in the U.S. born between the years 1946 and 1964, with the difference due to immigrants of that same age.[262] This "graying of America" has political, economic, and vast cultural implications. For instance:

1. Baby Boomers will redefine what it means to age. For one thing, they are aging at "an opportune time" because the "nature of aging is changing." Boomers feel younger than their parents did at the same age, and that is "not just in their imagination."[263] Life expectancy is longer, older people are far healthier than they used to be, and thus life after retirement is an active life. Boomers are working longer, going back to school, are taking on second careers, are volunteering their time and contributing their resources.[264] Many are aware of the "selfish" label and will seek to atone for it by "giving back" to society. In a sense, they refuse to age, because "sixty is the new forty!" It could be said that Boomers refuse to grow old, an attitude both commendable and perhaps reflective of Boomers' perpetual immaturity.

2. At the same time, however, because such a large group will be aging America may be facing an "economic time

bomb." Boomers will place heavy demands on government entitlement programs such as Social Security, Medicare, pensions, and long-term care. Furthermore, Boomers have notoriously not saved enough for retirement, so there is a great "fear of outliving our money."[265] The irony is that while Boomers may be better off than their parents in retirement because they have enjoyed higher incomes, the same generation that "wouldn't trust anyone over 30" also "never planned on a 30-year retirement" and thus saved less and spent more.[266]

3. Because the "nature of aging is changing," how aging in general is viewed by American society is liable to change, also. Westerners, and Americans in particular, have often been criticized for worshipping youth and disregarding the wisdom and experience of old-age. Compared to Eastern cultures, we have little regard for the elderly. The graying of America, however, may help change that shortcoming, even though it may be driven (selfishly?) by the same group that will benefit from it. That is, if a significant percentage of the population is older, still working, still influential, and still economic viable, they will demand to be listened to. The first to realize the importance of aging Boomers, of course, are the marketers and advertisers. Although marketing is usually and primarily geared toward the 18 to 30 year old age group, a significant amount of marketing is now geared toward Boomers. Just listen to the music used in television commercials – when music from the sixties and seventies is used, the obvious target is Boomers.[267]

Lower birth rates, smaller families, and longer, healthier lives all translate into a massive demographic and cultural shift for America. Just as the Boomers changed American culture when they were younger, they will continue to do so for the next quarter of a century. One day we will all be gone (and some will say "thankfully!"). In the meantime, any American missiology has to take into account the graying of America. Aging Boomers are a mission field unto themselves. Many actually had a church background as children and youth, but left out of rebellion. Hitting old age and still looking for that elusive meaning, many will return to the church full of questions. On the positive side, many churches will suddenly find that their largest and most energetic working force (and the one with the most time) are retired Boomers. If these are not utilized in creative and challenging ways, they will channel that energy outside of the church in travel, sports, and new business opportunities. They are a mission force waiting to be tapped in to.[268]

This is America: Missiological Implications and Challenges

In Part 3 I will address many specific missions strategies that apply to a changing America. Here I want to mention some conceptual and attitudinal implications:

First, as we approach America as a mission field, we must do so with a clear understanding of the Biblical gospel. As much as possible, we must attempt to identify and separate our own politics and ideology from the gospel, and make sure we clearly distinguish between the multiple implications (fruit and results) of the gospel from the gospel itself. In particular, we must not identify the gospel with the American way of life. International missionaries have known this for a long time. They know that any implication that Christianity is American or Western will hinder the proclamation, hearing, and acceptance of the gospel. The same holds true more and more in America. For the sake of reaching the nations who come to us, for the sake of reaching the postmodern generations, and for the sake of not diluting the message of the cross, we must keep these concepts separate.

Again, I am not saying that the implications of the gospel are not important. I am not saying that political and ideological issues are not important – I have my own. I am most certainly not saying that the fruit of the gospel is not important. I am simply saying that whereas the content of the gospel is non-negotiable, trans-cultural, and trans-generational, the fruit of the gospel – how we love each other, how we fight poverty and injustice, what marriages and families look like, how society is transformed – may look differently from time to time and culture to culture, even as it transforms lives. For example, the Bible is clear that husbands are to love their wives and wives are to submit to their husbands (Eph. 5:22-33). What that looks like may vary from culture to culture. We are also told to ""Carry one another's burdens" (Gal. 6:2), to accept "one another in love" (Eph. 4:2), to "be kind and compassionate to one another" (Eph. 4:32), and "to be rich in good works" (1 Tim. 6:18). How each of those plays out may vary from culture to culture and from situation to situation. Those of us who are slaves are also instructed to "obey our masters with fear and trembling" (Eph. 6:5; 1 Tim. 6:1-2). What that looks like…well, I rest my case. The message of the gospel is trans-cultural. The working out of the gospel will be within a culture at the same time as it transforms that culture. At the very least, we need to be careful not to identify how these look with any one earthly culture or generation.

Second, we are going to have to learn more and more to speak to a third-culture. That is, with immigration, globalization, high mobility, inter-racial and inter-cultural marriages, and with the ease with which younger generations accept and live multiculturally, more and more people are what is called "third culture." Originally, the term "third-culture" referred to children who were raised in a different culture than the one they were born in – missionary, military, embassy, and international business kids.

More and more it also refers to those who, although they may not have lived abroad, are products of more than one culture and who have the "mindset and will to love, learn, and serve in any culture, even in the midst of pain and discomfort."[269] This is more and more the future of America. Some worry that it means the end of American values and way of life. I don't think so, because third-culture people have the ability to appreciate, value, and celebrate multiple cultures and the best in many cultures. Therefore, it doesn't mean the end of the American way of life, it means a new American way of life. Missiologically, once again it means that we will have to present the unchanging and trans-cultural gospel as the meta-narrative for all times, all peoples, and all cultures. In a sense, the gospel *is* third-culture.

Third, all this means we can rejoice. We rejoice in what we have been as a nation and how far we have come, but we look forward to where God is taking us and what He is going to do in the future. In particular, we give thanks and rejoice for our Christian heritage, however we may define or explain it. God has guided and blessed us. At the same time, however, we must be realistic about our faults and flaws, for we have failed miserably in many areas throughout our history. This does not mean that patriotism is diminished; it does mean, however, that we should not allow patriotism to turn into idolatry. Consider the analogy of family and church. I love my family. There is something about blood ties that hold me to even extended family I have not seen in years. But my family, on both sides, is far from perfect. There has been alcoholism, depression, many divorces, abuse, prison terms, and broken relationships, all mixed in with ministry, long and successful marriages, loving relationships, meaningful lives, and contribution to both kingdom and society. But, it is my family. The same analogy applies to the bride of Christ. How can we not love Christ's body, both in its universal and local expression. The history of the church, however, is replete with corruption, persecution of fellow believers, materialism, alignment with dictators and despots, and contamination with the world. But, it is still the Bride of Christ. The same is true for America. My spine tingles when I hear the Star Spangled Banner (if sung correctly!). Tears come to my eyes at the foot of the Statue of Liberty, at the Viet Nam memorial, and any time I hear about a World War II veteran. Yet I don't want to whitewash the sins of our country. They are to be faced and confessed, and restitution made if necessary. Then, we are to forget what lies behind and look and move forward.

Finally, we need to remember that we have been here before. Every generation looks to the past and yearns to return, because every generation has a selective memory about an idealized and romanticized past.[270] We have throughout our history undergone demographic, generational, and economic change. Racial, ethnic, religious, political, and moral issues have always seemed more manageable and better in the past. That is not to say that our current issues are not critical and important and should be ignored. It is to say that we must maintain perspective about our present and our past. Once again, more importantly, we must maintain the right perspective about our future. God is sovereign, he has a plan, he has a plan for our nation. We look to the past to remember what he has done and rejoice. More importantly, we look to the future and rejoice in what he is going do to.

America is a mission field. America is changing. Some of that change is good and some of it is definitely not. Our faith, however, is one of hope – we look forward to all that God has in store for us. Without a doubt, there is uncertainty and some fear, but what an adventure!

Looking for Utopia:
Living with Fear, Boredom,
and Loneliness

Listen to my prayer, O God, do not ignore my plea; hear me and answer me. My thoughts trouble me and I am distraught at the voice of the enemy, at the stares of the wicked; for they bring down suffering upon me and revile me in their anger. My heart is in anguish within me: the terrors of death assail me. Fear and trembling have beset me; horror has overwhelmed me. I said, "Oh, that I had the wings of a dove! I would fly away and be at rest – I would flee far away and stay in the desert; I would hurry to my place of shelter, far from the tempest and storm."...But I call to God, and the LORD saves me. Evening, morning and noon I cry out in distress, and he hears my voice....Cast your cares on the Lord and he will sustain you; he will never let the righteous fall....But as for me, I trust in you.

Psalm 55:1-8, 16-17, 22, 23c (NIV).

This Psalm of David is an "individual lament,"[271] in which David expresses to God his fear, his anxiety, his troubling circumstances, and finally his trust in the only One who can save him. Unlike some of David's other psalms, we don't know the exact circumstances of this one. What we can tell from the content of the lament is that his troubles have been caused by a "companion," a "close friend" (v.13). This former friend is now an enemy who has brought to David distress, fear, anxiety, and even the threat of death. This new enemy has also turned others against David and they have reviled the king and brought suffering upon him, perhaps both physical and emotional. David is simply responding as any normal human being would in a situation of betrayal and danger: he trembles with fear, he is horrified at what has happened, he is internally anguished.

David's first response to his trying circumstances and anguished feelings is also quite normal: he wants to escape them. As soon as he expresses his troubles and his feelings he wishes that he could simply "fly away," leaving his troubles and enemies behind. He pictures himself away from it all, in his "place of shelter," far from the dangers that surround him. Psychologists tell us that most humans initially have either a "fight or flight" response to dangers and threats. Without a doubt, David was a fighter when he had to be. Here, however, his first reaction is to flee. The situation is apparently so dangerous or so emotionally trying because a former friend is involved, he would rather just avoid it.

After he talks through the situation a bit more, David's final response is what it usually is: he turns to God for comfort and protection. Rather than just randomly voicing his complaint, he turns his cry of distress to the Lord. David rests, as he so often does, in the power of God to comfort him, rescue him, and take care of his enemies. Because God has been and is faithful, David then encourages the godly to do what he has done, to cast their own cares, whatever they may be, on the Lord. It is only the Lord who can sustain them and who will faithfully protect them. David concludes his song of lament with a very pointed statement reflecting his decision: he will trust in God.

Although this psalm deals with one individual's specific struggle with danger, anxiety, fear, and faith, we can draw parallels to many human situations, both individually and corporately. Life is full of dangers. People in all walks of life experience and express a variety of anxieties and fears, real and perceived. Like David, the first response for so many is to flee, to find some kind of relief and escape, possibly to avoid dealing with the harsh realities of life any more than they have to. Because flight is not possible for an entire society, the solution for many of the dangers and fears we face – so we think – is to "fight" and make every effort to remove anything that may cause fear and danger. Sometimes this is appropriate, sometimes it may not be. In the end, however, we are left with the reality of sin and a fallen world. Missiologically this is important to know about America. We are a nation that craves peace of mind, safety, and even comfort. We will do anything we can to remove threats, whether real or perceived, to these "rights." We are, it seems, convinced that somehow and in some way, the best and most advanced country in the world should also be the one free from danger and immune to calamity. That conviction, and the inevitable disappointment when it is not fulfilled, is full of missiological implications.

The Business of Fear: Shouting for Your Attention with 24/7 News and Statistics

On Sunday, May 20th, 2012 I was at home when ABC World News Tonight came on TV. The top four stories were: a devastating earthquake in northern Italy, a devastating tornado in the Wichita, Kansas area, the development of Tropical Storm Alberto off the coast of South Carolina, and the ongoing wildfires in central Arizona. Because this was network television, only a few minutes was spent on each story. I am sure that had I turned to one of the twenty-four hour cable news stations, each of these situations would have been examined at much greater length. In fact, I am confident the Weather Channel was spending most of its time on Alberto. Furthermore, these and other stories of the day (and it was Sunday, a slow news day) will be dissected, explained, and analyzed AD nauseum on the 24/7 news channels. And at that, these stories were weather and natural disaster related. When the stories are about political crisis or involve crime and violence, the repeated showing, analysis, and dissecting is tenfold. This simple Sunday night news observation reflects three realities about the American landscape, the latter two consequences of the first, and all important for understanding the American psyche.

All news, all the time

This first reality has five characteristics:

1. What was once far away is now here, and vice versa. The ease of world travel and the speed of communication in our flat world mean that the other side of the world is no longer that far away. What used to happen in distant and isolated lands we now know about instantly, often before it is over. A natural disaster, a military coup, an act of violence – these are not only reported instantly, in many cases people all over the world can witness them in real time. What is happening "there" can be experienced immediately "here." What is happening "here" goes "there" during the actual event.

2. What once few knew about, we now all hear shouted again and again. This ability to give immediacy to any event is because the technology to report "live" is now not only in the hands of the professional journalist, but also in the hands of anyone who owns a cell phone. On the one hand,

there is the professional "24-hour" or "24/7" news cycle. In one sense, this is not new. Newspapers have always had "late editions" to cover the latest news developments. Radio and early television could interrupt any programming with breaking news. The desire for journalists to scoop a story and gain both the first and the biggest audience has been part of journalism for over a century. The difference now is technology and the number of all-news television stations. They are in fierce competition and have twenty-four hours of time to fill up with interesting programming or viewers will switch to the competition.[272] This means the four weather stories mentioned above will be hashed and re-hashed. Political intrigue, crime and corruption, violence, and the private lives of celebrities are the subjects of the most intense examination and voyeurism. You know news coverage of an event has gone too far when journalists (or celebrity reporters) are interviewing their peers because there is no one left to talk to. And that follows the examination of every psychological, economic, political, sociological, and environmental implication of the event in question. In the end, a heinous murder in Belgium, for example, can be reported and analyzed worldwide before the bodies are in the coroner's care. Positively, this amount of news reporting means that there is no excuse for being misinformed about world events. It is all available now. Negatively, the competition is so fierce and often so ideologically driven that the average person tends to follow a particular personality or ideology driven news vehicle with little filter or content analysis.

On the other hand, "news" is no longer solely the purview of the professional journalist. Cell phone videos, blogs, Facebook, and Twitter mean that any person in the world can "report" on any event. Sometimes this is valuable and groundbreaking. On occasion, entire "revolutions" are text and Twitter based, as were the student demonstrations in Iran a few years back. Sometimes information about atrocities can only be reported because a local person posted it, as has happened recently regarding atrocities in Syria. Furthermore, professional journalists often compete with bloggers for scoops and influence. Unfortunately, this lay reporting is often inaccurate, out of context (not that professional journalists do it perfectly), and difficult to verify. Positively, there is a level playing field and a democratization of news reporting. Anybody can put forth an opinion and show the "truth." Negatively, the overwhelming quantity of this reporting can be disconcerting and in great need of filtering; and, consequently, the "truth" can be even harder to distinguish from mere opinion and ideological rants.

3. Over reaction is the norm. Immediate over-reporting on 24/7 news services, blogs, and personal opinion vehicles, and the ability to respond to these immediately, also means that knee jerk reactions and shouting have displaced thoughtful debate. I will not agree with the opinion that our political discourse is that much more divisive and uncivil than it used to be – previous centuries were often worse. What is different is that political, economic, and social/cultural discourse is now done primarily in sound bites and tweets. This means that not enough thought goes into a statement and even less into the response. Rather than having to read a well thought out position paper or op-ed, we watch a two minute video on YouTube, read a 140 character tweet, or listen to a 12 second sound bite on TV. Response, or more often overreaction, is immediate and even less thoughtful. In the end, the winner is the one who can shout the loudest or come up with the cleverest retort.

4. Privacy is virtually non-existent. This is both good and bad. Positively, it is harder and harder for scoundrels to hide. Corruption, unethical, and even criminal behavior is easier to find and expose. Be sure that a blogger will out your sins. Negatively, unintentional lapses in judgment, honest mistakes, and youthful indiscretions are paraded publicly and never forgiven. Furthermore, so much reporting noise contributes to our society's celebrity worship. Although celebrity worship is nothing new,[273] 24/7 television accessibility floods us with the mundane and incredibly unimportant details of the lives of sports and entertainment celebrities.

5. The line is blurred between news and entertainment. This confusion has been discussed and debated for decades, but is getting worse because the technology is available for anyone to tell the story and even participate in the story. Through social networking media, viewers and readers can respond to a news story almost immediately (in the case of television and the internet; the next day in the dying newspaper medium). In fact, many news broadcasts show Twitter responses on the screen as they report the story. Is this news, entertainment, or social networking, or the blurring of all three? How is it possible for thoughtful discussion to take place in this environment of immediacy? It seems that it is getting harder to separate facts, opinions, and simple entertainment.

Irrational and unreasonable fear rules

This constant, and too often unfiltered and unreliable, reporting of news and information contributes to the second reality: We are too afraid of the wrong things. That is, fear of calamity, disaster, terrorist attacks, crime, disease, and accidents increase disproportionately to reality.[274] Barry Glassner in *The Culture of Fear: Why Americans are Afraid of the Wrong Things* shows how the improper use of statistics, poor research, irresponsible journalism, alarmist reporting, and politically driven fear mongering have caused Americans to overreact about the wrong things. Although the context of some of his examples and explanations are dated, his analysis of the culture of fear and its causes and effects is right on. Moreover, what he says is even more the reality now with the increased influence of the internet. Consider that a survey of parents found that, when it comes to their children, they worry most about: 1) Kidnappings, 2) School snipers, 3) Terrorists, 4) Dangerous strangers, and, 5) Drugs. All these fears are based on real incidences (in particular drugs), and are among the most spectacular events reported in the media. Compare parents' worries, however, with what actually kills or hurts kids the most: 1) Car accidents, 2) Homicide (2/3 of the time by a parent), 3) Abuse (more than 2/3 of the time by a parent), 4) Suicide, and, 5) Drowning. What gets reported? What is the most spectacular and fear inducing – drowning in a backyard swimming pool or the very rare instance of a school shooting?[275]

What is going on? Why do we fear the "wrong things"? The bottom line is that we panic when: we have incorrect and out of context information, when that event being reported is new to us, when the event is spectacularly disastrous, and when it is over reported. Some examples to illustrate these four points:

1. Incorrect and out of context information. The old saying is that "statistics don't lie, but the people who use statistics do." All too often statistics and studies are trotted out to prove a point. Unfortunately, "a new study has shown" does not mean that anything has been definitively proven. Researchers know that, especially for first time studies. They will usually draw tentative conclusions at the end of

their report and qualify all of it by saying "further research is needed." The breaking news we hear, however, is that a "new study has shown" this or that discovery, it gets reported repeatedly as a new fact, and we start to worry. Is coffee good for you or not? Is chocolate good for you or not? Is this particular medical procedure necessary or more harmful? Is crime up or down?

Some incorrect information sticks around for so long that it becomes urban legend. A common belief, held by every responsible parent, is that there are sadistic people who put razor blades and needles in Halloween treats. The parental *modus operandi* now is to reject apples (no one gives them anymore), and homemade or unwrapped treats, as these may have harmful objects. Furthermore, when the child comes home, all candy should be inspected. This is based on the "real" incidences way back in the late 60s and early 70s when children were harmed by razor blades and needles. The reality is, as Glassner (and others) point out, this myth was exposed by a sociologist who studied "every reported incident since 1958." The conclusion? There was never a single death or serious injury reported, and only a couple of incidents of minor cuts resulting from "young pranksters" and not evil adults. The two actual cases of child death resulting from poisoned Halloween candy were family related.[276] Still, ask any parent what their greatest fear is around Halloween and the answer will probably be fear of tainted candy.

2. A new and unfamiliar event. Without a doubt we fear the unknown far more than the known. When a danger becomes familiar, we no longer treat it as a danger. For example, Americans regularly agonize over new and unknown strains of flu like the avian flu, "which to date

[2006] has killed precisely no one in the U.S." At the same time, people have to be convinced that their yearly flu shot is important even though the common flu "contributes to the deaths of 36,000 Americans each year." Which strain of flu should we really fear? Similarly, we freak out over a bag of spinach that probably doesn't really have E.Coli, but we will load up on sodium, cholesterol, and fat, which will kill us more slowly.[277] If it is new, it is more frightening. Remember how frightened we were when HIV/AIDS was first discussed in the eighties?

3. We fear the disastrous more than the commonplace. Try to convince a person who fears flying that they are statistically safer in an airplane than in an automobile driving to the airport. Besides the emotional reality that they have no control in an airplane, one plane crash that kills 250 is emotionally more disturbing than 250 people killed in a hundred auto crashes. And, don't further confuse them by pointing out that poisoning by drugs (mostly prescription) kills more people than do car crashes![278] Likewise, in the last year two cruise ship accidents led many people to state they would never take a cruise, completely overlooking the fact that worldwide there are thousands of cruises every year without any mishaps. The spectacular scares us.[279]

4. Our fear increases due to over reporting. The question is simple: Is it happening more or are we hearing about it more? The evidence may be that crime is decreasing, wars are fewer, diseases are being cured, and life is generally safer than it has ever been. The problem is that the crime, war, and diseases that exist get reported far more often and in far more detail than they used to. The perception is, therefore, that there is actually more of it. For example, if a family was murdered by a father in Cleveland in 1970,

those in Phoenix may have heard about it on the evening news or may have read about it the next day in the paper. They would have considered it an awful crime, but it was a long ways off, and was soon forgotten. Today, that same crime is reported and analyzed instantly and continually until someone calls it an epidemic and we feel as if it happened next door.[280]

Contrary to popular belief, recent research has shown that the "decline of violence may be the most significant and least appreciated development in the history of our species." This conclusion, reached by three different authors, "runs counter to what the mass media is reporting and essentially what we feel in our guts." The Cold War ended without nuclear weapons being used, the death toll in wars is significantly lower now than it used to be (due to smart weapons and better medical care), genocide deaths are lower, more countries are ruled by democracies than dictators, and murder and rape is significantly down in both Europe and America.[281] Yet, we think the world is more violent. Why? For one, the past is inaccessible to most of us. We forget or don't realize how violent the world has been for most of its history. Second, of course, 24/7 immediate and intimate news reporting brings it right close to home. War and casualties of war are no longer faceless statistics, but are realities brought into our living rooms that very day.[282] Third, our religious culture is fascinated with apocalyptic scenarios. There was a fear increase toward the end of the 1990s, especially regarding the much overhyped Y2K computer bug. Our post 9/11 worldview is one filled with terrorists and potential terrorists. Certainly, novels, movies, and television help promote these fears through fictional, yet highly entertaining and highly unlikely scenarios. Finally, our culture is far more open than it used to be. Are crimes, including child abuse, for example, simply being reported more today than in past decades?[283] It would appear so. Not only are the reporting mechanisms more prevalent and efficient, but there is greater awareness about crimes, in particular those unreported "hidden" crimes that used to be swept under the carpet as family secrets. We are hearing more about "it," for there is less silence than there used to be.[284]

Life in the Bubble +
Zero Tolerance = Utopia

When irrational and unreasonable fear rules, there is another consequence – a third reality: we work as hard as we can at creating a safety utopia. We do this in two ways: One, we create a "bubble" existence in which as much risk and danger is removed as possible, and, two, we enforce a "zero tolerance" to anything that might be considered risky or dangerous. If we can do these two things well, we believe we will be able to live in a safe and risk free utopia.

The problem with creating a bubble, however, is that we don't all agree on what constitutes real danger. In fact, as Tulley argues in his definition of "dangerism," we have developed a belief system about what is dangerous and risky based more on "cultural histories, taboos, and traditions rather than science, statistics, or concrete evidence." That is, danger is relative. Some consider walking through fields and forests too dangerous because of all the snakes. Not so a country boy. Some see the big city, especially downtowns, as threatening and scary, although many downtowns are the safest parts of a city and home to millions of people. Some parents would never give their child a pocketknife; others give their sons a new one every birthday. Furthermore, when it comes to children, and especially our own, we lose all perspective and rationality. When there is a 1% chance of something bad happening, we become afraid, forgetting that there is a 99% chance that it won't happen. Essentially, when it comes to danger, we are irrational.[285] To soothe our fears we create a bubble – we don't let our children play in the front yard anymore, we teach them to automatically fear strangers, and we remove any toys or games that have been declared potentially hazardous. We are unaware that what is really driving the hazard warning is corporate fear of a lawsuit, not actual danger. So, whatever happened to dodge ball, tether ball, and playground monkey bars? Apparently at some point someone had an accident, the manufacturer and others were sued, the media reported it, a decision was made to remove the offending item because it was so dangerous, and the fear cycle began.[286] Together with the government, we just know that if we try hard enough society can be a safety utopia.[287] If it is not, then we need to find someone to blame.

The problem with zero tolerance, which is one of the ways we build a bubble, is twofold: there is no room for honest mistakes and for second chances and it leads to paranoia and guilt. In the first case, the effort by government, schools, and sometimes businesses to enforce zero tolerance for questionable behavior leaves no room for growth and learning. Certainly, many of the behaviors the zero tolerance policy is meant to control are unacceptable. A misbehavior, however, can sometimes lead to overreaction, excessive punishment, and remove the teaching, correcting, and rehabilitative moment. The teenager who accidentally leaves his hunting knife in the back of his pickup is suspended from school. The high school prank that called for genuine correction and discipline results in excessive punishment and humiliation. The first time youthful offender is locked up with older hardened criminals who will teach him how to be a better criminal. Correction and punishment may certainly be called for. In some instances, zero tolerance may be called for.

In too many cases, however, a "one-strike and you're out" policy is simply an overreaction based on unreasonable fear. It certainly may provide harsh consequences, but will it teach character?

The result of a zero tolerance attitude, whether official or unofficial, can also lead to paranoia and guilt. In the first case, some parents, for example, are fearful of corporally disciplining their children in public for fear of being turned in for child abuse. And in our society, in an accusation of child abuse, you are definitely guilty until proven innocent. In the second case, some parents who may have a more permissive attitude toward child rearing may allow their kids more freedom…until they are criticized for being irresponsible and non-caring.

In the end, trying to enforce a zero tolerance policy and attitude toward human blunders (or differing opinions) reflects a desire to manage and control a fallen creation. Biblically we have been given dominion over creation, but sometimes that is interpreted as abuse of creation on the one hand and absolute control on the other. Although a theology of creation may not even cross the mind of secular America, there is often a cultural belief, grounded in modernity, that we should be able to control creation just enough to remove all danger and risk.

Certainly, we should take precautions and be as safe as we can be. As Tulley says, "a little bit of dangerism is a good thing." However, sometimes accidents happen and sometimes people misbehave. We need to be aware of these situations, study them, and do what we can to "recognize and mitigate danger." What we don't need to do is to live in fear and over react to every hiccup in nature and human behavior.

Conclusion

The world is definitely a dangerous place, for it is a fallen world affected and infected by sin. The Bible is clear that human nature is inherently sinful and that all humans will sin by choice. Furthermore, the entire natural creation is also affected by the fall. Consequently, all that is dangerous and threatens our wellbeing is directly or indirectly caused by sin. That is the world we live in. Natural disasters will continue. There will be wars and rumors of war. Crime is a daily reality in every human community. There is regular economic and political uncertainty, oppression, and calamity. Every single person could be affected any day by an accident, a disease, or some sort of violence. We should be reasonably afraid, which means we must be careful, cautious, and concerned about our families. What is unreasonable is a culture of fear that is driven by misinformation and then too often manipulated for political and economic gain.

Just as King David wanted to flee on the wings of a dove to some place far away from the dangers that surrounded him, so we sometimes deny, try to escape, or attempt to remove any and all threat or risk. Again, every responsible person, parent, community, and government should take serious and reasonable steps to ensure as much safety as possible. Sometimes, however, that line is crossed into panic, a persistent and unreasonable fear, and unreasonable expectations for safety. We then feel as if we could pass the right laws, regulate more behaviors, and remove most threats we could live in a social, political, and economic safety bubble.[288]

Missiologically, the reality of our fallen world, and even the unfortunate culture of fear, provides an opportunity to:

1. Argue for the reality of sin and its consequences. The Good News is not good unless there is first some bad news and the bad news is that we are all sinners by nature and by choice. The bad news is that humans can work to improve the world (and should), but that perfect safety is impossible; in fact, there will be times and seasons when things get worse. Missiologically, the opportunity is there

for us to clarify that creation – nature and humans – are not neutral or indifferent in regards to God, but are estranged and in need of redemption. Consequently, . . .

2. We can explain the truth of a loving God who seeks to reconcile his creation to himself. Yes, all of creation is estranged from God. Yes, all of creation is hopeless if left to itself. The Holy God of love and justice, however, provided the means by which sin could be dealt with and reconciliation with him achieved. This allows us to . . .

3. Introduce Jesus Christ as the one and only mediator, redeemer, and reconciler. His life, sacrificial death, and resurrection are the one and only solution to sin, whether corporate or individual. Furthermore, we can . . .

4. Trust Jesus Christ as the only one who can remove fear from our lives, both eschatological and temporal. That is, not only does saving faith in Jesus Christ mean we do not have to fear death, the final judgment, and our eternal destiny, it also means that we can rest in him while living in the midst of fearful and dangerous times. We have to be careful, however, to . . .

5. Present the full gospel as a "dangerous" alternative to a dangerous world. In a world full of both real danger and exaggerated fear, a superficial therapeutic gospel is not enough. We do preach that Jesus saves, that Jesus heals, that Jesus is the refuge from danger and fear. We do not preach that Jesus is simply one who "meets all your needs" or "makes you happy and prosperous," for he may not, at least in the sense that many expect. He does not guarantee that he will remove all danger, need, and want. To the contrary, he calls us to die to self and to sacrifice

for others. Discipleship can be a dangerous journey; the Great Commission is a dangerous call; being salt and light could be costly. On the one hand, unbelievers need to hear this full gospel: Jesus saves from sin *and* he calls you to die. On the other hand, believers need to avoid building "safe" Christian ghettoes that keep them isolated from those who need to hear the gospel. Consequently . . .

6. The gospel story is *the* story, and we get to both report it and participate in it. Just as there is a blurring of the lines when it comes to news, entertainment, and social networking that allows people to participate in the story, so the gospel and the Christian life is a full participatory event. We cannot simply observe. We cannot simply hear and not do. We invite others to participate in the telling of the greatest story that can ever be told and to participate in the ongoing story of life in Christ. There are, therefore, no hard and fast lines between evangelism, discipleship, and Christian ethics. At the same time, our participation in the story is a life-long one – it is a journey. This should encourage us to engage in thoughtful participation (discipleship) and not knee-jerk, sound bite, bumper sticker Christianity.

The Pursuit of Happiness: 24/7 Entertainment on Demand

An underlying aspect of our fear is our comfort. That is, there is a sense in which our fear is a product of our affluence. Most Americans do not have to worry about tribal violence, rampant disease, or where their next meal is coming from. Most of us don't have to work in the fields from sunup to sundown for pennies a day. Most of us don't live with twenty members of our extended family in a one room shack or urban apartment. People who do have to live like this and do have to worry about making it through the day don't have the luxury of worrying about the latest child car seat, child proof medicine bottles, tainted trick or treat candy, plane crashes, or a suspected foreign bacteria or virus. To a large degree, much of our fear is a reflection of our affluence – we can *afford* the time and effort to worry and fret.[289] And what else can we afford? The time to be bored.

Boredom, pain, and a Band Aid

For over a century we have imagined, worked for, and created the means by which we could be more efficient in our work and thus have more leisure time. A shorter work week, longer weekends, more vacations – we all love them. The trade off, however, is too much time on our hands. At the risk of overstating this American (and increasingly, global) problem, we have invented more and more ways to fill our time, but we are less and less satisfied with these activities and the meaning (or lack thereof) they bring. Too many in our society are simply too bored with their lives. The solution, or better said, the result is obsession – with eating, with sex, with sports, and with entertainment. So many of us are so bored that "massive boredom industries designed to help people find escape"[290] fuel much of our American economy. It seems we have to do more and more, multitask more and more, and get busier and busier so that we don't have to stop and reflect on our pain and emptiness. And, the more we do, the more unsatisfied we are – it becomes a vicious cycle.[291]

The growing boredom in American society is not new.[292] Its increasing prevalence, however, is reflected by how much we spend to cure it. The chances are that an American family spends more on entertainment than on groceries, gasoline, or clothing once all expenses for movies, cable, music, and other forms of entertainment are factored in.[293] The size of the sports industry is over $200 billion, twice the size of the auto industry and seven times the size of the movie industry, which is immense in and of itself.[294] According to one market research company it is estimated that in 2004 Americans "spent $705.9 billion on entertainment, a figure equivalent to the entire gross national product of Canada" and Australia. That figure continues to grow every year, regardless of the economy, and reflects "consumers' need for 'self-actualization'."[295]

Going to extremes

The previous caveat about statistics and studies still holds true: it all depends on who is measuring what and then how the results are interpreted and reported. That is, these figures may or may not be accurate, but they are still astounding. As Americans we have the affluence of both time and money to address our boredom through a thousand different activities. This is not in and of itself wrong. The people of Israel had regular times of rest, refreshment, and celebration. Jesus and his disciples "partied" at weddings and celebrated with others often. There is nothing wrong with refreshing oneself through literature, music, a good movie, and sporting events. It does become a problem when we become obsessed to the point of idolizing sports and entertainment celebrities, when we overspend on entertainment, and when we engage in these activities not as a temporary distraction but as a way to avoid the real issues of spiritual, emotional, and relational barrenness. Rather than face the reality of the pain brought on by emptiness, we put an entertainment Band Aid on it.

A time comes, however, when the Band Aid no longer works, and more extreme measures are taken: spend more money, spend more time, take more risks, and seek more thrills. Witness the phenomenal growth and interest in extreme sports and fighting events. Why are all these so popular? They are countercultural, they are youth oriented, some are really a lot of fun, and they are marketed quite well. I would argue, however, that there is a direct connection to our affluence of time and money. We become desensitized to the Band Aid, still feel the emptiness, and do anything to feel truly alive, even if it involves extremely risky behaviors.[296]

An example of the extremes to which we may go is seen in the movie *Fight Club*, a grim but culturally important movie that addresses both the emptiness (mostly generational in the movie) and the actions taken to fill it. In the movie, young men in their twenties join a secret fight club in which the voluntary pummeling they give each other is the only way they can feel alive. "'I bleed, therefore I am' serves as [their] rallying cry."[297] Similarly, to quote the song written by Trent Reznor of Nine Inch Nails and covered so hauntingly by Johnny Cash: "I hurt myself today, To see if I still feel, I focus on the pain, The only thing that's real."

Conclusion

Rest, relaxation, and even entertainment are good things. Excess, abuse, and extremes of these, however, mask boredom, emptiness, and meaninglessness. Our missiological opportunity is not to avoid sports, entertainment, and leisure activities. Our missiological opportunity is to introduce the gospel of Jesus Christ as the solution to boredom, emptiness, and meaningless. Therefore:

1. We can communicate and demonstrate that knowing Jesus and being a member of his kingdom can be the thrill of a lifetime, fill our souls with hope, and give our lives all the meaning we can handle.

2. We do not, however, present this in the form of a magical formula: "Believe in Jesus and all your struggles will go away." No, even believers will struggle with some boredom, the occasional empty feeling, and times of meaninglessness. Sometimes the Christian life can be one

of simply perseverance. Dry times will come. Difficult times will come. Walking with Jesus, we need to explain, is a journey and it takes us through those times. Our hope is that he is with us in and through them.

3. We will want, therefore, to reject any trend toward formula Christianity and over-promising the Christian life as if we were in competition with extreme sports and adrenaline junkies. I am not saying that we need to eliminate all practical Christian teaching, or do away with "Christian" sports activities, outdoors events, and entertainment. I am not saying the Christian life cannot be and should not be fun. I am saying that we want to be careful not to *reduce* the gospel and the Christian life to just these, for the follower of Christ is primarily called to die to self, sacrifice, and even suffer. The victorious Christian life is not always seen in prosperity, success, and happiness. It is more often seen, Biblically and historically, in a life of sacrificial giving, excruciating faith, and exhausting perseverance. Fun is good, but the storms will come also and we should not present an incomplete gospel that will leave the new believer unprepared.

We may still go to movies, play sports, read books, play video games, and so forth. They are fun! They will, however, be genuinely experienced as occasional times of needed rest and not a temporary and counterfeit salve for unaddressed spiritual issues.

Where Everyone Knows Your Name: Social Networking

Plenty of cultural observers have commented on the loss of, and desire for, authentic community in American society. The close knit rural and small town communities of past decades are fewer and fewer. Homogenous neighborhoods with front porches, sidewalks, and neighbors who looked after each other's children are memories, primarily replaced by larger homes with highly transitional residents who barely know their neighbors. A transitional society, urban sprawl with long work commutes, diversification of backgrounds and interests, and the abundance of in-home entertainment options mean that we can cocoon in our homes without having to live in any kind of geographic based community.[298] That is, the community which in past days developed naturally from geography rarely exists anymore. The problem is that human beings were not created for social isolation; to the contrary, we were created to interact and be interdependent. When there is a lack of social contact – community – the result is loneliness, depression, and hopelessness.[299] Community has to be sought out and chosen.

The explosion in social networking over the last decade has revolutionized the way many Americans seek and create community. It is probably too early to tell what kind of long-term social and cultural impact these networking sites will have, but we can be sure that our society will never be the same. Whether through Facebook, MySpace, LinkedIn, Twitter, or dozens of other networking vehicles available or yet to be created, Americans are building community. But, how effective is it? Is all this technologically driven community really pulling us together or actually making us lonelier?

Stephen Marche, in an article published in *The Atlantic*, argues that "research suggests that we have never been lonelier (or more narcissistic)" than we are in the midst of our "densely networked" lives. Social media sites like Facebook have really only created more anxieties: "interfering with our real friendships, distancing us from each other, making us lonelier... and ... spreading the very isolation it seemed designed to conquer." Facebook, for example, appeals to us because of "its miraculous fusion of distance with intimacy," but is really giving us the "illusion of distance with the illusion of intimacy."[300] But is this true? According to the most recent research by the reputable Pew Research Center, the latest communication technology and social networking are not as bad for us as some have thought. Their research has discovered, first of all, that "Americans are not as isolated as has been previously reported." The qualifier is that, yes, there is more isolation than in in the middle of the twentieth century, for example, but the extent of that isolation has not changed since 1985. To the contrary, the new technology of mobile phones and the internet actually are "associated with having a more diverse social network" and do not significantly affect community or social involvement.[301] More specifically, Pew research on social networks users revealed that they: 1) are more trusting than others, 2) have more close relationships, 3) get more social support than other people, 4) are much more politically engaged than most people, 5) have revived dormant relationships, and, 6) are more open to opposing points of view.

Now, there is plenty more that can be said about some of the negative aspects of social networking, including bullying, narcissistic behaviors, vulgarity, and a lack of good judgment in posting. Be that as it may, the phenomenon of social media is still unfolding, its full implications yet to be known. No understanding of America, however, especially of the younger generations, will be possible without considering and studying social networking.

Conclusion

Perhaps one area where the church fails most often and most miserably is in being both an authentic and an open community. That is, we may actually function quite strongly as the family of God, loving and supporting each other. The problem is that it is so easy to turn inward and become functionally closed, even unintentionally and unaware that it has happened. Yet, we must not give up. The body of Christ, the family of God, the fellowship of saints, the fellowship of the Holy Spirit, the community of believers – all these are Biblical and theological ways to express what we are and what we are to be this side of heaven. Perhaps our failure to be more open is twofold: One, we place unrealistic expectations on each other and often communicate these to the world. Consequently, the world looks at the church and expects us to be more perfect than we can be or even expect to be ourselves. Or, they look at us and perceive that they would never be accepted in our "perfect" community. They either perceive us as closed or in reality we become closed. Two, perhaps we close up out of fear. We simply don't know how to handle the fast and ever changing world around us. We see a hostile and confusing world and retreat into our fortress.

Missiologically, therefore, we have the opportunity to live out what it means to be the church. If Jesus' statement that "all people will know that you are my disciples, if you have love for one another" (John 13:35) is true, then our communities of faith – local churches – should and could be ones that lonely and empty people are scrambling to join. In a fragmented and fearful society, where better for love, acceptance, and community to be found?

Missiological Summary

This chapter has only skimmed the surface of the sociology and psychology of our technologically driven society. Furthermore, the implications of such are vigorously debated and still being understood. The theological and missiological opportunities are many. The methodological responses are also numerous (see Part III). In summary, our missiological response to a society characterized by so much fear, boredom, and loneliness can be expressed in four words:

1. Sin. The truth is that we live in a fallen world tainted by sin. As a result, the world is full of danger, fear, meaninglessness, and human isolation. We must be realistic about our human condition, our human responsibility, and the temptation to turn our fears, our needs, and our solutions into idols.[302] Whatever the danger and whether the resulting fear is reasonable or not, and whatever the solutions we seek for boredom and loneliness, there is ultimately only one final and ultimate answer.

2. Gospel. Our message of Jesus Christ must be the Biblical gospel of him dying for our sins and not simple a "gospel lite" of "Jesus meets your needs." That is true, but it is insufficient and inadequate. We can teach people how to handle their money, how to raise their children, and how to improve their marriage. We can provide ministries that help people find jobs, improve community life, and address social issues. But sin, both individual and corporate, must be addressed. And, the truth of a dangerous discipleship cannot be downplayed, especially in a world and a society that is becoming more and more anti-Christian.

3. Witness. We must offer an authentic alternative to life in the world. Our words must be accompanied by action: we must show the reality of a loving, accepting, and even struggling, community. The cliché is that the church is a hospital for sinners, but sometimes clichés are true. Yes, the church is a redeemed community made up of regenerate believers. Yes, there should be accountability and discipline in the church. But it is a messy spiritual

hospital where "Corinthian" type believers begin the long
process of learning how to follow Jesus.

4. Serve. We not only demonstrate in our action what it
   means to be the Body of Christ toward each other, but
   we also demonstrate in our action what it means to love
   and serve the world. Authentic and open communities of
   faith work at finding ways to meet people at their points
   of need, demonstrating through service the love of Christ,
   and thus gaining an opportunity to verbally share the
   gospel of forgiveness of sin.

Fight or flight. Take the world head on or find ways to escape
and ease the pain. There are days when all of us feel pulled one
way or another. Neither option will ultimately address the core
human problem of sin or meet our deepest God-designed human
needs. In a society where most insist on shoving God aside, the
missiological opportunity is to present the one, true God who is
Lord over all of creation and in whom we can trust.

You Gotta Serve Somebody: The Myth of Absolute Freedom

No one can be a slave of two masters, since either he will hate one and love the other, or be devoted to one and despise the other. You cannot be slaves of God and of money.

Matt. 6:24

Paul, a slave of Christ Jesus....Do you not know that if you offer yourselves to someone as obedient slaves, you are slaves to that one you obey – either of sin leading to death or of obedience leading to righteousness?

Rom. 1:1; 6:16

In the Matt. 6:19-24 section of the Sermon on the Mount Jesus challenges his hearers about priorities, possessions, and loyalty. He warns against prioritizing the gathering of earthly possessions, for these are temporary and subject to loss and decay. He instructs his hearers to instead collect for themselves treasures in heaven, for these are safe and eternally secure. The choice one makes – prioritizing earthly possessions or heavenly treasures – reflects one's internal condition. That is, the treasure collected reveals the heart. Jesus continues to explain what he means with an analogy. In vv. 22-23 he refers to the eye as the lamp of the body and explains that what the eye beholds, prioritizes, and treasures will affect the whole body. If the eye is "good" then the body is "full of light." If the eye is "bad," then the body is full of darkness. What one seeks, prioritizes, and works to collect reflects one's interior condition.

Jesus concludes this section of his sermon by pointing to the core issue: loyalty. Dual loyalties are impossible to keep for very long. Eventually the tension leads to disloyalty and even hatred toward one of the parties. If a person prioritizes the collection of earthly possessions in his life – mammon, money, wealth – that means he is a slave to these things, and not to God. Trying to live loyally to both is an unbearable tension; it cannot be done. Jesus states it in stark terms: "You cannot be slaves to God and of money."

In the opening of the letter to the Romans, Paul refers to himself as a slave of Christ Jesus. Later in chapter 6, he addresses the issue of spiritual, but quite real, slavery. Like Jesus, he argues that divided loyalties are impossible. In this case, one is either a slave to sin or a slave of obedience. Like Paul, we can offer ourselves – commit ourselves – to be slaves of Christ Jesus, or we can offer ourselves to someone or something else. The problem is that being a slave to anything or anyone other than Christ Jesus is being a slave to sin. There is no other option. What we prioritize in life, what we seek to possess in life, what or who we follow in life will be our master and we its slave. Paul is just as stark in his statement as Jesus: ". . . you are slaves to that one you obey."

In our American society there are few ideals as dear to us as our freedom. We fought for it, we cherish it, we sing about it, we are proud of it – "let freedom ring." We do not like the idea of being a slave to anything (although the application of that principle came very slowly in our history). We value and promote the ideal of individual freedom and autonomy. And we should, within reason and within limits. Even at a time when we trail many other developed nations in science and math scores, in quality of health care, in quality of public education, and even in economic stability, the world still comes to us because they know they can be free. Certainly, most Americans believe there can be no such thing as "absolute freedom," defined as having no societal restrictions so the individual can act as he pleases regardless of consequences to himself or others. The great majority would also reject the various forms of anarchism, most of which include no role for the state.[303] However we may define and express our freedom, and we do differ, we agree that there are limitations.

Our political and social freedom is real, but it is ultimately both driven by and directed toward someone or something. That is, there is a spiritual reality (whether we are aware of it or not), that encompasses our political and social freedom. From the Biblical perspective, we are in one of two camps: either we are slaves of sin by nature (driven by sin) and choice (directed toward sin), or we are slaves of Christ Jesus in and due to a new nature (driven by the Holy Spirit) and choice (directed toward righteousness). Whatever freedom we may have politically, socially, and economically, it is encompassed by the spiritual reality of slavery, either to sin or to Christ. To be clear, within the realm of political and social freedom a person may do many good things and still be spiritually enslaved to sin. We may be free, but we are still slaves to something or someone, perhaps even to the very ideal of freedom. The bottom line, as Bob Dylan sang, also in stark terms, "You gotta serve somebody."

When we offer ourselves up to someone "as obedient slaves," we are turning that someone or something into an idol. What we serve, in other words, is or becomes what we worship. In American society, where we have so much freedom and so many options in which to express our freedom, it is easy to turn some of these options into our masters and gods. That may sound exaggerated because we usually identify idols with pagan cultures and animistic worship. It is true that many idols throughout human history are directly related to demons, things within the created order, and to things made by human hands. Still, at the root "of all idolatry is human rejection of the Godness of God and the finality of God's moral authority."[304] It is simply putting something else in his place, sometimes even unaware that we are guilty of idolatry. For example, when we reject his authority on human sexuality we are elevating our sexuality and its "free" expression to an ultimate authority. We make sex our "god." Or, when we ignore the fullness of meaning and purpose found in a relationship with God and seek constant activity, diversion, and entertainment to deal with our boredom and lack of meaning, we are idolizing both our needs and these activities. We are, in essence, slaves to entertainment.

These two examples also illustrate that idolatry involves the perversion of the goodness of God's creation and of the good gifts he has given us. Whether material possession, sexuality, rest and recreation, personal relationships, individual freedom, governing authorities, and the desire to worship, all are essentially and originally good within God's plan. They are his gifts to us. It is when we pervert these, abuse them, take them to extremes outside of his moral authority that they become idols and we become slaves to them.

Idolatry, therefore, is a reality in every society. It is a missiological issue because mission must "engage the gods" and "expose and unmask them."[305] Corporately, as an American culture and society, where there are numerous opportunities for us to express our freedom, there are consequently numerous opportunities for us to build idols and serve the corruption of God's good gifts. These American idols may not be obvious to us and they are certainly not unique to us. As we engage and expose these gods – as we engage them through our missiology – we are proclaiming exactly what Jesus, the Apostle Paul, and even Bob Dylan on one of his good days said: Absolute, unfettered, and unlimited freedom is a myth. You are either a slave to God or a slave to something else – you gotta serve somebody.

Designer Morality: Postmodern Fallout

It is too easy and a cop-out to blame Postmodernism for everything that is wrong in our American society. Immorality, idolatry, materialism, and the rejection of the Bible's ultimate authority is certainly not just the fault of postmodernism or post-modern people. Moderns were just as sinful. And so were pre-moderns. A key difference, however, is the understanding of authority. Pre-moderns believed that ultimate authority was in revelation given to society's leaders, whether kings, prophets, and eventually the Church. Obviously, not everyone obeyed or followed that given revelation, but the general worldview was that there was one revealed authority. Moderns placed ultimate authority in reason, logic, science, and human ability to exercise these objectively and correctly. Even for many Christians authority was in the "reasonable interpretation of the Bible." For the postmodern, there is suspicion of anyone or anything claiming final authority, for ultimate truth cannot be known. The Bible, therefore, is one of many religious writings to be compared to others for its usefulness. [306] Postmoderns, therefore, have a "pluralistic view of knowledge." They are even willing to "allow competing and seemingly conflicting constructions side by side," for the issue is not correctness but usefulness and "outcome." Therefore, truth, and especially moral truth, is "local." There is no overarching "metanarrative," only personal narratives.[307]

Dan Kimball humorously and truthfully explains this construction of a personal narrative (or identity) in the title to a chapter in his book: "Born (Buddhist-Christian-Wiccan-Muslim-Straight-Gay) in the USA." He goes on to explain how postmoderns believe there are "lots of religions to choose from," so "we piece together our own stories." This includes a "self-determined morality and diverse ideas about sexuality." If there is no "universal reference point," then who is to say what is right and what is wrong?[308] This is the postmodern fallout: there are no absolute reference points for morality and ethics; therefore, I am able to design my own morality. The biggest immorality is to "impose" any one morality on another person.[309] It all boils down to freedom with limited restraints, personal choice, and tolerance (defined as acceptance and encouragement) of all points of view. The problem is that freedom without objective restraints grounded in absolute truth leads to idolatry and enslavement.

American Idols

There are five major American idols to which we are enslaved that are missiologically significant. There are certainly more than these, and these five are not uniquely American. Again, these five idols are not directly caused by a postmodern worldview. They are grounded in the Modern experiment, propelled by Enlightenment views, and simply a reflection of humanity's sinful nature. They are perversions of God's good creation and God's good gifts, and really nothing new to the human condition. The reasons they are missiologically important are: One, they are currently dominating our society in both activity and discussion. They fill the air waves; they drive and reflect much of our economy, and dominate our public and private conversations. Two, the Postmodern fallout means that there are fewer and fewer grounds, from the point of view of intentional and aware practitioners, by which to critique these idols. In other words, relativism is the default position, if not ideologically then certainly practically, for all these idols. Unfortunately, the unintentional and unaware practitioners (the rest of us?) are too often oblivious of what we have bought into.

These idols are both the result of misunderstanding freedom as being without restraints and without consequences, and the cause of our slavery unawares. These American idols also overlap and influence each other. They build on each other, and each has numerous forms by which they manifest themselves in daily life.

The Right to Have Rights:
Radical individualism

The freedom we Americans live, fight, and die for is primarily expressed as individual rights. The "unalienable rights" endowed to us by our Creator – "life, liberty, and the pursuit of happiness" – we have understood primarily as the rights of each person. Without a doubt, what these rights are and should be has been debated and violently fought over throughout our history. The Civil War was all about rights, including state rights and the right to be free from slavery. Women marched for the right to vote. Laws were passed against child labor so children would have the right to a safe and healthy childhood. The rights in our Bill of Rights are regularly challenged ideologically and judicially: What is allowed under the right to free speech? What constitutes freedom of assembly? What can the press say without falling into libel? What is freedom of religion really supposed to mean? Many Americans have stood up for and fought for the rights of others who were oppressed and marginalized. We may not have always agreed with the cause or the methods, but many historical figures are considered heroes because they stood for the rights of those who could not or would not speak for themselves: slaves, women, children, the poor, the homeless, migrant workers, immigrants, religious sects, the unborn, and … some now say, the Gay population.

However we may see them play out in daily life, we hold these individual rights dearly. But what happens when individual rights – "my rights" – become the criteria by which we judge all concepts of freedom and happiness? Individual rights then become radical individualism. On the one hand, we agree with John Kennedy that the "rights of every man are diminished when the rights of one man are threatened." On the other hand, when individual rights are at the expense of good taste, morality, and the greater good of the American community, then rights – individual rights – have become an idol.

The political and sociological tensions between individual rights and community rights, or what constitutes acceptable individual freedom according to the Constitution will not be solved here. Neither will the opinions on morality and good taste. My point is that one of our great ideals has become one of our great idols. The beauty and necessity of individual rights have turned too many of us toward selfishness.[310] We want what we want regardless of others. We want what we want, because it is our right, no matter what the community may think. The societal and moral consequences are many. A few include:

1. A litigious society where every real or perceived slight is grounds for a lawsuit. The goal is not to see that justice is actually accomplished, but to force the other side to settle before the case has to go to court.

2. A society where no-fault divorce is the norm. If "my rights" are not met in this marriage or if this marriage is not making "me happy," then I have a right to get out of it and be happy. Even Christians fall into this trap, for certainly, as I have heard many times in marital counseling, "God wouldn't want me to be unhappy."

3. A society where the "right to choose" and "women's reproductive rights" automatically overrule the right to life. In this case, as in many cases of radical individual rights, a significant and often unaddressed underlying cause is the belief in the right to convenience. That is, how many abortions are really not about the right to choose, but about the "right" not to have one's life inconvenienced?

4. A society that is willing to redefine traditional understandings of sexuality, gender identity, and marriage based on the "right" to exercise one's sexuality. Of course, the issues of homosexuality and gay marriage are much broader and more complex than just demanding one's rights. However, when the debate is white hot, whatever is said about morality, traditional marriage, and the causes of homosexuality is trumped in the eyes of its defenders by an appeal to "rights." Note, even the issue – gay rights – is wrapped in the entire language of rights.[311]

In these four examples, and many others, what could be more American than appealing to one's rights? For many that is the crux of the argument. It is not morality, Biblical authority, or the opinion of the majority that matters, but rather one's individual rights. When have we gone too far with individual rights? Perhaps the question we should ask is not the specific question of, "Does this individual have this particular right?" but whether we have elevated the concept of individual rights to such a degree that they are an idol. The answer one gives is determined by his understanding of fallen human nature; that is, a Biblical view of fallen, sinful humanity has no difficulty in talking about freedom and rights within limits and restraints. If left to our own devices, we know the result will be like the book of Judges – everyone will do what is right in his own eyes and chaos will ensue.

Bigger and Better: Materialism

The nature of the American Dream was covered in the first chapter in the discussion of the Consumer Jesus. The Dream is itself driven by "rugged individualism" and Horatio Alger type opportunities where anyone with enough inventiveness and hard work can be "better, richer, and happier." Because we are an immigrant nation, and because a great number of people left poverty in Europe to find or make their riches here, socioeconomic upward mobility is weaved into our worldview as much as individual rights. In fact, such upward mobility is the expressed content of the American Dream. It is what we are all about; it is our right.[312]

Working hard to improve one's lot in life is good. Working hard to make life better and easier for future generations is good. Working to improve one's material status becomes an idol, however, when:

1. It erodes marriage, family, and other relationships. There are times in any job or business when time with family and friends is cut short. When deadlines are due, when a special project is underway, during certain cycles, or in times of financial straits when overtime or an extra job is needed then relationships may be sacrificed short term. When that sacrifice becomes a self-imposed pattern because the alternative would be less profit or a smaller paycheck, then the idol of materialism has crept in. Certainly, many people of limited economic means have to work long hours and many days – they wouldn't eat if they didn't. That is not idolatry but survival. In that case the spouse and the children understand and often pull together; the sacrifice is even seen as something admirable. But when the attitude is "just a few dollars (or a few million) more

and I will be satisfied," the family can't be fooled. They know they have taken a back seat.

2. It leads to unethical practices. Perhaps the temptation is not to neglect the family, but to cut ethical and legal corners. To cheat an employer, an employee, a customer, or the government, no matter how little or how much, indicates that the bottom line has become an idol.

3. It becomes an end rather than a means. None of this is to say that wealth is in and of itself sinful. Without a doubt the Bible warns against the dangers and enticements of riches (Ps. 49:6; Prov. 11:28; Matt. 19:23-24; Luke 8:14), but God can also bless with riches and wealth if he so chooses. In most cases, those whom God so blesses see their wealth not as an end, but as a means to the end of helping people, supporting missionaries and ministries, and as a tool to expand God's Kingdom.

4. It deteriorates into consumerism. Consumerism is the American Dream gone wild and out of control. No longer does demand drive supply, but marketing creates a demand. More and more is produced, and the trick is to convince consumers that they need all these products in order to experience fulfillment and to fit in with their peers. In one sense this is nothing new to the American scene; however, too many Americans are no longer purchasing out of need or even with their disposable income. We buy what we don't need with money we don't have, and eventually the debt load catches up. This is nothing short of idolatry, for the focus of attention and the spending of resources is far from God.

The idol of materialism is broad and can negatively affect many other areas of our society. For example, being in business is not a bad thing — materialism and business should not be equated, although Materialism can corrupt and ruin many a good business. Similarly, science and technology are not bad things. We all benefit from new discoveries and inventions in transportation, medicine, communications, the delivery of utilities, farming, and so forth. But these, too, can be corrupted by a spirit of Materialism. The same can be said about any domain of society, including education and government. In the end, like the rich young ruler, we have so much stuff, we just can't fathom giving it up.

"If we can put a man on the moon": Science and technology

It was noted earlier that one of God's good gifts to human culture is the ability to be creative, to invent, to discover, and to build. This gift can be used for God's glory and for the good of people: the Temple, city walls, shelter for families, places of business, hospitals, schools, and artistic monuments. This gift of science and technology can also become a tool of idolatry and an idol itself. Humans can build temples to Baal, Asherah poles, and even attempt to build a tower that would reach to the heavens (Gen. 11:1-9). Science and technology can also be used to build places of sin, weapons of destruction, and monuments to the selfishness of men.

The temptation for Americans is to turn science and technology itself into an idol, one that will somehow, in some way and at some time solve all our problems. The Modern worldview has held to this belief in inevitable progress and the inherent goodness of science for centuries. To a degree that faith is based on reality: diseases have been cured, means of transportation are quicker and safer, communication is instant, and so forth. That faith in progress, however, was shaken in the twentieth century with the devastation of World War I and the discharge of the atomic bomb at the end of World War II. Although science and technology have always been used for destruction and evil, the twentieth century most clearly demonstrated the ambiguity of science. Postmoderns, as discussed earlier, have a love-hate relationship with science and technology. They will use every gadget and bit of technology available, but do not have the faith of the Modern in the ability of science to cure our problems. In fact, they will point out that it is science and technology that has caused many of our problems: pollution, global warming, chemical contamination of food sources, and the use of cancer causing agents.

So, how are Americans still idolizing science and technology? One, we still believe to some degree that science will get us out the mess we have created. If we can put a man on the moon, then we ought to be able, with the right minds, the right amount of money, and the right time, to cure cancer, stop global warming, stop aging, and eliminate every inconvenience of life. Certainly science should be used for these – it is God's gift to us. But, are we expecting it to do things that cannot and should not be done? Where do we ultimately place our faith?

Two, we look to technology to fill the meaninglessness and hopelessness in our lives. As stated in the previous chapter, we look for a cure to our boredom, and we often look at technology. Movies, television, music, video games, motorcycles, motorboats, gadgets and toys may be pleasant and healthy ways to find rest and recreation. However, when science and technology combine with materialism to convince us that we must have all these to be happy … then we have an idol on our hands.

Avoiding the Silence, Filling the Space: Entertainment

To reiterate what was stated previously, rest, recreation, and having fun is not wrong. In fact, it is mandated by God and was practiced by the people of Israel and by Jesus and his disciples. Our difficulty is that we do not really know how to rest and truly recreate. We fill our time with countless and extremely expensive activities so that we can be distracted, titillated, and stimulated. Sometimes some of these activities lead to rest; at other times they are simply activities of a different kind used for simple distraction.

The billions of dollars and millions of hours spent on sports, music, movies, eating out, concerts, video games, gadgets and toys reflect a cultural obsession. Moreover, it is an obsession that only begs for more. More sports leagues than ever, and when that is not enough, we create fantasy leagues. More amusement parks, which "generate $12 billion in revenues each year." More ways to spend money on entertainment in all kinds of: cable television ("estimated revenues of $74.7 billion in 2007"), listening to music (MP3 players alone "generated $5.4 billion in revenue in 2007"), movies ("more than $10 billion in 2009"), video games ("Americans spent $13.5 billion on home video and computer games in 2006"). [313] That is just scratching the surface, but it proves that the entertainment industry is a very profitable one and apparently scratching a cultural itch.

One of the more distressing and fastest growing forms of entertainment is the "gaming" industry, called thus by those in the industry to avoid the actual negative connotations of gambling. Consider, however, that two decades ago only two states had legalized gambling. Now, only two (Utah and Hawaii) don't. Furthermore, "[g]ambling generates more revenue than movies, spectator sports, theme parks, cruise ships and recorded music combined," and is now a "40 billion dollar per year industry in the United States." No wonder, considering that just in Las Vegas "players lose $6 billion per year."[314] Besides the traditional gambling meccas of Las Vegas, Atlantic City, Shreveport, and Biloxi, there are "approximately 400 Indian gaming establishments" in the country.[315]

Also distressing and mind boggling is the growth of state lotteries. Doubtless, the enticement to win multiple millions of dollars is attractive . . . to the person who has not thought it through. The chance of winning the lottery is about "1 in 54 million" or less. Most studies show that the typical lottery player is already poor, less educated than the average person, and, increasingly, a senior adult. Furthermore, the economic benefits are always oversold, for the lottery never seems to solve the problems it promised to (usually education) and simply creates more (addiction to gambling).[316] The lottery is simply a tax on the poor without them realizing it. It is a way to exploit every desperate person's hope for a quick financial fix . . . and the government approves.

Related to our obsession with entertainment is the American (global, really) obsession and near worship of celebrity. *People* magazine, *The National Enquirer*, the *Star*, and multiple other tabloids; TV shows like *TMZ, Entertainment Tonight*, and *Extra*, and a countless number of talk shows that major on celebrity visits and stories – we are fascinated by the lives of the rich and famous even when their lives are messed up and they have nothing significant to say. In fact, nothing really fascinates us more than a celebrity life gone haywire: a messy divorce, an arrest, or a movie set meltdown. It seems as if we can't help but be attracted to celebrity "train wrecks." The celebrity's exhibitionism and our voyeurism are both fed by the *paparazzi's* thirst for profit and the shallow argument that the celebrity has a "right" to act as he or she wishes, and "the people have a right to know." Certainly, a general interest in celebrities can be harmless, especially as a teenager. It is the obsession with every detail of a celebrity's life, the inability to separate reality from the fantastic life of the celebrity, and the projection of inordinate knowledge, wisdom, influence, and even a sense of "normalcy" to that celebrity that is idolatry. And, usually, they don't even make good role models.

I do not want to come across as a grumpy, stick in the mud spoil sport. I also do not mean to imply that every single American is guilty of entertainment idolatry; besides, I am plenty guilty myself. It does not take much cultural examination, however, to realize that we work hard at avoiding any kind of silence or "space" in our lives by filling them up with entertainment. How many families are burdened because their children are involved in far too much – sports, band, ballet, etc? Can you name the last time you went to a restaurant or any public space that wasn't blaring music? I love music, but is anyone really listening? Have you counted the number of channels on your TV? How many are really worth watching? How often do we watch them just because they are there? We are tempted to do whatever we have to and spend however much money we can to avoid the boredom, meaninglessness, and loneliness of the empty space and silence in our lives. That is idolatry.[317]

Free Love at Last:
Our obsession with sex

Among all of God's good gifts to humans, perhaps none has been as misused, abused, and perverted as that of sex. He created us as sexual beings, an identity that far exceeds the mere sex act. Sex was part of his original design for men and women, to be perfectly expressed within his plan of the permanent union of one man and one woman loving each other, learning to understand each other more and more every day, and procreating to fill the earth. Obviously, the fall of Adam and Eve distorted the gift: both the security and stability of God given sexual identity and the fulfillment of the physical act of sex have been stunted, corrupted, and manipulated according to sin's twisted desires. The result throughout history and across all cultures has been frustrated, abusive, and self-centered relationships. Certainly, not all humans have expressed their fallen sexuality in the worst of ways; however, the potential, the temptation, and the threat simmer just under the surface in all of us.

This is not just an American problem – it is global. In fact, there are many cultures where sex, either overtly or covertly, is perverted almost beyond belief. The sex markets of Bangkok, the red light district of Amsterdam, the world sex slave business, the abuse of women in Muslim countries, pedophilia in Mormon polygamist sects, the explosion in online pornography, the sickening growth of child pornography, worldwide prostitution – no society or culture is free from the effects of sin on God's good gift of sex.

But this is a book about American missiology, and America has made an idol out of sex. We use sex to market and sell cars, beer, perfume, clothes, vacations, and even milk.[318] We hesitate to talk about how much money we make, for that would be ill mannered, but are willing to publicly talk about our sex lives. Magazines at the grocery store checkout lines have scores of articles on how to improve your sex life, how to turn him or her on, or new secrets about what he or she really wants, and they publish the same thing every single month. Television ads appeal to male insecurity offering all kinds of remedies, prescription and natural, for all kinds of ailments, real or perceived. It seems that every television sitcom that eventually runs out of good writing ideas (and they all usually do after a couple of seasons) turns to storylines full of raunchy sexual situations, some of which may be funny to a twelve year old just discovering what sex is about. And, it seems as is every television show has to introduce either a gay character or couple just to reinforce the view that such is perfectly normal.

And that is just scratching the surface. Wait till the marketers, and worse, pornographers can afford, master, and sell three dimensional holographic-type technology.[319] There will be a time when a person can have an encounter with a virtual prostitute and never have to leave home. It will cost money, it will involve lustful actions, but the excuse will be that no "real" person was involved. Wait till homosexuality and gay marriage is completely accepted and normalized by society.[320] Then all the raunchy ads and marketing we see now will also involve same sex images. American society is moving through three general attitudes toward sex: One, from an era when sex was a taboo subject that was practiced in private, and when even sinful acts were kept private. Two, through an era of "open and free love" in which sex had been "freed from its shackles" and idolized. Three, toward a rapidly developing era in which sex has become so open, commonplace, routine, and marketable that it carries no more meaning to people than having lunch together, an attitude already common in some European countries and found in such shows like "Sex and the City." Then, our slavery will be complete. We will think we have achieved full freedom regarding our sexuality and our sexual activity, but the truth is that the idol will have achieved its purpose: it will no longer even be noticed, its control complete.

Missiological Implications

These five idols are certainly not the only ones we struggle with; there are many others. But in relation to these, how do we face them, confront them, and eventually defeat them in our society? How do Christians remove these idols from their own lives and demonstrate to American culture what it means to be free as a slave of Christ?

1. We must unmask the idols by naming them. The missiological challenge is just what Wright said is the purpose of missions: to unmask false gods. That starts by naming, and thus admitting to, the idols in our society. We do this naming, which implies and includes confrontation, through both word and deed. Doing it by word does not mean we stand on the street corner (or in a television broadcast) and yell out that our neighbors are idolaters.

It means that we continue to preach and teach that idolatry is anything that interferes with, distracts from, or takes the place of, *on a regular, patterned basis,* our faith in and dependence on God.[321] More difficult, and more importantly, is to practice what we preach! We have the opportunity to demonstrate in our lifestyle what it means to be a slave to Christ, which is the true definition of freedom. Practically, this may mean simplifying our lives materially, reducing our obsession with, and maybe even participation in, "accepted" diversions, and cutting back on our addiction to busy-ness. This is not a call for a return to a legalistic view toward "wordly" entertainment; it is a call for an honest examination of priorities and investment of time and resources.

2. We must be willing to give up our individual rights. We can demonstrate appreciation for our American political, economic, and social freedom, and especially the individual rights that come with those. We can also demonstrate what it means to stand up for justice – for the rights of those who cannot speak and fight for themselves. At the same time we can demonstrate that being a slave to Christ means being willing to give up certain rights for the sake of Christ and others. We don't always have to be right. We don't always have to win. We don't always have to be compensated for a loss.

3. We must articulate and practice a Biblical theology of life. At the same time that we passionately argue for the rights of the unborn, our greater missiological challenge is to present a comprehensive Biblical theology of life. That is, we need to carefully articulate a pro-life stance that addresses not only the unborn, but the aged, victims of crime and war, and even the disconcerting number

of wrongful convictions that have led to misapplication of the death penalty.[322] We have done well in providing life affirming options through crisis pregnancy clinics, adoption ministries, and other counseling. Our growing aging population may demand similar "right to life" action for the growing numbers who will not be able to care or speak for themselves.

4. We must articulate and demonstrate how rights demand responsibility. For many of us this was modeled and taught to us by our parents. That does not appear, unfortunately, to be any longer the common cultural experience. To the contrary, the common cultural experience is that of entitlement and little conception of consequences.[323] The "right" to have promiscuous sex includes the consequences of disease or pregnancy and the responsibility of an unexpected child. The "right" to free speech includes the consequence of being rejected or not liked for what is said and the responsibility for the hearing rights of others. The "right" to have a job includes the responsibility of showing up on time, working hard, and paying taxes. The "right" to use this earth includes the responsibility of taking care of it. And so on. What would seem to be so elemental is lost in our idolatry of radical individualism.

5. We must practice simpler lifestyles and demonstrate generosity. We can demonstrate appreciation for our abundant material blessings, but also demonstrate what it means to generously give, to live simply, and to live by faith. As believers we can model staying out of debt, purchasing and owning less, and not pursuing the latest gadget or fad. Preachers often bemoan that contemporary Christians don't stand out from the world, and mainly point to hair, tattoos, and dress styles. They may have a point, but what

if Christians were known as those who live simply because they give away most of what they make? That would really stick out.

6. We must keep science and technology in perspective. We can make full use of science and technology, especially for the sake of the gospel. We need to be fully aware, however, that they are human constructions and temporary – they will fail us. The opportunity exists to appreciate what science and technology have to offer us, in spite of scientism and Darwinism, but yet preach, teach, and demonstrate that our faith is ultimately in God's provision and plan.[324]

7. We must learn and practice what the Bible means by Sabbath rest. We need to learn and then demonstrate that Biblical rest and re-creation need not be a burden financially, on our families, and on our time. We need to learn to model a weekly Sabbath rest, moderation in extra-curricular family activities, and regular re-creation times that don't require exorbitant expenditures.

8. We must practice sexual purity. This is perhaps the most difficult missiological challenge. We must learn to demonstrate sexual purity while speaking the truth about God's plan for sexuality. We must continue to speak the truth in love about adultery, pornography, and homosexuality, but always with compassion and grace for those trapped in these idolatrous sins and humbly guarding against our own failures. Essentially, we must practice what we preach. Confronting and defeating the sex idol is difficult for several reasons:

    •   There is no human being that is not a fallen sexual being. No one is guilt-free.

291

- There is probably no other sin that so affects a Christian's witness, especially that of Christian leaders. When a pastor falls into immorality, it is big news.

- There is probably no other sin that Christians (at least men) struggle with so much and so secretly. It is estimated that "70% of churchgoing Christian men have secretly surfed pornographic websites in the last year," that "50% of pastors have too,"[325] and that "thirty percent of women" are addicted to porn.[326] When the reality of church members' marital unfaithfulness, pre-marital sex, divorce, and struggles with homosexuality are taken into account, it is hard to have a prophetic voice in a sex obsessed society, because we are, too.

- Sexuality, especially homosexuality and gay marriage, will be the defining issue for evangelical witness in the coming decades. As we take a Biblical stand on human sexuality and the Biblical definition of marriage, we will be condemned, ridiculed, falsely accused of hate speech, and eventually susceptible to legal action for that perceived hate speech. The greatest challenge we will have as parents and grandparents will be convincing our children and grandchildren that our now "abnormal" views are, in fact, the Biblical and still normal views. As the normalization of the gay lifestyle and gay marriage continues, and as we hold to Biblical truth, the missiological challenge is to maintain a compassionate and loving attitude. To a large degree, if the gospel of Jesus Christ is to be heard by the gay world, it will not be only with our words, but because we love each other and love the world with Christ-like love.

Conclusion

You gotta serve somebody. There is no person who is totally and absolutely free. What freedom we do have is oriented towards service to someone or something, whether or not we know it or admit it. The myth is that freedom means no shackles to anyone; the reality is that true freedom is only found in being free from sin, from idols, and from self, and being shackled to Christ. That freedom, however, is not be used "as an opportunity for the flesh," but in service to "one another through love" (Gal. 5:13). Missiologically, that freedom is also to be used to express in word and deed the truth of the One who has set us free. Some of the ways we can do that will be examined in the next section of the book.

PART 3

Introduction
What Are We Going To Do?
Context and Response

Reality checks

We have formulated a Biblical Christology and we have examined the nature of our mission field, the United States of America. The subsequent practical and ministerial question is "What are we going to do about it?" If America is a mission field and we have the message that addresses the needs of both individuals and society, how do we tell the story in a way that it can be heard, understood, and responded to? How do we communicate hope, healing, and salvation in a society that has changed so much and continues to change faster and faster?

Before missiological strategies can be put into place, the uncomfortable reality checks of who we are must be recognized and stated. These include:

We have already lost the culture...
if we ever really had it

More than ever, the mixed, diverse, and post-Christian nature of our culture is apparent. With the growing influence of non-

Christian world religions, the continuing secularization of culture, and the growing influence of postmodern pluralism, the reality is that we have "lost" the culture. That is, the dominant worldviews, the prevailing morality, and the aspirations of both individuals and society are not Biblical. Of course, did we ever really "have" the culture? There was a time when our country operated primarily within a Judeo-Christian ethic, but even at its very best the American culture was still fallen, was still run by fallen men and women, and was still guilty of numerous sins. Today, the reality demands not that we "take it back" or return to a presumed ideal state of affairs, but that the cross of Jesus Christ be proclaimed as the ultimate solution to both individual and corporate sin. Where God takes the country from there will be his business.

We have already sold out to the culture … and we hardly even noticed

The reality is that Christians accommodated morally and ethically to the culture long ago. And, like the proverbial frog in the boiling kettle, we hardly even noticed. For example, we have slowly accepted coarseness, vulgarity, violence, and other sinful attitudes and behavior until we are almost immune to their effects. Consider the uses of h*** and d*** by Archie Bunker in the show *All in the Family* in the seventies. That was "ground breaking" and "progressive" or "vulgar" and "offensive," depending on your point of view. Slowly but surely, however, vulgar language became "acceptable," especially on cable television, so that now a character can say almost anything without us even raising an eyebrow. The same can be said for violence. We have gone in our entertainment from cheesy, bloodless, and unrealistic violence, past the portrayal of bloody and realistic violence, to gory, glorified, and, once again, unrealistic violence. The result is that we are desensitized. These are simple examples, to be sure, but the point is that, in one sense, we have all sold out and hardly noticed.

Care should be taken, however, as we consider the "selling out" accusation. Although the complaint that Christians and the church have "sold out" is true in many ways, too often the target is actually church practices and refers more to cultural preferences, sentimentality, and comfort zones than to Biblical principles. How often have we heard of a pastor who has "sold out" because he preaches in jeans and a t-shirt? Or that such and such church has "sold out" because it uses a band instead of an organ? Or, worse yet, they project the words to hymns and praise songs onto a screen? The reality is that most of what the traditional church does in worship is a reflection of somebody's culture. Pews, pulpits, architecture, suits and ties, 11 a.m. services – all these have a cultural basis. As we seriously reflect on areas where we have compromised the gospel, morality, and Biblical ethics with culture, we also need to carefully distinguish between those and cultural church practices.

We are not doing the job ... and by definition we are insane

The old *cliché* is that the definition of insanity is "doing the same things over and over again and expecting different results." If that is the case, then much of what we are doing missiologically in America proves that we are insane. Although evangelical churches have held their own for the last decade, overall church attendance and growth is not keeping up with population growth.[327] As we debate what has gone wrong and what we need to do, too often we overlook the fact that many of our churches and ministries are perfectly suited for life in the 1970s. We may be aware that the world has changed, but once we step inside the doors of the church building, we are seduced by the familiarity and the sentimentality of "how we have always done things." This is not a knock on tradition, for there is much to celebrate, protect, and hold on to in tradition. It is rather a concern about *traditionalism*, which is when comfortable and known ways override the mission of reaching people for Christ. The issue is not really about music styles, dress styles, or liturgy. The issue is a Christendom driven, purely attractional (come to us) world view versus a post-Christendom, missional, "we must go to them" worldview. It is rejecting the comfort of the Christian sub-culture and moving into a challenging and Biblically illiterate mission field. In essence, the issue is recognizing that the message hasn't changed, but the audience certainly has.[328]

We are never free from ideology … so my politics may not be the answer

We often hear that the "next election" is the most crucial in America's history, and often it is. We often hear that the "only hope for America" is for us to elect the right people or Bible believing politicians, or for this or that legislation to be passed or defeated. There is certainly nothing wrong with having strong political convictions, putting them in practice, voting, and passing or defeating legislation. These can become problematic when they are ideologically driven more than anything else. The danger is when we confuse Biblical Christianity with a particular political ideology, left, right, or in between. That is, the temptation is either to believe that our ideology is the only solution or to identify the gospel with our ideology. Politics, elections, and legislation can do a lot of good. They need to be pursued. We all have an ideology. We do need to be careful, however, to recognize our particular preferred ideology and make sure that the saving message of the gospel is partisan and ideologically free.

Having said that, however, the reality is that the gospel *is*, in the broader sense, political. Living out the implications of the gospel requires addressing lifestyle concerns and issues related to poverty, justice, war, and peace. The transformative power of the gospel is not just applicable to individual lives, but also to communities, cities, and nations. That inevitably requires political action within political systems. The challenge is to critically analyze a particular sociopolitical issue from a Biblical perspective, admitting to and being aware of one's own preferred ideology, and work at applying a Biblical solution regardless of the political *status quo* or the prevailing partisan ideology. Admittedly, this is difficult and a constant struggle, and will be addressed in more detail in the last chapter.

We don't have to give up yet ... or, maybe we should.

Should we be optimistic or pessimistic about the American mission field? Should we face the reality that the culture continues to deteriorate morally and spiritually, do what we can to spread the gospel, and simply wait for the second coming? Obviously, the answer one gives significantly reflects one's eschatology and understanding of the Kingdom of God. I have no desire to discuss millennial views or interpretations of the signs of the times. I also don't want to take a completely optimistic view reflective of postmillennialism or a completely pessimistic view reflected in some premillennial extremes. The middle ground I propose is this:

1. Jesus is coming again; but, no person knows the day or hour (Matt. 24:36: Acts 1:7). Trying to figure out more than that is an exercise in futility.

2. The signs of the end times are "signs for all times," because the end times began with the death, burial, and resurrection of Jesus Christ.

3. Jesus has inaugurated the Kingdom, which will be consummated at his return. In the meantime, the Kingdom grows like the wheat and tares; that is, it is a mixed bag of good and evil.

4. Our task while we live "between the times" is to "tell the old, old story" – to proclaim the gospel of the Kingdom, live as representatives of the Kingdom, and work to improve the present world as much as possible in preparation for the restoration and redemption of the creation.

5. We can be, therefore, both optimistic and pessimistic. There are periods when revival and awakening comes to different nations. There are periods of world war, famine, and great increases in evil. Nations rise and fall; tyrants come and go; sin persists, the Devil attacks, but the Holy Spirit of God is at work. We mourn when evil temporarily prevails. We rejoice when we see a spiritual response to God's work. Ours should be a realistic view of the world: it is both good and bad, with both rising and falling in different ages and in different regions of the world. Furthermore, we have to take care not to have an ethnocentric eschatology. That is, just because our own nation seems to be going backwards spiritually does not mean that God is not doing a great work in other parts of the world. In spite of what may or may not be happening on the American mission field, God has and is working a global plan.[329]

6. So, we don't need to give up, except in the sense of realizing that this is God's creation and he is at work accomplishing

his will and his plan of redemption. We don't go passive, but we may need to "give up" striving so much and trust in his timing and his work. Our hope is ultimately not in a political ideology, our ability to legislate morality, or even in our missiological strategies and methods, but in the story of Jesus and his love.

Part 3, therefore, will deal with the task of telling the gospel story. Four underlying assumptions drive the content of this third part:

One, the gospel must be *proclaimed verbally*. This means that the story of God's redemption offered in the person of work of Jesus Christ must at some point be spoken person to person, in small group discussions, in teaching groups, or by preaching from the pulpit.[330]

Two, the gospel must be proclaimed through *ethical and responsible* living by the individual Christian and by local churches. More than ever and because of social networking, rapid communication, and a hostile media, our public testimony is under close scrutiny and carries a broader influence.

Three, one of the most effective methods for telling the gospel and fulfilling the Great Commission task of making disciples is through *church planting*. There is probably no other missions strategy as effective, as popular, and as misunderstood as church planting.

Four, influencing all three of these principles is the principle and practice of *contextualization*, which is the effort to tell the gospel story in a Biblically faithful and culturally relevant manner. As common sense as that sounds, it is not easy and not without significant controversy. Much has been written about contextualization, but, as I will argue, it is a critically important principle that affects all that is done in missions. Therefore, it bears examination and discussion early on.

As was mentioned in the opening **Introduction**, this book is not a "how-to" manual covering every aspect of missions strategies and methods. There are scores of excellent books from far more effective and successful practitioners. My approach is to address the principle-driven big picture in order to stimulate thought, both encourage and challenge existing views as necessary, and encourage those already working at facing and making change. I pray the reader will see his mission field in a new light and prayerfully and carefully examine the doors of mission that God is opening in America.

The Gospel and Contextualization: Worldviews Matter

Then they traveled through Amphipolis and Apolonia and came to Thessalonica, where there was a Jewish synagogue. As usual, Paul went to them, and on three Sabbath days reasoned with them from the Scriptures, explaining and showing that the Messiah had to suffer and rise from the dead, and saying: "This is the Messiah, Jesus, whom I am proclaiming to you."

Acts 17:1-3

Then Paul stood in the middle of the Aeropagus and said: "Men of Athens! I see that you are extremely religious in every respect ... Therefore, what you worship in ignorance, this I proclaim to you.... God now commands all people everywhere to repent, because He has set a day on which He is going to judge the world in righteousness by the Man He has appointed. He has provided proof of this to everyone by raising Him from the dead."

Acts 17:22, 23b, 30a-31

The Apostle Paul considered his primary mission to be the proclamation of "Jesus Christ and Him crucified" (1 Cor. 2:2). Wherever he went on his missionary journeys, whoever he met, and whatever he did – healing, preaching, debating, or casting out demons – Paul's purpose was to get to the story of Jesus and his work on the cross. In the first few verses of Acts 17 we see Paul doing what he usually did when he entered a new city: he went straight to the Jewish synagogue and reasoned with the Jews that Jesus was the Messiah and the fulfillment of the entire Hebrew Scriptures. His strategy was to begin with the existing knowledge and understanding of synagogue attenders. He could assume they were believers in the one true God, had strong Biblical knowledge, and were looking for the Messiah. Starting there, he only needed to convince them that Jesus, the crucified and risen one, was the Messiah. Paul understood the context of his hearers – their language, worldview, presuppositions, hopes, fears, sufferings, and their expectations of the coming Messiah. That is, he contextualized the gospel so that it was clearly understood, and if rejected, it would be rejected for its content and not for any artificial reason Paul may have created.

Later in the same chapter of Acts we see Paul in Athens, the known world's center of philosophy and pagan spirituality and a city "full of idols" (v.16). He had already spent time, as usual, in the synagogue reasoning with the Jews and other God fearers. When he encounters some philosophers, they invite him to the Aeropagus so he could explain his strange teachings to the intellectuals who gathered there. Once again, Paul understood the context of his hearers. These probably had some familiarity with the Jewish religion, but were mostly steeped in philosophies that were polytheistic, moralistic, and anti-materialistic (that is, they believed in the immortality of the soul, but rejected any goodness in the material body). Thus, they had little or no Biblical knowledge, were certainly spiritual in the broadest sense, belonged to various competing schools of philosophy, had an abundance of intellectual confidence, and were interested in new ideas. Paul's strategy is quite different than it was in the synagogue. He assumes there is nothing monotheistic, Jewish, or Biblical about his hearers. He commends them for their religiosity, points to their statue of "an unknown God," and moves in his argument from that God whom they worship "in ignorance" to the One Creator God, who is above and distinct from his creation, to the "Man" through whom judgment will come and who has been raised from the dead. Paul's beginning point was completely different than it was with the Jews, but his ending point was the same – the Man Jesus Christ. Paul contextualized the message of the gospel so that it was clearly understood, and if rejected, it was rejected for its content (in this case, the resurrection) and not for any artificial obstacle Paul may have created.

Like Paul, our task is to tell the old gospel story of Jesus and his love on the cross. The inevitable question is, how? We certainly want to tell the story faithfully, accurately, completely, and effectively. We want the telling of the story to bear fruit. At the same time, fruit that is borne should reflect the true story and not an aberration. To put it in Great Commission words, as we make disciples we want those disciples to reflect and obey the Biblical Jesus, not a defective, incomplete, or modified Jesus of our own making. Doing this requires holding firmly to Biblical truth and communicating that truth in a culturally appropriate manner so that it can be heard, understood, and responded to. Being Biblically faithful and culturally relevant requires the practice of contextualization.

What It Is and What It Is Not

Contextualization simply means to put something within a context. Just as the Biblical interpreter should be careful not to take a passage *out* of context, the preacher, evangelist, and missionary must take into account the context to which he is applying the Biblical message. Questions that must be asked before the gospel message is shared include: What is the language spoken? What is the makeup of the audience, whether one person or thousands? What is the level of education and Biblical knowledge? Are they literate or non-literate? What are the cultural characteristics of the hearer? How do they think and make decisions? What is their current spiritual worldview; that is, what do they think of when they hear the words God, creation, Jesus, sacrifice, cross, and so on? The information the gospel teller wants to discover is: What is the worldview I am dealing with and how will that affect the understanding of the gospel message?

The communicator, therefore, is trying to "present the supracultural message of the gospel in culturally relevant terms."[331] He is trying to take the unchanging, transcultural, trans-generational, ever true and ever applicable gospel message and communicate it to and within whatever context God has called him to. This may require some significant adjustments on the part of the communicator such as learning a new language, spending years understanding the receptor culture, explaining a passage numerous times from numerous perspectives, and learning to use illustrations that make cultural sense to the hearer (as Jesus did). On the other hand, it may involve such simply adjustments as using an easier to read Bible because of the age or education level of the hearer, foregoing esoteric theological terminology, or never assuming the audience knows anything about the Bible…because they may not!

Contextualization is not, however, changing or excluding part of the message of the gospel to make it more palatable to a person, a culture, or to a dominant worldview. It is not allowing the prevailing culture to determine the meaning and application of Scripture. It is not even changing the terminology of Scripture – words such as "Father," "cross," or "blood" – to appease or not offend the hearers. It certainly may require patient explanation of a term or even the introduction of new terminology, but the Bible must be allowed to speak for itself. Inappropriate or extreme contextualization compromises the message; appropriate contextualization honors, respects, and engages the hearer and her context while faithfully, lovingly, and carefully presenting the truth of the gospel of Jesus Christ.[332]

Why Contextualization Matters

Contextualization that is thoughtful and careful is essential to communicating the gospel for three reasons:

1. It is biblically and theologically sound. The first example of contextualization is that of the revelation of God himself to human beings. His ways and thoughts are higher than ours (Isa.55:8-9), so he accommodated himself in ways that could be understood by his creation. He spoke in human language and he acted within his creation. Perhaps there is no greater example of contextualization than the incarnation of the Son of God. He became flesh as he identified with humanity. He grew, ate, drank, slept, and was tempted in every way as we are. When Jesus spoke, he spoke in the language of the people. When he spoke in parables or used illustrations, he used images people were familiar with – fishing, farming, weddings, and housecleaning. On the day of Pentecost, the Holy Spirit gave the disciples the gift of languages so that all hearers could understand what was being proclaimed. As seen in Acts 17, the Apostle Paul took into account the cultural, philosophical, and religious backgrounds of his hearers so that he could communicate the truth of the gospel clearly. The practice of faithful and appropriate contextualization is simply taking the Fall of *human kind* into sin seriously.

It recognizes that all cultures are sinful and require serious and patient definition of terms, explanation of concepts, and application to life.[333]

2. It is historically and culturally inevitable. That is, true evangelism and missions are practically impossible without the process of contextualization. The Bible was written in Hebrew, Greek, and Aramaic. It therefore needs to be translated and in ways that make sense to the readers.[334] Communication has to be in the language of the hearers and with an understanding of their worldview. For example, in Japan there is no word for sin, and the concept of shame is far more culturally significant than sin. The evangelist or missionary, therefore, cannot assume that his hearer understands transgression against God or another human being in the same way as he does. Patient explanation will be necessary. Similarly, assumptions and presuppositions on the part of the communicator have to identified, admitted, and set aside if improper or an obstacle to the communication of the gospel. A Western missionary also has to take care not to communicate that Christianity or the Christian life is to be identified with European or American dress, music, politics, or social practices. The reality is that we all contextualize in some form or fashion, but we are often unaware of how it happens within our own culture and how some of that contextualization has become "the right way to do things." Therefore, we think the worship service should be at 11 AM, which was an accommodation to rural American life. We think that a certain order of service, certain types of music, particular ways of dressing or designing worship space are godlier than others, when they are generally cultural accommodations from the past.[335] Contextualization must and will take place. The challenge is to do it carefully and thoughtfully.[336]

3. It removes artificial barriers to the gospel. Every person deserves to hear the gospel in a way that he can understand and respond to. This is, of course, easier said than done. The goal, however, is to communicate the gospel in such a way that the only stumbling block for the hearer is the gospel itself. That is, if the gospel is rejected by the hearer, we want the rejection to be because the gospel of the cross is the stumbling block, and *not* our person, our demeanor, our presentation, our explanation, or our inability to communicate in a way that the hearer can understand and respond. Contextualization is, therefore, "an act of love."[337]

Thoughtful, careful, and appropriate contextualization that is faithful to the Bible and critically aware of the culture is absolutely necessary for the effective communication of the gospel. Without an effort at contextualization, we run the minimal risk of identifying our styles, methods, and strategies with the only proper way of doing evangelism and missions, and the maximum risk of confusing our own cultural practices and preferences with the gospel message. Either way, the results can be a rejection of the gospel because it is "foreign" or "irrelevant" to the hearer or acceptance by the hearer of a truncated, distorted, and unhealthy gospel.

The Dangers of Syncretism

So far I have described contextualization in terms of "thoughtful" and "careful." That is because careless and thoughtless contextualization can lead to syncretism. Missiologist Gailyn Van Rheenen explains that syncretism often "is birthed out of a desire to make the gospel relevant" in a particular culture. The problem occurs when there is an "over-emphasis upon the cultural context." That is, the passionate desire to communicate the gospel can overcome, if one is not careful, the need for clarity in truth. Eventually, cultural "accommodations become routinized, integrated into the narrative of the Christian community and inseparable from its life,"[338] and we can't really tell where Biblical Christianity ends and our culture begins.

Syncretism, moreover, is a two-way danger. That is, the gospel message proclaimed by the evangelist or missionary may already be distorted by his own cultural influences, and the gospel message received by the hearer may become distorted by his cultural influences. This phenomenon, although quite serious, is nothing new. Throughout church history the dominant culture, whether communicating or receiving, has had a tendency to blend its own cultural beliefs and values with the gospel.

Having said that, it is important to understand that the gospel is *always* communicated within a culture and to a culture. It also must be culturally relevant – contextualized – so that it makes sense, can be responded to, and is applicable to the daily life of the recipient. Syncretism is not simply cultural accommodation. It occurs, rather, when cultural elements change the message of the gospel. For example, if a missionary teaches that the newly converted Christian must also become a believer in capitalism, that is syncretism. Now, capitalism may be the best economic system available, but it is not part of the gospel message. There have been many and are many Christians who are not capitalists. On the other hand, the hearer may receive the message of the gospel, believe in Jesus, but may not abandon (often due to cultural pressure) a belief in the veneration of and prayer to the saints.

In our American mission field, we have often confused the desired results of the gospel with the gospel itself. For example, some have too closely identified the gospel with behavior and lifestyle patterns. In fact, the gospel is often caricatured as being against this or that particular behavior. Changed behavior, however, is not the gospel; it is rather the fruit and the evidence of the gospel believed and received. For example, even something as important as being pro-life is not the gospel. Hopefully, a pro-life position will result from receiving the gospel, but it is not the gospel. Changed behavior should and must take place, but the gospel is repentance, belief and faith in Christ, regeneration, and *then* follows the evidence of changed behavior.

Practicing Biblical and effective contextualization and avoiding syncretism is not easy. It requires active study of the Scripture, taking a hard look at one's own cultural biases and presuppositions, and adopting a humble attitude toward the culture of others.[339] It requires an effort to find not only connection points and bridges to cultures, other religions, and worldviews, but intentionally pointing out the dissimilarities of Biblical Christianity with these.[340] However difficult it may be, an American missiology will not be effective and fruitful if it does not tackle contextualization and syncretism. Debates about culture, accommodation, and "going too far" will always be with us and should be. Biblical faithfulness and cultural relevance is always the goal.[341]

Some Principles of Contextualization

How can the practice of contextualization be summarized? What are some guiding principles? Although the study of contextualization can involve complex discussions of communication theory and anthropology, consider the following simple principles for careful and thoughtful contextualization.[342] These principles apply internationally and in America. They apply when doing missions cross-culturally and among sub-cultures or affinity groups within one's own culture.

1. Stay grounded in Scripture. The only way to avoid relativism and the corruption of the message when contextualizing is to stay grounded in the study of Scripture. The Bible is our standard for doctrine, faith, and practice. It is timeless,

trans-cultural, trans-generational, and without error. If this is so, then when a conflict arises, real or perceived, between the gospel being communicated and the hearer's culture, then it is back to the Bible. Scripture is the final judge of all cultures, whether the dominant one or a subculture, whether the culture of the preacher or that of the hearer. Failure to hold to this standard will result in "caving" to cultural pressure and re-interpreting the Bible according to a current and temporal norm. No example is more relevant at the time of this writing than how some denominations have set aside Biblical authority and long-held interpretations in order to accommodate cultural demands for the acceptance of gay marriage.

2. Consider other disciplines of study. Any serious attempt at contextualizing will include taking advantage of knowledge found in other disciplines such as history, sociology, demographics, anthropology, and linguistics. The one sharing the message of the gospel will be far more fruitful if he heeds the old public speaking adage, "know your audience." Information gleaned from these disciplines will inform the missionary as to a culture's makeup, worldview, and social structures. He will understand the struggles, issues, economic difficulties, and past events that have shaped the people and their religious and spiritual beliefs and practices. Knowing these will help the gospel story teller carefully choose his approach, his timing, his terminology, his illustrations, and his applications. They will help him anticipate barriers and objections, understand superstitions, suspicions, and fears. They will, in essence, make him far more fruitful.

3. Recognize that the process is never ending. Contextualization is not a "one time and done" process.

Cultures change; generations are different, and social, political, and economic circumstances influence and affect people. That is, contextualization can become dated quickly. The fruitful missionary, whether in America or around the world, will always be asking how the message can be better communicated. She will always remember that the gospel is about reaching people for Christ, and that the job is not done until people have heard, understood, and had the opportunity to respond.

4. Take into account all of Christian faith and life. Contextualization begins with the most basic task of translating Scripture and explaining its concepts, doctrines, and theology. It must not, however, end with theological formulation. Contextualization must also deal with worship, church structure, ministry issues, and what it means to live as the Body of Christ and in the world. That is, contextualization is both propositional and practical. It is concerned with truth statements and with true living. It declares the truth and then teaches how to live out that truth in real and practical ways within one's culture.

5. Remember sinful human nature. This simply means that no one's effort at contextualization is perfect. Because all humans are fallen, even the one communicating the gospel can have personal agendas, present a distorted version of the gospel, be prideful, and have plenty of spiritual blind spots. This is a reminder that the contextualization process demands humility, prayer, accountability, and a dependence on the Holy Spirit to both empower the communication of the gospel and the hearing of the gospel in spite of our mistakes and sinfulness.

6. Stay humble and learn from them, also. Humility in the contextualization process also means that much can be learned from the hearer and her culture, also. As we interact with a person, a group, an affinity, a population segment, or a people group, we encounter new ways of thinking and of seeing the world. Certainly, the Bible judges these elements just as it judges our own culture. Still, as we listen, watch, and learn we may uncover ways that our own cultural preferences, personal experience and background, and misunderstandings have distorted how we understand, live, and communicate the gospel. For example, a church planter may have a strong sense of time and the importance of timeliness. In fact, he has often spoken of the "spiritual stewardship of time" to the point that he has evaluated some people's spiritual maturity by how conscious they are of the clock. As he plants cross-culturally, however, he is soon frustrated by the apparent disregard for time and timeliness in other cultures. After some conflict, some effort, and eventually some humble learning, he realizes that he had almost turned time and timeliness into an idol. He had distorted the definition of discipleship by an overemphasis on time. He realized this as he learned that other cultures don't have the same concern over time and value other things more than he does. This did not make him or them more or less spiritual, just different.

These principles should make it clear that the process and practice of contextualization is dynamic, involves hard work, and must rely on prayer and the work of the Holy Spirit. In the end, however, how far can we go in contextualization? Put another way, what can be "given up" and what must be held on to no matter what, and how do we decide?

What Matters and What Doesn't ... or Shouldn't

The difficulty with most contextualization discussions among American evangelicals is that they usually start from an American, mostly Southern, middle class, white expression of Christianity. The question that should be asked is "How do we translate and communicate Biblical Christianity to _____?" The problem is that the often implied and unintended question is "How do we translate and communicate *our* understanding and version of Christianity to _____?" That may be an inevitable and understandable starting point, but it is the wrong one. A case in point: My missionary father was once at a missions conference with a display table that included a Spanish Bible. A well-meaning church member saw the Bible and asked Dad, "Is that the King James Version?" My Dad responded "No, it is the Spanish version." The gentlemen insisted "But, is it the King James?" really asking, of course, whether it was translated directly from the King James. The Bible in question was the Reina Valera, a translation from the original languages that actually predates the KJV. This brother, however, could not conceive of a translation that did not begin with his preferred English one.

Similarly, in contextualizing the gospel, including all the elements of ecclesiology, discipleship, and the Christian Life, the question should be "How should Biblical Christianity be communicated, expressed, and lived out in this particular context." Granted, it is impossible to completely separate one's own culture in the contextualization process, but every effort should be made to do so.

Again, this is true not only in international cross-cultural missions, but also in the American mission field. As we do evangelism, make disciples, and plant churches, the question is not "How do I lead them to do it like I do?" but "What does a disciple of Jesus or a New Testament church look like in this particular community, affinity group, population segment, or people group? Some principles to follow that help us distinguish how far we can go – how much can be "given up:"

1. Meaning matters, so don't give it up. The most important issue in contextualization is meaning. As hard as it may be at times in translating and communicating, the last thing we want to do is to change, alter, or distort the meaning of Scripture. If the gospel message is never changing and applicable to all, then the utmost care must be taken not to leave anything out or to incorporate any other views that may change that message. For example, it is going too far to speak of God as our "heavenly parent," for that radically changes the revelation of God himself to us. It is distorting the message to argue that because the Bible says Jesus died for the sins of the world that all people are ultimately saved. It is confusing the message to present Jesus as the "pig of God" to a New Guinea people group because they owned pigs and had no idea what sheep were (the inevitable consequence is having to completely redefine the image of God as Shepherd, to change the parable of the lost sheep, to drop the metaphor of humans as sheep gone astray, and on and on). Meaning matters. It may take time to explain unknown images, symbols, and concepts, but the effort is required so the message will not be compromised.[343]

2. Dissimilarities matter, so point them out. As the message is being presented, especially in a cross-cultural setting, there is often the opportunity to connect or bridge to a familiar concept in the hearer's religion or worldview. This can be quite effective and acceptable, *as long as* the dissimilarities and differences are also pointed out. Paul

did this on Mars Hill in Acts 17. For example, it is not going too far to say that Christians and Muslims are similar in that both are monotheistic. It is going too far, however, to say that the God of the Bible is the same as the Allah of the Koran. The dissimilarities are too vast. Our God is Trinitarian, he is and has revealed himself as Holy and Loving Father, as sinless incarnate Son who died and rose again, and as Holy Spirit who resides in his children. And that is just the beginning of the differences. Similarly, an evangelical could point out to a Roman Catholic that we also honor Mary and consider her a special and blessed woman. That is not going too far. The differences, however, must be pointed out. We do not accept the immaculate conception, her bodily assumption, and much less any hint of co-redemptrix. Bridges and connections help make the initial evangelistic contact – they open up the conversation. To leave it at that, however, compromises the message.

3. Forms don't matter, but principles do. In an American missiology the debates and controversies are often about forms. Ed Stetzer notes that "many biblical commands are often expressed through culturally appropriate actions," and that some biblical principles and commands "have *meaning* that can only be expressed through *form.*"[344] For example, we are commanded to gather as believers, to share testimony, to read the word of God, to pray, to worship, to fellowship, and to minister one to another. Exactly how each of those activities may be expressed can differ significantly from culture to culture, from people to people. The form does not really matter. The kind of music, whether praying while kneeling or with lifted hands, with heads bowed or eyes toward heaven, silently or all speaking aloud – these are cultural forms. Similarly, there are

Biblical principles of modesty and respect that can only be expressed in cultural forms. Clothing style, covered heads, men and women seated together or separately, and what is permitted or forbidden in the sanctuary are culturally driven.[345] As we attempt to contextualize, we must be careful not to dogmatize and absolutize our own cultural forms, for it is the principles behind them that matter.

4. Distractions and confusion matters, so beware. Thoughtful and careful contextualization, especially as it relates to forms, will try not to create distractions or confusion. In other words, and this is often the case in the American context, there is such a desire and passion to reach the lost and be relevant that it becomes less about missiology and more about making a point. Whether anti-traditional, whether infatuated with the latest fad, or even having a grim determination to stay traditional, the result is often nothing more than distraction and confusion. It becomes all about the exterior, the style, the expression, the form, and not the message. This can be a significant problem when the traditionalist and the non-traditionalist butt heads. Both are contextualizing (although the traditionalist often doesn't realize it), and both too often allow conflict over the form ("the right way to do things") to overshadow any thoughtful missiology. It appears too often that both are more interested in making their own point and taking a dig at the other than working together for the gospel. Therefore, whether attempting to hold on to existing contextualized forms or attempting to contextualize in new forms, style can quickly overcome substance. For example, a traditional church may stubbornly refuse to use projection equipment and video, all the while missing out on an incredible opportunity to illustrate the gospel in new ways, especially to younger people. Conversely,

a contemporary church may be so eager to be cutting edge in its audio-visual that the medium drowns out the message ("That was really cool ... whatever it was supposed to mean").[346]

5. Sentimentality and preferences don't matter, so get over it. We can make the issue of forms even more personal. Many times our worship, ministry, and even personal spirituality forms are more matters of personal preference and sentimentality than anything else. We grew up with them, we are comfortable with them, and we like them. I have often asked people why they objected to a particular form change in a church. Many times the best response they can come up with is "Well, I just don't like it." This applies to all of us. We all have comfort zones and personal preferences, and there is nothing wrong with that. It is a problem when these override and get in the way of more fruitful evangelism, missions, and ministry. Does it really matter whether worship music is sung with piano and organ or with a band? Does it really matter or not whether the pastor wears a coat and tie? Does it really matter whether the service starts at 10:45 or 11:00? Apparently it really does to some.

6. Cultural expressions matter both ways, so be flexible. There is a sense, however, in the process of contextualization when cultural expressions do matter. The ideal is that the gospel be lived out within a particular culture and can reflect that culture, its language, its music, and all its social flavors. Yes, the Bible judges all cultures. Yes, some elements in all cultures are evil and must be challenged and avoided. Yes, forms don't matter for the most part, except that all cultures need to be able to express their devotion to God and live out their faith within their culture. Thus, Africans

may sway when they sing hymns. In corporate prayer some Asians may all pray aloud at the same time. African-American preachers may whoop. Cowboy churches may meet in a rodeo arena, wear jeans, boots, and hats, and be led in worship by a fiddle player. Churches reaching young urbanites, middle class suburban churches, rural country churches, multicultural churches, and ethnic churches of a hundred varieties will and should reflect the best aspects of their cultures. Therefore, whether one is the gospel communicator or the recipient culture, both live within a culture and both should humbly respect and learn from each other.

Conclusion

Contextualization is a critical and inevitable process for developing an American missiology, and one that requires care. As is often the case with theological and missiological issues, the best way to accomplish appropriate contextualization is through humble and eager discussion with others. Learning from others is crucial. Mutual accountability is essential, but harsh criticism and thoughtlessly assuming the worst about the intentions of others is not helpful or even Christian. Contextualization can certainly be a difficult and controversial subject, but we also need to remember the principles Paul expressed in 1 Cor. 9:19-23 and in Phil. 1:15-18. In the first instance, Paul is willing to be and do whatever he has to in order to reach some for Christ. In the second, Paul is willing to overlook and not be too concerned about what others are doing or saying what their motives are – "What does it matter? Just that in every way, whether out of false motives or true, Christ is proclaimed. And in this I rejoice."

Obviously, Paul is not downplaying the significance of doctrinal truth and an accurate message. He argues for these in many other places. Still, it appears that he does not appear as concerned as we often are over motives and forms. We don't want to go "too far," but we must be willing to forego any cultural, personal, traditional, and preferred view, expression, or activity that may be an obstacle to telling the old, old story.

When Worldviews Meet: Evangelism and Contextualization

He left Judea and went again to Galilee. He had to travel through Samaria...A woman of Samaria came to draw water. "Give Me a drink," Jesus said to her..."How is it that You, a Jew, ask for a drink from me, a Samaritan woman?" she asked Him. For Jews do not associate with Samaritans. Jesus answered, "If you knew the gift of God, and who is saying to you, 'Give Me a drink,' you would ask Him, and He would give you living water...whoever drinks from the water that I will give him will never thirst again – ever! In fact, the water I will give him will become a well of water springing up within him for eternal life"..."Go call your husband," He told her, "and come back here." "I don't have a husband," she answered. "You have correctly said, 'I don't have a husband'," Jesus said. "For you've had five husbands, and the man you now have is not your husband. What you have said is true." "Sir," the woman replied, "I see that You are a prophet. Our fathers worshipped on this mountain, yet you Jews say that the place to worship is in Jerusalem." Jesus told her, "Believe Me, woman, an hour is coming when you will worship the Father neither on this mountain nor in Jerusalem. You Samaritans worship what you do not know. We worship what we do know, because salvation is from the Jews. But an hour is coming, and is now here, when the true worshippers will worship the Father in spirit and truth. Yes, the Father wants such people to worship Him. God is spirit, and those who worship Him must worship in spirit and truth." The woman said to Him, "I know that Messiah is coming. . . When He comes, He will explain everything to us." "I am He," Jesus told her, "the One speaking to you."

John 4: 1-26 passim

As he usually did, Jesus breaks all convention and traditional norms in this passage in order to reach a person (a town, really) who needed to know him. He is on his way from Jerusalem back to Galilee to get away from the Pharisees for a while. The usual route from Jerusalem to Galilee for a devout or strict Jew was to cross the Jordan River to the east, travel north, then cross the river west back into Galilee. Going this way a "fussy" Jew could avoid any contact with the despised Samaritans. The quickest way, of course, was straight through Samaria and that was the route Jesus took.[347] There are four actions Jesus took in this passage that are instructive for the practice of contextualized evangelism:

1. Jesus went to an uncomfortable place and engaged in an uncomfortable conversation. Jesus was used to going against convention. This was his regular practice when tradition and the cultural *status quo* interfered with truly knowing and obeying God or took precedent over loving and ministering to people. In this particular case the Samaritans were despised by the Jews for past slights (Ezra 4:2f), for peculiar worship practices, and for their mixed ethnic makeup.[348] Jesus took the direct route to Galilee

through Samaria, an action that would have been frowned upon by those Pharisees who were already criticizing him and seeking ways by which to discredit him. Although Jesus personally had no dislike or fear of the Samaritans, his choice of travel routes was one that probably made some of the disciples uncomfortable, opened him up to criticism by the religious establishment, and would create awkward situations when having to interact with the Samaritans themselves. This is exactly what the Samaritan woman thought. Jesus asked her for water, an act that took her by complete surprise. Yet, he ignores her statement, because he has a gospel agenda in mind.

2. Jesus turned a common conversation toward spiritual matters. "Give me a drink." A simple request about a common need. There was nothing aggressive, spectacular, or theological about Jesus' request. He was, in fact, thirsty. He also knew how to turn that request and the subsequent conversation to spiritual matters. He brushes off the Samaritan woman's objection, because the history between the Jews and the Samaritans was not what interested him. It was, rather, the woman's spiritual condition. This is important to note: Jesus did not get sidetracked, was not offended, and did not get defensive over what was a loaded political, sociological, and second tier theological issue. He focused on the woman and her need. If the woman only knew, he says, who was talking to her and what kind of water he could provide, she would never thirst again. In modern parlance, the woman responds with a "What in the world are you talking about? Whatever it is, give some to me."

3. Jesus then engaged the woman at the point of her spiritual need. Once Jesus got the woman spiritually interested,

he personalized the conversation. That is, he moved the spiritual conversation from an abstract theological concept to a personal spiritual need. When the woman confesses she doesn't have a husband to bring to Jesus, he points out her immoral and ungodly lifestyle. Apparently, his comment about her five husbands hit a sore spot. She comments that he must be a prophet, but then she immediately turns the conversation back to the religious differences between the Samaritans and the Jews. Jesus had hit too close to home. Rather than talk about her personal spiritual need, which was so evident in her immorality, she tried to move the conversation away from herself. What better way to avoid being confronted with one's sin than to bring up a controversial topic? People do it all the time. Jesus plays along, but only because he was going to bring the conversation full circle.

4. Jesus confronted the woman with the reality of his person. The woman tries to derail Jesus with the controversy between Jews and Samaritans over the proper place to worship. Jesus' response does two things: One, it corrects the woman's (and the Samaritan) misunderstanding about worship. The Jews are, in fact, correct. Two, Jesus introduces the new concept that, one day, and it is now, worship will not be centered in a particular place, but rather in the heart of the person. God is seeking true worshipers, and these will be worshipers from all peoples and in all places. The woman tries one more time to gain control of the conversation. "I know that Messiah is coming . . . when He comes, He will explain everything to us." That is, she is saying, "Thank you, sir, you can stop it now, for one day Messiah will straighten it all out." Then Jesus drives home the point that gets the woman's attention and excites her enough to go get her entire village: "I am He." Whatever

direction the conversation went, and whatever objection the woman presented, Jesus was going to take her to a confrontation with who he was.

These four strategic actions Jesus took offer a set of principles for evangelism as we develop an American missiology. I define evangelism simply as "telling the good news of Jesus Christ with the goal (if not always the reality) that the hearer would trust in Christ for the forgiveness of sin and the promise of eternal life." That is obviously a practical definition and not a fully developed theological one. I am aware of the place of the sovereignty of God, of election, of free will, of the work of the Holy Spirit, and the issues of repentance, faith, and regeneration. I am also aware of the differences of opinion regarding the *ordo salutis* (order of salvation) on the Calvinist-Arminian spectrum. Those discussions are for other books. My concerns here are the missiological tasks and implications of a contextualized evangelism. Therefore, what follows assumes that the Holy Spirit is the one who goes before the evangelist preparing the heart of the hearer, the one who convicts the hearer of sin and his need for salvation, and the one who does the work of salvation (regardless of one's understanding of the order of salvation).

When the lost person doesn't fit my box

One of the hardest things to do in evangelism is to move outside of one's comfort zone, to get "out of the box" and think, go, and do differently than what one is used to. In the American mission field, getting outside of one's evangelism box is more necessary than ever. Our growing religious, ethnic, cultural, and lifestyle diversity means that more and more lost people are further and further away from any semblance of a receptivity point. They are, rather, in the negative on the receptivity scale. They do not have even a basic Judeo-Christian worldview or ethic that serves as the starting point for presenting the gospel. They may not have grown up in the "American church culture." They may be from a different religious worldview, may be hostile toward Christianity, or may even be atheists. The challenge, therefore, is to move them from wherever they are intellectually, spiritually, and emotionally toward "zero" before there is a context where a gospel presentation even makes sense.[349] Therefore, contextual evangelism in the American mission field means:

We must be willing to be uncomfortable

Just as Jesus did when he went to Samaria, we have to leave our Christian bubble and engage uncomfortable people in uncomfortable situations with uncomfortable conversations. Many authors have written quite well about living missionally and incarnationally. In essence, what they are saying is that we can no longer expect many lost people to show up at our church willing to hear the gospel. If they come, it is usually because someone has already gotten out of their comfort zone, built a relationship, and invited them. However, more and more Americans are hostile to church (or their misconceptions of church) and will refuse to set foot in a church building. We must take the gospel to them (and take church to them, as the next chapter will discuss). An increasingly diverse, postmodern, and hostile culture means that evangelism will be more and more about going to our Samaria, relating to difficult, hard to understand people, and being involved in uncomfortable, out of the box, conversations. The Samaritans were the despised peoples of their day (according to the Jews); in our evangelism we must be willing to engage the "despised" peoples of our day, whoever and wherever they may be.

Leaving the Christian bubble does not mean that we no longer assemble together or that the local church is less important. It does mean that local churches may have to re-prioritize programs, activities, and events. Spiritual faithfulness cannot be solely measured (if at all) by the number of times a Christian attends church programs and activities. Fortunately, more and more churches understand and practice this. They teach, encourage, and empower their members to live a missional lifestyle. That is, spiritual health is not measured by a heavy "inside the church" workload, but by engaging the world in ministry and missions. Members are encouraged to not only bring their friends to church, but are encouraged and empowered to be, go, and do in and for the community. They are not encouraged to just sit, but are sent out.

Leading and empowering church members to go into uncomfortable situations with uncomfortable people acknowledges two realities:

One, it can be *dangerous*. Although we don't usually think of the American mission field as dangerous in the same sense as we think of a Middle Eastern country being dangerous, for example, it can still be. There are the obvious dangerous situations where witnessing and ministry may take place: among gang members, prostitutes, drug addicts, pornography pushers, radicals of all stripes. There are also the not so obvious dangerous situations, but ones which could seduce us as well: among pluralists, New Agers, hedonists, materialists, entertainment addicts, and all sorts of good people who are getting along fine without God. The most dangerous thing about engaging uncomfortable people in uncomfortable situations, however, is that we may come under conviction and see them as Jesus does! We may begin to see our own racist tendencies, prejudices, biases, and our distrust of "different" people challenged and begin to disappear. We may start to see every human being as made in the image of God, loved by God, and deserving of hearing the good news of Jesus

Christ. The Holy Spirit may choose to put us into contact with the very "despised Samaritans" in our own lives, whether they be people of a different race, ethnicity, language, socioeconomic status, or religious background. Even more radically, we may be put into the situation of having to love and share Jesus with a criminal, an alcoholic, a drug addict, a prostitute, someone with AIDs, or self-identified as part of the LGBT[350] community. The "danger" is that I may be changed in the process and become more like Jesus – full of grace, love, and truth, and who sees all humans as made in the image of God and worthy of hearing the gospel.

Consequently, the second reality is that *accountability* is needed. Jesus sent the disciples out two by two. As we head into uncomfortable situations, it should not be as the Lone Ranger. Accountability is needed both for the protection of the one doing the evangelism, and for the protection of the testimony of the church. In essence, we need to hold each other accountable so that no door is open to bring harm to the name and the cause of Christ, whether through moral failure, doctrinal confusion, or simple burnout.

We must work hard at understanding worldviews

It should be acknowledged right off that no lost person ever fits, in an important sense, my worldview box. After all, a lost person is dead in his sins and trespasses, spiritually blind, and living in darkness. He may be a family member, but the box – the worldview – is foundationally different. At the same time, however, there are many important connecting points; that is, there are many overlapping "boxes" we may have in common: language, nationality, place of origin, education level, interests, cultural background, and so on. An effective contextualized evangelism will take into account the person's worldview, work hard at finding out the assumptions, biases, and beliefs of the one being witnessed to, and then make every effort to build bridges in order to communicate the gospel in a way that is understandable within that person's worldview. There are several issues to consider:

One, we must learn as much as possible about the person or group ahead of time. If they are from a Muslim, Hindu, Buddhist, Sikh, Baha'i, or a tribal religious background, find out as much as possible what the foundational beliefs are, what the potential objections to the gospel may be, and what cultural barriers may hinder the communication of the gospel. For example, it is critical to understand that the Muslim believes in radical monotheism, rejects the Trinity, accepts Jesus only as a prophet, and considers the Bible to be corrupted. The issues in evangelizing the Muslim, therefore, will be considerably different than the Hindu, who believes there is one God with millions of manifestations, that Jesus could certainly be one of those manifestations, and that adding a belief in Jesus to a belief in other gods may be the prudent thing to do.

Two, we must listen and learn more than we talk. This is part of building any relationship and earning a right to be heard. Do we really care about the person? Are we listening so we can really learn about the person's culture, background, family, interests, and spiritual needs? Practically, it is part of listening for and discovering connections points. This is what Jesus did with the Samaritan woman. He listened carefully to every answer and statement she gave and built from it. His was no canned presentation; rather, he directed the conversation where he wanted it to go based on what she said. Listening is foundational to contextualized evangelism. We have the truth that will radically save and change a person. We believe we have the answer, and we do; but, do we know the questions? Are we listening close enough to build on what a person is saying? Can we show true interest in the person's response and guide a conversation to spiritual matters? Or, is it apparent that we are not really listening and not really interested, but simply waiting for a pause so we can insert our next point? Moreover, many evangelistic opportunities are spontaneous and unanticipated. Consequently, we don't have the time to learn about the person's worldview ahead of time. In this case, thoughtful questions and careful, humble listening are essential.

Three, we cannot assume anything. Many of the evangelism presentations we have learned, and many of the commonly used tracts, are ineffective with a growing number of the population. Too many of these assume a common starting point that is no longer true for many Americans, namely, a belief in God, trust of the church, a belief in the afterlife, and some acceptance of the authority of the Bible. I am not saying these presentations and tracts are not *eventually* and *often* effective once some kind of common ground has been achieved. We cannot, however, assume that the common ground exists. In secularized America the person we are witnessing to probably missed the first thirty years of Sunday School. Just as Jesus did with the Samaritan woman, we are going to have to bring the person along until common ground is discovered or established. This is, in itself, hard work and sometimes uncomfortable. Depending on a scripted presentation is certainly helpful and comforting in many cases, but it can often lull us into a false sense of effectiveness. In reality, most of these presentations were never intended to be used slavishly and verbatim, but are tools to be adapted to a variety of situations. For some of us, the true discomfort is learning to engage in authentic conversation, letting the Holy Spirit go to work, and carefully leading the conversation to spiritual matters. Fortunately, there is a much greater emphasis today on teaching believers to share their faith more naturally, without the fear of having to learn scores of bullet points and Bible verses, and simply taking the first step of being and making a friend.[351]

We must be relational and personal

Evangelism has to involve relationships. Unexpected and occasional evangelism still takes place – it happened to me at a car wash when the Lord put a person in my path ready to hear and receive the gospel. Increasingly, however, because of differing cultures, religious backgrounds, and growing suspicion of Christianity, we will have to spend more and more time with people. This is particularly true of peoples from Middle Eastern and Asian backgrounds, for which a relationship begins with eating meals in each other's homes and spending hours talking. In some cultures to simply begin a relationship requires more involvement and takes more time to establish than we are willing to give.

Similarly, emerging generations are loaded with institutional mistrust, are culturally and educationally predisposed toward pluralism, reject absolute metanarratives, and, although seeking relationships and community, feel they have already been let down by too many people in their lives. It has often been noted that the traditional "believe first, then belong" sequence has been turned on its head among emerging generations. Because of their mistrust, they will often seek to belong first and then believe. They may visit local churches, attend worship services for a long time, hang around believers, listen to the preaching, participate in corporate worship, and even attend small groups. Once they have seen the authenticity of Christianity in the lives of church members and have already experienced a sense of belonging, then they will take the plunge into full belief. Is this not, however, the progression of belief we see in Jesus' disciples? They travelled with him, they listened to him, and they lived life with him. Full-fledged belief, however, came only after a time spent with him. Therefore, it is commendable to invite, include, and welcome anyone and everyone to "belong" to the community (this does not mean they are church members) prior to belief. They are invited to "taste and see."[352]

Jesus consistently took the initiative to build relationships and be personally interested in people. Certainly, his goal was to understand, identify, and point out the person's spiritual need. He did this quickly with the Samaritan woman. He invited himself to Zacchaeus's house, something that sounds odd in a Western culture. He joined Matthew and a crowd of sinners for dinner. He knew how to ask probing questions and, as best as we can tell, never interrupted an answer. Evangelism, we must always remember, is about people – people who are lost and need to hear the gospel clearly and in a way they can understand it and respond to it. Although there are times and reasons for apologetic arguments and debates, evangelism is about people coming to know Christ as Lord and Savior. It must involve making personal connections and helping the person understand the reality of their personal spiritual need.

We must lead the person to a confrontation with Jesus.

Just about any discussion about evangelism methods eventually leads to a debate over "confrontational evangelism." On one side are those who believe that evangelism can only be and should only be "confrontational," in the sense of being direct and to the point. They argue that "friendship" or "relational" evangelism is meek and weak, takes too long, and runs the risk of never getting to the point of sharing the gospel. On the other side are those who react against "in your face" evangelism, because they see confrontational evangelism as too aggressive, not considerate enough of the person, and runs the risk of not being very effective because the hearer stops listening well before the gospel is ever presented.

The reality is that both sides are right...about the caricatures of the other. I have witnessed both extremes: On a mission trip to a Middle Eastern country, one person in the group felt compelled to move quickly to a strong presentation of the gospel almost immediately after meeting a Muslim. When he stated that Jesus Christ had died on the cross for our sins, the Muslim hearer obviously objected. From then on, it was a matter of argument and who could speak the most, the fastest, and the loudest. Nothing was accomplished other than this gentlemen being able to say he was only being bold for Christ. That he was; but fruitful he wasn't.

On the other extreme, I was having a conversation with a couple of pastors who had started playing basketball with a group of non-believers. Their stated intent was to build relationships that would lead to spiritual conversations. Their strategy was to play, be Christ-like in their behavior, actions and reactions, and wait for the other players to ask them what it was that made them so different. So they waited, and waited, and waited.

What is the best approach to personal evangelism? Both! If anything must be learned about contextualized evangelism it is that the situation, the context, and the person should shape and direct the approach, the method, and the style. Sometimes one only has a few minutes for a quick presentation that is direct and to the point. In other situations, where hostility is detected, where a completely different religious worldview must be answered, or where there are raw emotions involved (grief and anger, for example), relationship will have to precede presentation. A lot of "pre-evangelism" relationship and ministry, which takes time and patience, will be required. At the same time, every evangelistic presentation, method, approach, relationship must at some point lead the hearer to confront the reality of the person and work of Jesus. That does not mean we have to be "confrontational" in the negative sense, but we must confront the person with the truth of the gospel. It does not have to be ugly, loud, or argumentative, but every individual must at some point come to an existential encounter – confrontation, if you will – with Jesus.[353]

This is exactly what Jesus did with the Samaritan woman, and what he did time and again in his ministry. "I am He" he told her. "Do not be amazed that I told you that you must be born again," he told Nicodemus (John 3:7). Deny yourselves and "follow Me" he challenged his disciples (Matt. 16:24-28). "The Son of Man is the Lord of the Sabbath" he said to the Pharisees (Luke 6:5). Peter proclaimed to the crowd at Pentecost that they must "Repent and be baptized, each of you, in the name of Jesus the Messiah" (Acts 2:38). Paul told the Philippian jailer that he should "Believe on the Lord Jesus, and you will be saved" (Acts 16:31). In every case, whatever the situation – immediate, relationship established, friendly, hostile, a crisis, one-on-one, or to a group – a confrontation with the person of Jesus was inevitable.

Therefore, whether evangelism is door-to-door, handing out a tract, acts of service, friendship, or even event and mass evangelism, if there is no point at which the hearer is confronted with his sin and with Jesus' substitutionary atonement, then the process is incomplete.[354] This is not to say that every evangelistic encounter will make it to that point and that if it doesn't we have failed. No, some plant, some water, and some harvest. It is to say that any evangelistic approach that does not include a moment of confrontation with the gospel is not really evangelism. Contextualized evangelism will be careful, thoughtful, dependent on the Holy Spirit, and more interested in the hearer's spiritual need for the gospel than on the comfort of the gospel teller.

What about mass evangelism?

A few words about mass evangelism; that is, evangelism that targets groups of people. Once again, in the contemporary debates over evangelistic methods, there are two extremes to be avoided.

On one side, there are those who argue that the days of mass evangelism are over. Billy Graham and others of his generation were successful at it, but people simply do not respond to that method anymore. On the other side, are those who pine for a return to the days of "crusade" evangelism, full stadiums, and city-wide joint revivals. The church is in decline, they sometimes argue, precisely because we have left these tried and true methods.

The extremes and caricatures once again don't hold up. Yes, large stadium crusades are not as well received and fruitful as they were several decades ago. Times change, people change, churches change, and our methods certainly must change. Still, all mass evangelism is not the same and it should not all be discarded. Perhaps we should not expect tens of thousands in stadiums any more, but groups of people can be reached through mass evangelism strategies such as:

- Community driven events. Many churches use Harvest festivals, block parties, concerts, and other events to connect and share the gospel with their immediate neighbors and friends.

- Coordinated home groups. Some churches do mass evangelism broken down into bite sized pieces. They recruit host homes, train the leaders, plan the evening agenda, and then simultaneously invite friends and neighbors into homes for food, fellowship, and gospel. In one night, scores of homes can reach hundreds of people.

- Technology driven evangelism. Some churches have discovered that their pastor's sermons are downloaded by hundreds of people all over the world. Similarly, podcasts, web based seminars, and other social networking provides the opportunity to reach masses of people.

- Niche conferencing. With marriages falling apart, families struggling, and personal debt out of control for so many people many churches find that offering practical seminars on these issues attract people from the community. The conferences are Biblically based and end with a clear presentation of the gospel.

- Social ministry. Feeding the hungry, sheltering the homeless, clothing the poor, providing medical and dental clinics, free health fairs – all these are ways for churches to meet the immediate needs of people and their community and evangelize groups.

Rather than criticize the methods that others use, we would be far better off as we develop our American missiology to "think like a missionary."[355] That is, a missionary (at least a good one) to another country would not arrive with pre-packaged strategies and methods. Instead, she would spend time learning the language, the culture, listening to the people, and working hard at understanding their worldview. The question she would be asking is, "What is the best, quickest, most faithful, and fruitful way for me to share the gospel so that it is understood and can be responded to?" In America the same commitment is needed, whether doing personal evangelism or mass evangelism, whether speaking to a neighbor or a stranger, whether talking to one of similar culture or one of a totally different culture. That is, what will we have to be, do, change, adjust, learn, give up, forget, or sacrifice in order that the gospel be heard and believed?

Conclusion

A missiology for the American mission field is grossly incomplete if it does not take into account evangelism, the intentional and unapologetic task of clearly communicating the gospel of Jesus Christ with lost people in order that they may have the opportunity to respond to Jesus Christ as Savior and Lord. Evangelism, therefore, is a non-negotiable for an American missiology. At the same time, doing evangelism that is uniquely and exclusively Christocentric will be more and more condemned by our culture as intolerant, arrogant, and narrow minded. Responding to hostility toward Christian evangelism will require courage, firm boldness, and a much greater display of grace, patience, and love. We will have to be, in our evangelism, more and more like Jesus.

The non-negotiability of evangelism also means that evangelism must be contextualized. The point is not to blurt out the facts of the gospel just so we can claim that it was done. The point is to work hard and creatively so that the gospel can be communicated – explained, illustrated, applied – in every situation, to every situation, and every person. The gospel is true, timeless, cross-cultural, cross-generational, and relevant to every human being in every situation. Our challenge is, then, to find every way possible to make the connection between the living truth of Jesus Christ to every person and every situation. We move into uncomfortable situations, we love uncomfortable and unlovable people, and we make every effort possible so that we, our methods, and our style are not the reasons for a person's rejection of the gospel. We have the answer, and the answer is too important for us to be flippant, unconcerned, or non-creative in the way we deliver it.

Leading the Way:
Church Planting and
Contextualization

When Jesus came to the region of Caesarea Philippi, He
asked His disciples, "Who do people say that the Son of
Man is? And they said, "Some say John the Baptist; others,
Elijah; still others, Jeremiah or one of the prophets." "But
you," He asked them, "who do you say that I am?" Simon
Peter answered, "You are the Messiah, the Son of the living
God!" And Jesus responded, "Simon son of Jonah, you are
blessed because flesh and blood did not reveal this to you,
but My Father in heaven. And I also say to you that you
are Peter, and on this rock I will build my church, and the
forces of Hades will not overpower it."

Matt. 16:13-18

I discussed in the first two chapters the responses to Jesus'
questions "Who do people say that I am?" (as recorded in Mark)
and "Who do you say that I am?" As noted, Peter's response was
the correct answer: Jesus is the Messiah, the Christ, the Son of
the living God, the Anointed One. Mark records that Jesus told
his disciples to keep that information to themselves for the time

being. It was not yet time for Jesus to reveal publicly all of who he was and had come to do. Matthew gives a bit more detail about Jesus' response to Peter's declaration. Peter, Jesus says, is blessed because he did not gain this understanding from any person, but rather it was revealed to him by the Father. Peter, at this particular moment, demonstrated a spiritual insight that pleased Jesus. Jesus goes on to make a statement that has been one of the most controversial in church history; that is, ". . . on this rock I will build my church, and the forces of Hades will not overpower it."

Volumes have been written on the meaning of "on this rock" and whether Peter is explicitly, implicitly, or not at all given primacy and authority by Jesus in this statement. This is not the place to review that entire debate. Suffice it to say that the historical Protestant and evangelical interpretation is that the "rock" Jesus refers to is Peter's confession of faith in Jesus as the Messiah, the Son of the living God. Peter became an important leader in the early church, but there is no scriptural evidence that he claimed or was given apostolic primacy. Jesus is simply and importantly declaring that Peter's statement of Jesus' personhood and work is what his church will be built on.[356]

What are the implications of Jesus' response to Peter? What does it tell us about the church?

1. The church universal belongs to Jesus. That is, the people of God, the redeemed believers of all the ages, belong to him. He is the head of the church, which is vividly described in the Bible by many images, including the Body of Christ, the People of God, a Royal Priesthood, and the Bride of Christ. It is the church that Jesus Christ "loved" and for which he "gave Himself" on the cross (Eph. 5:25b).

2. The church, therefore, has a Christological foundation, identity, nature, and purpose. The church, as the Body

of Christ, finds its being, purpose, nature, and mission defined by the person and work of Christ. The church is built upon a specific confession of faith, namely that Jesus is the "Messiah, the Son of the Living God," with all that implies as to his person and work. One implication, not directly mentioned in this passage but evident throughout the Synoptic gospels, is that the church is directly related to the Kingdom of God, which Jesus preached (Mk. 1:15; Luke 4:43). The church is a sign, an agent, and a manifestation of the Kingdom in this age.[357]

3. Local churches, consequently, are the local presence of the Body of Christ and are local expressions of the Kingdom of God. Therefore, they also belong to Jesus. Whatever the denomination, the polity, the model, style, ethnicity, location, or identification, they belong to Jesus. A significant qualifier to that statement: Unless a local church agrees with Peter's confession of faith in Jesus as Messiah, it is not truly a local expression of Christ's church. It may be a religious gathering, a community of activists, or a fellowship of like-minded individuals, but it does not qualify as a church.[358]

4. The church, and local churches, will never be defeated. There is no power, no entity, no crisis, and no authority on earth or in history that has or can wipe out the church. The church may recede in influence, she may become filled with corruption, she may grow cold, and she may be disobedient, ineffective, and fruitless. She will not, however, as the Bride of Christ, perish from the face of the earth. This is no reason for triumphalism and arrogance. It is rather, reason to have humble confidence and loving boldness. The church's survival, renewal, health, and growth are totally Christ dependent. While we exist and work in

these last days between the two advents of Christ, there will be some temporary victories and some temporary defeats, for we live in the "already, but not yet." Our hope is in Christ, and our confidence is that nothing Hades can throw at us will ever ultimately defeat the church. In the American mission field, this means we may be seriously concerned, but we must never despair.

5. Finally, the church, and local churches, must be proactive, moving forward, engaging culture, and battling Satan and evil. The forces (the word is literally "gates" as many translations have it) of Hades will not overpower, prevail against, or defeat the church. The image is not of Satan and his forces attacking "fortress church," but of an advancing church battling Satan and the forces of Hades. Although the image is one of battle, of Christian soldiers, and of aggressiveness, we must remember that "our battle is not against flesh and blood" (Eph. 6:12) but against the real evil of Satan, whether in his person or his influence in the world.

As we consider the American mission field and the numerous spiritual, moral, and demographic changes and challenges it presents, the evangelical church of Jesus Christ must respond missiologically. The church can withdraw completely from society into a Christian fortress and create Christian ghettoes where all our needs are met by like-minded individuals and institutions. The church can change doctrinally and morally to accommodate itself and be more acceptable to the prevailing culture. Or, the church can intentionally and strategically expand its presence, ministry, and influence throughout society. The first option is unacceptable, although some evangelical churches have chosen in part or in whole to withdraw (it could be argued that in doing so they give up a significant aspect of what it means to be evangelical, namely, being salt and light in society). The second option is certainly unacceptable. Methodologically, churches do need to change and adapt in order to spread the gospel (thus this chapter), but to give up Biblical doctrines and morals (not necessarily traditional, cultural customs) also means to give up what it means to be evangelical and Christocentric.

That leaves the third option, and it is the hardest and most challenging one. We must seek to intentionally, strategically, and purposefully expand the presence, ministry, and influence of the church in America. There are many ways to do this, and some will be addressed in subsequent chapters. Missiologically, the critical beginning point is church planting, the starting of New Testament congregations in every possible location, for every possible people group and population segment, to reach every possible person with the gospel of Jesus Christ.

What is the point of church planting?

Anyone who is involved in church planting in America for any length of time will eventually be asked why more churches are needed. The objections to church planting range from "we already have enough and can't even fill them" to "all they will do is steal members from existing churches." These types of objections are mostly voiced in the Bible Belt, in the case of the first, or come from a misunderstanding of what church planting is supposed to be about, in the case of the second. These objections also stem from logistical, practical, territorial, and human concerns. The justification for church planting, however, is grounded in theological principles, Biblical commands, and missiological concerns:

TERRY COY

One, the universal church always exists in local expressions. Jesus responded to Peter in Matt. 16 that he is building his church, the redeemed body of believers of all ages and all nations. In Scripture, however, this universal church is always seen in local expressions. Whether started through the dispersion of persecuted Christians or directly by the Apostle Paul and his team most of the New Testament is about or addressed to local churches. Historically, regardless of ecclesiological belief and practice, all legitimate Christian denominations and movements have had at the center of their life, as their beginning point, or as their stated end, local expressions of the church. When denominations or movements have been illegitimate or gotten off track, they have forgotten or abandoned the local church or congregation.[359]

Two, making disciples leads to local churches. The Great Commission given in Matthew 28:18-20 is to make and teach disciples to obey all that Jesus taught and commanded. He gave the command, therefore, to make disciples who would follow him. The theological and logical progression is that as people are evangelized, baptized, and taught, they are incorporated into the Body of Christ and subsequently, necessarily, and inevitably into local expressions of his body. This is what Paul did on every one of his missionary journeys. He shared the gospel, made disciples, and led them to congregate as a local church. In this way, believers are in Christ and Christ is in them, both individually and corporately. This is precisely what Paul means when he says the Corinthians "are God's field, God's building" (1 Cor. 3:9), that the Romans "are one body in Christ" (Rom. 12:5), and that the Ephesians, a local body, are also part of "one body and one Spirit" (Eph. 4:4). Individual believers, in whom the Spirit of Christ dwells, are also part of a local church, in which the Spirit of Christ dwells and which is a local expression of the Body of Christ.

348

Three, local churches are the means to do Kingdom work. As local expressions of the universal church, the Body of Christ, local churches are indispensable for his Kingdom work. It is precisely through local churches that God has chosen to do his Kingdom work on earth. Although evangelism, discipleship, and ministry can and do take place outside of the walls of a church building and on an individual basis, they are meant to take place within the context of a local church's authority, blessing, and sending. Without a doubt many local churches fail in this respect. They become ingrown, self-centered, spiritually stagnant, and end up discouraging those who seek to fulfill the Great Commission. In some cases, the obedient and the motivated leave the local church in order to carry out their calling. They may do much good, but the healthiest and most fruitful scenario is for Kingdom work to be in the context of the local church. This is not to identify the Kingdom with the church, either universal or local. It is to say that God's chosen instrument for Kingdom work, as seen throughout Acts and the Epistles, is through the local church. [360]

Four, planting local churches is the most effective way to take the gospel to the American mission field. Local churches are planted, therefore, because they are local expressions of the universal church, are local signs and agents of the Kingdom, and are the most effective way to make disciples and to be salt and light in society. None of this removes personal responsibility from the individual to be a witness and to be salt and light on a daily basis wherever she may be. It simply means that neither the Christian life nor Christian mission is meant to be done alone. Greater fruitfulness, needed encouragement, important edification, and essential accountability come with membership in the local church. So, how to take the gospel to every person in every location and from every background in the American mission field? Many ways, but the most critical and most effective way is through church planting. [361]

What church planting is not

Many of the objections to church planting come from a misunderstanding of what church planting is and should do. Briefly, church planting:

(handwritten margin note: See CP + local chres as a team working together)

1. Does not reject of the ministry of established churches. Certainly there are individual established churches that are unhealthy and which have lost their vision and passion for the Great Commission. In principle, however, church planting respects, builds on, and depends on the prayers, ministry, encouragement, and financial support of established churches, all of which were a new church plant at some point. Church planting should be about embracing and honoring the ministry of those who have gone before.

2. Is not supposed to grow primarily by transfer growth from other churches. Yes, some transfer growth is inevitable. Yes, there are split, splinter, and conflict situations where a new congregation is started at the expense of an established church. And, yes, sometimes a new church is started by a prominent pastor and primarily grows by drawing members from other churches. New congregations that start when a church divides or that are based on drawing members from other churches is not a true church planting strategy. The intent of church planting, when done correctly, is to grow primarily from evangelism and making new disciples.

3. Should not be driven by the church planter's disappointment in a previous church, desire to emulate another planter, or misplaced confidence that he can do it "the right way."

To the contrary, church planting must be driven by God's specific call and shaped by the context of the community and people who need to hear the good news through the ministry of the new plant. That is, the planter should not plant the church he has always wanted to attend, but plant the one God desires to use in a particular context.

4. Should not be only the church planter's calling and vision, although in practice it too often is. Yes, God calls a particular planter and his family to start a particular new church. Yes, the church planter is specifically called by God to lead the new church plant. The qualities, skills, wiring, and personality of the church planter are critical, and the planter will be the visionary driving force behind the church plant. The American mission field will be reached, however, only when local churches themselves take on the responsibility of leading out in church planting. Like the church in Antioch (Acts 13:2-3), American churches are to intentionally and prayerfully call out and send out missionaries and church planters into the harvest.

5. Should not be limited to a particular model, style, strategy, or size. When it comes to size, at one extreme are those who claim that a church happens wherever "two or three are gathered together in My name" (Matt. 18:20). At the other extreme are those who argue that a "real" church requires full programming, a paid and ordained pastor, a building, and all the accoutrements of an established church. In the case of the former, the promise by Jesus that he would be present when two or three are gathered in his name simply means that he promises to be present among them as they resolve conflict. The context is church discipline and agreement in the church on issues

of correction, discipline, and restoration. The context is
not the definition of a church. In the latter case, however,
expectations have moved beyond what is Biblical to
traditional, cultural, and ecclesiastical customs and
requirements. These may be good and acceptable in and
of themselves, but they are more than what is required to
be a church.

It appears, however, that the disagreements over the
definition of a church, especially as it relates to a church
plant, are often due to confusion over the nature of a new
church and the goal and ideal of a healthy established
church. That is, the debate is over two different things.
Many definitions of a church are actually ideal definitions
of a healthy, established church (Biblical, certainly, but
still ideal). A new church rarely, if ever, comes close to
manifesting or practicing the full definition for some time,
and often gets criticized for this. The new church has yet to
grow and mature. It would be like saying a newborn baby
is not really a human because he has not yet manifested
all the characteristics of an adult human being. The issue,
then, is the beliefs, values, and practices the new church is
founded on and is growing toward practicing. Paul called
the Corinthians saints and a church, but they certainly
had a long way to go to fit most definitions of a healthy
and mature church.

What should a new church look like?

So, what should a new church look like? The first answer many
give often refers more to a particular model, style, or personal
preference. These are important, but the first issues to settle are

theological and missiological. Consider the following essential principles for a new church plant:

1. It should reflect New Testament functions. Discussion on the functions of the church usually centers on Acts 2:41-47. The list of church functions derived from this passage varies, but usually includes evangelism or missions, discipleship, fellowship, worship, prayer, and ministry. Some simplify the list by including worship, outreach, discipleship, fellowship, and ministry, all of which are undergirded by prayer. Whatever one concludes from this passage about the functions of the church, there are two observations to be noted in regards to new church plants: One, a new church plant should build into its original vision, mission, strategy, and organization all the functions of the church. Although it is difficult for a church of any size or age to be perfectly balanced at all times, that should be the intentional goal. Two, it should be understood that in a new church plant, these functions are mostly aspirational at the beginning. That is, a new church plant strives and works toward balanced functions, it doesn't start out with that balance in place. What is often overlooked in church planting (especially by its critics) is that the church of Acts 2 was composed of religious people with solid Jewish backgrounds. Their leap of faith was from being God-fearing Jews anticipating the coming Messiah to believing that Jesus was Messiah. In comparison, consider the Corinthians, a church composed in large part of pagans who had to make a huge leap of faith. Although they were "God's church" and were "sanctified in Christ Jesus and called as saints" (1 Cor. 1:2), they still struggled with their pagan background, with immorality, and suffered from divisions, pride, envy, and other sinful behaviors. They were a legitimate new church, but they

were at the beginning of their journey toward balanced functions. In other words, in church planting the road to an Acts 2 type church is usually through Corinth!

2. It should practice New Testament ordinances. If a new church plant is growing primarily and mostly through evangelistic growth, it will soon have the opportunity to baptize new believers and lead them to participate in the ordinance of the Lord's Supper. Certainly, it may be a few weeks or months before the first baptisms, and maybe even longer before sharing communion. Still, belief in and being organized for the practice of the ordinances are keys to the identity and health of a new church plant.

3. It should reflect New Testament organization. Churches and church planters go from one extreme to the other when thinking about organization. On one end are those from an organic or simple church model who may resist being "over organized." At the other end are those who make vast use of charts, plans, systems, leadership theory, and organizational science, sometimes allowing the organization to be more important than ministry and people. The reality is that whether a church begins and intends to stay as a house church of fifteen or begins with a launch team of seventy-five and grows to five thousand, some organization is required. At the very least, there are New Testament elements of organization which must be considered and implemented:

   a. Pastoral leadership (1 Tim. 3: 1-7; 4:14; 1 Pet. 5:1-5). Whether called overseers, elders, or pastors, the New Testament is clear that someone is to take the primary lead of a local church. Whether that person is paid or volunteer, seminary trained or not, ordained or not, a New Testament congregation requires a pastoral leader.

b. Servants (Acts 6:1-6: 1 Tim. 3:8-13). More and more church planters seem eager to avoid having deacons in their new church. This is usually because their experience and observation has been that of a traditional (and non-Biblical) Deacon Board which administered a church, and probably with a heavy hand. Too often, planters have noted, this led to a quenching of the Spirit, emasculated pastoral leadership, a decision making bottleneck, and the impetus for divisiveness rather than unity. The solution, however, is *not* to avoid having deacons. That is unbiblical and impractical. Most church planters eventually discover that God places servants in their congregation for a reason. They end up with a "servant council," with "servant leaders," or some other non-traditional name and system. They are, however, still deacons; that is, servants.

c. Congregational participation (Acts 6:2-6; 13:1-3; 14:27; 15:22; 1 Cor. 5:4-5). Although the level of congregational participation may vary, especially in a new church plant where so many are neophytes, the New Testament church is one where the congregation is involved in ministry and at some level of decision making. Again, this may be something the individual church grows into, the speed of which may depend on variables such as Biblical knowledge and maturity, cultural issues, and educational level, but there is no New Testament basis for authoritarian rule by a pastor or small group of people.[362]

d. A regular meeting time (Acts 2:46; 5:12; 1 Cor. 11:20; 14:26). Some people debate how often the church should gather, on what days, and at what times. Most of the sides taken in this debate are based on cultural, traditional, practical, or preferential issues. It is clear from the New Testament that local church believers gathered regularly for corporate worship, prayer, mutual edification, and the preaching and teaching of God's word. To do this regularly and effectively takes organization and planning.

e. Ministry intentionality (Acts 4:32-36; 6:1-7; 11:19-30; 2 Cor. 8: 16-9: 5). Whether it was evangelism, preaching and teaching, ministering to each other, or raising money for the afflicted, the New Testament church planned, organized, and implemented intentional ministry. A new church plant depends absolutely on the power and provision of the Holy Spirit; however, much of that power and provision is manifested through the intelligence, abilities, and gifts that he has given the church planter and the members of the body. Depending on the power of the Spirit, therefore, does not exclude planning and putting a plan into action, for the Spirit knows the needs of the church well ahead of time and empowers the members of the Body to carry it out.

4. It should preach, teach, and live out the New Testament message. Peter says that "Christ also suffered for sins once for all, the righteous for the unrighteous, that He might bring you to God, after being put to death in the fleshly realm but made alive in the spiritual realm" (1 Pet. 3:18). The New Testament message is that Jesus Christ has paid the price for sins in order that sinful human beings could be reconciled to God. This is the message of the gospel and must be the message of every

new church plant that calls itself Christian. There are three implications to consider:

a. Christocentric doctrine (Acts 4:12; Col. 1:13-23). Every new church plant will have essential doctrinal beliefs. Some of these will reflect its evangelical identity, some will reflect its denominational distinctives, and some may reflect a special emphasis of the church itself. Because the church is the Body of Christ, and because the message of the cross is at the center of our Trinitarian God's plan of redemption, the new church's doctrine must be Christocentric.

b. Christocentric preaching and teaching (1 Cor. 2:2). A new church should ensure that the entire word of God is preached and taught at various times and in various ways. There are also times when special concerns, topics, and events may dictate what is preached and taught. Life application of the gospel is essential to all preaching and teaching. All topics, series, and themes, however, must submit to and be in the context of the gospel of Jesus Christ and him crucified. No matter the occasion, the topic, or the passage of Scripture, there should be no doubt that "this new church preaches Jesus."

c. Christocentric outreach and ministry (Rom. 12:1-2; Phil. 2:5-11; Col. 3: 1-11: 1 Pet. 2:11-20). In a new church plant all external outreach and all internal ministry is grounded in and reflective of Christ and him living in every believer. Morality, ethics, community and family relationships, sharing with lost people, fellowshipping with believers, giving generously to all – these actions are because of Christ and for his glory.

5. It should be indigenous, contextual, and culturally appropriate. Being indigenous simply means that the church "fits well into a local culture."[363] That is, the new church seeks to reflect as much as possible the host culture *without* compromising the gospel message. It practices contextualization as it seeks to be culturally appropriate. As we saw earlier, the new church will work hard at understanding the community in which it is planted. The planter and other key leaders will seek to understand the culture, the worldview, and the ways of thinking and acting of the people they are trying to reach. This is not so the culture can shape the message, but so the new church can avoid or remove artificial obstacles and deliver the message of Christ as quickly, clearly, and freely as possible. Some contextual issues to consider in church planting include:

   a. Whether to use the homogeneous or multi-cultural/racial/ethnic approach. There are those who argue passionately for one and against the other approach. Those who promote the homogeneous approach say that it is the best way to take the gospel to people in their "heart" language and culture. Lost people, it is argued, will not cross cultural barriers in order to be hear the gospel and be saved. Not enough believers, in fact, ever cross those barriers after they are saved. The proponents of a multi-cultural approach counter that the homogeneous unit approach is non-Biblical and propagates racism. The Gospel breaks down all cultural barriers and new churches ought to lead the way.

      The reality is that both approaches are legitimate and needed. It all depends on the context. The homogeneous unit must still be used when there are language barriers and when there are significant cultural differences and divisions. The hope is that these barriers are eventually broken down through the power of the gospel, but to deny the use of any homogeneous approach fails to recognize that cultural distinctions are real and important to people.

The multi-cultural approach can and should be used as much as possible. Still, it is a "homogeneous" unit in the sense that it appeals to multi-cultural people – mixed marriages, bi-racial children, Third Culture kids, and so on. They are a "target group" precisely because they are multi-cultural in outlook. Furthermore, most multi-cultural churches still have a dominant culture, ethnicity, or race, and often are really mono-racial (Asian, for example) but multi-cultural (Chinese, Vietnamese, etc). Or, sometimes they are multi-racial (white and Black), but mono-cultural (military backgrounds, middle class). Both approaches should be used and encouraged as the context requires.

b. Following a particular model or style. Too often church planters adopt a model or style based on their own preference, what they have experienced, seen, or read about. There is no guarantee, however, that a model that worked five years ago in another state will transfer to the present day in a new location. A church planter should learn as much as he can from all models and styles, but should be willing to adapt his methods to the context – people and community – in order to bear the most fruit.

c. Forms related to worship, music, architecture, order of service, teaching, and preaching. There are numerous cultural variations for each of these. How they manifest themselves in a church plant will largely depend on the ethnicity, generation, and background of those being reached. We can agree that the Bible says we should "Let the message about the Messiah dwell richly among you, teaching and admonishing one another in all wisdom, and singing psalms, hymns, and spiritual songs, with gratitude in your hearts to God" (Col. 3:15). What we often disagree over is how that teaching and admonishing should take place, what singing and the accompanying music should sound like, and how the indwelling Messiah will be manifested in ministry and good works. Without a doubt, there are limits to what we do and how we do it. There are lines that can be crossed, but a church plant must at least ask the questions and struggle with appropriate, careful, and thoughtful contextualization.

d. Cultural norms related to time, conflict resolution, decision making, leadership, and organization. The Bible is replete with proverbs and specific instructions on how we are to deal with time, make decisions, be leaders, and treat one another. The principles are clear – for example, answering gently (Prov. 15:1), making the most of the time (Eph. 5:16), not lying to each other (Col. 3:9), being at peace with each other (1 Thess. 5:13), loving each other (1 Pet. 4:8), and many more. Exactly how each of these will look on a daily basis and in each congregation will largely depend on cultural norms. That is, cultures determine how time is viewed, how conflicts are properly resolved, and how leaders are selected and how they lead. If there is ever an occasion to evaluate any of these, it should be through the lens of the Bible and not one's own cultural norms.

When I am moved out of my comfort zone

Anyone who has been involved in church life and ministry for very long has at some point been in a worship service or a church ministry setting that made them squirm a little. Whether it was the music, the preaching, the order of service, the length of the service, how the people interacted with each other or with guests, how business was carried out, or how ministry and outreach were done, we have all been pushed out of our comfort zones. How do we evaluate what is done differently in churches, particularly in new church plants? Four questions should be asked when one is standing on the edge of comfort:

1. Is it Biblical? Is my discomfort, my objection, Biblical? Is it rising from a Scriptural or theological concern? If I believe it is, then I need to be specific about my objection. What is the specific Scripture principle or doctrine being violated or compromised? In some cases, the doctrinal objection is clear cut. For example, if a church denies or even minimizes the deity of Christ, there are ample grounds for objection. At other times, qualifying one's discomfort may not be as easy as it first appears. People often know that something is "not quite right," but cannot immediately explain the doctrinal concern. Perhaps there is not a "chapter and verse" to point out, but there are theological and ethical implications and applications that must be evaluated. For example, the Lord's Supper may be practiced, but is it acceptable to use pizza and Coke? Where is the line between being casually dressed and being immodest? What are the long term implications of a pastor led church as opposed to congregational polity? What does it mean to become a member of this particular

361

local church? If, however, being out of my comfort zone cannot be traced to a Biblical basis, then I need to ask another question.

2. Is it cultural? Is my discomfort and objection rising out of my cultural background? Is what I am experiencing really a reaction to the way another group of people worships and lives out church life? If it is, there are still two questions to consider: One, is it a cultural expression of church that is essentially neutral, regardless of how I feel? Two, is it a cultural expression that still needs to be judged and evaluated by Scripture? That is to say, churches (and especially church plants) need to reflect the culture they are in, but not entirely, for all cultures are fallen. In the American mission field, there are many culturally driven forms and practices of church that we rarely thing about…unless we are of another culture. Consider "traditional" churches (and I use traditional in the broadest sense): We consider 11 a.m. as the sacred meeting time; we place an American flag at the front, which seems quite odd to some cultures; we insist on punctuality; we prefer relatively "short" sermons; we often sit while singing and reading the Bible; we don't mind if men and women sit together, and so on. Similarly, consider "non-traditional" churches: We don't like to point out guests; we like to use video and other technology; we stand the entire time we sing; the Bible is on the screen; the offering plate is not passed; altar call invitations are rarely given, etc. Now, consider other cultural expressions: late to start and finish whenever; children freely move around the sanctuary; sermons can be very long and very expressive; music can be loud and expressive; men and women may sit separately; women may have their heads covered, and the list could go on.

New church plants must be culturally relevant in whatever culture they are planted. The challenge is to understand that there are boundaries; however, these boundaries are not always clear. It takes hard and prayerful work, therefore, to "search the Scriptures and understand the culture before determining the boundaries," and knowing which cultural elements should be kept and which should be discarded.[364]

3. Is it a preference? Perhaps my discomfort and objection is nothing more than a challenge to personal preferences. The truth is that we all have preferences in worship and church life. Most of these are grounded in our personal experiences, especially if we grew up in the church. To simply not like the way something is done is understandable from a human perspective, but is inexcusable from a missiological one. We simply cannot let our own preferences dictate or be obstacles to evangelism, church planting, or ministry in the American mission field.

4. Can I tell the difference? Unfortunately, many cannot tell the difference between Biblical and theological issues, cultural expressions and forms, and personal preferences. All these just melt into "the right way to do church." There is a difference between each of these, and they are important. Taking the gospel of Jesus Christ to the American mission field through church planting demands the hard work of identifying the differences so my culture and my preferences will not be an obstacle. We do not want to confuse the "earthen vessels" in which we received the gospel with the "treasure" itself. That is to "confuse faithfulness to the gospel with perpetuating and extending cultural forms in which we received it."[365]

Evaluating one's discomfort with church models, forms, and styles requires, therefore, prayer and wisdom. Planting a new church to be culturally relevant requires even more of both. Two questions should accompany whatever is done in a new church plant, whatever is kept in an established church, or whatever is changed in any church: One, why are we doing (or holding on to) this? If there is not a solid Biblical and missiological reason, then it should be seriously questioned. Two, will this violate principles of order or modesty, cause unnecessary offense, unnecessary distraction, or unnecessary division? If it does, then it should be carefully reconsidered. The desire is to be Biblical and wise, and not be foolishly sold out to either traditionalism or fad.

Missiological Implications

Jesus is building his church among all peoples, in all places, and through all times. This means that:

1. Local churches are the means for Kingdom work; therefore, more local churches are needed in the American mission field.

2. Church planting is the most effective way to fulfill the Great Commission and the best way for the Body of Christ to live as salt and light in whatever community if finds expression.

3. Church planting, therefore, involves all kinds of new churches to reach all people in all locations.

4. Church planting models and strategies must be Christocentric, striving to be both Biblically faithful and contextually appropriate.

5. All churches were new at one time. New churches will struggle, be out of balance at times, and sputter in their efforts to grow into a healthy established church. When what they do pushes us out of our comfort zone, we need to be careful that we are not allowing cultural norms and personal preferences to sour our attitudes toward them. New churches and church planters need the encouragement, the prayers, and the loving accountability of established churches. Even as they push us to the edge of our comfort zones, we should celebrate that, however it is done, "Christ is proclaimed" (Phil. 1:18).

His Word Will Not Return Empty: Proclamation and Contextualization

> For Christ did send me to baptize, but to preach the gospel – not with clever words, so that the cross of Christ will not be emptied [of its effect]. For to those who are perishing the message of the cross is foolishness, but to us who are being saved it is God's power.... For since, in God's wisdom, the world did not know God through wisdom, God was pleased to save those who believe through the foolishness of the message preached. For the Jews ask for signs and the Greeks seek wisdom, but we preach Christ crucified, a stumbling block to the Jews and foolishness to the Gentiles. Yet to those who are called, both Jews and Greeks, Christ is God's power and God's wisdom, because God's foolishness is wiser than human wisdom, and God's weakness is stronger than human strength.
>
> 1 Cor. 1:17-18, 21-25

After Paul opens his first letter to the Corinthians with the obligatory (but theologically rich) greeting, he deals with the first controversial issue on his list of concerns: divisions in the

Corinthian church. Several factions had developed in the church, each claiming a different head or leader: Paul, Apollos, Cephas, or Christ. Paul rejects such divisions, for the body of Christ cannot be divided in such a way. He then expresses his strong displeasure that his name has been appropriated by one of the groups. He was not the one who was crucified. He baptized only a few of the Corinthians, and never so that he could build his own following. Whatever any of the factions may think, Paul's primary purpose when he arrived in Corinth was to preach the gospel. Regardless of the multiple needs of the city and the issues to address, the starting and ending point in Paul's missionary strategy was to "preach Christ crucified." Note how Paul elaborates on his preaching and its content as he corrects the divisive Corinthians:

First, Christ sent him to preach the gospel. Paul is not minimizing the importance of baptism, but will simply not allow anyone to use baptism done by anyone, even himself, as the basis for factions in the church. The important thing for the Corinthians to remember and recognize is that Paul's priority when he arrived in their city was to *euaggelizesthai*; that is, to evangelize or be "a gospelizer."[366] There were many other issues to address, doctrines to teach, problems to solve, but they all flow from and are grounded in the gospel. Without the initial preaching of the gospel – the good news – there is no basis on which to address any other question.

Second, Paul did not allow his style or method to distract from the message of the cross. He says he preached "not with clever words," meaning literally not with "*sophia*" or wisdom of words. Paul will address the content of his preaching in the next few verses, but here he is addressing form or style. There was in the Greek rhetorical tradition not only an emphasis on philosophical content, but also on rhetorical ability.[367] Therefore, Paul is stating that his preaching was not flowery, smooth, superbly articulate, or brilliant (see 2:1 also), for that would have distracted from the content of the cross. Certainly, Paul was capable of articulate speech, but that was never his concern or intent. No one would be able to say that Paul made a convincing argument with his words; if anyone believed him, it was because of the message he was proclaiming.

Third, Paul is not surprised that the message is foolishness to the lost. Paul could not have drawn a greater distinction between the gospel and the prevailing worldviews than he does in the next few verses. The gospel message of the cross was so contrary to the prevailing religions and philosophies of the day that the first response of many was "foolishness!" When the Jews heard Paul some of them responded to such foolishness in anger (Acts 13:50). When the Gentiles heard such foolishness, they often ridiculed Paul (Acts 17:32). Yet, some in both groups also believed and became disciples of Jesus (v. 24; Gal.3:28). Regardless of the form or style of Paul's preaching, his point here is that the content draws the definitive line: foolishness or the power of God. For those who are lost and dying, the content is foolish. For those who are being saved, it is the power of God. Of course, it is only after a person hears and believes "the foolishness of the message preached," and is saved by God that the power of the message of the cross is so obvious. This message, then, is what the Corinthians ought to be passionate about, not petty cliques based on personalities.

Fourth, the message of the cross clashed with core beliefs of the prevailing worldviews. The cross is foolishness in content to both the Jews and the Greeks because its message collides with the core expectations of the two prevailing world views. On one side were the Jews, who demanded miraculous signs of anyone who would claim to be their Messiah. They had been waiting a long time for the Messiah and were expecting a mighty and powerful deliverer who would "simply repeat the Exodus, in still greater splendor." There was nothing quite as convincing to them as the display of divine power through amazing signs. On the other side were the Greeks, who "were zealous for every kind of learning," for their civilization had contributed to the wisdom and philosophies of the world as none other had ever done. There was nothing quite as important to them as the reasonable formulations of the human mind. These demands, however, were idolatrous, for they were exalted above all else and decidedly came between the Jews and the Greeks and acceptance of the message of the cross.[368] That is, in the foolishness of the cross neither group got what it was looking for – power and wisdom – in the way they defined and desired power and wisdom.

Finally, Paul clearly states the content of the gospel – Christ crucified. The Jews expected powerful divine signs. The Greeks wanted powerful and convincing human wisdom. What they got was the message of a crucified Messiah, the incarnate Son of God, who died and rose again on the third day. The Jews stumbled over the thought of a weak Messiah who could be defeated by the Romans. The Greeks laughed at the idea of God taking on flesh, dying, and then living again. This message – Paul's preaching – is foolish to those who cannot or will not believe. But "we" (Paul, his fellow missionaries, and the Corinthians themselves), he reminds his readers, keep on preaching the message of Christ crucified for it is God's power and wisdom. Amazingly enough, what seems foolish and weak to the prevailing worldviews, is stronger and wiser than anything that could be conceived in and by the world.

In the midst of religious pluralism, pagan dominance, gross immorality, and constant ridicule and hostility, Paul reminds the Corinthians why he came to them, what they heard, and what they must stand for: Jesus Christ crucified. As he continues to encourage the Corinthians in verses 26-31, he reminds them that God has chosen them, many from an insignificant and even despised status in the world, to demonstrate his power and wisdom in the cross. No matter the conditions in the church or in the world, this is the message of the gospel – this is what is proclaimed – Jesus Christ and him crucified.

It should be apparent from our examination of the American mission field in Part 2 that twenty-first century America is a lot like Corinth; that is, a thriving cosmopolitan crossroads, diverse in its religious and philosophical views, and proud of its moral openness and freedom. Paul's reminder to the Corinthians is also a reminder to the church in the American mission field, pluralistic, pagan, immoral, and hostile though it may be. Our proclamation must be about the crucified and risen Christ. All other issues flow from and follow this core message.

Definition of Preaching

Just as it is with evangelism and church planting, there is ample contemporary controversy over the purpose, nature, and appropriate methods of preaching. Significantly, much of the controversy over preaching style (expository, narrative, topical, etc) is primarily over preaching done in the church to believers. Most instances of preaching in the New Testament, however, and especially that of Peter and Paul, was proclamation or heralding of the gospel to non-believers for the purpose of leading them to conversion. Preaching done to the Christian community was usually referred to as "teaching" and was primarily for instruction and edification.[369]

Be that as it may, preaching now commonly refers to the public proclamation of God's word, whether evangelistically to mostly non-believers or primarily to believers in a church setting. In the former case, just about anybody would refer to Billy Graham's famous evangelistic messages as "preaching." A church setting is assumed in the latter, for example, when John Stott defines preaching as such: "To expound Scripture is to open up the inspired text with such faithfulness and sensitivity that God's voice is heard and his people obey him."[370] Similarly, Albert Mohler defines "to preach" as "reading the text and explaining it – reproving, rebuking, exhorting, and patiently teaching directly from the text of Scripture. If you are not doing that, then you are not preaching."[371] Mohler's definition could also apply to evangelistic preaching, because evangelistic preaching must involve reading from the text, explaining it, and then calling for repentance and faith in Christ.

My intent in this chapter, therefore, is to focus on preaching as gospel proclamation in and to the American mission field. Following Paul's example as he "gospelized" in and to Corinth, what are some missiological principles for the proclamation of the gospel in the American mission field?

One size will not fit all

Any quick survey of the New Testament will show that Jesus' preaching, and later preaching about Jesus by the Apostles, was done in every way possible for that day. Jesus preached the gospel of the Kingdom in synagogues, in the Temple, from a hillside, along the road, in a crowded house, from a boat, one on one, in his home country, in Samaria and across the Jordan, to the Roman invaders, to lepers, sinners, and tax collectors, and to the religious. He used parables, quoted the Hebrew Scriptures, asked many questions, engaged in debate, performed miracles, healed people, often left people perplexed or amazed, and explained the entire Scriptures.

The Apostles preached in upper rooms, to large crowds, to individuals, in homes, in synagogues, in the Temple, before the Sanhedrin, before Roman rulers, in jail, on ships, in large cities, and in the countryside. Paul walked, traveled by ship, wrote letters, debated the Hebrew Scriptures with the Jews and philosophy with the Greeks, confronted the demon possessed, stood up to idolaters, almost convinced governors, appealed to his Roman citizenship, took a Nazirite vow, and became all things to all people for the sake of the gospel.

As a result of our cultural diversity, pluralism, the tribalizing effects of postmodernism, and as a consequence of media saturation, we have to proclaim the gospel to a niche driven population. The saving message of the cross is exactly the same for every single person. Communicating it, however, will require greater contextualization efforts to smaller niche and affinity groups as never before. One "size" or type of proclamation will simply not do (if it ever did). Just as Jesus and the Apostles addressed each person and every crowd differently, so must the gospel be communicated contextually to hundreds of niche groups. The advertisers and retailers in America have figured this out. So did Paul. He "always preached the gospel but never the same with different people."[372] Language differences, immigration, the growing number of Third Culture people, generational preferences, learning styles, linear and non-linear worldviews – all these demand that we work hard at proclaiming the universal message of the cross to particular people. We must work hard at not making worldview and cultural assumptions. We must practice one of the basic tenets of communication – know our audience.

Know our audience

Paraphrasing the standard caricature of philosophical reflection the question is, "If a preacher speaks to a crowd and no one understands, has he just made noise?" That is, if the message of the cross of Jesus Christ is not heard accurately and understood well enough so that the hearer can either accept it or reject it, has preaching taken place? This question is not to devalue the work of the Holy Spirit in illuminating the mind of the hearer. It is, rather, to emphasize the responsibility of the church and the preacher, in whatever context, to prayerfully and seriously work at proclamation so that it is not a wasted effort. Some of the hard work of understanding the audience includes:

1. Knowing language and cultural barriers. This may seem to be the most obvious of observations, but it is not always as apparent as is often assumed. We understand that people speak different languages, but we don't always realize that conversational English (or conversational ability in any language) does not mean there is an ability to understand theological or Biblical concepts, or insider church language. Whether proclaiming through preaching, personal evangelism, a written tract, a television ad, or a billboard, we cannot assume understanding in cross cultural proclamation. Even asking a person or a crowd if they understand or whether we are making sense will not always help. Some people may hesitate to admit they do not understand for fear of appearing ignorant or being shamed. Furthermore, in some cultures the responsibility for effective communication falls more on the hearer than the speaker, meaning that the hearer may claim understanding in order to save face. The lesson to learn is that we cannot automatically assume our message is understood just because we have proclaimed it.

2. Orality and literacy issues. Most Americans do not realize it, but "[o]ral communicators still compose at least fifty percent of the population in the United States and other Western nations such as Canada, France, and the United Kingdom." These are people who communicate primarily through "oral narrative rather than through writing," due to either a lack of skill or out of preference.[373] This simply means that for fifty percent of Americans highly literate proclamation, whether preaching, written materials, or even long lecture filled videos, will not connect. One problem is that this issue is not often discovered or recognized until the oral learner has stopped listening, moved on, and apparently "rejected" the message. I once worked with a

bivocational church planter who was insightful enough to pay attention and adjust to the people he was reaching. Mark planted a church in deep East Texas among the extremely poor. During a quarterly progress review meeting, this mechanic-church planter told me that he was preaching and teaching using the King James Version of the Bible, but realized that his people just "didn't seem to understand anything he said and would not respond." He switched to the New International Version, but got the same response. He told me, "I then realized they could not read. So, I got some videos from Child Evangelism Fellowship. I play part of the video, stop it, and then we discuss the stories. They are excited, learning, and participating like never before." Certainly, a great ministry would be to offer literacy classes and increase the reading ability of the people. The point is that this wise planter communicated the gospel to the people in a way they could clearly understand and respond.

3. Learning styles. Not every person learns the same way. Our traditional educational system has been strongly geared toward the logical style, although it is now understood that there other learning styles besides the *logical*, including *visual, aural, verbal, physical, spatial, social*, and *solitary*. Some people have a dominant style, but most of us are mixed.[374] Proclaiming the gospel effectively means being aware of and addressing all styles. To concentrate on simply one style means we run the risk of missing a significant part of the population. Jesus knew this. He told stories, he used illustrations and metaphors from everyday life, his miracles were visual lessons, he used logic with the scribes and Pharisees, and he even drew in the sand. Good preachers know this. That is why the most basic preaching class will teach exposition, illustration, and application.

The aha! moment comes at different points for different people, usually depending on their learning style.

4. Educational background. When we proclaim the gospel in spoken word, through the written word, or even through images, what is the educational background of the audience? We never miss the child, teen, and adult divides, but even with these divisions (especially with adults) we cannot assume educational background. Like Mark, the church planter who discovered that his people could not read, we should consider the educational background of the audience. Certainly, we want to work to "bring them up," but where are they now? What can and must be said at their level of education so they can understand it?

5. Spiritual and religious background. A critical consideration, especially in our growing secular and pluralistic society, is finding out the spiritual and religious background of people. Again, nothing should be assumed. In evangelism, in church planting, in any form of proclamation, we cannot assume that the recipients of the message have any Christian church background. More and more people in America "missed the first thirty years of Sunday School," or even have non-Christian backgrounds. We cannot assume they know anything about the Bible and much less understand any of our terminology. Again, we will want to teach to increase their knowledge, but the starting point may be Creation and the very existence of One God.

6. Life context. We know Jesus Christ and his work on the cross is the answer, but what are the questions people are asking? What is their life context? What are their real needs, their struggles, their fears, their ambitions, the crisis they are undergoing, and their pain? What are the

questions they are asking about meaning, about purpose, about eternity, about relationships, and about making it day to day? Yes, they need to recognize they are sinners in need of forgiveness. Yes, they need to understand Jesus and his sacrifice on the cross. But at times even Jesus listened to, asked about, and met physical needs on the way to addressing the core spiritual need. The danger, however, lies in stopping at the need, whether real or felt. The danger also lies in proclaiming Jesus only as one "who meets all your needs" without a call to repentance and turning from the sin that directly or indirectly contributed to those needs. That is, our proclamation can and should begin on many levels, and it can and should address many needs and situations in life. If our proclamation only reaches those points, however, then we have failed to communicate the essential gospel of the cross of Christ and his call to discipleship. To the contrary, we make Jesus into a spiritual Santa Claus, only an ethical teacher, a sage with pithy sayings, or a holy vending machine ready to meet every selfish need. We make Jesus into "a person who helped us discover ourselves" rather than he who "asks for all of our lives, not just a 'spiritual' segment."[375]

Therefore, we should not only know our audience, but we need to . . .

Lead our audience

There are those who complain that spending too much time or effort in knowing the audience, whether community, focus group, or people group is dangerous because it allows the lost world to set the agenda for proclamation and ministry. In other words, surveying a community before planting a church, discovering the "felt needs" of a community, or discovering the worldview of a people is to allow "them" to determine the shape of the church plant or the focus and content of preaching. As it is with many missiological concerns and complaints, the answer is both yes and no. Certainly, a church or a preacher can over-contextualize and allow the context to determine what is done and said. When that happens, proclamation loses its prophetic edge and is indistinguishable from a motivational talk. The other extreme is to ignore the needs, issues, concerns, and struggles of the intended audience and never connect with them. In this case proclamation is a wasted effort.

The solution is to thoroughly know and understand as much as possible about the audience, its needs, conflicts, worldview, and problems, not so they will determine or change proclamation but to *inform* and *direct* proclamation so that it gets as quickly as possible to the heart of the matter. For example, Jesus brought up the five husbands and live-in boyfriend to the Samaritan woman not so he could offer marriage counseling or even condemn her immorality, but to get quickly to the reality that he was the Messiah she and others were waiting for. Jesus went to have a meal with Zacchaeus not just because Zacchaeus was a lonely, bitter man in need of a friend, but because Jesus intended to lead him to repentance and salvation. Similarly, Paul engaged the philosophers at Mars Hill not just to win a philosophical argument but to quickly get to the truth of the resurrected Lord. In each case, Jesus and Paul were *leading* their respective audience from the point of contact to an encounter with the truth of Jesus Christ. In all proclamation, whether it is written, one to one, a billboard, a tract, sharing a personal testimony, evangelistic preaching, or preaching in the local church, there is an initial connection point with some reality in the audience. That reality is the door through which the proclaimer – the preacher – walks through, takes the audience by the hand, and leads them to an encounter with the cross of Jesus Christ.

Therefore, knowing your audience well is so the proclaimer, whether the church or a preacher, can fashion the delivery of the message of the cross so that it is heard, understood, and can be responded to by the hearer. Proclamation, therefore, must:

1. Lead to understand. Knowing the audience well, including people's worldview, their real and perceived needs, their struggles and problems provides the proclaimer with the questions that are being asked. The proclaimer must not stop, however, at answering those questions. He must continue to lead the audience to the ultimate and eternal questions of sin and redemption. Jesus did not just tell the Samaritan woman she had five husbands, implying God did not like it. He led her to an encounter with himself. Likewise, our proclamation cannot stop at "Jesus can help you be a better husband, wife, and parent," but we must lead the hearer to understand that "Jesus died to save you from your sins" and that "Jesus calls you to follow him fully and completely, and that will make you a better husband, wife, and parent."

2. Lead to respond in faith. The purpose in leading our audience to understand is so that they will respond to Christ in faith. Of course, this may take time, especially if the audience is steeped in a sinful lifestyle, has absolutely no Biblical background, or is a devout practitioner of another world religion. Still, the point is not to simply condemn, inform, debate, win an argument, or even to simply love them in a Christ-like manner. The ultimate goal is to lead the person to repentance and a faith response to the message of Christ.

3. Lead to grow in grace and truth. Once a person has repented and received Christ, continued proclamation

takes place. The purpose now is to lead the person – the audience – to grow in grace and truth. This does not mean they try harder or work at becoming a better person, but that they continually surrender every aspect of their lives to the Lordship of Jesus Christ. They understand more and more what it means to walk and live in the grace and truth of Christ in them and them in Christ. They become disciples of Jesus, truly "little Christs."

Tell the Story

One of the most challenging, necessary, and yet overlooked aspects of our proclamation is telling the story, that is, the entire story of God's mission and purpose for his creation.[376] What do I mean? What we too often do is:

1. Get theologically, ethically, and morally out of balance. On the one hand, there are times and seasons to emphasize particular theological, moral, and ethical concerns. For example, in our American society there has certainly been reason over the last several decades to emphasize the Biblical reasons for a pro-life and pro-marriage position. In a particular congregation, a pastor may choose to preach more often than not on the sovereignty of God and the exclusivity of Jesus Christ in response to prevailing questions about the "openness" of God and the plurality of world religions. In general, most para-church organizations and other Christian "movements" have a particular emphasis. These are usually in response to either a real or perceived need in the church. On the other hand, the preaching of, for, and in the local church should seek to tell the whole story – from creation to eschatological restoration. It certainly can't be done all at once and

must be done creatively, but telling the story should be intentional and systematic. And, applying it to all of life must be intentional and systematic. We preach Jesus crucified, but do we tell how the entire history of creation and all of the Old Testament leads to him? We want to make disciples of Jesus, but do we talk of all aspects of life – individual, marriage, family, community, and world? Do we stay on pet issues, narrow concerns and passions, and specific applications, or do we talk about being a disciple in all realms of society – education, science, environment, government, the arts, and the economy? We must proclaim, preach, and teach the whole counsel of God's word.

2. Develop a "canon within the canon" for our preaching. My seminary preaching professor challenged us students to take a clean, unmarked Bible and highlight the passages we preached from. After a few years, he said we would be able to tell whether we had developed a "canon within the canon" of favorite passages. Perhaps one might argue that teaching from the Gospels or the Epistles is more profitable than teaching from Leviticus. The problem is that Leviticus and all the other sixty-five books are equally inspired and authoritative. One solution is to preach systematically through all the books of the Bible, even if not in sequential order. However one preaches, the temptation must be avoided to preach only from the pastor's or the congregation's favorite passages. If this is done, the whole story will not be told, heard, and understood.

3. Atomize Scripture beyond recognition. That is, taking an overly scholarly and analytical approach to the Bible. There are certainly occasions to break down the verse, do word studies, and delve into the sentence structure. This

may certainly be needed for sermon preparation, but is rarely needed in most local church preaching. To analyze and break down each verse and word to such a degree can lead the audience to think of the Bible as a book that can only be interpreted by the technically adept, as one with hard-to-find hidden meaning, and as inaccessible to them on a daily basis. If this reductionist approach is taken too regularly, the audience can't see the forest (the whole story) for the trees (the technicalities).

4. Treat the Bible only as a helpful handbook for life. That is, using the Bible haphazardly as an instruction manual full of sayings for meeting the needs of life. On the one hand, the Bible does have instructions for life. Proverbs and other wisdom literature even lay many of these out in topical and pithy form. They should be preached and taught appropriately and regularly. On the other hand, the problem with preaching only topically turns the entire Bible into a book of pithy sayings. That is, a topic or problem or issue is laid out, and then dozens of verses from all over the Bible are taken out of context and often misinterpreted and misapplied to address the topic or solve the problem. As true and as valuable as the verses may be, and even as well applied as they may often be, the audience never hears the whole story from creation to restoration.[377]

5. Focus on making quick converts in evangelism and fail to make disciples. This is often a legitimate criticism of evangelists and evangelistic methods. It should never be, however, a legitimate criticism of the church as a whole and of local churches in particular. The Great Commission is about making disciples – baptized followers of Jesus who obey all that he taught and commanded. Evangelism

is not complete until discipleship takes place, discipleship is impossible without evangelism, disciples are evangelists, and discipleship is not an event but a life-long journey. Nothing in the process should be neglected, and the entire process is about knowing God, his story, and his whole purpose for life.

So how do we make sure we are telling the whole story?

First, keep the purpose, the goal, the end game in mind. We are about making disciples of Jesus Christ, and if there was one thing that was distinctive about the early disciples, it is that they knew the story. If they were Jews, they had the background. If they were Gentiles, they learned the background. What they heard from Jesus, and what the early church heard and read from the apostles was a whole and balanced theology and ethic. Therefore, being a disciple of Jesus means growing in grace and truth, meaning knowing the whole story and how it applies and works out in individual life, community life, and in the world.

Second, proclaim Jesus and him crucified as the driving theme. Telling the whole story, proclaiming and preaching the whole counsel of God, does not mean there is not a core theology that drives it all. Whether we are talking about the mission of God in the world, the Kingdom of God, the Great Commission, the life of the church, or even individual repentance and salvation, the core doctrine – better yet, the core event – that drives every single one is the cross of Jesus Christ. Jesus made it clear to his disciples that he had to go to Jerusalem to suffer, die, and be raised again (Matt. 16:21; 20:18; Lk. 18:31-32). For this he was born. Paul told the Corinthians that he "determined to know nothing among" them but "Jesus Christ and Him crucified" (1 Cor. 2:2). This was not because everything else was insignificant, but because everything else revolves around this core event – the suffering, death, burial, and resurrection of Jesus Christ.[378]

Third, preach the whole counsel of God. How to do this is precisely where the debates and controversies over preaching take place. Should preaching be expository? Verse by verse expository? Topical? Narrative? Doctrinal? The short answer is "yes." In the broadest sense, all preaching should be expository, when defined as "preaching that takes as its central purpose the presentation and application of the text of the Bible. All other issues and concerns are subordinated to the central task of presenting the biblical text."[379] The best way to do this is in a planned, organized, and systematic way – preach through books, preach doctrinal themes, do character studies. At the same time, the occasional topical preaching is appropriate as long as it is text driven and in context. For example preaching on the topics of wisdom, family relationships, dealing with worry and anxiety, or addressing a current event can all be addressed through proper exegesis and in proper context.

The good news for preachers trying to reach the younger "postmodern" generations is that they are truly interested in what the Bible says. Certainly, the same assumptions about Biblical authority and worldviews cannot be made; that is, they want to know what the Bible says, but will not automatically take the preacher's word for it. Furthermore, although they want to know what the Bible says, that does not mean they want a one-way monologue. Dialogue, visual illustrations, and audience participation are more the mode of learning for many in the younger generations. The content or preaching, however, must be Biblical. In fact, Dan Ingram argues that the "emerging church needs to elevate public reading, preaching, and teaching" more than ever. The audience may have changed and the specific methodologies in proclamation may have changed, but there is a "renewed hunger for theology and an interest in discussing the mysteries of God." Therefore, rather than "simply give messages on 'three easy steps' to solve a problem," Ingram calls for straightforward Biblical preaching on human sexuality, on the Biblical model of marriage and family, on hell, on the trustworthiness of Scripture, and on the real messiness of the Christian life.[380] The bottom line is to preach the Bible. Current situations in the lives of people should be addressed; however, unless current situations are related "to the eternal Word of God" then "relevant sermons" are simply "pulpit trifles."[381]

Use Technology

Using technology in the proclamation of the gospel seems like an obvious step to take, but it is not without its controversies and dangers. Doubtless, the church should take advantage of every possible technological advance to spread the gospel, including the internet and social media. The last twenty years should tell us that we have just scratched the surface of communication technology and do not yet have a realistic idea of how much more society will be changed by technology. The church cannot afford to fall behind.[382]

The gospel and social media

The challenge, however, is that the world is drowning in media messages. There is so much "noise" and so many voices clamoring for attention, it is harder and harder for anyone or any entity, especially the church, to get its message heard. We have hundreds of television and radio stations, millions of websites, dozens of social networking sites, and constant advertisement on each of these and in magazines and billboards. There are ranting voices along the political spectrum, scores of social and political movements, and thousands of charities and faith based organizations. It is surprising that any one is actually heard. The media window in which to be noticed and heard is small. For the church to effectively proclaim the gospel of Jesus Christ in this environment is going to take all the creativity, perseverance, and faith we can muster. In fact, to even be noticed, much less heard and heard accurately, is a challenge like none previously known.[383] Yet, as difficult as it may be, it must be done.

Lest the reader who may be overwhelmed by technology be discouraged by such intense competition and not even try, there is hope. It is precisely because we are so inundated by filth, nonsense, and meaningless messages that people are willing to find and listen to words of light and life. The pastor or leader who is tech savvy has probably already figured out how to use technology to spread the gospel and increase ministry effectiveness. The pastor or leader who is not tech savvy can learn. Just ask a young person to guide you. Furthermore, although there is some monetary investment in some technologies, some of it is cheap or free. Therefore, using technology is not just for large and wealthy churches. For example, the pastor of a two hundred member church can:

1. Make sure the church has an attractive, user-friendly, and up to date website. Clearly, a church's website is now its front door. Visitors will check out a website before visiting the physical address of a church. It does not have to be the most sophisticated, but it does have to be updated, easy to maneuver, and with sufficient information to lead the visitor to go from the website to the actual church on Sunday morning. With a little more cost and time investment the church's website can be a provider of all kinds of resources for the person seeking spiritual help: Bible studies, counseling materials, frequently asked questions about faith and the Bible, and so forth. Many pastors are choosing to include podcasts of their sermons. The beauty is that all these resources and these sermons can be downloaded and listened to by anyone anywhere in the world.

2. Create both a church and a personal Facebook account. This is an easy and free way to communicate church events, share devotional thoughts, testimonies, post videos, helpful links, and reach out to hundreds of people who may never come to church. Sunday School classes, small groups, and different church ministries can have their own Facebook pages. Like a website, however, a Facebook account has to be fresh and updated.

3. Write a blog. This scares a lot of people, but a pastor's blog is a good way to regularly share insights from God's word. He can prepare people for upcoming sermons, reflect on the sermon just delivered, and even do a little "training." A blog can be started at no cost, but time must be invested. Again, freshness, regularity, and staying updated are keys to success.

4. Use Twitter. This scares more people than a blog, and with some reason. Just as any technology and social media can be misused, perhaps none is as much as Twitter. The reality, however, is that a pastor has followers, and not only in his congregation. There are many in the community who are interested in hearing something from the pastor – if not a thirty minute sermon, then maybe 140 characters. Tweeting daily can be a way to share the gospel with hundreds of people immediately and consistently.[384]

The resources and time that could be put into technology are endless. But, it doesn't take much to get started. The future is communication technology and social media. Although it may be a bit scary for some, never in the history of mankind have we had so many different vehicles by which we can proclaim the gospel of Jesus Christ. The fact is that one church or ministry sitting in a small town in the middle of nowhere can reach thousands of people all over the world. The airwaves are full and getting fuller, but the effort to fill some of it with the gospel is well worth it.

Preaching and technology

The use of technology in local church preaching is sometimes even more controversial than social media. The particular question is how image and video should be used. Some argue that any use of video or imagery detracts from the proclamation of the word of God. Others argue that we live in an ever increasing visual culture, and, just as Jesus used stories, parables, and metaphors to communicate with an oral culture, there is nothing wrong with using visuals to communicate and illustrate Biblical truths. In fact, many would argue that using visual imagery enhances and is necessary to help a visual generation understand Biblical truth.

The use of visual imagery, and any technology for that matter, could detract from the message. Moreover, any visual image originally designed to teach and aid in worship can eventually become an idol itself, as it often did in Roman Catholic history. In contemporary settings, lights, music, and video images can aid in worship and illustrate preaching, or overwhelm the actual teaching of the word of God. The question for any technological, and particularly visual, aid is whether it enhances and clarifies the meaning of the message or whether the "cool factor" distracts and detracts from the message.

Take, for example, the use of video in sermon introductions and as illustrations. Some use movie or television clips. Others have used "stock" clips bought and downloaded from the internet. Those who have the resources often make their own clips. Whatever is used, the criteria for using video during a sermon should be the same as for any illustration:

- Is it relevant to the main point? Does it illustrate, explain, or apply the primary teaching point? Will its use help many in the congregation "get" what you are explaining?

- Is it appropriate? If it is a movie or television clip, are the content and the context appropriate? Is the language, the violence, or the relationship portrayed offensive? Is the context surrounding the clip one that would distract? In other words, does the clip come from a movie that is offensive in itself? Disclaimers may be necessary.

- Is it forced? This is true of any illustration. Is it being shared because it is funny, exciting, or emotive and just interesting to watch? Or, does it clarify the truth being taught?

- Does it distract? Most of what has already been mentioned could mean that the video distracts; however, when the congregation walks out, will they be talking about the video illustration or about the message proclaimed that was illustrated by the video?[385]

In the final analysis, perhaps the contemporary use of visual images can be compared to the medieval use of stained glass windows. Stained glass (and other architectural features) was used to tell the story, to assist people in knowing and remembering the Biblical story. It was never meant to replace or distract from the actual preaching and verbal explanation of the Bible. As we move more and more into a visual culture with visual learners, preaching can be enhanced through visual means. The perpetual danger, however, is to allow the effectiveness and even the beauty of the stylistic aid to overshadow and even replace the substance of what is being proclaimed.

Missiological Implications

1. Proclamation (in the broadest sense) and preaching (in the narrow sense) of the gospel is a non-negotiable of the Christian faith. They may be done in a variety of settings, in multiple venues, through numerous vehicles, and to different audiences, but they must be done.

2. The content of our proclamation and preaching may begin and initially connect with the audience at different points, be it a real or perceived need, a personal, congregational, or cultural problem, a crisis, or a question. It must lead, however, to Jesus Christ and his work on the cross. We may speak of the family, of rearing children, the Levitical law, Queen Esther, Solomon's wisdom, or of loving each other. We may be teaching on creation, Noah's ark, David and Goliath, the role of deacons, or spiritual gifts. We may be preaching through Judges, Psalms, Joel, Romans, or Hebrews. There are innumerable Biblical topics, themes, doctrines, and concerns to address. In every case, however, missiologically speaking, every verse, topic, or problem addressed should eventually lead to Jesus. That does not mean we allegorize, take verses out of context, or force meaning onto certain passages. It does mean that we must never forget that we preach Christ crucified.

3. Proclamation, therefore, will involve the hard work of contextualization – knowing the audience and making sure the gospel is communicated faithfully and appropriately so it will be heard and can be responded to. Furthermore, whether an audience of one, of one hundred, or untold millions through a mass media campaign, the audience must be led to an encounter with Jesus.

Finally, we cannot fear technology. We have always eventually used new technology, including microphones and loudspeakers, lighting, acoustic technology, and projection equipment. We must still use it and use it to the fullest. We use it carefully and judiciously, knowing that we will make mistakes and have to learn the limits of its use. Technology is a tool, and as with all tools, it can be misused and abused. Using it will not always be easy or cheap, but technology, and particularly communication technology, will only inhabit our lives more and more. Let's use it more and better than the devil will.

Salt and Light: Christian Life and Contextualization

> You are the salt of the earth. But if the salt should lose its taste, how can it be made salty? It's no longer good for anything but to be thrown out and trampled on by men. You are the light of the world. A city situated on a hill cannot be hidden. No one lights a lamp and puts it under a basket, but rather on a lampstand, and it gives light for all who are in the house. In the same way, let your light shine before men so that they may see your good works and give glory to your Father in heaven.
>
> Matt. 5:13-16

Jesus is delivering the Sermon on the Mount. He has just listed the Beatitudes, detailing the attitudes and actions of Kingdom disciples. They are to be humbly dependent on God, merciful, gentle, peacemakers, pure in heart, and searchers for righteousness. They will also experience persecution because of their righteousness, both because of the righteousness of Christ in them and the practice of righteous behavior; that is, both for who they are and for what they do.

Following that list of Beatitudes, Jesus uses two metaphors to describe Kingdom disciples which explain the reasons for their righteous behavior. Why do they practice these behaviors that are so blessed? Because they are the salt of the earth and the light of the world. Significantly, Kingdom disciples do not practice righteousness in order to become salt and light, but because they already are salt and light.

These Kingdom disciples are described as salt for three reasons: One, because they stave off further corruption of the world. Just as salt preserves meat and other food, holding off the rotting process, so should Kingdom disciples hold off, delay, and prevent society from further rotting. Two, just as salt adds and enhances flavor in food so should Kingdom disciples add to and bring out the best in people and society. The presence of believers should enhance everything from politics to the arts, from science to technology. Three, as "salty" Christians come into contact with the lost world the impact of that saltiness should create a thirst for living water, the only water that can slake the thirst of lostness.[386] The last thing disciples should want is to be like tasteless salt: useless, disposable, and just plain blah.

Furthermore, Kingdom disciples are described as light for two reasons: One, because they chase darkness away wherever they may be. Just as the light always wins out over the darkness, so should the presence and the behavior of Kingdom disciples chase away darkness. Two, when light shines in and overcomes darkness, it is an active and even aggressive phenomenon. Kingdom disciples, in other words, are not to be passive, withdrawn, or in their own fortresses and ghettoes. They are certainly not of the world, but this passage leaves no doubt that they are to be in the world shining brightly. They are on a hill, on a lampstand, giving out light boldly and confidently.

There is a purpose, Jesus points out, for disciples to be salt and light and to practice the blessed attitudes and behaviors he has listed. It is not so the disciples will be honored. It is not so they will win every theological argument. It is not so they will take over the government, rule society, build their own kingdoms, or even change the behaviors of every person in the world. It is so people who see Kingdom disciples living out their lives, loving one another, and behaving righteously, will give glory to the Father. It is as the world observes us – children of God, Kingdom disciples, the church – living out what we say we believe that they will come to the conclusion that God is real and worthy of glory.

As we consider what the church's response should be to the ever changing mission field that is America, we have noted the non-negotiables of contextualized evangelism, church planting, and proclamation. These are the usual strategies expected of evangelicals for engaging the world. They are where we put the greatest amount of resources, training, and effort. Living as salt and light in the world gets a bit more complicated. For one, it is much more personal. We are now talking about lifestyle…my lifestyle, in fact. That is not to say that evangelism and proclamation cannot be and should not be part of our lifestyle. But when we start talking about being salt and light, or of living a missional lifestyle as it commonly referred to, we are talking about the most personal aspects of life – attitudes, relationships, morals and ethics, practicing and experiencing love. As the old saying goes, we have moved from preaching to meddling.

Two, whether we are talking about an individual's personal holiness or the church being corporate salt and light, we are now talking less about strategies and methods and more about people being Godly people. Certainly, being salt and light requires intentionality, strategy, and methods, but because every person and every life is unique, the expressions of salt and light are as diverse as there are people. There are Biblical principles to follow, but God's calling, gifting, and the context of every person's and every church's life is different.

The reality that we are all different means, third, that our discussions on being salt and light can quickly deteriorate into legalism if we are not clear and careful. The temptation is often for one person to impose his situation on another or expect all believers to live out their witness in the exact same manner. The danger is to read a challenging and well intentioned book on the missional lifestyle and feel guilty and condemned (convicted is OK) because we are not practicing every suggestion perfectly…and no one is. Again, there are Biblical principles to follow, and often there are very specific commands. In many cases, however, how we "love one another," behave gently, seek after righteousness, rejoice always, love our husbands and wives, and are filled with the Spirit may not look exactly the same in every situation. A long list of what to do and not to do is easy; walking in the Spirit by faith is a little harder. Checking off a list of missional suggestions is satisfying; living one's daily life in the Spirit, open to his movement and direction, paying attention to people around us, and being fruitfully engaged in the community is hard – thus the Spirit.

Having said that, both the individual Christian and the church should be salt and light in the American mission field.[387] The list of ways this could be done through ministries, activism, and movements would fill another book. So, instead of a long list of ministries and activities, I want to suggest some contours for both personal and corporate action as we live as Kingdom disciples in a fallen world. The overarching principles is that we move from what we already are (salt and light) to what we should do (flavor and illuminate), all to draw attention to the Creator and Redeemer God in Jesus Christ.

Being a saint in a sinful world

There are few aspects of Christianity that are as misunderstood as that of being a saint. At one extreme is the "saintly" image found mostly within the Roman Catholic Church. In this view a person may be canonized as a saint after a lifetime of observable righteous behavior, evidence of performing miracles, and, in some cases, martyrdom.[388] The lifestyle of these people is often honored and respected even by non-Catholics, as was, for example, Mother Teresa's. Saints, therefore, are special people who have achieved a higher and more notable spiritual status than the rest of Christians.

At the other extreme is the worldly understanding of saint. In this case being called a saint is usually a pejorative term. A self-righteous, holier-than-thou person is referred to as arrogant for thinking he is so saintly. Or, a meek, goody-goody person is ridiculed as being a saint. In the best of cases, someone who has actually displayed exceptional behaviors is called a saint, as in, "she must be a saint to put up with him," or "my mother was a saint – she raised five boys."

The Biblical concept of a saint, however, is both broader in application and more specific in definition. A saint is *anyone* and *only that one* who has been saved by grace through faith and is now a child of God. She is a saint not because of behavior but because she has been set apart *for* God and *from* the world. A believer is a saint, therefore, because of God's action and for God's purposes. As believers, this is who we are in Christ – saints.[389] This is a positional reality made possible by the redeeming work of Jesus Christ on the cross. The reality of this sanctification is such that the Apostle Paul had no problem referring to the Corinthians, the Galatians, or other struggling believers as saints.

Our positional sanctification is just the beginning. The New Testament is full of principles, instructions, and commands on how to live out our sainthood – the process of being sanctified. All these "to do" passages, however, are based on the "being" passages; that is, being in Christ, being a saint, being redeemed, being forgiven, and being a child of God. We must know who and what we are before we can do. Otherwise, what we do can turn into self-righteousness, self-seeking, and outright legalism while simultaneously judging and condemning others.

Being a saint in a sinful world, therefore, means living out one's positional holiness in the journey to actual holiness, which is reflecting in our thoughts, attitudes, behaviors, and relationships what we already are in Christ. This perspective should remove any self-righteous arrogance about being a saint, and does not have to result in milquetoast blandness. It may certainly lead to criticism and ridicule by the world, but it will be Jesus in us they are criticizing and not our own self-righteousness or legalism.

In the American mission field, what are a few of the specific areas of life in which as Christian saints we can demonstrate actual holiness, if not perfectly, at least hopefully and aspirationally? What are some ways we can do good works that will point people to the Father?

Grace and forgiveness

Perhaps there is nothing we like to personally receive but struggle more at giving than grace and forgiveness. These are at the very core of Christian faith and experience. They are perhaps what most radically distinguish Christianity from all other world religions. Other religions may include compassion, justice, righteousness, mercy, and maybe even merited forgiveness, but the Biblical God is the only One who acts toward his creation with undeserved grace and unmerited forgiveness. We are the only ones who could write and sing "Amazing Grace."

At the same time we struggle at living out, practicing, and offering grace. It goes, obviously, totally against our human nature. If it didn't, it would not be amazing. Even as believers and recipients of God's grace and forgiveness and as those who write about, preach about, and talk up grace and forgiveness, we still suffer from the Romans 7 syndrome – we are made of flesh, sin still lives in us, and we don't always do what we want to do but do that which is evil. And, is there anything more subtly evil than acting ungracefully and withholding forgiveness?

The world's way is to hold a grudge and seek retribution and revenge. Individuals, families, clans, peoples, and nations won't forgive, refuse to forget, and seek ways to get even. Centuries-old grudges keep nations at the brink of war, real or perceived slights keep tribes and clans distrustful of each other, and personal offenses eat at individuals and families for generations. In one sense the world knows a lack of grace and forgiveness is ultimately destructive, yet we still celebrate "righteous revenge" over and over in our folklore, our stories, and our movies (we all love a good revenge action movie). There is, however, something about a story of grace and forgiveness that grabs the world's attention. When the already overextended family takes in an orphan; when a passerby risks his life to pull a stranger from the path of a subway train; or when a donor offers her kidney to a stranger who needs it. When the former POW forgives his captors' abuse; when the wrongly incarcerated prisoner forgives his accusers and the justice system; when the rape or pedophilia victim forgives her attacker; or when the abandoned son forgives the father who left him when he was born. When these actions take place, and they are sometimes the actions of Christians, the world knows that is how it should be ... in a perfect world.

Unfortunately, we don't live in a perfect world. But as disciples of Jesus we have been given both an example and a command that reflect the perfect world that was before the fall and will be when all is restored. We are to live in grace, live out grace, and offer forgiveness again and again. What are some ways these could be lived out?

1. As was discussed earlier, one of our American idols is that of individual rights. As Kingdom disciples we must stand up for the rights of the helpless, hopeless, and the defenseless. We can find ways, however, to demonstrate

what it means to give up our own rights. In a contentious society, we don't always have to win. In a litigious society, we don't always have to sue. In a selfish society, we certainly don't have to be first. Perhaps a good question for every Christian to ask himself every morning is "what right can I give up today?"

2. Jesus said the world would know us and believe because of our unity and love for one another. Is anything more confusing in the American mission field than the lack of love shown among Christians? This is not a plea for us to "all just get along," or to overlook truth so that we can have "peace at any costs." It is a challenge to examine some of the issues we fight over and to ask if in some cases we can live with being wronged, misjudged, and falsely accused. What better way to show the world grace and forgiveness than to show it among ourselves first?

3. Perhaps the most difficult and controversial application of grace and forgiveness is on the corporate and national level. As individuals we are supposed to turn the other cheek, but what about the nation? As individuals we are supposed to forgive, but what can and should a group – institution, company, organization – overlook and forgive? How does all this grace and forgiveness stuff apply to the criminal justice system, national defense, and even daily business ethics? There are a variety of opinions that go from one extreme (no application whatsoever in a world of *realpolitik*) to the other (absolute pacifism, for instance). Christian ethicists have long struggled with the tension between turning the other cheek, loving your enemies, and the reality that the "government is God's servant, an avenger that brings wrath on the one who does wrong" (Rom. 13:4b). My intent is not to offer an

answer but to challenge us to at least ask the question from a missiological perspective. What would grace and forgiveness look like if the church practiced them both as individuals and as a body? What would grace and forgiveness look like and what societal impact would we see if the church insisted that they be practiced daily in business dealings, in politics, and even in national domestic and foreign policy? What missiological impact would loving your enemies have at these levels?[390]

Marriage faithfulness and commitment

Although the actual statistics on divorce, adultery, and pornography use by married men (and women) in our culture are debatable and often confusing, they are still high enough to be depressing.[391] Committed church-goers (of any religious persuasion) do better, but we, too, still struggle in these areas.[392] If there were, however, any one visible witness by the saints that could impact the lost American mission field more than anything else we said or did, it would probably be a radical turn around in these statistics. As Mormons become more mainstream and accepted as a "Christian" denomination, what is the one thing they are usually praised for? Strong marriages and traditional family values (at least on the surface). Certainly having a strong marriage, being faithful to one's spouse, and avoiding the entanglement of pornography does not make one a Christian (just as it doesn't for a Mormon). Neither is preaching on marriage and family alone or primarily a balanced missiological strategy. Bottom line, the American mission field needs to hear the gospel of the cross of Jesus Christ. The challenge is to not allow our failed marriages, or any other aspect of our lifestyle, to become an obstacle to hearing and responding to that message or any other lifestyle message. For example, although we can confidently oppose gay marriage on Biblical and theological grounds, our voice is much more likely to be heard if we were to more consistently practice Biblical marriage as a whole.

Moderation in lifestyle

David Platt's book *Radical* challenged the church to reconsider the pitfalls of the American Dream out of control; i.e. materialism and consumerism. Platt calls on Christians who have also fallen into the grips of these idols and suffered the consequences of debt, bankruptcy, and a lack of generosity to repent and radically change their lifestyles. Whether or not one accepts all of his views, Platt's is a prophetic voice that needs to heard and heeded. Denominations bemoan the lack of giving and stewardship by churches. Pastors grieve and fret over the lack of giving and generosity by church members. We all work hard at helping them get out of debt through financial seminars. We certainly recognize the problem and some of the cause. Yes, it is a lack of obedience. Yes, it is a lack of discipleship and stewardship. It is also a buy-in to the rampant materialism and consumerism in our society, and too many pastors and church leaders lead the way. Churches build facilities they don't really need and go deep into debt to do so. When times get tough, pastors preach on trusting God and giving generously, but lead their churches to slash their own missions giving budgets. We have certainly been rich Christians in a poor world; now we are more like indebted Christians in an indebted and needy world.

Every good evangelical preacher has at some time spoken about being a saint – set apart from the world and for God – and described that in terms of what a saint does not do. Over the decades it has been said that a good Christian avoids everything from movies, bowling alleys, pool, mixed bathing, worldly entertainment, eating out and shopping on Sunday, smoking, drinking, dancing, and so on. Some of these prohibitions were simply cultural. Some were appropriate prohibitions at the time (you could only play pool in a bar, for example). It is still a pretty good idea to avoid some of these. How often, however, have we preached against materialism and consumerism and for a simpler lifestyle? How often have we said that the most distinct way to stand out from the world would be to live simply and give away fifty percent of one's income? Similar to moderation and simplicity in finances, how about the same applied to the use of our time? Being overly busy is often a status symbol and an implied measure of spirituality. Yet, Jesus regularly took time to slow down, retreat, and reflect. Why do we feel we don't need the same? I certainly am not "there" yet on any of these issues, but I wonder if we realize what kind of impact that type of saintly lifestyle would have in the American mission field?[393]

I warned earlier about how easy it is to fall into legalism when talking about being a saint in a sinful world. All that I have mentioned, as Biblical as they may be, could easily be used to puff ourselves up or to judge others for not doing so. That is not the purpose of suggesting these. In the final analysis, the most important aspect of being a saint in a sinful world is to know and proclaim that, although a sinner and although still dysfunctional, imperfect, and a struggling sojourner, we have experienced God's grace and forgiveness. When all else fails, we tell the world we are saints not because we are so good, but because he is so good and has forgiven us.

Being the church in a sinful world

Being salt and light in a lost world is not only the privilege and responsibility of the individual Christian, but also is a command for the church. That is, although there is an individual responsibility, there is no room for individualistic Christianity. Just as the church is a sign of the Kingdom, and just as the local church is a contextual manifestation of the Kingdom, so is the church to be salt and light. And, again, that begins and is most transformative when the local church – each local church – seeks the best ways to be salt and light in its community and its people. The following four suggestions for being salt and light in the sinful world apply to the universal church of Jesus. They are universal, cross-cultural, and cross-generational principles. Each local church, wherever and whenever it exists, must ask itself how each of these plays out missionally in its local context. Remember, the intent is missiological – being salt and light in and to a lost world. This is not a definition of church, an explanation of a healthy church, but a challenge for the church and each local church to reflect and consider how to live out the gospel contextually.[394]

Loving the God of all creation

Is it just me or is the flippant and over the top "Praise Jesus" or "I give all glory to God" spoken after so many touchdowns and by so many celebrities at awards ceremonies irritating and sound almost blasphemous? On the one hand, there is something commendable and encouraging about giving praise to God at every opportunity, especially when millions are watching. On the other hand, when the celebrity's lifestyle is highly questionable and when the implication is that God is on the winning team's side then God has been reduced to a talisman and a purveyor of personal ambitions. Similarly, we have all cringed at the ease with which some preachers and congregations manipulate Scripture and use God's name in vain to shore up their particular point of view, activity, or agenda. Even when they have a good point, the lack of humility gives reason to be concerned.

So, how can the church express love for God in a way that would have a missiological impact on the American mission field? We love the Lord, we are commanded to tell of and sing his praises, but how do we do that in a way that puts all the attention on him and not on us? We can begin by:

1. Acknowledging the Lordship of Jesus over every aspect of life. Easy to preach, harder to practice. The reality is that both individual Christians and churches tend to compartmentalize God. We allow him into certain areas of our lives, but keep him at arm's length in others. This is often noted by unbelievers. They see a deacon acting pious on Sunday, but cheating his customers on Monday. They see a Sunday School teacher blessing the Lord on Sunday, but gossiping about the neighbor during the week. They see a church arguing vehemently for a pro-life position, but then making operations and personnel decisions along business rather than Biblical principles. They see a denomination publicly condemn the purveyors of pornography, but then turn a blind eye to the corruption on Wall Street.

   Acknowledging and practicing the Lordship of Jesus in all these areas does not mean we flippantly bring up his name every time we can, like the phony celebrity. It does mean, first, that we seek him and his will in every decision, whether personal or corporate, acknowledging that we may struggle with understanding what should be done in every situation. Some situations are black and white; others may be a little bit more ethically messy, which is the nature of a fallen world. Second, it means that we can and should acknowledge him verbally and publicly as often as we can. The difference is what we acknowledge him for. We thank him for health and opportunity, not necessarily for the touchdown or the victory. We thank him for guidance, wisdom, and opportunities in education and business, not necessarily for our success over the failures of others. We acknowledge what he has done in our lives, but are careful that we don't set ourselves up as the deserving winner or victor.

2. Holding to a sense of fear, reverence, and mystery. This is a corrective to some of the flippant over familiarity expressed toward God in both the world and in society. We certainly have a personal and intimate relationship with our Father God in and through Jesus Christ. We have the right and privilege to call him "Abba" (Rom. 8:15). We are the friends of Jesus. Yet this does not excuse flippancy and disrespect. For example, there are few people who know me as well and love me as much as my own father. He and I have a close and intimate relationship. I call him "Dad" or even "Daddy." Still, I honor and respect him enough that I would not call him "dude" or "man," or even by his name, "Frank." He is my father and my friend, but I still want to honor and respect him, especially in public.

Missiologically, as we speak of and refer to God in the world, we should do so in balanced terms: He is our Father through Jesus Christ. At the same time, he is Almighty and Holy God, and a healthy fear of him is called for. Furthermore, we should always speak of him and for him in humility, holding to a sense of mystery, acknowledging that he is God and we are not, that he has all the answers and is absolute, but that we "see through a glass darkly." This does not mean watering down the truth or refusing to stand for truth. It simply means speaking the truth in humility and love.

In the same vein, our humble and reverent talk about God will help us from manipulating him as a heavenly vending machine or thinking of him as one who is susceptible to "spiritual laws" by which he must bless and prosper us. It will also keep us from manipulating him politically and ideologically. That is, we will want to make sure we are on his side, rather than carelessly claiming he is on our side.

3. Worship corporately in a Biblically "seeker sensitive" way. What we do and how we act in our corporate local church worship is missiologically important. The world often judges us (sometimes misjudges us) based on what takes place on Sunday when we come together. All kinds of controversies have embroiled evangelical churches in the last few decades over corporate worship issues – the music wars, preaching styles, architecture, video and imaging, the dress of the preacher, and on and on. Those issues will not be settled here, if ever. I would propose, however, that every local church needs to be "seeker sensitive" along the 1 Cor. 14:23-24 principle. In this passage Paul tells the Corinthian church that speaking in tongues all at once and in a disorderly fashion will cause unbelievers who come in to the assembly to wonder if the believing Corinthians were out of their minds. Two points to notice: One, Paul expected unbelievers to attend the gathering of believers from time to time. Two, he is concerned about how these "seekers" would respond.

The immediate context is tongues, of course, but the principle remains – don't do anything in your corporate worship service that will cause unbelievers to stumble, leave before hearing, and write you off as crazy. Whether it is music, preaching, video, public expressiveness, tedium, or anything else, there is a Biblical principle of not letting anything be a stumbling block for the visiting unbeliever, except for the gospel itself. This does not mean that the unbelieving world determines how worship is carried out.

It does not mean that anything should be watered down or that the message should be compromised. It does mean that some in the world are seeking truth and we don't want to be the cause of them not finding it. If the unbeliever who comes to worship wants to think we are crazy because we believe the gospel, then that is acceptable. If she believes we are crazy because of our behavior, or way of speaking, or of any way we may be mis-representing the Lord, then we have a problem.

Loving God is what we want to do and express. Doing it thoughtfully, carefully, and with humility will have a missiological impact on the American mission field. America has already seen and heard too many extreme views. She has heard enough from self-proclaimed prophets. She needs to hear from Kingdom disciples who love the Lord with all their hearts, souls, and minds, and with all humility.

Loving the people of God

The night of his arrest Jesus gave the disciples the clear command to "love one another" (John 15:17). During his prayer for the disciples, Jesus made it clear that the unity and love expressed among his followers for each other should be such that the world would pay attention (John 17:23). Subsequently, John lays out in his first letter the importance, significance, and practicality of that command to love one another. The spiritual bottom line is that to know God is to have love and to love one another (1 John 4:7-8). Loving the people of God – one another – is therefore not only an ecclesiologically driven command and reality but a missiological imperative and strategy.

When people in a local church practice love for another – not perfectly, but intentionally, consistently, and gracefully – the church then acts as that shining city on a hill. It becomes a community that some would want to join and belong to. There are four aspects to loving one another that must all be practiced for the community to shine the light missiologically:

1. Loving one another is more attitude and action than emotion and feeling. Unfortunately, too much of our understanding of love revolves around feelings. That is certainly part of it, and certainly the most enjoyable aspect of love. Loving one another in a Kingdom way may involve affection and feelings, but these are not a prerequisite. True love – Biblical agape love – is unconditional. It begins with an intentional decision and attitude to act in love regardless of feelings and regardless of merit. Practically, this may be as simple as greeting a person one would rather avoid. It means speaking well of someone who doesn't deserve it. It means returning good for evil rather than seeking revenge. Would that every believer felt affection for another; however, that is unrealistic and not even Biblically required. What is required is love in action, one for another, regardless of feelings.

2. Specifically, loving one another means caring for each other's physical needs. In this case, charity begins at home. Acts 2:45 tells how the early church took care of each other materially to the point that no one had need. James tells us in 1:27 that pure religion is caring for orphans and widows in distress. These examples and commands are a counter to those who may talk the love talk and act affectionately, but not be really doing the things that demonstrate sacrificial love. The Biblical truth, argues Sean Cordell, is that the highest in priority are the members of the Body of Christ. That does not diminish nor excuse our social responsibility for those outside the church, but it

does keep us from neglecting our own.[395] If the church did what it was commanded to in terms of caring for its own, would there be very many occasions for someone to go hungry, to be unable to pay their bills, or be forced to seek government assistance? If this were the reputation of the church, would it not proclaim something about the gospel to the lost community?[396]

3. Loving one another includes rebuke, correction, mutual accountability, and truth telling. Loving one another does not mean a lack of conflict, accountability, or speaking truth when necessary. Leaders are instructed to "rebuke, correct, and encourage with great patience and teaching" (2 Tim. 4:2) even as they shepherd and love the flock. Those who are "spiritual" are to confront and gently "restore" a person who "is caught in any wrongdoing" (Gal. 6:1). The priority of love for Christ and his church often means that individuals who are sinning and damaging the body need to confronted directly and quickly. Thus Ananias and Sapphira (Acts 5:1-11). Thus Paul's direct and frank letters to the Galatians and the Corinthians. Missiologically, the world needs to see, understand, and believe that the church is serious business. Sin is taken seriously, unity is taken seriously, responsible membership is taken seriously, and care for one another is taken seriously. We don't go to one extreme and become legalistic, negative, and brow beat each other all the time, but we also don't go to the other extreme and refuse to address sin, hoping that everyone will be happy, positive, and just get along famously. Being the church is hard work, and taken it seriously is in itself a missiological statement.

4. At the same time, loving one another means learning to live with conflicts, disagreements, and differences. Love

certainly "covers a multitude of sins" (Prov. 10:12; 1 Peter 4:8), which means that we have to often just overlook an offense and move on. That is, love for one another does not mean that every single offense, disagreement, or problem has to be addressed. Sometimes we just need to "get over it." Sometimes, we can do everything in our power to act in grace, to love and forgive, and these will not be reciprocated. Paul recognized this when he instructed us "if possible, on your part, live at peace with everyone" (Rom. 12:18). Sometimes there will be conflicts and disagreements and even a parting of ways (as with Paul and Barnabas). This does not mean that love stops. It does not necessarily ruin our testimony in the community. If handled correctly, with patience, and with good intentions, and followed up with kind and good words for each other, the lost world can learn how conflict can and should be handled.

The lost world will not always understand the inner workings of a local body of Christ. We should not expect them to. Missiologically, however, God can and will use the testimony of how we love one another to draw lost sheep unto himself.[397]

Loving the creation of God

"The earth and everything in it, the world and its inhabitants, belong to the Lord" (Ps. 24:1). This truth did not change with the fall. In fact, the restoration of all things is possible because "the Redeemer and the Creator are not two different gods but one and the same Lord God almighty, Maker of heaven and earth." The One who created the perfect earth, the One who has preserved, provided for, and given common grace to a fallen earth, and the One who will restore all things, which also involves a new heaven and new earth, is the same God. There is, therefore, no basis for "false dichotomies between the kingdom present and the world, the spiritual and material realms, the eternal and the temporal, the soul and the body, redemption and creation, and evangelism and social action."[398]

This insistence on a vigorous and unified monotheism, an understanding of the Kingdom presently inaugurated, and believing there will be some sort of continuity between this present earth and the new earth[399] specifically provides the foundation for a Christian environmentalism. That is, there is no Biblical foundation for interpreting the dominion command (Gen. 1:28) as anything other than that of a careful, loving, and protective stewardship of God's creation. If God is in the process of restoring his creation, then how should we treat that creation? The attitudes and actions the church takes toward the care of the earth, our stand on environmental policies, and our individual exercise of ecological stewardship carries significant missiological weight.[400] A young urban church planter working among the "bohemian" community of downtown Dallas once told me that he often had to answer the question, "Why is it that you Christians say you love God, but mistreat his world?" Perhaps the question was often a pet misdirection, but the point was made. We do not have the reputation for being "creation lovers." We preach love of God, we preach of obeyinghis commands, and we preach of Christ's Lordship of all life, but fail to always connect that to environmental stewardship.

Unfortunately, as is often the case when trying to practice Biblical theology at the intersection of culture and social policy – all in a fallen world – we run into numerous understandings, applications, and philosophical extremes. Combine that reality with a missiological concern (our proclamation and our visible witness), and it is even more complicated. How do we proclaim and practice a Christian environmentalism that shows America that we love the God of creation and his creation…without going too far? Some principles to consider:

1. The basis for our environmentalism is a Biblical creation and redemption theology. A Biblical stewardship of the environment holds off two extremes: On the one hand, we love God and his creation, and thus we are good stewards of it. We do not love creation or nature in and of itself. A Biblical stewardship wards off any idea of pantheism, panentheism, or nature worship, for "nothing in creation is in itself divine."[401] If one wants to be a "tree hugger," it is because God created that tree, not because we have some sort of "universal oneness" with that tree or that it is somehow endowed with divinity. Moreover, God created that tree to be wisely used by humans, not worshiped. Human beings, then, are stewards, managers, wise users, and wise conservers of creation, not "almost a parasitic presence" as some extremists posit.[402] A Biblical understanding of creation stewardship will also hold in check extreme views of animal rights, most of which posit little distinction between animals and "human animals," thus demeaning humans, who have been crowned by God with "glory and honor" (Ps. 8:6). Without a doubt, it is a sin to torture or mistreat animals, to hunt species into extinction, and even to farm and raise animals in torturous conditions. It is a sin, however, not because they are almost on par with the human "animal" but because they are God's creatures and we are to be good stewards of them. There is nothing wrong, therefore, in choosing to be a vegetarian or a vegan for health reasons; however, most philosophical or "spiritual" reasons fall far short of a Biblical understanding of creation stewardship.[403]

    On the other hand, a Biblical stewardship corrects a flippant, uncaring, or even abusive attitude toward creation. Understanding God's creation and our responsibility to care for it does not allow for thoughtless development, farming practices, mining, forestry, over fishing, and so forth. Fortunately, we have learned our lessons to some degree and have made corrections. We still have a long way to go when we consider the amount of food we waste and the increasing amount of natural resources we use in this country. This is not a call to stop it all, for that is unrealistic and impossible. It is a call for individual Christians and the local church to take the steps necessary to publicly demonstrate that this is our Father's world and we will take care of it as he has commanded.

2. We practice what we preach individually and corporately. We need to counter the objection my church planter friend regularly encountered by practicing environmental stewardship personally and corporately. Slowly but surely, we are making progress, even if it is forced upon us. Recycling, driving more efficient cars, better insulating our homes, being aware of and careful with the use of chemicals, and shopping with greater care and wisdom are some of the practical ways this can happen. Churches can both preach and practice environmental stewardship. Too often, evangelical churches fail to include creation stewardship in their preaching. If there is practical environmentalism in the church, it is to improve the bottom line (savings on heating and air conditioning, for example) and not to proclaim a theology of creation and restoration. Avoiding the extremes mentioned above, the church – and every local church – should lead the way in testifying to God's goodness as demonstrated in his creation, his gifts and provisions, and to our own joyful stewardship of all that he has created, sustains, and will one day restore. What we will be doing is behaving "as we were originally created to and as we will one day be fully redeemed for."[404]

3. We learn to live with tensions and differences in application. To some this call for Christian ecological

stewardship, especially with a missiological view, will sound too idealistic and unrealistic. Granted, the practical, social, political, and ideological issues are complex. The same, however, holds true for any social and political issues. The challenge can be met as we hold two attitudes: One, we start somewhere. We struggle with the Biblical text, we develop a theology of environmental stewardship, and we begin to practice it personally and corporately. Like it or not, this will be a major twenty-first century issue, and we must be ready with a Biblical response. Two, we will have to be comfortable with some tension and disagreement among ourselves. Even if we avoid the extremes mentioned above, how environmental stewardship is implemented through policies will create tension and conflict. There are business concerns, agricultural issues, industrial and mining priorities, and so forth. These are driven by both monetary and philosophical concerns, all of which may be represented in a local church. There are differing positions on the ozone layer, on global warming, and deforestation, on farming techniques, and how to keep from polluting the air and the water. Wherever one may land on these issues – their causes and their solutions – the reality is the environment is in trouble and environmental issues will be at the forefront of political and economic conversations. The challenge is for the church to keep going back to a Biblical theology, practicing stewardship personally, and then graciously proclaiming care for God's creation and working together toward corporate implementation.[405]

Loving the world of people

"For God so loved the world" (John 3:16), meaning the world of people. And so should we. Jesus "saw the crowds" and "felt compassion for them" (Matt. 9:36). And so should we. Paul's dramatic salvation experience coupled with his clear understanding of sin and Christ's work on the cross, compelled him (2 Cor. 5:14) to obey the "heavenly vision" (Acts 26:15-20) and take the message of salvation to the Gentiles (the known world). And so should we. Because of God's mission and his love for the world, can we – can I – love the world's people? Certainly, it is not the same love that we express and feel within the body one for another. Perhaps there is rarely any feeling at all; however, can we love the world of people by choice, in obedience, and compelled by God's love by our actions? To love the lost world is this way involves three perspectives:

1. The right perspective of people. From the outset we have to remember that all people are created in God's image. That image is marred and disfigured. All people are fallen, are sinners, and have fallen far short of God's standard. The expressions of that universal fallen nature are individual; that is, all people are sinners, but some really manifest sin in the most evil ways possible. Still, we have to see people as Jesus does, with the *imago Dei*, as those for whom he felt compassion, as redeemable, as potentially believers and children of God. Remembering this truth about all people should keep us from demeaning any gender, group, race, ethnicity, culture, or socioeconomic class. It should also remind us that every individual, no matter how despicable and evil, deserves to hear the saving message of the cross.[406]

   Conversely, although we love people who are made in the image of God, we should not act surprised when they behave like lost people. Christians who should know better misbehave sometimes. Why are we shocked and surprised when a lost person acts lost? Certainly, we can bemoan the loss of common decency and morality, but we should not be too surprised.[407]

2. The right perspective of God's work. If the Kingdom of God can be described as God's eternal rule and reign over all that is, then we must recognize that he can be and is at work in the world even if the church is not yet present. In the darkest of places, in the most corrupt society, and in the most evil of hearts, God can work. His command to go is based on the realities that "the Holy Spirit has come upon you" (Acts 1:8) and that Jesus with us "always" (Matt. 28:20). These promises, the omnipresence of God, and the love of God for the world imply that God is at work well ahead of any evangelistic and missionary effort. He is at work in the world of people, in individual hearts and among cultures, societies, and groups. The only thing lacking in many cases is one who will proclaim in word and deed (Rom. 10:14). We can be excited about the lost world because God is at work in the world and invites us (commands us!) to join him there.

Furthermore, he is at work in all domains of society. In fact, Jesus is also Lord over every domain of society. A missional church will seek to move into and influence every domain of society rather than retreat into a Christian ghetto. This does not mean that we stop preaching prophetically about the sinfulness of society. It does mean that we disciple our people and then encourage them to go into business, government, education, health, the arts, and all domains of society to be salt and light. God is already at work in every one of these areas. A missional church will find ways to get out of the Christian sub-culture and influence culture at large. In this way, the local church is not trying to be at the center of society impacting every domain of society, but is equipping and empowering believers to go into the domains of society and be "Christians in the city."They are missional disciples right where they live and work every single day.[408]

3. The right perspective of strategies. Much ink has been spilt in the debate over whether the church should be attractional or incarnational. Michael Frost and Alan Hirsch say a church is "attractional" when it "plants itself within a particular community, neighborhood, or locale and expects that people will come to it to meet God and find fellowship with others."[409] This approach is a "come and see" one. If a lost person is going to hear or experience the gospel, it will be primarily within the walls of the existing church. In contrast, an "incarnational" approach is one where the church "embodies the culture and life of a target group in order to meaningfully reach that group of people from within their culture."[410] This is a "go and tell" approach. Understand that the incarnational approach does not eliminate the Biblical command to gather as believers, nor does it eliminate the need for a gathering place. The difference is a matter of emphasis and of world view; that is, as the church seeks to love the world of people and reach them for Christ, is the primary method to first attract them into a building where they can hear the gospel or to go among them with the gospel and then congregate into a culturally relevant church? Is the primary idea to get them onto our turf or to meet them on theirs?[411] The reality is that both are biblical and both are strategically important, and that importance is often shaped by the context.

Why should a church think and act incarnationally? What is wrong with doing all that is possible to attract people with powerful and relevant sermons, stirring music, comfortable environs, and numerous ministries and events? In and of themselves, these are not bad. If they are all that is done or relied upon for outreach, however, then the church will:

- Attract people mostly like those already in the congregation.

- Miss out on reaching all kinds of groups – languages, ethnicities, classes, affinities, sub-cultures – who would never set foot in that particular church.

- Miss out on reaching the radically uninterested and disconnected lost. That is, people for whom church is not an option and not even on their radar, no matter how attractive it may be.

- Fool itself into thinking it is growing by reaching people when the majority of their baptisms are children and teenagers from families already in the church. Certainly, we want these to be saved and baptized, but they are not from the lost community.

- Unintentionally find itself in competition with other churches. The competition is in attracting either churched people or sympathetic lost people. Again, these need to be reached and need a church home. The problem is that the "slice of the demographic pie" that includes these people is small and getting smaller. More and more churches compete for the same shrinking demographic, and avoid having to cross significant and challenging cultural barriers to reach the growing general population that is completely detached from the gospel.[412]

The call, therefore, is to love the world of people, that world that "God so loved" that "He gave His only begotten Son." That is to be done on a personal and individual level as believers live in communities, work, go to school, and play. It is also to be done corporately as the church models Christian community and reaches – goes – into the lost world proclaiming and living out the gospel. The church is both "an imperfect social incarnation of God's inbreaking reign of love and reconciliation, joy and freedom, peace and justice,"[413] and the missional point of God's mission in and to the world.

Missiological Implications

If we are to be salt and light in the world – among and to the lost sheep for which Christ died – it will take intentionality, commitment, and a willingness to die to our own comforts, preferences, and selfish desires. Some implications include:

1. Taking personal responsibility to lead the way. Many of us do not naturally or easily leave our comfort zones and love people. We will have to choose to think and act missionally, to take the first steps ourselves, and then lead our families to act in love toward the lost world. At the very least, our lifestyle should be different, noticeable, and cause others to ask us "why?" This we must do; this I must do.

2. When we speak of God and about God we need to be careful. For one, we need to always speak with a sense of humility, respect, and never flippantly. God is not our pet deity. We also need to be careful that we are not carelessly speaking *for* God. Certainly, there are times for a prophetic word, and times for rebuke, correction, and edification. What we say must line up with Scripture and

with a healthy and balanced Biblical theology. We must do this; I must do this.

3. We are and we will be noticed. As a church, a local body of believers, the world notices how we treat or mistreat each other. Our unity, our love for one another, how we meet each other's needs, and how we live openly as a Christ-centered Kingdom community will be and should be an open book of testimony. When we fail to do so, it is probably what is most noticed and criticized by the world. When we do so well, it is probably the most attractive aspect of an attractional strategy. We must do this; I must do this.

4. We must practice what we preach – or preach it if we don't – about the stewardship of God's creation. We may argue about the specifics, but we must witness to our care and concern for the world that God created and gave us to steward. We must do this; I must do this.

5. The church – and all local churches – must envision, redirect, and restructure themselves to be primarily incarnational. This is absolutely necessary in today's diverse and fractured society. This means:

    a. Avoiding building a Christian ghetto and getting trapped in the Christian sub-culture. That is, we don't hide behind the walls of our "distinct community" but rather go into the "surrounding communities as salt and light."[414]

    b. Seeing ourselves primarily as a missional or a sending entity. That is, we would be as interested in how many go out as in how many come in.

    c. Developing parallel and new cultures. On the one hand, the church itself is a "new community, a culture not of this world."[415] On the other hand, the church is called to make culture by moving into all domains of society.[416]

We must do this; I must do this.

6. More specifically, being incarnational means taking on significant social responsibility: feeding the hungry, clothing the poor, healing the sick, standing up for the oppressed, doing all that is possible to give hope to the hopeless, both spiritually and physically. Social responsibility involves both social ministry (ministering to those in need) and social action (organizing to change unjust social structures). The latter means that the church will be involved in politics, something that is inevitable in order to defend the sanctity of life and the Biblical definition of marriage or to confront the structural causes of poverty, systemic racism, rampant violence, defense profiteering, and irresponsible greed by the powerful.[417] In the midst of carrying out our social responsibility, however, we must remember that wherever and however we start in meeting human need, ultimately we cannot be content until the gospel of Jesus Christ is proclaimed in a way that it is heard, understood, and the opportunity is given for a response of repentance, faith, and commitment.[418] This we must do; this I must do.

7. Finally, we are limited missiologically only by our vision, passion, and obedience. Becoming salt and light is not an issue of resources, but of how we view the world, how we view people, how we view our call, and how we choose to obey Christ's command to go. This we must do; this I must do.

Conclusion

What is the future of the American mission field? Are we on the same track as Western Europe, where the church has been declawed, defanged, and tamed beyond recognition? Many believe that is our future. The good news is that we have never had a state church, which historically has only led to corruption, syncretism, and, I would argue, has sped up the decline of the church in Europe. Our continued moral decline, rapid cultural change, demographic changes, economic uncertainty, and the growth of world religions and postmodern relativism – what do these mean for the American mission field?

The case for pessimism

1. Our flat, globalized world and increasing immigration means that world religions will continue to grow and influence America. Moreover, although Mitt Romney was not elected president, Mormonism is almost accepted as another branch of Christianity. All this means a further confusion of Biblical Christology.

2. The acceptance of world religions is made possible partially because of our increasing postmodern worldview. Pluralism and relativism reign. The Christian metanarrative will

increasingly be seen as intolerant. Ironically, that also puts pluralism on a collision course with Islam.

3. Simultaneously, the continued decline of morals and the continued rejection of the church's relevance mean that non-Biblical worldviews and lifestyles will continue to grow and gain acceptance. Perhaps nowhere will this be so obvious as in the acceptance and promotion of gay marriage.

4. The response of many denominations and churches will be doctrinal compromise. Of course, this is nothing new in Christian history. For some, to survive, be relevant, and have any kind of societal acceptance requires re-interpretation of the Bible and significant doctrinal compromise.

5. For those who refuse to compromise, even if they do so lovingly, there will be an increasing loss of religious liberty. More and more, as evidenced already in Western Europe and in Canada, the only acceptable form of intolerance will be against evangelical Christians. For example, it is not inconceivable that "hate speech" laws will soon be passed that prohibit preaching or working against any homosexual agenda. Even prohibitions against evangelism are not unimaginable.

The case for optimism

1. All of the reasons listed for pessimism may simply mean that a purging of the church is taking place. Biblically and historically, there have been times when Christians could no longer remain lukewarm. Many bemoan the decline of cultural Christianity, but it may be the best thing that ever

happened to the American church and to the American mission field.

2. The flip side of our growing immigrant population is that many are coming to Christ when they enter America, and, more importantly, others are often bringing with them a revitalized Christianity. Many, in fact, are coming as missionaries to what they see as a lost America. If there is any future for the evangelical church in America, it may just be among the often marginalized and culturally invisible immigrant and ethnic church.

3. As uncomfortable as that immigrant Christianity may make some American Christians, it will force us to evaluate our Christianity, particularly our commitment and practice. That is already happening. This does not mean that every innovation, idea, or practice brought to ours shores is Biblically acceptable, but it will force us to rethink what Biblical Christianity is and should look like in America.

4. There are indications that the younger, emerging generation (especially younger church planters) are bringing with them a passion and commitment to the unvarnished gospel as we have not seen in generations. They are less and less interested in all the accouterments of traditional and cultural Christianity. They simply want to make disciples of Jesus Christ.

5. As overwhelming and intimidating as technology may be, never before have there been so many ways to evangelize and disciple people. We are still learning how that will work out, but distance, numbers of people, languages, educational levels, and worldviews are more easily (not

perfectly) transcended than ever before. Yes, the same technology can be appropriated by wolves in sheep's clothing and by every religious huckster around, but these have always been with us. Still, the opportunities are limitless.

Realistic tensions

1. We are living between the times. Biblical history is linear history. It is headed to its final consummation, the details of which we love to argue about. In the meantime, however, from a human perspective there are advances and setbacks, cycles and the repeating of history. Some things in life are a whole lot better than they used to be; others, not so much. It is a bit like the advice a stock market investor gets: Take the long view. Watching the stock market every day will only drive you crazy. We have to keep things in the big two thousand year plus perspective.

2. Therefore, change is inevitable, both good and bad change. We influence what we can, we fight some of it, we embrace some of it, and some we avoid. Most often we simply have to ride the wave of change. When a surfer encounters a giant wave, he does not stand up to it or he will be smashed. He does not swim in it, for that compromises his whole purpose and he may drown in the roiling water. When the wave of change comes, the church cannot stand up to it or she will be smashed into quaint irrelevance (witness the Amish and other separationist groups). She cannot swim in the wave or she will not live out her purpose and drown in compromise (witness liberal Christianity). The church must ride the wave of change, moving forward, staying above the roiling temptations of compromise, staying

focused on the end goal, and coming out victorious in the end. Metaphors always break down, but the point is that the church has always found a way to survive in the best and worst of changes, and we will this time, also.

3. Therefore, we must remember that God is in charge. And, not only is he in charge of America, he is in charge of so much more! Creation, history, and the future – he has a plan, it will not be thwarted, and it will all come to pass. Our struggle is to stay Biblically faithful in times of rapid and discontinuous change. Easy to preach, harder to practice.

Epilogue

Most preachers have had the experience of preaching to themselves. They have carefully prepared a sermon, are delivering it with passion, and realize somewhere in the process that God is speaking to them as much as anybody else. This has certainly been my experience while writing this book, especially in Part 3. My observations and suggestions for responding to and engaging the American mission field does not come from one who has practiced it all very well. The challenges I put forth are as much a challenge for me as they are for my home church, my denomination, and all evangelical Christians and churches. The reality is that most of us don't need more knowledge and information – Biblical, theological, demographic, methodological. For the most part we know enough. Yes, there is always more to learn, a new way of looking at things, greater insight to be gained, and new ways of applying that knowledge. At some point, however, we must act, we must obey.

My hope is that this book will have challenged some to see things differently, encouraged some in what they are already doing well, and stimulated some to further action and good deeds. My desire is never to be critical; to critique, yes, but to do so in a way that will ultimately encourage and spur to action. Conviction is up to the Holy Spirit, and, as usual, he has convicted me first. In the end, I pray that this book will encourage American evangelicals to trust in God and act in faith, knowing that he has a plan and has invited us to be part of that plan wherever we are planted. The American mission field is his. America's future is his. At the risk of some eisegesis, Paul's word to the Philippians can apply to the church in America and perhaps to the nation as a whole: "I am sure of this, that he who started a good work in you will carry it on to completion until the day of Christ Jesus." We have a task to do. We are to be faithful to his calling and his command. We do need to remember, however, that the plan, the work, and the results are his.

Endnotes

1   Having grown up in Latin America, I am well aware that "America" is much more than the United States. However, for ease and simplicity, when I refer to the United States I will use "America." That in no way is intended to denigrate or minimize Canada, the United States of Mexico, or any of the other countries on the American continent.

2   When I say "church" I am referring to those who are broadly referred to as evangelicals. They hold to the historical orthodox doctrines of the faith, including the authority, veracity, and inspiration of Scripture, the exclusivity of Jesus Christ, salvation by grace through faith, the necessity of personal conversion, the reality of heaven and hell, and a belief in fulfilling the Great Commission both personally and corporately. Therefore, using "the American church" is an oversimplified and practical term, not intended to express any particular ecclesiological or denominational agenda or belief.

3   Thus, carrying out the Great Commission within one's own cultural, socioeconomic, ethnic, or language grouping for the purpose of assimilating new believers into established churches is evangelism, not missions. Admittedly, the distinction is somewhat artificial and one sided, for

missions without evangelism is impossible. Wilbert Shenk, "The Culture of Modernity as a Missionary Challenge," *The Church Between Gospel and Culture*, eds. George R. Hunsberger and Craig Van Gelder, Grand Rapids: William B. Eerdmans Publishing Company, 1996, 77-78, points out that "there is no biblical or theological basis for the territorial distinction between mission and evangelism. To accede to this dichotomy is to invite the church to 'settle in' and be at home." Instead, he argues, a Kingdom approach would mean that the church always sees itself as an "outsider" to the culture and never is comfortable and at home in any culture. I agree this should be the church's understanding of itself. The church should always see itself on mission in its own and in any culture; however, doing missions in an intentional and strategic way is more effective and fruitful if seen as cross-cultural. This can help prevent the church from becoming too comfortable.

4   The book is not, however, a detailed "how to" book. To be so would require multiple volumes, and there are already many books available that specifically and practically address the how to of ministry and missions.

5   Alex Stepick "God is apparently not dead," in *Immigrant Faiths: Transforming Religious Life in America.*" Edited by Karen I. Leonard, Alex Stepick, Manuel A. Vasquez, and Jennifer Holdaway (Lanham, MD: AltaMira Press, 2005), 13.

6   R. Laurence Moore, *Touchdown Jesus: The Mixing of Sacred and Secular in American History* (Louisville: Westminster John Knox Press, 2003), 43; Jenna Weissman Joselit, *Immigration and American Religion* (Oxford: University Press, 2001), 71-97 passim.

7   Richard Robinson, "Judaism and the Jewish People," in
     The Compact Guide to World Religions." Edited by Dean
     C. Halverson (Minneapolis: Bethany House Publishers),
     1996, 126; Arthur, Hertzberg, "Judaism and the Land of
     Israel," in *Understanding Jewish Theology: Classical Issues and
     Modern Perspectives.*" Edited by Jacob Neusner (New York:
     KTAV Publishing House, Inc. 1973), 86.

8   Louis Jacobs, *A Jewish Theology* (London: Darton, Longman
     & Todd, 1973), 292-99.

9   Ellen T. Charry, "The Uniqueness of Christ in Relation
     to the Jewish People: The External Crusade." In Sung
     Wook Chung, ed., *Christ the One and Only* (Grand
     Rapids: Baker Academic, 2005), 140; Karl Rahner and
     Pinchas Lapide. Translated by Davis Perkins. *Encountering
     Jesus – Encountering Judaism: A Dialogue* (New York:
     Crossroad), 104-107.

10   Samuel Sandmel, *We Jews and Jesus* (New York: Oxford
     Press, 1965), 35-78 passim.

11   John P. Newport, *Life's Ultimate Questions: A Contemporary
     Philosophy of Religion* (Dallas: Word Publishing, 1989), 365;
     Jacob Neusner and Bruce Chilton, *Jewish-Christian Debates:
     God, Kingdom, Messiah* (Minneapolis: Fortress Press, 1998),
     215-216.

12   Timothy Miller, "New Religious Movements in American
     History," in *Introduction to New and Alternative Religions
     in America,* Vol. 1, Histories and Controversies. Edited by
     Eugene V. Gallagher and W. Michael Ashcraft (Westport,
     CN: Greenwood Press, 2006), 10.

13   Thomas A. Robinson and Hillary Rodrigues, eds. *World Religions: A Guide to the Essentials* (Peabody, MA: Hendrickson Publishers, 2006), 128. Dean C. Halverson, "Islam," in *The Compact Guide to World Religions*." Edited by Dean C. Halverson (Minneapolis: Bethany House Publishers, 1996), 107-08; John Alden Williams, ed. *Islam. Great Religions of Modern Man*, Richard A. Gard, Gen.Ed. (New York: George Braziller), 1962, 161.

14   Halverson, "Islam," 107-08; Walter Martin, *The Kingdom of the Cults*. Gen. ed. Ravi Zacharias (Minneapolis: Bethany House Publishers, 2003), 446-47.

15   Neal Robinson, *Christ in Islam and Christianity* (Albany: State University of New York Press), 1991, 6-7; Faruk M. Zein, *Christianity, Islam and Orientalism* (London: Saqi Books, 2003), 67-70. Williams, Islam. *Great Religions of Modern Man*, 31-32.

16   Newport, 383.

17   Michael McDowell and Nathan Robert Brown, *World Religions at your Fingertips* (New York: Alpha Books, Penguin Books, 2009), 200-01; Newport, 384-85.

18   Dean C. Halverson, "Hinduism," in *The Compact Guide to World Religions*. Edited by Dean C. Halverson (Minneapolis: Bethany House Publishers, 1996), 89-97.

19   Swami Satprakashananda, *Hinduism and Christianity: Jesus Christ and His Teachings in the light of Vedanta* (St Louis: Vedanta Society of St. Louis, 1975), 29-35.

20 Oscar MacMillan Buck, *Our Asiatic Christ* (New York: Harper & Brothers, Publishers), 1927. Unfortunately, Buck was a Missions and Comparative Religions professor whose approach was to present Jesus to Hindus not as the unique crucified Savior but as the perfect Hindu. Ronald Neufeldt, "Hindu views of Christ," in *Hindu-Christian Dialogue: Perspectives and Encounters.* Edited by Harold Coward (Maryknoll, NY: Orbis Books, 1989), 162-75.

21 Newport, 388-89; Jeff Wilson, *"Buddhism in America,"* in *Introduction to New and Alternative Religions in America*, Vol. 4, Asian Traditions. Edited by Eugene V. Gallagher and W. Michael Ashcraft (Westport, CN: Greenwood Press, 2006), 112-24.

22 Dean C. Halverson, *Buddhism,"* in *The Compact Guide to World Religions.* Edited by Dean C. Halverson (Minneapolis: Bethany House Publishers, 1996), 58-63.

23 José Ignacio Cabezón, "A God, but Not a Savior," in *Buddhists Talk about Jesus; Christians Talk about the Buddha*, edited by Rita M. Gross and Terry C. Muck (New York: Continuum, 2000), 21-23.

24 Ibid, 24-27.

25 Terryl L. Givens, "The Church of Jesus Christ of Latter-Day Saints," in *Introduction to New and Alternative Religions in America*, Vol. 2, Jewish and Christian Traditions. Edited by Eugene V. Gallagher and W. Michael Ashcraft (Westport, CN: Greenwood Press, 2006), 22.

26 Stephen Prothero, *American Jesus: How the Son of God became a National Icon* (New York: Farrar, Straus and Giroux, 2003), 186.

27   Two Mormons, Mitt Romney and Jon Huntsman, sought the Republican presidential nomination in 2012. Romney was chosen as the nominee, eventually losing President Obama. His nomination helped legitimize Mormonism as a "Christian" denomination.

28   Robert L. Millet, *A Different Jesus? The Christ of the Latter-Day Saints* (Grand Rapids: Eerdmans, 2005), 19-22; James E. Talmage, *Jesus the Christ* (Salt Lake City: Deseret Book Company, 1976), 4-10; President John Taylor, *The Mediation and Atonement* (Salt Lake City: Sevens & Wallis, Inc., 1950), 93-96.

29   Millet, 146-48.

30   Ibid, 82-88, 190-207. "So extraordinarily intense is the mediation of the corporately structured LDS church that Jesus becomes pragmatically unnecessary in the work of salvation." Harold Bloom, *The American Religion* (New York: A Touchstone Book, Published by Simon & Schuster, 1992), 123.

31   Ron Rhodes, "Christ," in *The Counterfeit Gospel of Mormonism* by Francis Beckwith, Norman Geisler, Ron Rhodes, Phil Roberts, and Jerald and Sanra Tanner (Eugene, OR: Harvest House Publishers, 1998), 135, 171.

32   According to Talmage, 32, the holy Trinity is comprised of "three physically separate and distinct individuals, who together constitute the presiding council of the heavens."

33   Joselit, 124.

34 Stephen J. Nichols, *Jesus, Made in America: A cultural history from the puritans to the Passion of the Christ* (Downers Grove: IL: InterVarsity Press, 2008), 10, reminds us that "Christians in all cultures and ages have the tendency to impose their understandings and cultural expression on Scripture and beliefs."

35 Winthrop Hudson, *Religion in America* (New York: Charles Scribner's Sons, third edition, 1981), 92-93; Veli-Matti Kärkkäinen, *Christology: A Global Introduction* (Grand Rapids: Baker Academic, 2003), 85-89.

36 Nichols, 46-73. Thomas Paine was the most notorious in rejecting the orthodox Jesus. Jefferson is known for cutting the supernatural out of two copies of the Bible and presenting the leftovers as "The Philosophy of Jesus of Nazareth," and "The Life and Morals of Jesus of Nazareth," which contained, according to him, the words and actions that were authentic. Jefferson was a follower of Jesus in the sense that he followed certain teachings of Jesus. He invoked God and the name of Jesus repeatedly. But what he understood and meant by "Jesus" is the question. Interestingly, Jefferson was denounced as an atheist by New England ministers when he was running for president in 1796. It should be noted that among the founding fathers there were those who held orthodox beliefs, including John Witherspoon and Benjamin Rush, although Rush ended up a universalist.

37 Prothero, 19-31.

38 John P. Crossley, Jr., "Liberalism," in Muser, Donald W. and Joseph L. Price, eds., *A New Handbook of Christian Theology* (Nashville: Abingdon Press, 1992), 285-87.

39   Justo L. González, *A History of Christian Thought: From the Protestant Reformation to the Twentieth Century* (Nashville: Abingdon Press, 1992), 348-61; Pelikan, 196-97.

40   Kärkkäinen, 95-96.

41   Ibid., 97-100.

42   Nichols, 102, 108-10.

43   Prothero, 32- 40.

44   Edward Feser, "Blinded by Scientism," http://www.thepublicdiscourse.com/2010/03/1174?printerfriendly=true, accessed 8/19/2011; Sholto Byrnes, "When it comes to facts, and explanations of facts, science is the only game in town." *New Statesman*, 10 April 2006, http://www.newstatesman.com/print/200604100019, accessed 8/19/2011.

45   www.centerfornaturalism.org, accessed 8/19/2011.

46   Michael Shermer, "The Shamans of Scientism." *Scientific American*. May 13, 2002, accessed 8/19/2011.

47   Mikael Stenmark, *Scientism: Science, Ethics and Religion* (Aldershot: Ashgate Publishing, 2001), 133-42.

48   Hudson, 175; Pelikan, 204.

49   Hudson, 184-88.

50   Unlike the other groups discussed in this section, there is debate and disagreement among evangelical scholars whether to call the Adventists a cult or not. They certainly

hold unorthodox views on the law, the Sabbath, the intermediate state, the destiny of the wicked, and other doctrines. Their understanding of the person and work of Jesus, however, is generally considered orthodox. My point was their attempt, and others', to "manage" Jesus as it relates to his second coming. See Walter Martin's *Kingdom of the Cults* (Minneapolis: Bethany Fellowship, Inc., Publishers, 1965) for a balanced discussion of what he calls the "puzzle" of the Seventh Day Adventists.

51   Martin, 46-51.

52   Hudson, 288-92.

53   Stanley J. Grenz, *A Primer on Postmodernism* (Grand Rapids: William B. Eerdmans Publishing Company, 1996), 2-4.

54   Ibid., 5-38.

55   Dan Kimball, *The Emerging Church: Vintage Christianity for New Generations* (Grand Rapids: Zondervan, 2003), 87-88.

56   John P. Newport, *The New Age Movement and the Biblical Worldview: Conflict and Dialogue* (Grand Rapids: William B. Eerdmans Publishing Company, 1998), 4-7.

57   Manly P. Hall, *The Secret Teachings of All Ages: An encyclopedic outline of Masonic, Hermetic, Qabbalistic, and Rosicrucian symbolical philosophy* (Los Angeles: The Philolsophical Research Society, Inc. 1977), 277.

58   Bruce G. Epperly, *Crystal & Cross: Christians and New Age in Creative Dialogue* (Mystic, CT: Twenty-Third Publications, 1996), 140-46; Hall, 178.

59   Ibid., 146-49.

60   Ron Rhodes, "The Christ of the New Age Movement." Reasoning from the Scriptures Ministries, http://home. earthlink.net/-ronrhodes/ChristNAM.html,   accessed 8/19/2011; Hall, 178.

61   Michael Scott Horton, *Christless Christianity: The Alternative Gospel of the American Church* (Grand Rapids: Baker Books, 2008), 159.

62   John T. Kavanaugh, *Following Christ in a Consumer Society: The Spirituality of Cultural Resistance* (Maryknoll, NY: Orbis Books, Revised Edition, 1991), 3-19, 32.

63   Bruce Shelley and Marshall Shelley, *Consumer Church* (Downers Grove: InterVarsity Press, 1992), 110.

64   Ibid.

65   Nichols, 178.

66   Robert S. McElvanie, *Grand Theft Jesus: The Hijacking of Religion in America* (New York: Three Rivers Press, 2008), 63.

67   David Platt, *Radical: Taking Back Your Faith from the American Dream* (Colorado Springs: Multnomah Books, 2010), 13; Michael Scott Horton, *Made in America* (Grand Rapids: Baker Book House, 2001); Horton, *Christless Christianity*, 19-21.

68   Davie E. Fitch, *The Great Giveaway* (Grand Rapids: Baker Books, 2005), 183.

69 Norman Vincent Peale, *The Positive Power of Jesus Christ* (Carmel, NY: Guideposts, 1980); *The Positive Principle Today* (Carmel, NY: Guideposts, 1976); *Imaging: The Powerful Way to Change Your Life* (Carmel, NY: Guideposts, 1982); *The Power of Positive Thinking*. Special 35th Anniversary Edition (New York: Prentice Hall Press, 1987).

70 Robert H. Schuller, *The New Reformation* (Waco: Word Books, 1982).

71 Ibid.

72 A good example of a book that trivializes Jesus' sayings in both a consumer and therapeutic way is Laurie Beth Jones, *Jesus CEO.: Using Ancient Wisdom for Visionary Leadership*. New York: Hyperion, 1995. She says that "nowhere in the Gospel does Jesus put himself down. Jesus was full of self-knowledge and self-love....His 'I Am' statements were what he became." Essentially, what Jesus was doing was giving himself and others motivational pep talks, most of which are good for business.

73 Horton, Made in America, 78-84.

74 Horton, *Christless Christianity*, 102. Joanna and Alister McGrath, *The Dilemma of Self-Esteem: The Cross and Christian Confidence* (Wheaton, IL: Crossway Books, 1992), 88, point out that the cross, in fact, is what "establishes the objective basis of Christian self-esteem. It is here that God has established His relationship with us. Sin has been dealt with. Where secular psychological theories close their eyes to the reality, the seriousness, and the power of sin, the gospel acknowledges them – but affirms strongly the reality, the seriousness, and the power of the cross of Christ to

defeat sin. We may rest assures that all that is necessary for self-esteem has been done – and done extremely well! – by God through Christ on the cross."

75   McElvanie, *Grand Theft Jesus.*

76   Clint Willis, *"Introduction"* in *Clint Wallis and Nate Hardcastle*, eds., Jesus is Not a Republican: The Religious Right's War on America (New York: Thunder's Mouth Press, 2005), x; J.M. Berger "Jesus Was Not a Republican, but St. Paul Probably Was" in Wallis and Hardcastle, 294. Horton, *Christless Christianity*, 26, says that "When the focus becomes 'What would Jesus do?' instead of 'What has Jesus done?' the labels no longer matter. Conservatives have been just as prone to focus on the former rather than the latter in recent decades."

77   Horton, *Christless Christianity*, 207; An example of the both the left and right abuse of Jesus is seen in one of Ann Coulter's online articles. In "The passion of the liberal," http://townhall.com/columnists/anncoulter/2004/03/04/the_passion_of_the_liberal/print (accessed 9/27/11), she discusses Mel Gibson's movie "The Passion of the Christ." She rightly criticizes those she calls "know-nothing secularists on television" who criticized the movie because it insisted on "rubbing our faces in the grisly reality of Jesus' death," and "spending so much time on Jesus' suffering and death while giving 'short shrift to Jesus' ministry and ideas'." She argues they just want to show the "nice" Jesus. Good point. Too often the liberal approach to Jesus is to ignore his demands. But Coulter then goes on to say that "Being nice to people is, in fact, one of the incidental tenets of Christianity." Perhaps being "nice" is not how Jesus or Paul put it, but there is an awful lot about love, kindness, mercy,

and even loving your enemies. Overlooking those teachings allows her to say in another article (obviously ideologically driven) that the U.S. should "be spying on all Arabs, engaging in torture as a televised spectator sport, dropping daisy cutters wantonly throughout the Middle East and sending liberals to Guantanamo." "Live and let spy." http://townhall.com/columnists/anncoulter/2005/12/21/live_and_let_spy/page/full/ (accessed 9/27/11).

78   Nichols, 214.

79   "Exaggerated patriotism is checked and tempered by the awareness that, while this is a homeland, it is, at the same time, a foreign country." Richard John Neuhaus, *American Babylon: Notes of a Christian Exile* (New York: Basic Books, 2009), 49-51; Russell D. Moore, "First Person: Alzheimer's, Pat Robertson & the true Gospel," http://www.bpnews.net/printerfriendly.asp?ID=36119 (accessed 9/16/11), notes that "Sadly, many of our neighbors assume that when they hear the parade of characters we allow to speak for us, that they are hearing the Gospel. They assume that when they see the giggling evangelist on the television screen, that they see Jesus. They assume that when they see the stadium political rallies to 'take back America for Christ,' that they see Jesus. But Jesus tells us He is present in the weak, the vulnerable, the useless. He is there in the least of these (Matthew 25:31-46)."

80   "Not thinking that 'Christ crucified' is as relevant as 'Christ and Family Values' or 'Christ and America' or 'Christ and World Hunger,' we end up assimilating the gospel to law." That is, we confuse what he did with what we are to do. Horton, *Christless Christianity*, 144-46.

81 See Kärkkäinen, *Christology: A Global Introduction*, 189-285; John Mackay, *The Other Spanish Christ* (New York: Macmillan, 1935); José Miguel Bonino, ed., *Faces of Jesus. Latin American Christologies* (Maryknoll, NY: Orbis, 1984). Vernon Grounds, "Psychological Evaluations of Jesus" in *Perspectives on Christology: Essays in Honor of Paul K. Jewett*, eds. Marguerite Shuster and Richard Muller (Cedar Rapids: Zondervan Publishing Company), 165-66, lists several works that have examined different conceptions of Jesus, ranging from "The Existentialist Rabbi" to "The Universal Man."

82 It is worth noting the warning by Pastor Alistair Begg: "Don't confuse the benefits of the gospel with the gospel." He points out that we can and do and should preach the benefits of the gospel and the doctrines that relate to the gospel; however, "they are not the gospel." Sermon delivered at the Southern Baptists of Texas Annual Meeting, 14 November,2011, Irving, TX.

83 In the Matthew 16:13-20 account of this exchange Jesus tells Peter he was blessed because the Father had revealed this truth about Jesus to Peter.

84 The unintentional consequence of a red-letter Bible is that some people end up thinking Jesus' words are more authoritative than the rest of Scripture. They fall into the same Jesus vs. Paul fallacy found in much of liberalism. Some critics have rightly pointed out that evangelicals need to pay more attention to Jesus' words and not place the epistles above the Gospels (and thus having a canon within the canon). For the authoritative nature of Scripture see F. F. Bruce, *The Books and the Parchments* (Westwood, NJ: Fleming H. Revell Company, 1963); and Josh McDowell,

The New Evidence that Demands a Verdict (Nashville: Thomas Nelson Publishers, 1999).

85   See James Leo Garrett Jr., *Systematic Theology: Biblical, Historical, & Evangelical*, Vol. 1 (Grand Rapids: William B Eerdmans Publishing Company, 1990), 529-30; Millard J. Erickson, *Christian Theology*, Unabridged, one-volume edition (Grand Rapids: Baker Book House, 1985), 665-75; Millard J. Erickson, *The Word Became Flesh: A contemporary incarnational Christology* (Grand Rapids: Baker Book House, 1991), 625-27.

86   Daniel L. Migliore, *Faith Seeking Understanding* (Grand Rapids: Wm. B. Eerdmans Publishing Co., 1991), 144.

87   The humanity of Jesus "is not an issue severely contested in contemporary Christology; for that matter, it is not contested at all. This is not to say that it is unimportant." Erickson, *The Word Became Flesh*, 14.

88   Garrett, 533-37; Erickson, *Christian Theology*, 712-16.

89   There are some intriguing passages in the Gospels related to Jesus' humanity, especially as it relates to his family and hometown (Matthew 12: 46-50; Mark 6:1-4; John 7:3-6). In John 7 his brothers seem to be egging him on to be more public in his works; however, v. 5 says his brothers did this because they did not believe him. In Mark 6, Jesus returns to his hometown of Nazareth, where he was well known. These who had known him the longest rejected him, for, after all, wasn't he just the carpenter's son? These passages seem to argue against the idea that Jesus stood out as a human being. Certainly, once he began his ministry of healing and performing miracles he stood out – people flocked to

him. But for the first thirty years he was apparently not too much unlike his brothers, friends, and neighbors. He was sinless, yes. But he was still a first century Jew who lived, worked, worshiped, and played pretty much like all others in his culture. He did not walk around with a halo, speak in somber tones, or have a spotless white robe while everyone else wore daily working clothes. Even Mary and Joseph, who experienced the unique circumstances of his conception and birth "did not understand what He said to them" (Luke 2:5), implying that they perceived him as simply their son who strayed from the village crowd.

90   Erickson, *Christian Theology*, 717-18.

91   A similar argument was famously made in the twelfth century by Anselm, the Archbishop of Canterbury in *Cur Deus homo* (Why God Became Man). He argued that we owe a debt to God that must be satisfied. We are incapable of offering that satisfaction due to our sin. On the one hand, only God can offer perfect satisfaction; on the other hand, human satisfaction is required for human sin. Thus, God became man in order to offer the satisfaction – it was given by a God-man. Anselm's theory has been influential throughout history, but has a variety of weaknesses. See Justo L. Gonzalez, *A History of Christian Thought. Vol. II: From Augustine to the Eve of the Reformation* (Nashville: Abingdon Press, 1971), 166-67; James Leo Garrett, Jr., *Systematic Theology: Biblical, Historical & Evangelical,* Vol. 2 (Grand Rapids: William B. Eerdmans Publishing Company, 1995), 21-22.

92   Gregory Nazianzen, Epistle 101. *The Nicene and Post-Nicene Fathers,* 2d ser, 7:440.

93   Erickson, *Christian Theology*, 707, suggests that Jesus's "body may have been more nearly perfect in some respects than ours, because there was in him none of the sin (neither original sin nor the personal sin common to every human) that affects health." Perhaps, but Jesus did live in a fallen world affected by sin, so childhood diseases, the common cold, and other illnesses may have affected him like any other person. These are consequences of the fall that even he had to live with and reflect in no way on his personal sinlessness. This hint of Docetism is also found in Norval Geldenhuys, *Commentary on the Gospel of Luke, The New International Commentary on the New Testament* (Grand Rapids: William B. Eerdmans Publishing Company, 1993), 122, when he comments on Luke 2:40 that Jesus grew up physically and spiritually "perfectly as no one before or after Him. He was truly Man, but a perfect Man, even in childhood." Geldenhuys then approvingly quotes an earlier scholar who said that Jesus' humanity was "a perfect humanity developing perfectly, unimpeded by hereditary or acquired defects." Again, I would agree that Jesus had no hint of original sin or a fallen nature. Yet, being a perfect human living in a fallen world, he was affected by the effects of the fall, both human and natural, that surrounded him. Just as evil men could torture and kill him, so could childhood diseases, for example, have sickened him.

94   Erickson, *Christian Theology*, 707.

95   Ibid., 709.

96   The Consumer, Therapist, and Ideological Christologies are assumed to be generally orthodox in their understanding of Jesus' deity and humanity. What is defective in them is

their understanding of the work of Jesus, either in its nature or purpose.

97 Erickson, *Christian Theology*, 694-97; Erickson, *The Word Became Flesh*, 47-52; Garrett, *Systematic Theology:* Vol. 1, 582.

98 Erickson, *Christian Theology*, 679.

99 The uniqueness of the incarnation can be denied in two ways: One, some would say that the one God has been incarnated numerous times in various people and at different times. Two, some would say that many gods can be manifested through many incarnations.

100 John Hick, *God and the Universe of Faiths*, rev. ed. (Glasgow: William Collins Sons & Co Ltd., 1973), 148-79.

101 Paul F. Knitter, *No Other Name? A critical survey of Christian attitudes toward the world religions* (Maryknoll, N.Y.: Orbis Books, 1995), 171-204. For a critical evaluation of Hick's and Knitter's positions, see Erickson, *The Word Became Flesh*, 277-304.

102 Thomas C. Oden, *The Word of Life, Systematic Theology: Volume Two* (New York: HarperCollins, 1989), 66.

103 Robert M. Bowman, Jr. and J. Ed Komoszewski, *Putting Jesus in His Place: The case for the deity of Christ* (Grand Rapids: Kregel Publications, 2007), 138-39.

104 Oden, 70.

105 Ibid., 71.

106 McDowell, 155-63.

107 Oden, 35.

108 Erickson, *Christian Theology*, 684, notes that "Jesus did not make an explicit or overt claim to deity. He did not say in so many words, 'I am God.' What we do find, however, are claims which would be inappropriate if made by someone who is less than God."

109 I. Howard Marshall, *The Origins of New Testament Christology* (Downers Grove: InterVarsity Press, 1990), 63.

110 Donald Guthrie, *New Testament Theology* (Downers Grove: Inter-Varsity Press, 1981), 275-81.

111 Bowman and Komoszewski, 246-47.

112 Guthrie, 306-12.

113 Ibid., 312-16.

114 Ibid., 332; Leon Morris, *The Gospel According to John: The New International Commentary on the New Testament* (Grand Rapids: William B. Eerdmans Publishing Company, 1971), 447, 623.

115 It should be noted that these instances of coming back to life were examples of resuscitation and not resurrection. Those who came back to life did so in the same fallen and mortal bodies they had at death. Thus, they were eventually going to die again. The resurrection of Jesus was much more than resuscitation.

116 "The form of the 'if' clause in Greek (*ei* + indicative) does not so much challenge his sonship as assume it to build a doubtful imperative. Satan was not inviting Jesus to doubt his sonship but to reflect on its meaning. Sonship of the living God, he suggested, surely means Jesus has the power and the right to satisfy his own needs." D. A. Carson, "Matthew" in *The Expositor's Bible Commentary*, volume 8 (Grand Rapids: Zondervan Publishing House), 112.

117 Morris, John, 41. Oden, 63, states that the "tendency of some modern critics to discredit the Johannine testimony is unjustified."

118 Oden, 64, notes that the "sonship of Jesus to the Father is the heart of the Johannine tradition."

119 "There cannot be any doubt but that John conceived of Jesus as the very incarnation of God." Ibid, 857.

120 Guthrie, *New Testament Theology*, 248-49, points out that "the position adopted by the 'Jesus of history' school, which regarded Paul's developments as perversions of the original simplicity of Jesus" is "itself a figment of the imagination." To the contrary, it is a "misunderstanding" to say that Paul discounts the "historical Jesus in favour of a spiritual appreciation of Christ." Because Paul is writing after the fact of the resurrection, he understands that "the messianic mission has been accomplished," and "develops his own reflections on the new-look messianic concept, which found fulfillment in the risen Christ, who inaugurated a spiritual kingdom." Paul "had to relearn a true approach to messiahship as expounded by Jesus himself" (emphasis mine).

121 F. F. Bruce, "The Book of the Acts" in *The New International Commentary on the New Testament*, rev. edition (Grand Rapids: William B. Eerdmans Publishing Company), 81-82.

122 F. F. Bruce, *Paul: Apostle of the Heart Set Free* (Grand Rapids: William B. Eerdmans Publishing Company, 1977), 116-17.

123 "There can be no doubt that in the usage of the New Testament writer, beginning from Paul, the title of 'Lord' is regarded as the title used of God in the Old Testament and now applied to Jesus....Increasingly, the title was understood in terms of the Old Testament and regarded as an acknowledgment of a status equal to that of God the Father." Marshall, 106, 108.

124 Garrett, *Systematic Theology*, Vol. 1, 270.

125 Erickson, *Christian Theology*, 703.

126 Oden, 51.

127 Erickson, *Christian Theology*, 703-04.

128 Oden, 165.

129 Erickson, *Christian Theology*, 725.

130 Oden, 169.

131 Garrett, *Systematic Theology:* Vol. 2, 608.

132 Ibid., 621.

133 Erickson, *Christian Theology*, 731-33.

134 Erickson, *The Word Became Flesh*, 78-86.

135 Erickson, *Christian Theology*, 735; Garrett, *Systematic Theology*, Vol. 1, 606; Oden, 79, says "The Son gave up the independent exercise of divine attributes and powers that constituted his equality with God....The text does not focus specifically upon what was emptied, but rather upon what the self-emptying called forth – the servant life" (emphasis his). Oden, 74-92, offers a detailed discussion of the emptying and subsequent exaltation of the Son based on Phil. 2. Alister E. McGrath, *The Mystery of the Cross* (Grand Rapids: Academie Books), 123, notes that "if God is omnipotent, he must be at liberty to set that omnipotence aside, and voluntarily to impose certain restrictions upon his course of action – to put it dramatically, but effectively, he must be free to have his hands tied behind his back. The Christian understanding of the omnipotence of God is that of a God who voluntarily place limitations upon his course of action" (emphasis his).

136 Ibid., 136, says the point being made is "a point which is so easily overlooked – that Christians proclaim a person, not an ideas. Ideas need to be defended, and tend to go out of fashion rather quickly – a person needs to be encountered, and the result of that encounter may be a lasting relationship."

137 "...whereas the idea of a coming Messiah was widespread among the Jews, the origin and character of the coming Messiah was not clearly understood. Different groups tended to visualize a Messiah who would be conducive to their own tenets...there is little doubt that popular

opinion leaned heavily towards hope of a coming leader who would deliver the Jewish people from the oppressive Roman yoke. When seen against this prevalent notion, it is understandable why Jesus avoided the use of the term." Guthrie, 238. Also, Garrett, *Systematic Theology*, Vol. 1, 552, points out that at "the time of Jesus, Judaism had numerous different ideas about the Messiah…but the theme of a political Messiah surely was dominant."

138   Guthrie, 237.

139   Ibid., 243. There are a few times in the Gospels when Jesus is referred to either directly or indirectly as the Messiah. For example, in Matt. 2:3-5 Herod asks the wise men where the Messiah will be born. In Luke 3:15 (cf. John 1:20-22), the people wonder if John the Baptist is the Messiah, which he denies, explaining that there is a coming One who is a far more powerful judge. In John 1:41 Andrew tells Simon that "we have found the Messiah," and in 7:26, 31, people are wondering about his connection to the Messiah. In John 6:15 the people tried to act on their misunderstanding of the Messianic King, which disappointed some of his disciples (6:66). In all these cases the understanding of Messiah was inadequate, incorrect, or incomplete. Ibid, 238-39.

140   Ibid., 408-410

141   Ibid., 410-413.

142   Russell D. Moore, *The Kingdom of Christ: The New Evangelical Perspective* (Wheaton, IL:Crossway Books, 2004), 85-86, notes that if "personal salvation means a transfer into the Kingdom (present, future, or already/not year), then the content of the Kingdom must inform the

redemptive priorities of Christianity." He goes on to quote Carl F. H. Henry saying that "the Kingdom has 'a social aspect as well as an individual aspect,' since 'redemption is nothing if it is not an ethical redemption'."

143 George R. Beasley-Murray, "The Kingdom of God and Christology in the Gospels," in *Jesus of Nazareth: Lord and Christ*, ed. Joel B. Green and Max Turner (Grand Rapids: William B. Eerdmans Publishing Company, 1994), 28.

144 Bruce, *The Books and the Parchments*, 106-13.

145 For a discussion of Paul's knowledge of and dependence on the teachings of the historical Jesus, see Bruce, *Paul: Apostle of the Heart Set Free*, 95-112. See also David Wenham, "The Story of Jesus Known to Paul," in Green and Turner, *Jesus of Nazareth: Lord and Christ*, 297-311.

146 Bruce, *Paul: Apostle of the Heart Set Free*, 99. Bruce also notes, 125, that "for Paul...the exalted Lord whose risen life and power are conveyed to his people by the indwelling Spirit is identical and continuous with him who lived among men as a servant, the crucified one, the historical Jesus."

147 McGrath, *The Mystery of the Cross*, 41.

148 Moore, 56.

149 Ibid., 93, notes that a "Kingdom-oriented view of salvation...cannot be construed as a flight from the world, or as the salvation of individuals from the condemnation of the material order." It should, rather, "be understood as the redemption of the cosmos through the messianic accomplishment of Jesus. This redemption is not escape

from creation but instead is a restoration of the created order. . . ." Lest there be fear that social action deteriorate into the Social Gospel, Moore, 121, points out that "the perennial debates over evangelism and social action are not, first of all, about social action, or even about the Kingdom of God, but about the nature of the gospel and the very definition of salvation." Keeping the regeneration of the individual as the beginning point and the core of Kingdom theology holds in check any deviation into some of the pitfall of the Social Gospel and an emphasis on the love of God devoid of his justice.

150   George G. Hunter, III, *Church for the Unchurched* (Nashville: Abingdon Press, 1996), 23. See George G. Hunter, III, *How to Reach Secular People* (Nashville: Abingdon Press, 1992), for a discussion on how the West became so secularized, the characteristics of secular people, and how they can be reached.

151   Alister McGrath, *The Passionate Intellect* (Downers Grove, IL: InterVarsity Press, 2010), 9, notes that in "2006 the movement now widely, if inaccurately, known as the new atheism exploded on the cultural scene." Its primary popularizers have been Christopher Hitchens and Richard Dawkins. The good news about this movement is that "[p]ublic interest in the God question soared." McGrath, 111, accurately points out that "the new atheism conducts its polemic against a notion of God that bears little relation to that of Christianity."

152   See http://www.usatoday.com/news/religion/story/2011-12-25/religion-god-atheism-so-what/52195274/1 for a story about the "apatheists" who just say "so what?" Accessed 3/17/12.

153 Moore, 110-11. This is, of course, easier said than done. Political ideals, cultural mores and expectations, and personal background and experience all influence how each believer and church understands, approaches, and confronts the "world."

154 I do not know if the phrase "the house we live in" used to describe culture originated with him, but I have heard Ed Stetzer use it several times in speaking.

155 Gailyn Van Rheenen, "A Theology of Culture: Desecularizing Anthropology," in *International Journal of Frontier Missions*, Vol. 14:1 Jan.-March 1997, 33.

156 "Unfortunately, today the term 'culture' is used to signify that which is contrary to Christianity or, in a more general sense, what people refer to as traditional values. However, I suggest that this understanding unfortunately advances unwanted and unintended perceptions of Christianity by those outside the Christian community. It suggests that Christianity sees culture as something contrary to Christianity, when, in fact, that is not the case (or I hope it is not the case)." Bruce Little, "Theology Engaging Culture," www.sebts.edu/faithandculture/pdf_docs/theology_engaging_culture.pdf, accessed 21 December 2011. It is worth nothing that many "traditional values" are also culturally driven.

157 Glenn W. Barker, "1 John" in Gaebelein, Frank E. gen. ed., *The Expositor's Bible Commentary*, Vol. 2 (Grand Rapids: Zondervan Publishing House), 321; Morris, *The Gospel According to John*, 126-28.

158 Kevin T. Bauder, "A Prelude to a Christian Theology of Culture," in *Missions in a New Millennium*, W. Edward

Glenny and William H. Smallman, gen. eds. (Grand Rapids: Kregel Publications, 2000), 238, agrees with the Organic Theory of culture as represented by poet T.S. Eliot when he says that "cultures are not the creation of God; they are the creations of humans." I would argue that because God created human beings and all their potentialities, set up the original human endeavors of marriage, family, work, and general stewardship of His creation, that He did create culture. Certainly, the complexities and varieties came later with the expansion of the human race.

159 Van Rheenen, 35-36.

160 Ibid., 37, also notes that "Generally speaking, culture cannot be easily categorized as good, bad, or neutral. The influences shaping culture are complicated and frequently contradictory, impossible [to] easily categorize."

161 The Lausanne Covenant, Article 10 on Evangelism and Culture states that "Culture must always be tested and judged by Scripture. Because men and women are God's creatures, some of their culture is rich in beauty and goodness. Because they are fallen, all of it is tainted with sin and some of it is demonic. The gospel does not presuppose the superiority of any culture to another, but evaluates all cultures according to its own criteria of truth and righteousness, and insists on moral absolutes in every culture," http://www.emeu. net/pdf/lausanne-covenant.pdf, accessed 1/4/12. It is true that the gospel does not presuppose the superiority of any culture to another, but there is ample Biblical evidence of some cultures considered more evil than others. Again, historically, there have been cultures and sub-cultures that few would deny are further down the "evil spectrum."

162 It is important to note that acknowledging different perspectives does not imply or lead to relativism. As D. A. Carson, *Christ & Culture Revisited* (Grand Rapids: William B. Eerdmans Publishing Company, 2008), 113, notes: " …whether we like it or not, we all perspectivalists." Contra a relativistic understanding of truth, Carson, 101, explains that "human beings may know objective truth in the sense that they may know what actually conforms to reality, but they cannot know it objectively, that is they cannot escape their finitude and (this side of the consummation) their fallenness, and therefore the limitations of perspectivalism, and thus they cannot know anything completely or from a neutral stance. What is this but another but another way of saying that all of our knowledge is necessarily interpreted knowledge?" Thus, we can know the truth, we just cannot know it perfectly, exhaustively, and completely objectively. In terms of our discussion, we are so entrenched in our own culture, we cannot see it objectively.

163 Lesslie Newbigin, *The Gospel in a Pluralist Society* (Grand Rapids: William B. Eerdmans Publishing Company, 1989), 196-97. "All of us judge some elements of culture to be good and some bad. The question is whether these judgments arise from the gospel itself or from the cultural presuppositions of the person who makes the judgment. And, if one replies that they ought to be made only on the basis of the gospel itself, the reply must be that there is no such thing as a gospel which is not already culturally shaped" Ibid., 186.

164 Bruce J. Nicholls, *Contextualization: A Theology of Gospel and Culture* (Vancouver, B.C.: Regent College Reprint, 1979), 10, quotes G. Linwood Barney as saying that culture

is made up of three layers: One, the deepest, includes ideology, cosmology, and world view. Two, derived from the first, is values. Three, following from the first two, are the institutions like marriage, law, and education. David J. Hesselgrave and Edward Rommen, *Contextualization: Meanings, Methods, and Models* (Grand Rapids: Baker Book House, 1989), 203 ff, explain that communicating the gospel involves addressing these areas of culture: 1) Worldviews, 2) Cognitive processes, 3) Linguistic forms, 4) Behavioral patterns, 5) Communication media, 6) Social structures, and 7) Motivational sources.

165 Bauder, 233.

166 Mary Hopper, "Music and Musical Instruments," in Elwell, Walter A., ed, *Baker Encyclopedia of the Bible*, Vol. 2 (Grand Rapids: Baker Book House, 1988), 1,501.

167 See John A. Thompson, "Trades and Occupations," in Elwell, Walter A., ed, *Baker Encyclopedia of the Bible*, Vol. 2 (Grand Rapids: Baker Book House, 1988), 2,083-93, for a list and description of the various trades in the Bible.

168 See Victor H. Matthews, *Manners and Customs in the Bible*, rev. ed. (Peabody, MA: Hendrickson Publishers, 1991), for a detailed study of the numerous cultural distinctives of the people of the Bible.

169 Charles F. Pfeiffer, *Old Testament History* (Grand Rapids: Baker Book House, 1973), 96-98, notes that sacrifices were "regularized by the Mosaic Law," and the "rite of circumcision was practiced by many peoples of antiquity, usually at the time of puberty."

170 Bob Deffinbaugh, "Cults, Christianity, and Culture (Acts 15:1-31)," http://bible.org/print/book/export/html/1343, accessed 1/10/2012

171 Ibid., makes the argument that the Jerusalem Council's decision "established a biblical precedent concerning the relationship between culture and Christianity. The Jewish culture (as prescribed by the Old Testament law) was not essential for salvation. To be saved, one needed only to believe in the shed blood of Jesus Christ. Christians, whether Jew or Gentile, could continue to practice their culture in any way that was not inconsistent with biblical morality. To have fellowship with those of other cultures, each Christian must be willing to refrain from his cultural liberties which prove to be either a cause of stumbling or a hindrance to fellowship."

172 Newbigin, 198.

173 Ibid, 195, says that "We have to say both 'God accepts human culture' and also 'God judges human culture.' There will have to be room in the Christian life for the two attitudes...."

174 H. Richard Niebuhr, *Christ and Culture* (New York: Harper & Row, Publishers, 1951), passim.

175 Christendom "evokes medieval European age of faith, of passionate spirituality and a pervasive Christian culture." It provided "a true overarching unity and a focus of loyalty transcending mere kingdoms or empires. ..."Christendom offered a higher set of standards and morals" than any individual kingdom could. It was simply a "primary form of cultural reference." Philip Jenkins, *The Next Christendom:*

The Coming of Global Christianity (Oxford: Oxford University Press, 2002), 10. Although Christendom was challenged by the Renaissance, was seriously damaged by the Enlightenment, and its collapse assured by the growing secularism of the twentieth century, it was still the presupposition of many in Western societies until the last quarter of the twentieth century.

176 Craig A. Carter, *Rethinking Christ and Culture* (Grand Rapids: Brazos Press, 2006), 111-212.

177 Carson, *Christ and Culture Revisited*, 218-22.

178 Ibid., 12, 62.

179 Ibid., 40-41. Carson, *Christ and Culture Revisited*, 81, lists the "non-negotiables" of Biblical theology as: "creation, fall, the call of Abraham, the exodus and the giving of the law, the rise of the monarchy and the rise of the prophets, the exile, the incarnation, the ministry and death and resurrection of Jesus Christ, the onset of the kingdom of God, the coming of the Spirit and the consequent ongoing eschatological tension between the 'already' and the 'not yet,' the return of Christ and the prospect of a new heaven and a new earth. One might expand or contract this list a bit, but the point itself must not be ignored." The "point" is that any stance on how to approach the Christ and culture issue must attempt to integrate these biblical issues or will fail to be "deeply Christian."

180 Ibid, 43, 207.

181 Justo L. Gonzalez, *A History of Christian Thought, Vol. 1: From the Beginnings to the Council of Chalcedon* (Nashville:

Abingdon Press, 1970), 261, notes that "the fourth century saw thousands of hermits flock to the Egyptian desert."

182 Robert A. Baker, *A Summary of Christian History* (Nashville: Broadman Press, 1959), 24, notes that because the Roman Empire was "fast declining," the Emperor Constantine needed "a strong internal unity that could engender both loyalty within and beat off attacks from without. Constantine proposed to attain this unity by making Christianity the cement of the empire." Historians note that Constantine's personal life and actions demonstrate that it "is hardly conceivable that [he] really became a Christian."

183 Carson, *Christ and Culture Revisited*, 21-22. He also quotes Niebuhr's admission that the synthesis approach leads to the "institutionalization of Christ and his gospel," and fails to "face up to the radical evil in the present world."

184 Niebuhr, 187-88; Carson, *Christ and Culture Revisited*, 25.

185 This privatized Christianity has often been identified with Modernity. However, although Postmoderns are more apt to insist on a consistent, broad, and non-privatized application of their faith, their definition of Christianity can often be rather unorthodox.

186 See John A. Mackay, *The Other Spanish Christ* (New York: Macmillan, 1933); Luis N. Rivera, *A Violent Evangelism: The Political and Religious Conquest of the Americas* (Louisville: John Knox, 1992).

187 Douglas F. Ottati, "Social Gospel" in *A New Handbook of Christian Theology*, eds. Donald W. Musser and Joseph L. Price (Nashville: Abingdon Press, 1992), 448.

188 Plenty has been written about how activist evangelicals of the last forty years have transformed from theological/ ideological pre-millennialists to practical post-millennialists. This "conversion" was made possible by the attention paid to evangelicals by Ronald Reagan and their subsequent political advances.

189 Jerry E. Shepherd, "Ecclesiastes," in Tremper Longman, III and David E. Garland, gen. eds., *The Expositor's Bible Commentary*, Vol. 6: Proverbs–Isaiah, rev. ed. (Grand Rapids: Zondervan, 2008), 287-91; Roland E. Murphy, "Ecclesiastes," in David A. Hubbard and Glenn W. Barker, gen. eds., *Word Biblical Commentary:* Vol. 23A: Ecclesiastes (Dallas: Word Books, 1992), 31-39.

190 Alan J. Roxburgh and Fred Romanuk, *The Missional Leader: Equipping your church to reach a changing world* (San Francisco: Jossey-Bass, 2006), 6-7.

191 "As humans, we have always faced the 'face of change,' whenever we attempted to find new ways of adjusting to or mastering our environments. The practice of introducing and managing new ideas, technology, and behavior in organizations is as old as humanity itself. Only the incessant rate of change is unique to our current time." Jerry Glover, Adaptive Leadership: When change is not enough (part one). *Organization Development Journal,* Summer 2002.

192 Exactly how fast the amount of available information is growing is apparently not immediately known. I found some who claimed that available information is doubling every two years, some who claimed that it is doubling every eighteen months, and even one claim that it is doubling every eleven hours.

193 Alan Hirsch, *The Forgotten Ways* (Grand Rapids: Brazos Press, 2006), 247-71.

194 Some argue that we are still entrenched in Modernity, and we are in significant ways. Others argue that we are already in a post- postmodern time, and we may be. After all that has been written on postmodernism, it seems to be less defined than ever. Surely, that is because cultural changes and movements are often best defined and described by historians well after the fact.

195 We often hear the complaint that America is falling behind the rest of the world in various areas. Perhaps we are; however, I wonder if the reality is not that we are falling behind, but that the rest of the world is catching up quickly. That is not the same thing.

196 Although reporting has changed and statistics can be skewed and interpreted in various ways, it is generally accepted that crime today is on the level it was in the early sixties. See http://en.wikipedia.org/wiki/Crime_in_the_United_States (accessed 2/4/2012), http://www.nytimes.com/2011/05/24/us/24crime.html (accessed 2/4/2012), and http://www.csmonitor.com/USA/2010/0524/US-crime-rate-is-down-six-key-reasons (accessed 2/4/2012).

197 See Charles Murray, "The New American Divide," *The Wall Street Journal*, www.wsj.com, January 21, 2012 on the fading of the American Way of Life, including marriage and religion. For his complete analysis, see Charles Murray, *Coming Apart: The State of White America, 1960-2010* (New York: Crown Forum, 2012). On pages 2-7 Murray describes life in America on November 21, 1963, the day before President Kennedy's assassination. That critical event

changed everything. November 22 "became the symbolic first day of what would be known as the Sixties." November 21, therefore, was the "symbolic last day of the culture that preceded it. . . ."The change in the American way of life from 1963 to the present day is radical, but it involves both good and bad change, for "America still had plenty of problems on November 21, 1963." Therefore, lest he sound too nostalgic for the past, Murray, 116, states that "if a time machine could transport me back to 1960, I would have to be dragged into it kicking and screaming. In many aspects of day-to-day life, America is incomparably superior to the America of 1960."

198 I have been frequently amused by the historical amnesia of political pundits and media commentators when they say something like "America has never been so divided politically as it is now." Really? Have they forgotten the Civil War? What about the sixties, with its constant anti-war demonstrations, riots, civil rights unrest, political assassinations, and the proverbial generation gap? Even when they bemoan the political mudslinging of today's political campaigns, as negative and ugly as it is, they are unaware of some of the awful political shenanigans of the nineteenth century. See http://en.wikipedia.org/wiki/American_election_campaigns_in_the_19th_century (accessed 2/6/2012).

199 *Modern Family* is a TV series that promotes the "new normal" – blended families, parents on their second marriages, gay partners adopting children, and so on. This is certainly not the first TV series to promote the "new normal," and, unfortunately, it does reflect what is all too common. Since the first draft of this chapter was written, NBC has actually premiered a sitcom entitled "*The New Normal.*" According to the NBC website, http://www.nbc.

com/the-new-normal/about/: "These days, families come in all forms–single dads, double moms, sperm donors, egg donors, one-night-stand donors... It's 2012 and anything goes." Furthermore, and most disturbing, is that the Disney Channel has announced that it will introduce a lesbian couple on the popular show *Good Luck Charlie*, http://www.theblaze.com/stories/2013/06/25/disney-channel-will-include-lesbian-moms-on-episode-of-popular-tv-show-to-reflect-diversity-and-inclusiveness/.

200   No example is more common (and now tiresome) than the worship wars. Changes in music style can certainly be uncomfortable and even irritating, but not inherently unbiblical or harmful. Certainly, there is both good and bad contemporary music, but there are some pretty weak hymns, too. Many other examples of preferences elevated to dogmatic status include worship times, the pastor's dress, the order of service, the architecture of the church building, the structure of Christian education, and so on.

201   Erickson, *Christian Theology*, 279, notes that some of the more traditional expressions of the immutability of God "have actually drawn heavily upon the Greek idea of immobility and sterility. This makes God inactive. But the biblical view is not that God is static, but stable. He is active and dynamic, but in a way which is stable and consistent with his nature." Garrett, *Systematic Theology*, Vol. 1, 218 notes that "God's changelessness should not be equated with immobility." On the other hand, both Erickson, 279-81, and Garrett, 218-19, warn against the errors of Process Theology.

202   One of the results of the paradigm shift from Modernity to Postmodernity is the rejection of a mechanistic (Newtonian and Cartesian) world view and the understanding that

the world is far more complex and even chaotic (Einstein and quantum physics) than previously understood. The Newtownian perspective viewed the universe mechanistically; that is, the universe was seen as a machine based on the ideas of cause and effect. Life and behavior was predictable. We understood how things functioned by breaking them down into component parts.

Along came Einstein and the later study of quantum physics. The shocking discovery was that reality is not as predictable as expected in the Newtownian paradigm. Life, it seems, is even more chaotic than we realized. A result of this shift in understanding was the study of all living systems and organizations, leading to the studies of chaos and complexity. Now, it must be understood that complexity and chaos are not necessarily negative. Chaos, or rather the edge of chaos, is an element – a desired element – of a complex system. When a system or organization faces the threat of stagnation, decline, or death, it will move to the edge of chaos. It is in that condition (chaos is not a location) where innovation takes place. Therefore, "moving to the edge of chaos creates upheaval but not dissolution.... The edge is not the abyss. It's the sweet spot for productive change," and "innovations rarely emerge from systems with high degrees of order and stability." Bottom line, the "science of complexity" views "all living things as examples of complex adaptive systems," which actually thrive on change. Order, stability, and no change ultimately means death. See Hirsch, 247-76; Richard T. Pascale, Mark Milleman and Linda Gioja, *Surfing the Edge of Chaos* (New York: Crown Business, 2000), 5-6; Tony Mobbs, *Adaptive Leadership in Today's Modern Society*, Copyright IBM Corp., 2004.

203 The same could be said for the repeating circumstances in Judges, e.g. "The Israelites did what was evil in the sight of

the LORD. So the LORD handed them over to Midian seven years, and they oppressed Israel." Judges 6:1-2a.

204 Strategic planning implies laying out the vision, the mission, goals, objectives, tasks, and methods to accomplish these within a particular timeline. What is done, who it is done for, and anticipated results are clearly delineated. The plan should certainly anticipate obstacles and uncertainties, and responses to these. Strategic preparedness focusses on the preparation of leaders, the instilling of values, the development of skills, and an emphasis on flexibility, fluidity, and the ability to respond quickly and creatively to unanticipated and unexpected scenarios. These two approaches are not mutually exclusive and one includes some of the other. The best strategic planning today, in fact, is short term and "on paper and not in concrete," as rapid change is expected.

205 David Evert, *And Then Comes the End* (Scottdale, PA: Herald, 1980), 31, quoted in Boyd Hunt, *Redeemed: Eschatological Redemption and the Kingdom of God* (Nashville: Broadman and Holman, 1993), 276.

206 See http://en.wikipedia.org/wiki/Ethnic_cleansing for a long and horrific list of ethnic cleansings in the last one hundred years.

207 This quote is variously attributed to George Orwell, Joseph Stalin, Hermann Goering, and most frequently, to Winston Churchill.

208 "Faith on the Move: The Religious Affiliation of International Migrants, Executive Summary." Pew Forum on Religion & Public Life, www.pewforum.org/

Geography/Religious-Migration-exec.aspx?print=true (accessed 3/8/12). However, "[w]hile the United States has taken in more immigrants than any other country, the share of the U.S. population that is foreign-born (13%) is about average for Western industrial democracies," and actually 26th among 159 countries. Ibid., "Spotlight on the United States" (accessed 3/8/12).

209 The reality of all this immigration does not mean, however, that all were always welcome. Theoretically, that might have been so. Practically, there were exclusions at various times on various groups of people. For more information on global people movements see https://genographic.nationalgeographic.com/genographic/lan/en/atlas.html (accessed 3/29/12), which obviously takes an evolutionary approach to anthropology. Still, the interactive maps on this site help visualize the vast people movements in history. See http://www.nytimes.com/interactive/2009/03/10/us/20090310-immigration-explorer.html (accessed 3/29/12) for an interactive map of immigration patterns in the U.S. See also http://www.historyworld.net/wrldhis/PlainTextHistories.asp?historyid=ab18 (accessed 3/29/12) and http://www.history.ac.uk/ihr/Focus/Migration/websites.html (accessed 3/29/12) for further information about migrations of peoples.

210 For a scathing criticism of multiculturalism as an ideology, see Alvin J. Schmidt, *The Menace of Multiculturalism: Trojan Horse in America*, with a Foreword by Dinesh D'Souza (Westford, CT: Praeger Publishers, 1997). On pages 3-4 he defines multiculturalism as "a leftist political ideology that sees all cultures, their mores and institutions, as essentially equal. No culture is considered superior or inferior to any other; it is merely different. Criticisms of other cultures

is labeled 'insensitive' or 'bigoted.' There is one major exception, however. The Euro-American culture with its Judeo-Christian underpinnings is not only criticized but often condemned, being accused of racism, sexism, and classism." He does emphatically clarify that "[m]ulticulturalism must not be confused with multicultural education, as it often is. Multicultural education presents and examines the values and practices of other cultures objectively and critically in a non-doctrinaire manner." His concern, therefore, is "multiculturalism as an ideology," which is "cultural relativism."

211 The homogeneous principle was first introduced by in 1955 by Donald McGavran, *The Bridges of God* (United Kingdom: World Dominion, Press), 1955. The basic principle is that "men like to become Christians without crossing racial, linguistic or class barriers," thus facilitating the growth of the church along natural lines and leading to People Movements (large conversions). The principle (or rather, the subsequent application of it) has been vigorously opposed by others who call it racist. For example, C. René Padilla, "The Unity of the Church and the Homogeneous Principle," in *Exploring Church Growth*, ed. Wilbert Shenk (Grand Rapids: Eerdmans Publishing, 1983), 301, concluded that the principle "has no biblical foundation" and is a "missiology tailor-made for churches and institutions whose main function in society is to reinforce the status quo." Padilla has a valid warning; however, to not at least look at real and existing homogenous groupings and start with them guarantees that some groups will eventually be overlooked and will fall between the cracks of a missiological strategy.

212 See Jenkins, *The Next Christendom*, and Soong-Chan Rah, *The Next Evangelicalism. Freeing the Church from Western*

Cultural Captivity (Downers Grove: InterVarsity Press, 2009).

213 "Introduction" in *America, Christian or Secular,* ed. Jerry S. Herbert (Portland: Multnomah Press, 1984), 18-20.

214 See http://www.wallbuilders.com/. One critic of Wallbuilders notes that "Barton's intent is not to produce 'scholarship,' but to influence public policy." Paul Harvey, "Selling the Idea of a Christian Nation: David Barton's Alternate Intellectual Universe." www.religiondispatches. org/archive/politics/4589/selling_the_idea_of_a_ christian_nation.html (accessed 3/5/2012).

215 Others trace America's Christian heritage all the way back to Christopher Columbus, who they argue, was driven by his Christian Faith to explore new worlds. See, for example, David C. Gibbs with Jerry Newcombe, *One Nation Under God: Ten Things Every Christian Should Know About the Founding of America,* 2nd edition (Seminole, FL: Christian Law Association), 2003-06.

216 Interview in "Is America a Christian Nation?" by David Roach & Tammi Reed Ledbetter, *Southern Baptist Texan,* June 24, 2012.

217 Farrell Till, "The Christian Nation Myth." http://www. infidels.org/library/modern/farrell_till/myth.html (accessed 3/30/12). See also http://www.nobeliefs.com/ index.htm.

218 "Contrary to the claims made by some from the Religious Right, America was not founded as a Christian Nation which was then later undermined by godless liberals

and humanists. Just the opposite is the case, actually. The Constitution is a godless document and the government of the United States was set up as a formally secular institution. It has, however, been undermined by well-meaning Christians who have sought to subvert its secular principles and framework for the sake of this or that "good cause," usually in the interest of promoting this or that religious doctrine." Austin Cline, "America a Christian Nation–Is the United States a Christian Nation?

It's a Myth that America is a Christian Nation." http://atheism.about.com/od/americachristiannation/a/AmericaChristianNation.htm (accessed 3/30/12).

219 Terry Eastland, "In Defense of Religious America," in *America, Christian or Secular,* ed. Jerry S. Herbert (Portland: Multnomah Press, 1984), 50, more accurately explains that neutrality. He notes that the "intention of the framers of the First Amendment was not to effect an absolute neutrality on the part of government toward religion on the one hand and irreligion on the other. The neutrality the framers sought was rather among the sects, the various denominations."

220 John Fea, "Is America a Christian Nation? What Both Left and Right Get Wrong." www.hnn.us/articles/42835.html (accessed 3/5/2012). Mark Weldon Whitten, *The Myth of Christian America* (Macon, Ga: Smyth & Helwys Publishing, 1999), 42, notes that only in recent history and for political reasons have "some evangelical/fundamentalist Christians of the Religious Right adopted a new tactic to promote a Christian America."

221 Reb Bradley, "America has never been a Christian nation." www.wnd.com/2009/04/95167/print/ (accessed 3/5/2012).

222 "Like that ancient empire [Constantine's], the United States abounds in Christian trappings. And yet the United States embraces virtually all the values that have been common to empires for centuries on end. It pays lip service to peace but thrives on violence, exalts the rich over the poor, prefers power to humility, places vengeance above forgiveness, extravagance above modesty, and luxury above simplicity. In a word, it rejects the values of Jesus. How then, can we claim that the United States is a Christian nation?" Richard T. Hughes, *Christian America and the Kingdom of God* (Urbana and Chicago: University of Illinois Press, 2009), 186. For a very critical view of American history see http://amwerner.hubpages.com/hub/Modern-America-Fears-The-Authority-of-Revisionist-History.

223 Richard Land, *The Divided States of America* (Nashville: Thomas Nelson, 2007), 32.

224 Mark A. Noll, George M. Marsden, and Nathan O. Hatch, *The Search for Christian America*, expanded edition (Colorado Springs: Helmers & Howard, 1989), 18-19.

225 Mark A. Noll, *One Nation Under God? Christian Faith and Political Action in America* (San Francisco: Harper & Row, Publishers, 1988), 4. Land agrees that both Liberals and Conservatives miss a lot in American history. In The Divided States of America he has two chapters on exactly what each are "missing."

226 Ibid., 8-9, 189. Within our own American history we see an example of claiming too much for God when both the North and the South in the Civil War claimed that theirs was a "just and holy cause" and had God on their respective sides. Similarly, Matthew Arbo, "First Person: Questioning

American Exceptionalism," http://www.bpnews.net/
printerfriendly.asp?ID=37753, (accessed 6/7/2012), warns
against the "doctrine of American exceptionalism," which
has "been used to justify aggression by insisting that 'normal'
rule do not apply to the country's actions....God blesses us
despite our national identity, not because of it. American
exceptionalism implies that God's favor extends to this
nation in a way the Bible promises only to the church."
Land, on the other hand, argues for a balanced and soft
sense of exceptionalism. He states, 54, that he will not join
in a call for a "Christian America" because that "can too
easily lead to government establishment of religion." He
does argue, however, in "Is America a Christian Nation,"
Southern Baptist Texan, June 24, 2012, that "there is room
for an American 'exceptionalism' defined as God having
chosen to intervene in American history in unique ways
for his purposes, and in his providence [having] chosen to
bless us in manifold ways throughout our history." Those
blessings, however, are "by definition, undeserved, and incur
obligations." In *Divided States,* 195, he states that American
exceptionalism means "a responsibility to seek to share, but
not impose, the blessings of freedom and democracy with
others." It is, 30, "a doctrine of obligation, responsibility,
sacrifice, and service in the cause of freedom, not a doctrine
of pride, privilege, and empire." Essentially, God's blessing
is to be shared, not hoarded.

227 Ibid., 9-10. John Wilsey, "Is America a Christian Nation?"
The Southern Baptist Texan, June 24, 2012, likewise "argues
that America was established as a nation with religious
liberty, but not as a Christian nation 'in the strong sense'."

228 Ibid., 9-12. Carson, *Christ and Culture Revisited*, 209 agrees
that, whether or not America is a Christian nation or

founded on Christian principles, it "would be more realistic to acknowledge that the founding of the nation was borne along by adherence to some Christian principles and not others. After all, there cannot be many today from any camp who want to return to slavery."

229 Land, *Divided States*, 32, notes that "the American government put in place by the Constitution was an attempt to wed Judeo-Christian values with Enlightenment ideas of self-government."

230 Christian Smith, *Christian America? What Evangelicals Really Want* (Berkeley: University of California Press, 2000), 26-37, 90, conducted a nationwide survey of evangelicals and noted that we cannot agree on what an evangelical is and much less on what "Christian America" means.

231 A great irony is how the content of our "Christian Nation" identity has changed. At our founding we were decidedly Protestant with a Roman Catholic minority. In the nineteenth Century we were Protestant with an anti-Catholic bias, although due to Irish, Italian, and Polish (among others) immigration Catholics became the majority. In the twentieth Century, that anti-Catholic bias kept many Protestants from supporting Alf Landon for President in 1936 and caused great concern for Protestants when John Kennedy was elected. Most recently, however, a strong practicing Roman Catholic, Rick Santorum, was the preferred Presidential candidate of many conservative Protestants and evangelicals.

232 "The United States continues to be a highly religious nation. Most Americans say they belong to a particular faith and large percentages agree with statements about key religious

beliefs and behaviors,'"Partisan Polarization Surges in Bush, Obama Years," Pew Research Center, http://www.people-press.org/2012/06/04/partisan-polarization-surges-in-bush-obama-years/, (accessed 6/7/2012). However, where's the fruit?

233 I am indebted to my good friend Dr. Robby Partain for this insight. Trevin Wax, "First Person: Southern Baptists, we're not in Zion anymore," http://bpnews.net/printerfriendly. asp?ID=37974, (accessed 6/7/2012), notes that "[i]t won't do for us to bemoan the disappearance of cultural Christianity. There were dangers then, too, included an often watered-down Gospel as well a cultural respectability that masked unregenerate hearts."

234 Civil Religion has several definitions, but essentially refers to the mixture of religion and culture to the point that each is identified with the other. Thus, for example, the "American Way of life" is often identified as the Christian way of life. Land, *The Divided States of America*, 37, strongly warns against making a patriotic idolatry, of "making a god of one's nation." He argues that statements such as "God is on our side," or "My country right or wrong" do just that. This is, unfortunately, the "besetting sin of conservatives," who "merge God and country as if they are virtually inseparable."

235 Secularists are notorious for taking this phrase out of context. Jefferson was addressing a specific concern of the Danbury Baptists about state encroachment on religion. He was assuring them that this would not happen. He was not, regardless of his personal heretical theology, arguing for the absence of religion in public life. Also, contrary to popular belief, this phrase does not appear in the Constitution. The First Amendment contains two clauses that must be held

in tension (and it has never been simple): "Congress shall make no law respecting an establishment of religion, or prohibiting the free exercise thereof." See http://www.loc.gov/loc/lcib/9806/danpre.html for Jefferson's letter.

236 See H. Leon McBeth's chapter on "Baptists in Colonial America: The Struggle for Religious Liberty", in *The Baptist Heritage. Four Centuries of Baptist Heritage* (Nashville: Broadman Press, 1987), 252-287.

237 Carson, *Christ and Culture Revisited*, 118, makes a pointed observation that "naïve Christians often think that these signs of residual civil religion and the Deism on which they are based constitute solid evidence of Christian commitments. Conversely, they see the erosion of civil religion, and the Deism on which they are based, as an erosion of genuinely Christian commitments. Neither assessment is realistic. Worse yet, some Christians, more knowledgeable but not necessarily wiser, are tempted to speak to public issues solely in the categories of Deism, hoping thus to gain wider exposure and establish a broader consensus. At a certain level of public policy, they may on occasion be right. But arguing for morality from the assumption of Deism is a far cry from upholding Christianity.... Deism is not a halfway house between secularism and Christianity; it is in fact a form of secularism."

238 Similarly, Carson, 195, makes the same argument with a global application. He notes that "[f]rom a Christian point of view, it is unhelpful to speak of the 'Christian West' or of 'our Christian nation' or the like. In America, this is not only because of the legal force of the First Amendment (however it is interpreted) but also because nowadays the numeric shift in numbers of Christians, from West to East and from

North to South, is so dramatic that such expressions sound increasingly parochial and out of date. Still more important, talk of the 'Christian West' actually stifles the advance of the gospel in parts of the world where countervailing religions and ideologies want people to believe in the stereotype of the Christian West so that Christian claims can be dismissed as merely Western. Above all, Christians who wish to be faithful to the Bible will remind themselves of their heavenly citizenship. Not to understand this is to identify too closely with the kingdoms and orders of this world, with disastrous results both materially and spiritually." See Jenkins, *The Next Christendom*, and also Michael Pocock, Gailyn Van Rheenen, and Douglas McConnell, ""The Disappearing Center: From Christendom to Global Christianity," in *The Changing Face of World Missions* (Grand Rapids: Baker Academic, 2005), 131-59.

239 The terms "urban," "metropolitan," and "metro area" are used in different ways. The U.S. Census Bureau calls any area over 50,000 people as urban. Others make a clear distinction between urban (as core or central city) and the suburb. I am using the terms "urban" and "urbanization" to refer to what is usually called a metro area. Some would object. See http://www.newgeography.com/content/002799-staying-same-urbanization-america.

240 "People: Urbanization of America." www.theusaonline.com/people/urbanization.html. Accessed 4/10/12; Bruce Katz, "A Much More Urban America." http://www.brookings.edu/opinions/2007/0723urban_katz.aspx?p=1. Accessed 4/23/2012.

241 William H. Frey, "Population Growth in Metro America Since 1980: Putting the Volatile 2000s in Perspective."

http://www.brookings.edu/papers/2012/0320_population_
frey.aspx?p=1, (accessed 4/23/2012).

242 In some cases the actual primary city of an urban are is
declining in population because it is landlocked or because
jobs have changed or moved out. Examples are Detroit, St.
Louis, and Cleveland, among others. Also, it is interesting
to note that "[N]ot counting immigration, the population
of the U.S. is barely growing, and probably won't double
for at least 150 years. But this near-zero population growth
disguises major shifts in the populations of U.S. regions.
In great numbers, Americans are fleeing the climatically
inhospitable and densely populated Northeast and Midwest
for the sunny South and the thinly populated West."
"Growing Cities of the West and the South." www.ti.org/
Metrogrowth.html, (accessed 4/11/2012).

243 Audrey Singer, "Immigrants in 2010 Metropolitan
America: A Decade of Change." http://www.brookings.
edu/speeches/2011/1024_immigration_singer.aspx?p=1,
(accessed 4/23/2012).

244 William H. Frey, "Melting Pot Cities and Suburbs: Racial
and Ethnic Change in Metro America in the 2000s." http://
www.brookings.edu/2011/0504_census_ethnicity_frey.
aspx?p=1, (accessed 4/23/2012).

245 See http://www.namb.net/overview-why-send/.

246 Eric Swanson and Sam Williams, *Transform a City:
Whole Church, Whole Gospel, Whole City* (Grand Rapids:
Zondervan, 2010), 30-36, give "six reasons to engage with
cities: 1. Cities have a transforming effect on people, 2. Cities
from a creative center, 3. Cities create fertile ground for

thinking and receptivity, 4. Cities can help people live more efficiently and productively, 5. Cities are valued by God, and 6. The early Christian movement was primarily urban."

247 In the 1990s I made several trips to San Francisco for a missions partnership. During my first trip I was impressed by the revitalization and gentrification of most of San Francisco, which had driven real estate and rental prices to unimaginable heights. When I asked the person giving us the tour "Where do the poor people live?" his ironic response was "Oakland." For a pro-gentrification view see Jeffrey Knowles, "Gentrification: What does it really do?" Next American City. http://americancity.org/buzz/entry/922/, (accessed 6/7/2010). For anti-gentrification views see "Urban Rights, an Anti-Gentrification Action, Houston, Texas." http://www.wakeuphouston.org/ (accessed 6/7/2010), and Gustav Landauer, "Affordable Housing in Austin – Tools to Fight Gentrification." http://www. monkeywrenchbooks.org/node/251, (accessed 6/7/2010). For a more balanced and pastoral approach to the inevitability of gentrification see Bob Lupton, "Gentrification with Justice." *by Faith Magazine*. http://byfaithonline.com/ page/in-the-world-gentrification-with-justice, (accessed 6/9/2010).

248 Just Google "anti-church zoning" and you will encounter scores of news reports and articles about cities hostile to church zoning.

249 See the research released by the Pew Research Center: "Most Say Homosexuality Should Be Accepted By Society." Released May 13, 2011. www.people-press. org/2011/05/13/most-say-homosexuality-should-be-accepted-by-society/, (accessed 4/26/2012); and "Ten Years

of Changing Attitudes on Gay Marriage." http://features. pewforum.org/same-sex-marriage-attitudes/download. php, (accessed 4/26/2012). Not too long after I wrote this chapter, President Barack Obama came out in favor of Gay marriage.

250 See Robert Steuteville and Phillip Langdon, "The New Urbanism: A better way to plan and build 21st Century communities." *New Urban News.* http://www. newurbannews.com/AboutNewUrbanism.html, (accessed 6/9/2010); and "New Urbanism." http://en.wikipedia.org/ wiki/New_Urbanism, (accessed 6/9/2010).

251 "Far from being dead, cities are experiencing a second life, fueled, in part, by their distinctive physical assets: mixed-use downtowns, pedestrian-friendly neighborhoods, adjoining rivers and lakes, historic buildings and distinctive architecture....We are, in short, a full-fledged 'Metro Nation.'" Katz, "A Much More Urban America."

252 "OECD report cites increasing income inequality in U.S." Los Angeles Times, http://articles.latimes.com/2011/ dec/06/business/la-fi-1206-oecd-income-20111206   , (accessed 4/10/2012). Compared to the rest of the world, income inequality in the U.S. "ranks near the extreme end of the inequality scale." Max Fisher, "Map: U.S. Ranks Near Bottom on Income Inequality." The Atlantic, http://www. theatlantic.com/international/archive/2011/09/map-us-ranks-near-bottom-on-income-inequality/245315/.

253 "The portion of American families living in middle-class income neighborhoods has declined significantly since 1970...as rising income inequality left a growing share of families in neighborhoods that are mostly low-

income or mostly affluent....The finding how a changed map of prosperity in the United States over the past four decades, with larger patches of affluence and poverty and a shrinking middle." Sabrina Tavernise, "Middle-Class Areas Shrink as Income Gap Grows, New Report Finds." www.nytimes.com/2011/11/16/us/middle-class-areas-shrink-as-income-gap-grows-report-finds.html? (accessed 4/10/2012). See also "The Causes of Rising Income Inequality." The National Bureau of Economic Research. www.nber.org/digest/dec08/w13982.html, (accessed 4/10/2012), for a more balanced explanation of the gap.

254 Danielle Kurtzlben, "The Myth of Economic Inequality." www.usnews.com/news/articles/2012/02/09/the-myth-of-economic-inequality_print.html, (accessed 4/10/2012).

255 "The Real Story Behind 'Rising' U.S. Income Inequality." http://Politicalcalculations.blogspot.com/2011/10/real-story-behind-rising-us-income.html, (accessed 4/10/2012).

256 Charles Lane, "Obama's simplistic view of income inequality." *The Washington Post*, http://www.washingtonpost.com/opinions/obamas-simplistic-view-of-income-inequality/2011/12/19/gIQAeVmR5O_story.html, (accessed 4/10/2012).

257 Murray, *Coming Apart*, 120.

258 Ibid., 124-207 passim.Murray, 149, specifically points out that "over the last half century, marriage has become the fault line dividing American classes." He also notes, 269, that although his studied focused on white Americans, his conclusions are applicable to all groups in the country. His solutions are, by the way, political and Libertarian.

259 However, it has been noted that the gap also increased between the 1980 and 1990 census, particularly when comparing the median incomes among the wealthiest and the poorest clusters in America. Michael J. Weiss, *The Clustered World*. Boston: Little, Brown and Company, 2000, 15. The news, however, could get worse. According to an article by Hope Yen, "Poverty in U.S. on track to hit 47-year high," *Fort Worth Star-Telegram*, July 23, 2012, census figures to be released in the fall of 2012 indicated that the "official poverty rate will rise from 15.1 percent in 20120, climbing as high as 15.7 percent" and "would put poverty at the highest since 1965."

260 William H. Frey, "Five Things the Census Revealed About America in 2011: V. Americans lost ground on income and poverty in the 2000s." http://www.brookings.edu. opinions/2001/1220_census_demographics.aspx?p+1 (accessed 4/23/2012). See also, "Immigration and Poverty in America's Suburbs." http://www.brookings.edu/ papers/2011/0804_immigration_suro_wilson_singer. aspx?p=1, (accessed 4/23/2012); and Alan Berube and Elizabeth Kneebone, "Parsing U.S. Poverty at the Metropolitan Level." http://www.brookings.edu/ opinions/2011/0922_metro_poverty_berube_kneebone. aspx?p+1, (accessed 4/23/2012).

261 Many demographers divide the Boomers into early Boomers (born 1946-1955), later Boomers, or, as some call it, "Generation Jones" (born 1956-1964). The first group remembers and was greatly affected by the assassinations of JFK, RFK, and Martin Luther King. They lived through the Viet Nam war and faced the draft. The latter group came of age after the draft ended, have little or no memory of the assassinations of the sixties, and identify more with

Watergate and the recession of the seventies. See http://en.wikipedia.org/wiki/Baby_boomer.

262 John Haaga, "Just How Many Baby Boomers are There? http://www.prb.org/articles/2002/justhowmanybaby-boomersarethere.aspx, (accessed 4/25/2012). See "Facts and Statistics About the Baby Boomer Generation." http://www.babyboomer-magazine.com/news/165/ARTIᴄᴇ1437/2010-04-04.html.

263 Alan Greenblatt, "Aging Baby Boomers." Published by CG Press, a division of Congressional Quarterly, Inc. www.cqresearcher.com, (accessed 4/25/2012).

264 "Baby Boomers Will Transform Aging in America, Panel Says." http://www.huffingtonpost.com/2012/04/02/aging-in-america-baby-boomers-arianna-huffington_n_1397686.html, (accessed 4/25/2012).

265 Maureen Mackey, "The Graying of America: An Economic Time Bomb?" The Fiscal Times. http://www.thefiscaltimes.com/Articles/2010/10/19/The-Graying-of-America-An-Economic-Time-Bomb.aspx#page1, (accessed 4/25/2012). "Today there are just over three (3.3) workers for every [Social Security] beneficiary. By 2030 there will be just over two (2.2)." "The Graying of America (statistics)." Family Giving News. http://familygivingnews.wordpress.com/2011/03/02/sidebar-the-graying-of-america/, (accessed 4/25/2012).

266 Greenblatt, "Aging Baby Boomers."

267 It should be noted that the "graying" phenomenon is not just happening in the U.S. Many other countries are

experiencing it and often to a greater degree. Canada, France Germany, Italy, Japan, and the United Kingdom all have larger aging populations than the U.S. Greenblatt, "Aging Baby Boomers."

268 Edward Hammett, "Meet the 'New Old': Ministry to and with Baby Boomers." Congregational Resource Guide. http://congregationalresources.org/meet-new-old-ministry-and-baby-boomers, (accessed 4/25/2012).

269 Dave Gibbons, *The Monkey and the Fish: Liquid Leadership for a Third-Culture Church* (Grand Rapids: Zondervan Books, 2009), 38. See also David C. Pollock and Ruth E. Van Reken, Third Culture Kids: Growing up among worlds (Boston: Nicholas Brealey Publishing, 1999), and www.crossculturalkid.org.

270 Alistair E. McGrath, *Mere Apologetics: How to help seekers & skeptics find faith* (Grand Rapids: Baker Books, 2012), 30, observes that "every generation believes it stands at a critical point in history. Augustine of Hippo, writing in the early fifth century, remarked on how many people of his time longed for the good old days, when Christianity was given support and security by the Roman Empire. Bernard of Clairvaux, writing seven hundred years later, wrote of the sense of nostalgia many then felt for the time of Augustine. And many sixteenth-century writers commented on how they longed to have lived at the time of Bernard of Clairvaux. Things were so much better then! We find it very easy to believe things were better in the past. We must remember that the past is easily idealized and romanticized, especially by those who feel alienated and displaced in the present."

271 Willem A. VanGemeren, "Psalms" in *The Expositor's Bible Commentary*, Vol. 5, Frank E. Gaebelein, gen. ed. (Grand Rapids: Zondervan Publishing Company, 1991), 392.

272 "According to former journalists Bill Kovach and Tom Rosenstiel, 24 hour news creates ferocious competition among media organizations for audience share. "24-hour news cycle," http://en.wikipedia.org/wili/24-hour_ newscycle, (accessed 4/26/2012). W. Joseph Campbell, "Media Myth Alert: 24/7 news cycle no new phenomenon," http://mediamythalert.wordpress.com/2011/01/25/247-news-cycle-no-new-phenomenon/, (accessed 4/26/2012), argues that the 24.7 news cycle is not "exclusive to the digital century," and that "[s]peed and time pressured are traditional elements of daily journalism." He is correct; however, he is overlooking both the "live" and the ubiquity element of news channels.

273 Movie star and sex symbol Rudolf Valentino's death in 1926 led to "mass hysteria" and suicide among his fans, riots in the streets, and an estimated 100,000 people lining the streets of New York City for his funeral. http://en.wikipedia.org/wiki/Rudolph_Valentino. 274

274 Christopher J. H. Wright, *The Mission of God: Unlocking the Bible's Grand Narrative* (Downer's Grove, IL: InterVarsity Press, 2006), 168, notes in a chapter on idolatry that the "idolatrous power of fear is enormous and seems to bear no direct relation to the scale of what is feared."

275 Barry Glassner, The Culture of Fear: *Why Americans are Afraid of the Wrong Things*, (New York: Basic Books, 1999). Remember that statistics can be confusing and stated in many ways to make one's case. See the National Institute

of Health and the Center for Disease Control for statistics that lend Glassner's claims support: http://www.nlm.nih.gov/medlineplus/ency/article/001915.htm and http://www.cdc.gov/nchs/fastats/children.htm.

276 Ibid., 30-31.

277 "How Americans Are Living Dangerously," http://www.time.com/time/printouts/0,8816,1562978,00.html, (accessed 5/18/2012),

278 Freeman Klopott, "Poisoning is a bigger killer than car crashes," *Fort Worth Star-Telegram*, May 23, 2012. Of course, as soon as I quote this newspaper report which uses a series of studies and statistics, I wonder if the reporting is accurate and in context!

279 "...vivid descriptions of horrific events can have an overwhelming impact on our decision making, no matter how rare the event or unlikely our involvement might be." Gever Tulley, *Beware Dangerism! Why We Worry about the Wrong Things and What It's Doing to Our Kids*, TED Lectures. Published in the United States by TED, 2011.

280 I mentioned earlier that the crime rate in America has declined significantly. "In 2009 America's crime rate was roughly the same as in 1968, with the homicide rate being at its lowest level since 1964. Overall, the national crime rate was 3466 crimes per 100,000 residents, down from 3680 crimes per 100,000 residents forty years earlier in 1969 (-9.4%)." The article is quoting statistics from FBI Uniform Crime Reports (http://www.disastercenter.com/crime/uscrime.htm), http://en.wikipedia.org/wiki/Crime_in_the_United_States, (accessed 5/18/2012).

281 "Think the world is getting more violent and dangerous? You're wrong, according to study," http://www.syracuse. com/news/index.ssf/2011/10/think_the_world_is_ getting_mor.html, (accessed 5/18/2012); Joshua S. Goldstein, "Think Again: War," http://www.foreignpolicy. com/articles/2011/08/15/think_again_war, (accessed 5/25/2012), comes to the same conclusion. War is not nearly as frequent and costly as it used to be.

282 According to http://www.fas.org/sgp/crs/natsec/RL32492. pdf the numbers of American casualties in some of our wars are:

- Civil War: at least 620,000 total deaths
- WWI: 53,402 battle deaths, 116,516 total deaths
- WWII: 291,557 battle deaths, 405,399 total deaths
- Korea: 33,739 battle deaths, 36,574 total deaths
- Viet Nam: 47,434 battle deaths, 58,220 total deaths
- Operation Iraqi Freedom: 4,301 total deaths
- Operation Enduring Freedom: 714 total deaths.

Now, consider that the millions killed worldwide in World War II were known about by the average American after the war. In fact, it was not until Germany surrendered that the Holocaust was officially verified. Even during the war reporting was sketchy, distant, and highly censored. Pictures of dead American soldiers were rarely allowed to be published. During Viet Nam, the evening network news started giving body counts and showing film of dead and injured American soldiers. That brought the war so close to home that many average Americans changed from supporters to opponents. (Marshall McLuhan noted that "Television brought the brutality of war into the comfort of the living room. Vietnam was lost in the living rooms

of America—not on the battlefields of Vietnam." http://
www.britannica.com/EBchecked/topic/355118/Marshall-
McLuhan/355118suppinfo/Supplemental-Information).
Today, the wars in Iraq and Afghanistan are immediate,
ubiquitous, and personal. Every soldier can be a war
reporter. Although the casualty rate is nowhere near WWII,
Korea, or Viet Nam, in some ways it is felt more intensely
by Americans because every single death and severe injury
is reported in detail by someone. These are not faceless
casualties, but men and women we can know everything
about. I am in no way demeaning the tragedy of those who
died and suffered in previous wars. My point is that the
more information we have about casualties and the quicker
we receive that information in real time, the harder it is for
us to take. Furthermore, it makes it near impossible for the
government to implement any kind of war policy without
constant criticism.

283 "Violent crime is at all-time low in our country…by most
accounts, violent crime constitutes just 3% of reported
criminal activity, yet is responsible for as much as 43% of
news coverage" What is worse is that "news stories about
children revealed that 43% were in the context of violent
crime." Tulley, *Beware Dangerism!*, calls this "pathological
fear mongering on the part of the networks."

284 Child abuse in America is still a national tragedy. UNICEF
reported in 2001 that the U.S. "has the highest rate of
deaths from child abuse and neglect of any industrialized
nation." http://en.wikipedia.org/wiki/Crime_in_the_
United_States, (accessed 5/18/2012).

285 Tulley, *Beware Dangerism!*

286 "…fear of lawsuits or other ramifications – independent of actual danger" leads to action whereby a product is removed or a warning is issued. That leads to the public belief that the product or activity really must be dangerous. The reality, therefore, is the warning was issued out of fear of a lawsuit (a real fear, by the way) and not actual harm. Ibid.

287 Comedian Jeff Foxworthy says that kids today will have no stories to tell. We have so overprotected them that they cannot point to a scar or a burn and tell the story of how they got it. According to Tulley, *Beware Dangerism!*, when "we strive to remove all risk from childhood we also remove the foundations of a rational adulthood, and we eliminate the very experiences that will help kids grow up to be the empowered, creative, brave problem-solvers that they can and must be."

288 An entire chapter could be written on economic fear, overreaction, and the attempts to create an economic utopia. Certainly, there needs to be some regulation and controls in a free market, but it is called "free" for a reason. Part of that freedom is that it will move up and down – sometimes unpredictably. Governments try to control that unpredictability through regulation. Traders and big companies try to leverage that unpredictability to their benefit. Individuals sometimes make knee jerk reactions based on that day's unpredictability. Once again, information is immediate: I can look at the Stocks app on my iphone and see stock market updates every twenty minutes. I cannot and should not go online every twenty minutes and move my stock around.

289 Gregory Rodriguez, "The perils of our play-it-safe society," *Los Angeles Times*/Article Collection, http://articles.

latimes.com/print/2006/mar/05/opinion/oe-rodriguez5, (accessed 4/26/2012), notes that "in this culture of anxiety, we no longer need to face danger to be consumed by fear," for "fear sells."

290 John F. Schumaker, "Boredom: The New Epidemic Facing America," http://voices.yahoo.com/shared/print. shtml?content_type+article&content_type_id=8182439, (accessed 4/26/2012).

291 "Our culture's obsession with external sources of entertainment – TV, movies, the Internet, video games – may also play a role in increasing boredom." That is, the more we seek entertainment to ease our boredom and the more saturated we become with stimuli, the more ineffective that stimuli is. Thus, more boredom. Anna Goslin, "Bored to Death: Chronically Bored People Exhibit Higher Risk-Taking Behavior," http://www.scientificamerican. com/article.cfm?id=the=science-of-boredom&print=true, (accessed 4/26/2012).

292 On August 21, 1921 Benjamin De Casseres wrote an essay in *The New York Times* entitled "The Leaden Age of Boredom," in which he discusses Albert Einstein's observation that Americans are "bored to death," and expresses the opinion that the "Era of Boredom is full upon us." Of course, this was at the beginning of the "roaring twenties" and pre-Great Depression and pre-World War II.

293 Damon Darlin, "How to Tame an Inflated Entertainment Budget," *The New York Times*, http://www.nytimes. com/2005/11/19/business/19money.html?pagewanted=all, (accessed 6/1/2012).

294 "Sports and Entertainment, http://nbaccorp.com/en/our-clients/industries/sports-and-entertainment, (accessed 6/1/2012).

295 Jackie Cohen, "America's Culture of Entertainment," http://www.marketwatch.com/story/americans-value-entertainment-studies-show, (Accessed 6/1/2012). To maintain some perspective, this figure also includes purchases of books and magazines.

296 "Feelings of boredom and deadness are becoming so intense that increasing numbers of desperate souls will even put their lives on the line in hopes of a life restoring 'rush'." Schumaker, "Boredom: The New Epidemic Facing America."

297 Craig Detweiler and Barry Taylor, *A Matrix of Meanings: Finding God in Pop Culture*, (Grand Rapids: Baker Academic: 2003), 172. The movie's "biting sarcasm and ferocious energy expose the spiritual bankruptcy of a consumer society bent on happiness..." Robert K. Johnston, *Reel Spirituality: Theology and Film in Dialogue*, 2nd edition, (Grand Rapids: Baker Academic, 2006), 211.

298 "...we've witnessed a long, slow retreat into the hermetically sealed comfort of our fortress-like homes...deep friendships replaced by screens, gadgets, and exhausted couch-potato stupor," Stephen Ilardi, "Social Isolation: A Modern Plague," http://www.psychologytoday.com/blog/the-depression-cure/200907/social-isolation-modern-plague, (accessed 6/1/2012).

299 "...on average, Americans have fewer intimates to confide in than they did a decade ago, according to one study. Another

found that 20 percent of all individuals are, at any given time, unhappy because of social isolation...," Katherine Seligman, "Social Isolation a Significant Health Issue," http://www.sfgate.com/cgi-bin/article.cgi?f=/c/a/2009/03/01/DDDB15VE34.DTL#ixzz1wZUTmUrW, (accessed 6/1/2012).

300   Stephen Marche, "Is Facebook Making Us Lonely," http://www.theatlantic.com/magazine/print/2012/05/is-facebook-making-us-lonely/8930/, (accessed 5/18/2012). Marche accurately points out that our American psyche is highly individualistic and has always celebrated the unattched loner, whether the explorer, the cowboy, or the astronaut – "Loneliness is at the American core."

301   Keith N. Hampton et al, "Social Isolation and New Technology," http://pewinternet.org/~/media//Files/Reports/2009/PIP_Tech_and_Social_Isolation.pdf, (accessed 6/1/2012). See also Aaron Smith, "Why Americans use social media," http://www.pewinternet.org/Reports/2011/Why-Americans-Use-Social-Media.aspx.

302   See Wright, *The Mission of God*, 136-188, for an excellent chapter on "The Living God Confronts Idolatry." He notes that as human beings we turn to idols the "Things that entice us," the "Things we fear," the "Things that we trust," and the "Things we need."

303   Richard T. De George, "Anarchism," in *The Oxford Companion to Philosophy*, ed. Ted Honderich (Oxford: Oxford University Press, 1995), 30-31

304   Wright, *The Mission of God*, 164.

305 Ibid., 163.

306 Kimball, *The Emerging Church*, 44.

307 Grenz, *A Primer of Postmodernism*, 43.

308 Kimball, *The Emerging Church*, 73. Kimball, of course, is describing how postmoderns think, not defending them.

309 Some have argued that Postmodernism is simply the inevitable outcome of Existentialism, in which the individual is the reference point for all existence and all meaning.

310 The philosophy of radical individualism (known as Objectivism) has been promoted and popularized by the author Ayn Rand in her books *The Fountainhead* and *Atlas Shrugged*. She promoted "rational egoism" or "rational self-interest," as the ultimate guiding moral principle. She argued that if every person were driven primarily by self-interest, particularly in business, society would inevitably benefit. This is because in laissez-faire capitalism the self-interested business person would not do anything harmful to his bottom line, including harming others. Although her fiction is at times compelling (the quality of her writing is greatly debated; it is often preachy and pedantic) and some of ideas are worth noting (although her philosophy is pedestrian and shallow), Rand's self-interest position was so radical that she belittled religion and any form of altruism. Two points to note in understanding her: One, she was a refugee from Communist Russia and thus was reacting to that extreme collectivism. Two, being anti-religion, she completely overestimated human nature. Perhaps her philosophy would work in a perfect world

without fallen human beings. See http://en.wikipedia.org/ wiki/Ayn_Rand and www.aynrand.org.

311 Homosexuality is being more and more accepted by society, especially among young people. The Pew Research Center notes that 63% "of those younger than age 50 ... say that homosexuality should be accepted." Similarly, opposition to gay marriage is declining. As of a 2011 study, "45% favor allowing gays and lesbians to marry legally, while 46% are opposed." Just two years earlier, in 2009, it was only 35% in favor and 54% opposed. "Most Say Homosexuality Should Be Accepted By Society," http://pewresearch.org/ pubs/1994/poll-support-for-acceptance-of-homosexual-ity-gay-parenting-marriage, (accessed 6/4/2012).

312 Jon Meacham, "Keeping the Dream Alive," *Time*, July 2, 2012, 26-39, notes that the First Charter of Virginia contains 3,805 words, of which 98 or 3% are about religion and the rest are about economics and exploitation of the land for its riches. See the article for a brief summary of the history of the American Dream and how it is currently a threatened reality. See http://avalon.law.yale.edu/17th_ century/va01.asp for a copy of the Virginia Charter.

313 http://www.researchamerica.org/research_cents (accessed 7/10/2012).

314 "Gambling Facts & Stats." http://www.pbs.org/wgbh/ pages/frontline/shows/gamble/etc/facts.html (accessed 7/ 10/2012).

315 http://en.wikipedia.org/wiki/Native_American_gaming (accessed 7/10/2012).

316 "The Facts About The Lottery," http://www.saneok.org/files/Facts&Stats/LottoFacts.pdf (accessed 7/10/2012).

317 As this chapter was being written the Penn State scandal continued to unfold. Besides the horrific sins and crimes committed against children by Jerry Sandusky, the scandal included the cover-up by Coach Joe Paterno and top university officials. That cover-up has led to much debate and discussion about our worship of sports in general and football in particular and how Penn State elevated its football program and own image well above the safety of children. There has been a lot of talk about this misplace "idolatry," but it is doubtful whether any significant social change will result.

318 The race car driver Danica Patrick is considered a sex symbol. She has used that image to advertise GoDaddy.com and to do the "Got Milk" ads.

319 See http://electronics.howstuffworks.com/gadgets/high-tech-gadgets/holographic-environment.htm, http://en.wikipedia.org/wiki/Holography, http://en.wikipedia.org/wiki/Pepper%27s_Ghost, http://en.wikipedia.org/wiki/Volumetric_displays, http://en.wikipedia.org/wiki/Musion_Eyeliner for some examples of this technology.

320 In the months since the writing of this paragraph, the Boy Scouts have voted to accept gay scouts into their ranks. The normalization and cultural acceptance of homosexuality and gay marriage has snowballed in 2012 and 2013.

321 We all struggle at times with faith and dependence. That does not automatically translate into idolatry, just simple Christian life struggles. Pattern and lifestyle is the issue.

322 The good news is that a recent Pew Forum report indicates that "polls conducted in 2009 have found fewer Americans expressing support for abortion than in previous years." Americans are now "evenly divided on the question." http://www.perforum.org/Abortion/Support-for-Abortion-Slips.aspx?print=true.

323 The culture of the sixties and the Baby Boomer generation often get blamed for this. Being one, I cannot help but wonder how much that is true. I clearly remember the prevailing view of the seventies being that good self-esteem, which included lots of rights and little responsibilities, would cure just about anything: poverty, crime, teen pregnancy, etc. How did that work out?

324 See Leonard Sweet, *Viral: How Social Networking is Poised to Ignite Revival* (Colorado Springs: WaterBrook Press, 2012).

325 Jim Miller, "Book Review: Surfing for God." www.thechurchreport.com/index.cfm?fuseacation=siteContent.default&objectID=155542 (accessed 6/4/2012). Mike Genung, "How Many Porn Addicts are in Your Church?" http://www.crosswalk.com/print/1336107/ (accessed 6/4/2012), points out that "Porn is reported to be a 12 billion dollar industry in the U.S....50 percent of men viewed pornography within one week of attending a Promise Keepers stadium event...54 percent of pastors said they viewed porn within the past year in a Pastors.com survey...in a 2003 Focus on the Family poll 47 percent of respondents said porn is a problem in their home."

326 "Thirty percent of women are addicted to it. Sixty-seven percent of men say they look at it at least once a month...

Perhaps even more shocking, 50 percent of pastors said they visited adult web sites at least once a week." "Pornography Harms Women, Invades the Church." http://www.christianpost.com/news/pornography-invades-the-church-53257/ (accessed 7/11/2012).

327 "The evangelical church has experienced a more encouraging story this millennium, but even evangelicals are experiencing a slowdown in a variety of key areas," and "While numeric church attendance will decline slightly from 52 million in 2005 to 49 million in 2020, the American population will grow from 296 million in 2005 to 336 million in 2020, causing a significant percentage decline." David T. Olson, *The American Church in Crisis* (Grand Rapids: Zondervan, 2008), 57-58, 176.

328 Ibid., 163.

329 Timothy C. Tennent, *Theology in the Context of World Christianity* (Grand Rapids: Zondervan, 2007), 241, insightfully notes that "[f]rom a Western perspective not informed by global realities, it is easy to become discouraged and pessimistic about the advance of the gospel because of the rapid decline of Christianity in the West. However, from the Chinese perspective, it seems that everywhere one turns – in the city and in the country, among the educated as well as the peasants – people are coming to Christ and new churches are emerging."

330 I will not be dealing directly with the written and the visual proclamation of the gospel through books, the internet, the arts, music, and movies. These are all legitimate and even necessary tools to communicate in the American mission field. My concerns are not specific technologies for sharing

the gospel, but the principles and issues of communication that lie behind all forms of proclamation.

331 Hesselgrave and Rommen, 1.

332 A discussion of contextualization can be quite technical and controversial. There are those who take extreme views in the discussion: One extreme argues that contextualization does not matter and should not ever be practiced. They are usually unaware or in denial about the contextualization they already engage in, such as speaking and reading in English. They are, in fact, already giving up too much to their own preferred culture and refuse to make any adjustments to the receptor culture. The other extreme accommodates to the receptor culture so much that the distinctiveness of the gospel is lost. These, also, identify the gospel too much with culture – any culture – to such a degree that the message is compromised or totally lost. Therefore, not all contextualization schemes are legitimate.

333 David J. Hesselgrave, "World-view and contextualization," in Ralph D. Winter and Steven C. Hawthorne, eds, *Perspectives on the World Christian Movement: A Reader* (Pasadena, CA: William Carey Library, 1981), 405.

334 "We simply cannot translate word for word, using words with equivalent meanings, for words, themselves, are products of a culture and reflect the basic values and assumptions of that culture. The fact is, there are no words in one culture that carry exactly the same meanings as the words of another culture." Paul G. Hiebert, "Culture and Cross-Cultural Differences," in Winter and Hawthorne, *Perspectives*, 375.

335 Bruce Riley Ashford, "The Gospel and Culture," in *Theology and Practice of Mission: God, the Church, and the Nations,* ed. *Bruce Riley Ashford* (Nashville: Broadman & Holman, 2011), 118, notes that "Scripture provides us examples of contextualization, that contextualization is inevitable," and, 120, that "every Christian alive today is actively involved in contextualization. Every American Christian worships in a contextualized church."

336 I just recently heard the story of a Sudanese pastor who left his village for "further training" and came back to his people ready to teach them the "right way to do things." He was now dressed in a white shirt and suit, preached in a highly literate manner that his people could not understand, and forbade Dinka worship songs because he was going to teach the proper English Christian songs. The two missionaries who witnessed these changes pleaded with him to drop them and return to what he was previously doing. It was only when his own people confronted him about it that he changed and went back to being a Sudanese Christian.

337 Quote by Tony Merida, presentation on "Preaching and Contextualization" at SEND North American Conference, Atlanta, GA, July 31, 2012.

338 Gailyn Van Rhennen, "Syncretism and Contextualization: The Church on a Journey Defining Itself," in *Contextualization and Syncretism: Navigating Cultural Currents,* ed. Gailyn Van Rheenen (Pasadena: William Carey Library, 2006), Evangelical Missiological Society Series Number 13, 7-8.

339 "It is important to remember that all our Christian understandings and life are in human contexts, and therefore

partial. This does not mean they are necessarily wrong, but we need to be humble in our stance and to seek unity in the church.…But there is always the danger that when we put the Gospel in human contexts that the essence of the Gospel will so distorted that it loses its message." Paul G. Hiebert, "Syncretism and Social Paradigms," in *Contextualization and Syncretism: Navigating Cultural Currents,* ed. Gailyn Van Rheenen (Pasadena: William Carey Library, 2006), Evangelical Missiological Society Series Number 13, 44.

340 Van Rheenen in "Syncretism and Contextualization," 9, quotes David Hesselgrave: "Both philosophically and theologically, a communication approach that is over-dependent upon the discovery and utilization of similarities is open to question. Dissimilarities between beliefs and practices may, in fact, be more important and utilitarian in the long run.…If one's objective is to convert and disciple, both the number and importance of these differences will far outweigh the number and importance of supposed similarities."

341 See David Hesselgrave, "Syncretism: Mission and Missionary Induced?," in *Contextualization and Syncretism: Navigating Cultural Currents*, ed. Gailyn Van Rheenen (Pasadena: William Carey Library, 2006), Evangelical Missiological Society Series Number 13, 72-90, lists five propositions regarding syncretism.

342 Adapted from Michael Pocock, Gailyn Van Rheenen, and Douglas McConnell, *The Changing Face of World Missions* (Grand Rapids: Baker Academic, 2005), 324-25.

343 An example of taking the time to explain a critical Biblical concept is that of God as Father. In our American society

there are far too many people who have a negative image of Father. They were abused, abandoned, neglected, or ignored by an absent father and can't conceive of God as a father without being haunted by their past experiences. The solution is not to drop the term, but rather patiently, graciously, and lovingly help the hurting hearer come to understand and experience God as the perfect Father.

344 Elmer L. Towns and Ed Stetzer, *Perimeters of Light: Biblical Boundaries for the Emerging Church* (Chicago: Moody Publishers, 2004), 41.

345 And how we dogmatize some of these forms! I remember in the 1970s how my Christian employer could not understand how I could be a Christian and have long hair (it was the seventies). What I couldn't understand was how he could be so concerned about my hair and at the same time be such a vocal racist.

346 Marshall McLuhan famously said the "The medium is the message," meaning that "the form of a medium embeds itself in the message, creating a symbiotic relationship by which the medium influences how the message is perceived." http:// en.wikipedia.org/wiki/The_medium_is_the_message.

347 "Strict Jews, like the Pharisees, disliked the Samaritans so intensely that they avoided their territory as much as possible. Their route from Jerusalem to Galilee lay through the region beyond the Jordan. This was considerable longer, but it avoided contact with the Samaritans. For those in a hurry the shorter way was a necessity." Leon Morris, *The Gospel According to John*, in The New International Commentary on the New Testament, gen ed. F. F. Bruce

(Grand Rapids: Wm. B. Eerdmans Publishing Company, 1971), 255.

348 Ibid., 256.

349 Ed Stetzer, *Planting Churches in a Postmodern Age* (Nasville: Broadman & Holman, 2003), 189-93, has a discussion on the Engel Scale, the Gray Matrix, and his own Evangelism Journey Process showing how many people have to move from hostility or complete ignorance of the gospel to a point of openness and receptivity.

350 Lesbian, Gay, Bisexual, Transgender

351 I am not denying the need for deeper learning, for apologetics, and for further Biblical knowledge. I am saying that all of these are not pre-requisites to doing the work of an evangelist.

352 Jim Belcher, *Deep Church: A Third Way beyond Emerging and Traditional* (Downers Grove, IL: InterVarsity Press, 2009), 101, points out that the danger is for them to never be confronted with the truth. He notes that, "yes, belonging is important, but we still have to believe at some point." Just as Jesus invited people to follow him, to "belong to the community," but at some point challenged them to commit to him, so must every person seeking to belong also be at some point lovingly confronted with the truth of the gospel. J.D. Greear, "Mission to Postmoderns," in Bruce Riley Ashford, ed., *Theology and Practice of Mission* (Nashville: Broadman & Holman, 2011), 288, similarly notes that evangelism to postmoderns "must prioritize relational engagement."

353 http://www.merriam-webster.com/dictionary/confrontatio
n?show=0&t=1344448147 defines confrontation as "a face-
to-face meeting" and "the clashing of forces or ideas."

354 George Robinson, "The Gospel and Evangelism," in
Bruce Riley Ashford, ed., *Theology and Practice of Mission*
(Nashville: Broadman & Holman, 2011), 89, notes that there
"are no set biblical guidelines for evangelistic methodology
beyond calling for a response." There are, however, "biblical
guidelines for content: we are admonished to proclaim
Christ crucified and risen."

355 I am not saying that every conceivable method in evangelism
is acceptable. There are many that are manipulative,
unethical, and too accommodating to the cultural status
quo. Although Jesus ate with the sinners, he didn't become
a sinner. We must do what we can to relate to people in
order to reach some, but there are moral and ethical limits.
Wright, *The Mission of God*, 423, notes that the "validity of
evangelism in principle does not legitimize any and every
method of evangelism in practice."

356 John Peter Lange, The Gospel According to Matthew,
Commentary on the Holy Scriptures, Volume 8, Matthew-
Luke (Grand Rapids: Zondervan Publishing House, 1960),
298, notes that "the words of Jesus only refer to Peter in so
far as by this confession he identified himself with Christ,
and was the first to upbuild the Church by his testimony."
The "expression refers not to the Apostle as an individual,
but … to the faithfulness of confession." Similarly, Archibald
Thomas Robertson, *Word Pictures of the New Testament*,
Volume I (Grand Rapids: Baker Book House, 1930), 132,
asks "What is the rock on which Christ will build his vast
temple? Not on Peter alone or mainly or primarily. Peter by

his confession was furnished with the illustration for the rock on which His church will rest. It is the same kind of faith that Peter has just confessed."

357 Erickson, *Christian Theology*, 1,042, says that the "church is a manifestation of the kingdom of or reign of God. It is the form which that reign takes on earth in our time." Stanley J. Grenz, *Theology for the Community of God* (Nashville: Broadman & Holman, 1994), 624, notes that the "church, therefore, is a foretaste of the eschatological reality that God will one day graciously give to his creation. In short, it is a sign of the kingdom."

358 Defining a legitimate and healthy New Testament church will require more detail than Peter's statement. My purpose here is to state the irreducible minimum of this passage: Peter's confession of faith is what the church is built on. There is no other foundation (1 Cor. 3:11).

359 There have been many Christian movements throughout history that have provided correctives, enlightenment, and renewal to the church that have not been directly local church driven. I would argue, however, that if they are overly individualistic, such as ancient contemplative hermits and some expressions of the "deeper life" movement, they are unhealthy and out of balance. Other cross-denominational, non-denominational, or parachurch movements and organizations that focus on evangelism, discipleship, counseling, social ministry and justice can be healthy, and helpful and edifying to the local church if they are truly para-church (to be side by side, or come alongside the church).

360 Hunt, *Redeemed!*, 219, notes that "As fare local churches, so fares the work of the kingdom of God! This is the crucial importance of the local church."

361 There are numerous excellent books that explain in detail the missiological, practical, and logistical aspects of church planting. See, for example, Daniel R. Sanchez, Ebbie C. Smith, and Curtis E. Watke, *Starting Reproducing Congregations: A guidebook for contextual new church development* (Cumming, GA: Church Starting Network, 2001); Ed Stetzer, *Planting New Churches in a Postmodern Age*; Rodney Harrison, Tom Cheyney, and Don Overstreet, *Spin-Off Churches: How one church successfully plants another* (Nashville: Broadman & Holman, 2008); and, Ed Stetzer and Warren Bird, *Viral Churches: Helping church planters become movement makers* (San Francisco: Jossey-Bass, 2010).

362 The Baptist Faith & Message 2000 of my own Southern Baptist family states that each local church "operates under the Lordship of Christ through democratic processes." That statement, however, is interpreted and applied all along the "democratic processes" spectrum. There are few churches that vote on every single issue; most operate in some sort of delegated committee, team, or staff-led form. It is certainly a matter of debate among Southern Baptists. See, for example, Chad Owen Brand, R. Stanton Norman, Daniel Akin and James Leo Garrett, Jr. *Perspectives on Church Government: Five Views of Church Polity* (Nashville: Broadman & Holman, 2004) for Southern Baptist views.

363 Pocock et al, *The Changing Face of World Missions*, 15.

364 Towns and Stetzer, *Perimeters of Light*, 45.

365 *Hunter, Church for the Unchurched,* 65.

366 Archibald Thomas Robertson, *Word Pictures in the New Testament,* Vol. IV, Epistles of Paul (Nashville: Broadman Press, 1931), 76.

367 Gordon D. Fee, The First Epistle to the Corinthians, *The New International Commentary on the New Testament* (Grand Rapids: Wm. B. Eerdmans, 1987), 64.

368 Ibid., 74-75.

369 P. H. Menoud, "Preaching," in *The Interpreter's Dictionary of the Bible,* Vol. 3, K-Q (Nashville: Abingdon, 1962), 868, notes that the "NT writers draw a clear distinction between 'to preach' and 'preaching' on the one hand, and 'to teach'…and 'teaching'…on the other. Preaching is the proclamation of the gospel to men who have not yet heard of it. Teaching is an instruction or exhortation on various aspects of Christian life and thought addressed to a community already established in the faith."

370 John Stott, "A Definition of Biblical Preaching," http://www.preachingtoday.com/skills/2005/august/2—stoff.html (accessed August 28, 2012).

371 R. Albert Mohler, Jr., *He is Not Silent: Preaching in a postmodern world* (Chicago: Moody Publishers, 2008), 52.

372 Tony Merida, SEND North America Conference.

373 Hayward Armstrong, *Tell the Story: A Primer on Chronological Bible Storying* (Rockville, VA: International Centre for

Excellence in Leadership, 2003), 3. See also http://www.churchstarting.net/biblestorying/.

374 See http://www.learning-styles-online.com/overview/ for an overview of learning styles.

375 Sweet, *Viral*, 147-49, also notes that "Christian spirituality is totalitarian." Jesus is Lord of all, not just the supplier of personal needs.

376 Although specifically speaking about evangelism, Robinson, "The Gospel and Evangelism," 77, notes that "[e]ach part of God's mission – creation, fall, redemption, restoration – is not only God's plan, but it is also his story." Robinson bemoans the fact that we so often fail to be "master storytellers."

377 Sweet, 149, bemoans what he calls "versitis," which is to think of Scripture as a long series of verses, and to consider each verse as a stand-alone statement." This approach fails to see the "bigger meaning of Scripture."

378 Robinson, 79, says that "[w]e have a story to tell, and there is a bloody cross at the center of that story." He also notes, 91, that the "only non-negotiable when it comes to telling the story is that every aspect must point to the bloody cross and resurrection of Jesus which stands as the climactic event of the entire mission of God." Belcher, *Deep Church*, 157, notes that "we preach Christ in every text."

379 Mohler, 65.

380 Ingram, *The Emerging Church*, 173-185 passim. Greear, "Mission to Postmoderns," 284, notes that postmodersn

"suffer from the loss of two things: a source of authority and a grand narrative uniting all of human existence." This means that our preaching must be "the expository teaching of the story line of the Bible," so that we "present the Bible as the one, authoritative story of Jesus Christ and his plan for the earth."

381 Haddon W. Robinson, *Biblical Preaching: The Development and Delivery of Expository Messages* (Grand Rapids: Baker Book House, 1980), 28.

382 Sweet, *Viral*, 161, asks whether "you can imagine doing ministry the last five hundred years and getting away with. 'Sorry, I don't do books'? Can you imagine doing ministry in the next five years and getting away with 'Sorry, I don't do Facebook'?" Sweet's book is all about social networking and the church's mission. Although he points out difficulties, uncertainties, and even threats due to this rapidly growing technology, he rightly points out that it is here to stay and will only become more and more influential. What will the church do?

383 We are in an "era that is so oversaturated with, and psychologically immune to, even highly sophisticated strategies of persuasion (thanks to the ubiquity of media in our lives), standard evangelism has slammed up against a concrete wall." Carl Raschke, *GloboChrist: The Great Commission takes a Postmodern Turn* in "The Church and Postmodern Culture" series, James K.A. Smith, ed. (Grand Rapids: Baker Academic, 2008), 59.

384 Sweet, *Viral*, discusses many ways that Twitter, Facebook, and other social media can be used to "ignite revival."

385 There are other ways to use technology during preaching – twitter feeds from the congregation on screen during the sermon, questions being texted to the pastor while preaching, and video feeds to overflow rooms or satellite campuses are just three examples. These, too, are controversial and can both enhance or distract from preaching. The last one, satellite campuses, brings up other ecclesiological issues. There are also other less technological ways to visually enhance preaching. For instance, a painter or sculptor could be at work during the sermon illustrating what is being said. The same criteria, however, should apply.

386 Alan and Katherine Carter, "The Gospel and Lifestyle," in Bruce Riley Ashford, ed., *Theology and Practice of Mission* (Nashville: Broadman & Holman, 2011), 129.

387 Alan Hirsch and Lance Ford, *Right Here, Right Now: Everyday mission for everyday people* (Grand Rapids: Baker Books, 2011), 33, note that it "will take both missional church plus missional disciples to make a missional movement." Furthermore, 23, they note that their desire is to "help Christians see the kingdom opportunities that exist on the pathways of their daily routines and lifestyle patterns and to live missionaly more than simply do mission activities."

388 http://www.catholiceducation.org/articles/religion/re0136.html.

389 Hirsch and Ford, 77, make the unfortunate observation that "[m]ost Christians are willing to give their afterlife to Jesus but want to keep their earthly life for themselves."

390 Ibid., 96-99, give some practical ways to practice "creative grace" towards others.

391 See, for example, http://psychcentral.com/lib/2012/the-myth-of-the-high-rate-of-divorce/all/1/ for an analysis of the conventional claim that "fifty percent of all marriages end in divorce."

392 See http://thegospelcoalition.org/blogs/tgc/2012/09/25/factchecker-divorce-rate-among-christians/ and http://www.edstetzer.com/2012/09/pastors-that-divorce-rate-stat.html for discussions on how wrong conventional wisdom is about divorce among church goers. It is better news than what we thought, but still troubling.

393 Alan and Katherine Carter, 133-143. They also offer a contrast between a "Wordly Model" of stewardship and a "Biblical Model," and challenge Christians to "purge our lives of that which does not help to advance God's mission on earth."

394 There are numerous definitions of the term "missional." Hirsch and Ford, 66, offer the following: "A working definition of missional church is a community of God's people that defines itself by, and organizes its life around, its real purpose of being an agent of God's mission to the world. In other words, the church's true and authentic 'organizing principle' is mission. When the church is on mission, it is the true church."

395 Sean Cordell, "The Gospel and Social Responsibility," in Bruce Riley Ashford, ed., *Theology and Practice of Mission* (Nashville: Broadman & Holman, 2011), 106.

396 Certainly, the issue is not as simple as I am making it out here. Consider that in many cultures and contexts, church members have learned not to share their needs for fear

of embarrassment or shame or loss of status. In other situations, there are those within the church who may be lazy, irresponsible, and who may take advantage of the generosity of others. Paul knew this was a reality (1 Tim. 5:8-16). Furthermore, many churches are made up primarily of the poor and needy, all of whom may all depend to some degree on government assistance. My intent is to make a missiological point, not address the complexities of poverty.

397 Darrell L. Guder, ed., *Missional Church: A Vision for the Sending of the Church in North America* (Grand Rapids: Wm. B. Eerdmans, 1998), 103-04, notes that "[b]efore the church is called to do or say anything, it is called and sent to be the unique community of those who live under the reign of God.... We are a noticed and watched people."

398 Hunt, *Redeemed!*, 96-97.

399 Ibid., 355, for a brief discussion of both continuity and discontinuity between the present and the new earth.

400 Wright, *The Mission of God*, 413, argues that "a biblical theology of mission that flows from the mission of God himself...must include the ecological sphere within its scope and see practical environmental action as a legitimate part of Christian mission."

401 Ibid., 400. Wright, 402, goes on to say that "[t]here is a fundamental difference between treating creation as sacred and treating it as divine...The sacredness or sanctity of creation speaks of its essential relatedness to God, not of it being divine in and of itself."

402 Moore, *The Kingdom of Christ, 125*, notes how "much of the ideology of contemporary environmental movements" are contrary to a theology of the Kingdom of God. Nature is sovereign over all in these views, rather than being under the Lordship of Christ.

403 See Norman L. Geisler, *Christian Ethics: Options and Issues* (Grand Rapids: Baker Book House, 1989), 293-310, for a brief overview of the materialistic, pantheistic, and Christian views of the environment.

404 Wright, 415. "Christians are more likely to be blamed for the ecological crisis than seen as bearing any kind of good news in relation to it."

405 See the work of *A Rocha*, an international organization of Christians working together for conservation. http://www.arocha.org/int-en/index.html.

406 If you are a Calvinist, that despicable person may be one of the elect. You don't know, so you still share the gospel. If you are not a Calvinist, you certainly share the gospel. Either way, you share the gospel with any and all. Wright, *The Mission of God*, 422-424, points out that the missiological implications of the image of God in humans means that: "All human beings are addressable by God," "All human beings are accountable to God," "All human being have dignity and equality," and that "The biblical gospel fits all."

407 Ibid., 429-432, discusses the effects of sin on all of human life, human society and history, and "the whole environment of human life."

408 Swanson and Williams, *To Transform a City*, 154, also note that "[b]elievers living out the gospel in their domains can have a potentially more powerful evangelistic effect, since the gospel spreads through the natural societal channels as opposed to being a 'religious' program." Ashford, "The Gospel and Culture," 125, argues for "thinking and acting 'Christianly' in the various dimensions of human society and culture, including the arts, the sciences, and the public square. In so doing, the Christian allows Christ to take possession of non-Christian societies and cultures." Moreover, 126, critically engaging in culture allows the church to "both read and write culture," the latter meaning "to create and construct works of culture within" arenas of society.

409 Michael Frost and Alan Hirsch, *The Shaping of Things to Come* (Peabody, MA: Hendrickson Publishers, 2003), 18-19. This does not mean that the church should not be "attractive," for it definitely should be. The point is that an attractional model depends almost exclusively on people coming to the building and then fitting in.

410 Hirsch, *The Forgotten Ways*, 281.

411 Ibid., 37. Jedidiah Coppenger, "The Community of Mission: The Church," in Bruce Riley Ashford, ed., *Theology and Practice of Mission* (Nashville: Broadman & Holman, 2011), 66, notes that "a kingdom ecclesiology recognizes that the King calls his church both to gather and scatter for the glory of God." Furthermore, 71, "The King's people must also understand that kingdom life can flourish as they are scattered throughout our villages, towns, and cities."

412 Ibid., 35.

413   Guder, 158.

414   Belcher, 192.

415   Guder, 115.

416   "This means that Christians are called to create public educational institutions, build businesses, organize neighborhood groups, create charities, be artists and musicians and writers, and start political action groups. We are to make culture." Belcher, 192.

417   See Cordell, "The Gospel and Social Responsibility," 92-108, for a brief Biblical theology of poverty and a balanced approach to care for the poor, which he defines as including the "weak, the lowly, the oppressed, and the hurting." Cordell acknowledges that the causes and cures for poverty are complex and due to "many contributing factors." Whatever the case may be, the gospel "alone has the power to change the heart of the unbelieving poor or the unbelieving oppressor."

418   Wright, 318-19, notes that "Mission may not always begin with evangelism. But mission that does not ultimately include declaring the Word and the name of Christ, the call to repentance, and faith and obedience has not completed its task. It is defective mission, not holistic mission."

CPSIA information can be obtained at www.ICGtesting.com
Printed in the USA
LVOW04s0023220814

400387LV00011B/218/P

9 781629 020778